Highly Competitive Warehouse Management

An Action Plan for Best-in-Class Performance

North American Edition

Jeroen P. van den Berg

Distribution Group
Boonton, NJ

Distribution Group

Copyright © 2012 by Distribution Group
ISBN 978-0-915910-65-6

All rights reserved. No part of this book may be reproduced or transmitted in any form or by any means, electronic or mechanical, including photocopying, recording, or by any information storage and retrieval system, without permission in writing from the publisher.

Cover: Eric Rugers (www.launderette.nl)
Photo: Maarten Corbijn (www.corbino.nl)
Questions: Workbook Company (www.workbookcompany.com)

workbook company®

Distribution Group
712 Main Street
Boonton, NJ 07005
www.DistributionGroup.com

To Godelieve.

Forever the best in my class!

"Highly Competitive Warehouse Management puts the nuts and bolts of warehouse management under a magnifying glass, but it also takes a broader view of aligning DC activities with the company's overall strategy."

Jeff Ostrowski
Editor-in-chief, Distribution Center Management, USA

"Successive incidents in global businesses like Toyota and Foxconn show that traditional management theory has made companies vulnerable. Highly Competitive Warehouse Management, in fact, provides an alternative to the endless pursuit of efficiency coined by JIT, Lean, Kaizen, etc."

Won Hee Yee
The Society of Professional Logisticians, South Korea

"In a time when many companies loose themselves in high profile software systems and complex mechanization, Van den Berg gets down to earth and mixes proven concepts with the capabilities of modern IT systems."

Duco Avis
Logistics Director, Blokker, The Netherlands

"Highly Competitive Warehouse Management follows a practical and systematic approach towards improving warehouse operations. Together with the accompanying materials it makes a concise teaching package."

Herman Lemmer
Lecturer Logistics Management, University of Pretoria, South Africa

"Van den Berg's focus on aligning the workers' personal goals with company-wide goals will help managers make the changes needed for highly competitive warehouses."

Dr Lorike Hagdorn-van der Meijden
Professor Transport Distribution and Logistics, VU University Amsterdam and Managing Director Transport and Mobility, TNO, The Netherlands

"Highly Competitive Warehouse Management is a must-have for every logistics professional."

Karel de Jong
Senior Vice President Supply Chain, Jumbo Supermarkets, The Netherlands

"Imagine yourself doubling the output of your warehouse with the same staff and space while collaborating with competitors in 2020! Jeroen van den Berg shows how to design and manage best-in-class warehouse processes that meet the tough challenges of the next decade."

Dr Walther Ploos van Amstel
Supply chain expert and
co-author of *European Distribution and Supply Chain Logistics*

"Most warehouses use modern systems and technologies. Highly Competitive Warehouse Management explains how to go forward and take full advantage of these investments."

Hanny Kapelle
DC Manager, Wehkamp.nl, The Netherlands

"Jeroen van den Berg unravels the many causes of improper warehouse management and, more importantly, provides a systematic way to improve warehouse performance, with often astonishing results. This book presents essential knowledge in an easily accessible way, together with guidelines and tools to implement changes, and is therefore highly recommended to both students and practitioners."

Dr Henk Zijm
Scientific Director Dutch Institute for Advanced Logistics (Dinalog) and
Professor of Supply Chain Management, University of Twente, The Netherlands

"Jeroen van den Berg enriches the rather conservative warehousing world with new scientific perspectives. He writes them down in an easy-to-understand manner, which ensures that people actually read his work."

Heres Stad
Editor-in-chief, Reed Business, The Netherlands

"Highly Competitive Warehouse Management shows how warehouses play a prominent role in the integrated supply chain."

Dr Ad van Goor
Emeritus Professor, VU University Amsterdam and
best-selling author of *Logistics: Principles and Practice*, The Netherlands

Contents

FOREWORD 9
HOW TO READ THIS BOOK 11
CHAPTER 1   HIGHLY COMPETITIVE WAREHOUSE MANAGEMENT 13
   1.1   Competitive Advantage 16
   1.2   Best-in-Class Supply Chain Performance 21
   1.3   The Clean Socks Experiment 24
   1.4   Four Elements of Warehouse Optimization 27
   1.5   Growth Path for Warehouse Optimization 32
   1.6   Warehouse Maturity Scan 36
   1.7   Summary 45

CHAPTER 2   THE CHALLENGE OF CHANGE 47
   2.1   Change Management to Facilitate a Change-Oriented Culture 48
   2.2   Warehouse Strategy to Give Direction 51
   2.3   Warehouse Action Plan to Organize Evolution 64
   2.4   Optimization Actions to Create Fun and Successes 71
   2.5   Project Management to Give Guidance 76
   2.6   Summary 80

CHAPTER 3   WAREHOUSING 81
   3.1   Warehouse Justification 84
   3.2   Material Handling 86
   3.3   Warehouse Services 90
   3.4   Warehouse Processes 96
   3.5   Inbound Processes 97
   3.6   Storage 102
   3.7   Wave Planning 103
   3.8   Outbound Processes 111
   3.9   VAL 118
   3.10   Cross-dock 119
   3.11   Summary 119

CHAPTER 4   WAREHOUSE MANAGEMENT SYSTEMS 121
   4.1   WMS Modules 123
   4.2   Real-time Communication 126
   4.3   Material Handling Control 129
   4.4   Interfaces 131
   4.5   Summary 145

Chapter 5 Effective Warehouse Management ... 147
- 5.1 Service Level Agreements ... 148
- 5.2 Standard Operating Procedures ... 159
- 5.3 Activity-Based Costing ... 161
- 5.4 Performance Indicators ... 171
- 5.5 Summary ... 186

Chapter 6 Process Efficiency ... 187
- 6.1 Service Level Improvement ... 188
- 6.2 Efficiency Improvement ... 192
- 6.3 Compact Storage ... 200
- 6.4 Summary ... 201

Chapter 7 Responsive Warehouse Management ... 203
- 7.1 Justification ... 205
- 7.2 Capacity Planning ... 207
- 7.3 Wave Management ... 218
- 7.4 Task Management ... 220
- 7.5 Summary ... 229

Chapter 8 Resource Utilization ... 231
- 8.1 Utilization Improvement ... 232
- 8.2 Cut ... 233
- 8.3 Activate ... 235
- 8.4 Postpone ... 237
- 8.5 Space Utilization ... 239
- 8.6 Summary ... 240

Chapter 9 Collaborative Warehouse Management ... 243
- 9.1 Discontinuities ... 245
- 9.2 Activity-Based Pricing ... 253
- 9.3 Synchronized Planning ... 256
- 9.4 Virtual Warehousing ... 263
- 9.5 Summary ... 270

Chapter 10 Service Alignment ... 271
- 10.1 Rationalize ... 272
- 10.2 Accelerate/Decelerate ... 275
- 10.3 Balance ... 278
- 10.4 Summary ... 284
- 10.5 What's Next? ... 284

Appendix A Maturity Scan ... 285
Appendix B Standard Operating Procedures ... 291
Appendix C Create Your Own Action Plan ... 297
References ... 307
Index ... 311
About the Author ... 319

Foreword

You are holding the revised second edition of this book. In 2007, I published the first edition under the original title *Integral Warehouse Management: The Next Generation in Transparency, Collaboration and Warehouse Management Systems*. In retrospect, I must admit that this title was ill chosen. Firstly, people did not pick up on the adjective *Integral*. Secondly, the ideas and innovations that I regarded as *next generation* concepts were hardly recognized as such by readers. In the end, the only phrase that stood up in the book title was *Warehouse Management*.

Nonetheless, the book was well received both by practitioners as well as students from universities around the world. In particular, readers appreciated the maturity model, a growth model for step-wise performance improvement that was introduced in the book. Soon after the book's release, the online version[1] of the warehouse maturity scan was published. The online scan calculates scores for the maturity of a distribution center and a corresponding savings potential. The results are stunning. The *warehouse maturity scan* has identified an average savings potential of 20 percent among distribution centers – a value that closely matches users' own estimates. Most importantly, people *acknowledge* the main bottlenecks pointed out by the maturity scan.

In my consulting practice, I have seen that the maturity scan creates awareness among my clients. Rather than expecting a warehouse management system to solve their problems instantaneously, managers are motivated to fight the root causes of their problems, which are often issues concerning dysfunctional operator behavior, poor process design, improper use of existing IT systems and the secondary position of the distribution center within the company. It has profoundly changed my work as a consultant. Projects have become more successful and create greater benefits for clients. I find it highly satisfying.

For these reasons, I have decided to rewrite my book. First of all, I changed the title to *Highly Competitive Warehouse Management*. The new title refers to the idea that a distribution center should create a competitive advantage for companies rather than stay in its subordinate position. The subtitle is *An Action Plan for Best-in-Class Performance*. Instead of *next generation* concepts, I

---

[1] Developed in collaboration with *logistiek.nl,* a Dutch logistics portal by Reed Business.

emphasized the maturity growth path. In fact, I further elaborated on the various steps and instruments in the growth path and turned them into a cut-and-dried action plan.

Another thing that I have revised in the second edition concerns the subject of warehouse management systems (WMSs). I am glad to see that WMSs have evolved since the publication of the first edition in 2007. Clearly, any book that discusses IT issues needs to be updated on a regular basis.

Finally, the second edition comes with a comprehensive set of questions throughout the book. The questions have been composed according to the Make Books Work method developed by Workbook Company. This method enables readers to make connections that help them to absorb information, to gain in-depth knowledge and understanding of topics and to immediately apply the information in daily practice.

I hope that this book inspires you to make a difference. If you are a manager, then I hope that you challenge the usual practices throughout your organization. If you are a WMS vendor, then I hope that you recognize that a WMS implementation is more than getting new software to work and that you help your clients to actually move forward in their performance. If you are a consultant, then I hope that you create awareness among your clients and help them to fight root causes of problems rather than symptoms. If you are a student, then I hope that you keep an open mind and challenge existing ideas once you start your career in practice.

Finally, I would like to thank a number of people who helped me to realize this project. In the first place, my clients who applied the methodology of highly competitive warehouse management in their distribution centers. This was where many ideas were born. In particular, I want to thank Major Peter van Winkel and Dennis van Hattem of the Royal Dutch Air Force, who were the first to adopt highly competitive warehouse management. Their ideas and dedication have had a great impact on the development of the methodology. Further, I am grateful to Martine van der Steeg of Workbook Company for adding the questions throughout the book. Also many thanks to Eric Rugers for the cover design. Finally, I want to express my gratitude to Steve Joel, Sander de Leeuw, Kees Gabriëls, Margaret DeWitt and the team at the Distribution Group for their valuable comments and suggestions that greatly helped to sharpen the contents of this book.

Jeroen van den Berg
Buren, The Netherlands, 2011

How to Read this Book

To make the content of *Highly Competitive Warehouse Management* applicable, accessible and useable for you, we integrated the Make Books Work method, developed by Workbook Company. This method helps you to get the most out of *Highly Competitive Warehouse Management*.

While reading the book, you will find questions along the way that will help you capture the content of *Highly Competitive Warehouse Management*. There are four types of questions:

- *Get it*. Knowledge and insight
- *Explore it*. Analysis and reflection
- *Do it*. Action and application
- *Case study*. Case study of a fictitious company called Foodies.

You will find the *Get it*, *Explore it* and *Case study* questions throughout the various chapters of this book. *Do it* questions are at the end of the book in Appendix C, where you create your own action plan.

If you want to adopt the methodology of highly competitive warehouse management in a distribution center, then we suggest that you answer all questions. However, if you have limited time, then we advise managers to pay special attention to the *Explore it* and *Do it* questions. Consultants should focus on *Explore it* and *Case study* questions. If you are a WMS vendor, then we suggest answering the questions in Chapter 4. And if you are a student, then *Get it* and *Case study* questions are most valuable.

For educators who use *Highly Competitive Warehouse Management* in their curriculum, the questions in the book are incorporated in an online homework tool that can be found at www.hcwm.net.

Good luck and make *Highly Competitive Warehouse Management* work for you!

Chapter 1

Highly Competitive Warehouse Management

Some warehouses, or distribution centers, have excellent performance with 99 percent-plus perfect deliveries, a productive and strongly motivated workforce and a flexibility that anticipates any changes in the market. The distribution center runs smoothly in close collaboration with other departments within the company and with other members of the supply chain. The manager (or director) responsible for the distribution center plays an important strategic role within the company, and is seen as an equal to other managers in sales, production, purchasing and other departments.

How striking is the contrast with many other distribution centers. Their performance is poor and unreliable. Staff are badly motivated and need the constant attention of the manager and team leaders. The manager is absorbed in his[2] day-to-day routine. Unexpected (and expected) events, special customer requests, delays of incoming goods and dozens of other issues require his immediate attention. Moreover, the distribution function is held in low esteem compared to other departments and is expected to cater to their whims.

Naturally, the manager wants to improve the performance of his distribution center. The distribution center is an essential link in the supply chain. It makes goods available when (and how) we need them and it creates efficiency in upstream and downstream activities. If the distribution center can provide competitive service levels with substantially lower costs, then this gives the company, or even the entire supply chain, a major advantage. However, despite the hard work of the manager, his efforts remain fruitless. Ironically, the manager is so busy with everyday *problem-solving* that he rarely has time to solve his problems and find a way out of this ordeal.

---

[2] For ease of reading, we use the male form in this book.

1. **Give your opinion about the performance of your distribution center with regard to the following aspects.**
   a. Estimate of perfect delivery rate
   b. Current productivity and motivation of workforce
   c. Flexibility to market changes
   d. Role of the manager within the company

In this book we introduce *highly competitive warehouse management* as an *action plan* for managers to successfully transform their distribution center from its current state[3] into a best-in-class operation. It helps the manager to escape the everyday *fire-fighting* routine and explains how to create a best-in-class distribution center. The action plan builds upon *best practices* that have proven to be successful in many operations. highly competitive warehouse management advocates a flexible approach and uses the best practices as modular building blocks for warehouse optimization. Since distribution centers differ, the model also identifies which best practice should be introduced next at any time. This decision is based on the *maturity* of the distribution center. Consequently, *warehouse maturity* serves as a core element of highly competitive warehouse management.

The approach is called highly competitive warehouse management because it not only attempts to save costs in the distribution center, it also aims to strengthen the competitive position of the whole company. This broad scope challenges the manager not only to run an excellent operation inside the walls of the distribution center, he also has to look beyond the limits of his own world. If he wants to have a real impact on the bottom-line business results, the manager has to collaborate with managers of other departments.

Highly competitive warehouse management transforms the distribution center into a strong link within the company and the supply chain. The methodology distinguishes itself by combining the following three elements:
- It advocates a line of thinking about logistics optimization that goes back to basics.
- It capitalizes on the detailed data captured by modern information systems.
- It strengthens the distribution center to become an equal partner to other members of the supply chain.

Before the massive introduction of IT systems in distribution centers, managers focused on understanding and analyzing *processes* and motivating and training *people* on the shop floor. Nowadays, with the capabilities of sophisticated IT systems, the attention of managers has shifted from people and processes to *technology*. Clearly, information technology is a powerful enabler and we will

---

[3] Use the scan in Appendix A to estimate the current state of your distribution center as well as the potential for further savings.

build on its potential in this book. However, without properly managing people and processes it becomes worthless. A well-organized operation together with a well-trained workforce lay the foundation for logistics optimization. Similar to existing logistics models such as Lean and Six Sigma, we advocate a focus on people and processes to seek optimization.

Modern information systems capture highly detailed data on logistics activities. *Warehouse management systems* (WMSs) can use this data to enhance operational performance. The methodology of highly competitive warehouse management uses the data to provide powerful analytics for performance evaluation and process analysis (*transparency*) and for aligning relationships in the supply chain (*collaboration*). Moreover, the model explains several advanced planning and control methodologies that capitalize on this detailed data. These methods seek to make WMSs more intelligent.

Oftentimes the distribution center plays a subordinate role within companies. However, since the distribution center serves as the de-coupling point between many business activities, it is highly dependent on decisions from other departments such as sales, marketing, customer service, production planning and purchasing. Many of these decisions create substantial inefficiencies through demand fluctuations, frequent deliveries, tough response times or inefficient order sizes. We realize that it is difficult to address these issues while the distribution center is in the underdog position. Hence, highly competitive warehouse management first aims to build a strong operation, so that the distribution center is ready to become an equal partner to other departments. Then it may jointly investigate what is best for the whole company. Only in this way, can the distribution center create competitive advantage.

2. **The title of this book is *Highly Competitive Warehouse Management*.**
   a. Explain the approach of highly competitive warehouse management.
   b. What are the advantages of this approach?

3. **Consider the role of the distribution center within your company.**
   a. How do you best describe its role?
   b. What do you think of this role?

1.1 Competitive Advantage

Outstanding performance within the distribution center may contribute to the competitive power of the entire company, not to mention the overall supply chain. We identify three areas where the distribution center may have an impact on corporate performance:
- Logistics costs
- Customer service
- Business alignment.

Logistics Costs

First, we consider logistics costs. Davis (2011) gives an indication of the average logistics costs for companies as a percentage of the sales price of a product (Table 1.1). The total logistics costs in Table 1.1 are on average 7.8 percent of the sales price. Naturally, this percentage varies between industries depending on product value and handling characteristics. The transportation costs in this table refer only to costs associated with the transportation of finished goods. If we were to include the inbound supply of raw materials and semi-finished goods, then the logistics costs would increase to approximately 11 percent. The average profit margin on these products is 4 percent (Ballou, 2003). Hence, a reduction of the logistics costs can have a substantial impact on the profit margin.

Table 1.1 Logistics costs as a percentage of sales price (Davis, 2011).

Category	Percentage of Sales
Administration	0.2
Order-entry/customer service	0.3
Inventory holding	1.7
Warehousing	1.8
Transportation	3.8
Total	**7.8**

Van Goor, *et al.* (2003) characterize the trends in logistics costs by comparing studies of Ballou, Davis and the European Logistics Association (ELA) over the years. They identify that the percentage of *inventory holding costs* has consistently declined due to initiatives like *just in time* deliveries and *lean thinking*. At the same time, advances in production technology and new management philosophies have reduced the cost per man hour and thereby the portion of *production costs* (not shown in Table 1.1) in the overall costs.

While the inventory holding and production costs dropped, the relative shares of *transportation* and *warehousing costs* steadily grew. Despite the technological progress in material handling equipment and IT, distribution centers have not been able to improve their productivity. This is due to the increased demands imposed by smaller, more frequent orders. Likewise, elevated fuel prices, traffic congestion and decreasing drop sizes have consistently enlarged the transportation costs component. Even after the recession hit in 2008 and fuel prices dropped dramatically, transportation costs continued to grow due to excess capacity still in place and ever-shrinking drop sizes with tight restrictions.

From these figures we may conclude that existing logistics models such as JIT, ECR, TQM, Kaizen, Lean and Six Sigma have proven to be highly successful in reducing inventories, shortening response times, eliminating errors and rationalizing process steps. We certainly recommend them for these purposes. However, after many years of successful application the question arises whether further reductions in these directions are still effective. Zero inventories (Hall, 1983) may sound great, but it eradicates all economies of scale in the supply chain.

We believe that the focus on warehousing costs will continue in the coming years. Companies will realize that reducing inventories at the expense of more complex warehousing and transportation activities is no longer a valid approach. Therefore, highly competitive warehouse management introduces an action plan that not only attempts to reduce inventories, shorten response times, eliminate errors and rationalize process steps, but also looks in other directions when necessary.

Customer Service

Poor performance from the distribution center immediately impacts customer service levels. Errors in deliveries cause empty shelves in stores or downstream warehouses, which results in lost sales. In time-critical situations it may even render the customer's operation ineffective. For example, if the customer needs spare parts for a defective machine, it can only be fixed after all parts are available. Late or partial deliveries seriously harm the operation. In particular, the distribution center must be able to sustain customer service levels during busy periods.

Customers become dissatisfied when goods arrive late or incorrectly. They complain, demand compensation or even switch their business to a competitor. In addition, incorrect deliveries must be returned and the correct goods shipped with substantial extra costs.

However, there is a flip-side to high levels of customer service. Managers should be aware that good customer service may necessitate high logistics costs. Hence, competitive customer service is not necessarily an exceptionally high level of service. In fact, a competitive service level represents the optimal trade-off between service and costs. This trade-off may vary between companies and depends on strategic choices of the company. For instance, if a company sells its products at low prices, then customers may be tolerant towards more moderate customer service levels. Highly competitive warehouse management will make the cost-to-serve transparent so that companies may decide upon the optimal trade-off between service and cost in their customer service strategy.

The distribution center may also improve its service to internal departments. For instance, many departments within a company rely on the distribution center to safeguard inventories and successfully forward goods. Hence, if the distribution center correctly manages and records inventory levels in the company's IT systems, then other departments can decide accurately how much can be purchased, produced or sold. As a result, inventory levels stay low and incidents resulting from inadequate data are prevented.

4. The distribution center may improve customer service.
   a. How does customer service affect corporate performance?

Business Alignment

The distribution center is the decoupling point between various business activities. Despite the attention paid to supply chain management, departments within companies still often operate as independent silos. Departments typically consider their own interests first when doing business. These interests may conflict with the interests of the company as a whole. For example, the objective of the sales department is to achieve high sales volumes. At first sight this objective seems logical. However, a sales department with a strong drive to achieve sales volumes is likely to promise special conditions to win customer orders. These conditions may easily lead to substantial handling requirements or exceptional peak volumes, which could make the sales volume highly unprofitable.

We may encounter similar effects when the production department wants to run excessively long production batches or the purchasing department wants to buy from a cheap (yet unreliable) supplier. If the distribution center merely copes with the outcomes of these poor decisions, or ironically becomes highly efficient in dealing with these issues, then the inefficiencies will never be resolved. As such, the distribution center has the unique advantage of being able to view the effects of departmental behavior. By making the implications transparent, the distribution center can help to align the various departments in accordance with company objectives.

5. Consider how your distribution center performs on the three elements that impact corporate performance: Logistics costs, customer service and business alignment.
   a. Logistics costs: What are the warehousing costs as a percentage of annual sales?
   b. Customer service: What are the actual service levels of the distribution center for services to customers?
   c. Business alignment: To what extent do departments in your company collaborate and consider overall company objectives?
   d. Think of a peer company. How is this company performing on these three elements?
   e. Consider the differences. Are these differences intentional? What are the underlying reasons?

1.1.1 Competitive Advantage for Third Party Logistics Providers

For private warehouses, reliable and efficient warehouse services give the company a competitive edge, which helps it acquire and retain market share. Moreover, the cost savings directly add to the profit margin. With an annual warehouse budget of several millions, a cost saving of 10, 20 or even 30 percent can be significant.

For third party logistics providers (3PLs) the situation is somewhat different. Operating the distribution center is their core business. In 2006, market leaders in third party warehousing each had global market shares between 1 and 5 percent. These percentages are remarkably small compared to many other markets. Furthermore, the Council of Supply Chain Management Professionals (CSCMP) claims that 20 to 25 percent of outsourcing relationships fail within two years; 50 percent within five years. A study by *Material Handling Management* magazine (Drickhamer, 2005) of 453 distribution centers in the U.S. revealed that only 11 percent outsourced to a third party logistics provider. Such figures are characteristic of an immature market.

There are exceptions, but quite often we see that 3PLs and clients focus on short-term results rather than lasting relationships. For instance, it is lucrative for the 3PL to hold high inventories and ship small order lines, since it earns a fee for each pallet in stock and each order line that is shipped. However, for the client company and the supply chain it may be more effective to reduce inventories and to consolidate order lines. Another complicating aspect is that neither party is willing to share information. The different interests and perspectives of the client and the 3PL may result in extended response times, elevated safety stocks and increased costs. Clients assume that running the logistics operation is the responsibility of the service provider, instead of a joint effort. Often they neglect their internal logistics expertise. Third party logistics providers spend a lot of time and effort in resolving the effects of poor collaboration, rather than improving overall performance.

Such behavior creates a lot of inefficiency in the supply chain. It adds to overall costs and compromises service levels to the client's customers. Hence, it is important that clients and 3PLs are aware of this situation and attempt to resolve it. In principle, the client company and the outsourced distribution center represent the same link in the supply chain. The challenge for both is to act as one. However, we believe that a strategy that focuses on supply chain objectives is more viable for a 3PL than one that focuses on its own short term objectives. As an account manager of a 3PL recently confided: "The cheapest service is one that does not need to be fulfilled."

Figure 1.1 illustrates in *cause-and-effect relationships* how highly competitive warehouse management helps 3PLs to overcome this situation. We hypothesize that the application of highly competitive warehouse management could help the 3PL provide reliable services as well as lower costs by 10 percent. The cost advantage can be achieved by creating transparency, using intelligent IT and developing a close collaboration with clients.

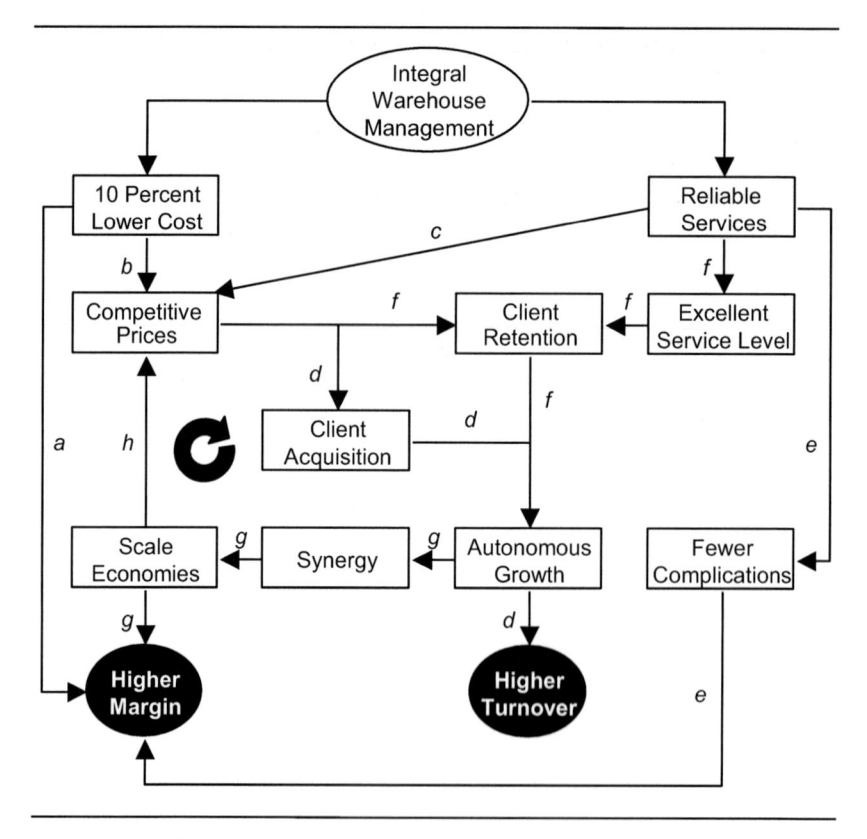

Figure 1.1 The effects of highly competitive warehouse management for third party logistics providers.

We elaborate on the various cause-and-effect relationships below.
 a. *10 Percent Lower Cost → Higher Margin.* A fraction of the cost advantage can be used to increase the profit margin.
 b. *10 Percent Lower Cost → Competitive Prices.* The remaining fraction of the cost advantage may be used to offer competitive prices.
 c. *Reliable Services → Competitive Prices.* When the 3PL knows upfront that it is able to provide reliable services in a sustainable way, then it does not have to include a substantial safety margin in its rates to compensate for future complications.
 d. *Competitive Prices → Client Acquisition → Autonomous Growth → Higher Turnover.* Competitive prices help attract new customers. The growth leads to a higher turnover.
 e. *Reliable Services → Fewer Complications → Higher Margin.* Similar to c, reliable services help prevent the cost of future complications. This improves the margin.

f. *Reliable Services → Excellent Service Level → Client Retention → Autonomous Growth → Higher Turnover.* Reliable services create excellent service levels for clients. They remain content with the logistics services and in combination with competitive prices do not consider changing to a competitor. This sustains the growth of the 3PL.
g. *Autonomous Growth → Synergy → Scale Economies → Higher Margin.* Sharing the warehouse capacities across different clients may create synergies, e.g., by using the same warehouse staff for multiple clients' operations. Synergy only comes about when products have similar characteristics so that they can be handled with the same systems and when volume fluctuations are complementary so that peaks are leveled out. The synergy creates scale economies, which further improves the margin.
h. *Scale Economies → Competitive Prices → Client Acquisition/Retention → Autonomous Growth → Synergy → Scale Economies.* Scale economies can also be used to lower prices. This triggers a continuous cycle that further advances scale economies and accelerates growth and profitability. This is the efficiency advantage enjoyed by market leaders.

To conclude, a strategy that is aimed at optimizing overall supply chain performance helps to achieve profitable growth for third party logistics providers.

6. **Figure 1.1 shows the effects of highly competitive warehouse management for third party logistics providers.**
    a. Explain the cause-and-effect relationships in your own words.

1.2   Best-in-Class Supply Chain Performance

International research shows that companies with best-in-class supply chain performance considerably outperform their peers:
- Accenture, INSEAD and Stanford University (Accenture, 2003) identify a strong correlation between superior supply chain performance and financial success in a study among large global enterprises in 24 industries. A high-performance supply chain not only provides cost advantages but also helps enhance revenues.
- Davis (2006) observes that best-in-class companies have logistics costs 32 percent lower than their laggard peers. This cost advantage increased their profit margins by more than 3 percentage points on average.
- Deloitte (2003) observes that companies able to master supply chain complexities are 73 percent more profitable than the laggards in a study among manufacturers across North America and Europe.

- Deloitte Netherlands (Scheper *et al.*, 2005) shows that companies that master complexity are 30 percent more profitable than the average in a follow-up study among Dutch manufacturing companies.
- Enslow (2007) reports similar cost differences between leaders and laggards in research by the Aberdeen Group among process industry companies. Moreover, the best-in-class achieve better performance metrics such as perfect order rate and forecast accuracy.
- Another study by the Aberdeen group (Enslow & O'Neill, 2006) identifies that one out of eight respondents have reduced their warehousing costs by more than 20 percent in the preceding two years. These operations excel in the application of information technology and management techniques.
- *Material Handling Management* magazine (Drickhamer, 2006) reveals a 31 percent difference in warehousing costs between the best-in-class and the laggards in a study among 457 distribution centers in the U.S. The leaders stand out in the application of warehouse management practices.

Based on the above studies, we draw the following conclusions:
- The overall *logistics costs* of best-in-class companies are approximately 30 percent below their laggard peers. We observe an identical gap in *warehousing costs*.
- Rather than investing in automated material handling systems or a new warehouse layout, the best-in-class primarily achieve this cost advantage by applying modern management techniques and IT systems.
- There is a relatively small group of companies with best-in-class characteristics who are well ahead of the pack. This performance gap suggests an enormous savings potential for companies in general[4].
- Moreover, best-in-class companies not only have lower logistics costs, they also provide better service levels and are financially more successful. The benefit of additional profit is comparable to the cost savings potential. In other words, better logistics has a double pay-off.

7. **Think of best-in-class companies that you know.**
   a. *Give two examples of companies with a best-in-class supply chain.*
   b. *Why do these companies have a best-in-class supply chain?*
   c. *What are the differences between these best-in-class companies and your company?*

---

[4] Enslow (2007) estimates logistics costs (inventories, transportation and warehousing) as a percentage of sales for best-in-class companies at 6 percent. This would be a 23 percent cost advantage compared to the average costs stated by Davis (2006) for the same year.

The above conclusions illustrate that warehousing and logistics are key factors in creating competitive advantage for companies. The cost savings and service improvements may be found across all elements of the supply chain:
- Production
- Purchasing
- Inventory holding
- Warehousing
- Transportation
- Order-entry/customer service/administration.

In order to be successful, it is necessary to consider all aspects in an integral manner. We believe that the distribution center plays a key role in this endeavor. By streamlining internal warehouse operations, we may reduce costs and improve performance levels. After many years of negligence and increasing warehousing costs, considerable savings must be possible. However, the distribution center also is the intermediary between production, purchasing, inventory control, transportation, sales, etc. If the distribution center focuses on overall company/supply chain objectives in its dealings with these departments, then the company will develop toward integral optimization.

In this book we introduce an action plan called highly competitive warehouse management that demonstrates how the distribution center can attain best-in-class performance, both internally and in its interaction with other members of the supply chain. In accordance with the studies mentioned earlier and based on our own research among a large number of distribution centers, which we will discuss in Section 1.6, we estimate that the methodology reduces warehousing costs by up to 30 percent. Of course, warehousing costs are only an element of overall logistics costs. However, since the methodology aims at integral optimization, it may create savings across other disciplines as well. Nevertheless, if a company seeks best-in-class supply chain performance, then separate improvements in other disciplines are also necessary.

8. **Investigate your company's internal costs for the last two years.**
   a. Estimate the costs in Table 1.2.
   b. What do you notice when you analyze the costs?
   c. In your opinion, which costs need to be reduced? And why?

Table 1.2 Internal costs in last two years.

Category	Costs last year	Costs year before
Production	$	$
Purchasing	$	$
Inventory holding	$	$
Warehousing	$	$
Transportation	$	$
Order-entry/CS/Administration	$	$
Total	$	$

The Clean Socks Experiment

In the previous section, we concluded that major savings are possible in warehouses. Now the question arises as to how these savings can be attained. We investigate this question by addressing a simple exercise from everyday fashion logistics.

> **Exercise: The Clean Socks Experiment**
> This experiment comes from the privacy of my own home, but it could just as well be yours. My wife, our two sons and I all wear socks, which need to be washed and returned to our drawers. Our family owns the usual equipment to help us with this chore: a washing machine, a dryer, a washing line and several laundry baskets. We wear various kinds of socks (dress socks, sports socks, cycling socks, hiking socks, etc.) in different colors and styles. We keep our clean socks, nicely folded in pairs, in our individual sock drawers.
>
> Managing our socks can be seen as a straightforward logistics process, so it is an interesting exercise to see if we can find ways to improve it. Personally, I have encountered two major bottlenecks over the years. The first bottleneck is that for no apparent reason socks seem to disappear in the process, which leaves our family with a bunch of single socks without pairs. The second bottleneck is that, although the overall process seems pretty efficient, it is particularly labor-intensive to find matching pairs from the diversity of clean socks.
>
> Now, I would like to ask you to think of ways to optimize this process and in particular to overcome the two bottlenecks. I suggest that you take precisely five minutes and write down as many improvements as you can. Do not bother about costs or feasibility. This is a brainstorming exercise. Anything that is legal and does not involve magic is allowed. Good luck!

9. Take five minutes to think about the "clean socks" process.
   a. *Try to list at least 10 possible options for improving the process.*

Did you take time to find possible solutions? If not, then please stop reading and do the exercise first. Next, we will discuss the solutions that you found.

1.3.1 Change the Process

Now that you have done the exercise, let us consider the ideas you wrote down. Here is a list of options; perhaps you found some similar options.

1. Tie pairs together before you put them in the laundry basket so that pairs stay together. Perhaps you could use the clothes-pins from the washing line to hold them together.
2. Put the dirty socks in separate laundry baskets by person/color group and wash them separately to simplify the sorting process.
3. Move the washing machine and dryer to the master bedroom to reduce travel distances.
4. Keep a registration of the socks in each stage of the process (e.g., dirty laundry basket, washing machine, dryer, washing line, clean laundry basket, closet), so that socks are not lost easily.

If you look at this list, you see that all of the solutions made changes to optimize the laundry process. In general, changes to existing processes may help to eliminate one or more activities (option 1) or to improve activities (options 2, 3 and 4). Such changes contribute to overall efficiency (more efficient sorting) and accuracy (fewer missing socks).

1.3.2 Introduce a Tool

However, there are more ways to optimize activities. Here are some alternative solutions:

5. Attach distinctive markers to identical socks so that you can easily find pairs.
6. Put dirty pairs in separate small bags that keep them together throughout the entire process.
7. Attach waterproof RFID tags to the socks and use automatic tag readers to track them in each stage of the process, so that socks are not lost easily.
8. Introduce an automatic sorting device and automate the process.

Notice that these solutions all use tools. In general, tools are excellent aids to optimize activities. In fact, the extensive use of tools has given the human race a competitive advantage over animals. This is illustrated by our ancestors in prehistoric times whose lives were predominantly defined by their tool-making technologies: stone age, bronze age and iron age. Clearly, the introduction of a new tool or technology creates many opportunities, which may lead to a breakthrough in performance.

1.3.3 Redefine the Problem

It may be that there still are some solutions left on your list. So, let us consider a third selection of options:

9. Accept that you wear non-matching socks and eliminate the sorting process.
10. Buy many identical socks and eliminate the sorting process.

11. Use disposable socks and eliminate the entire laundry process. However, purchasing and disposal processes are introduced instead.
12. Stop wearing socks and eliminate the entire laundry process.

Notice that these four options do not attempt to optimize the solution. Instead they redefine the problem. This is fundamentally different. To explain, we must first distinguish between two roles: the client and the service provider, each with distinct responsibilities. On the one hand there are the people who wear the socks, we will refer to them as clients. On the other hand there are those who clean and sort the socks, we will refer to them as the service providers. In this example, a person could be both client and service provider.

In general terms, the client provides the input and defines the output of the process, whilst the service provider executes the process. Note that in solutions 9 to 12, the client has relaxed the requirements that are imposed on the laundry process, which makes it easier for the service provider to execute the task. In particular, in option 9 the client slackens the requirements on the output of the process, in option 10 the client alters the input to the process and in options 11 and 12 the client eliminates the input altogether. In general, solutions that redefine a problem can be highly effective. Think of teleconferencing instead of meeting in person or downloading instead of buying music, movies or literature.

1.3.4 Persist in the Old Way

It may be that there are solutions on your list that do not change the process, do not introduce tools and do not redefine the problem. Here are some examples:
13. Practice extensively and become a highly-skilled socks sorter.
14. Pay the kids to do the laundry.
15. Hire a maid with outstanding household skills.
16. Outsource the laundry process to a low-wage country (off-shoring).

In these examples, we persist in the old way of working, only we train to do it more efficiently or we use cheaper labor to do the job.

Case Study: The Clean Socks Experiment
I persisted for many years in the frustration of sorting socks. For my 42nd birthday I threw away all my socks and bought 30 pairs of identical black socks. This not only eliminated the sorting process, it also helped to mitigate the missing socks issue: each time I lose a sock, I do not have to discard the whole pair. Furthermore, we no longer fold socks into pairs. Instead, we just drop the loose socks in the drawer. My wife often wears boots so she also threw away her socks and now wears the black socks from my drawer. For our two sons we did the same. We bought 30 gray pairs, which they both can wear.

1.3.5 Solution Categories

In general we may classify solutions in one of the following four categories:
   a. Persist in the old way
   b. Change the process
   c. Introduce a tool
   d. Redefine the problem.

10. Consider the list of solutions to the "clean socks experiment," which you compiled in Question 6.
   a. Classify all options in one of the four solution categories.
   b. Which category had the most options?
   c. Which category had the fewest options?
   d. Is this typical of your problem-solving approach?

Clearly, these categories do not apply to washing socks only. In fact, they apply to all repetitive activities that we encounter in our lives, either personal or professional. Warehousing involves a lot of repetitive work and we will exploit this categorization in our quest to find better ways to do that work.

11. While keeping the "clean socks experiment" in mind, consider the order-picking process in your distribution center.
   a. Identify one or two bottlenecks in the order-picking process.
   b. List as many solutions as you can think of to resolve the bottlenecks.
   c. Classify all options in one of the four solution categories.
   d. Look at the number of options per category. Try to think of one additional option for the category with the fewest answers.
   e. Which solution(s) will most likely help to improve the order-picking process in your distribution center?

1.4 Four Elements of Warehouse Optimization

In 1908, industrialist Henry Ford introduced efficient *mass production* for his Model T-Fords. This was a major accomplishment. Since that time, companies all over the world have enjoyed enormous *economies of scale*. However, this resulted in sky-high inventories, lengthy response times and limited room for customer-specific modifications or none, considering Ford's famous phrase "You can have any color you like, so long as it is black."

Supply chain management (*SCM*) changed this view of the world. The focus shifted from efficient manufacturing to reducing inventories and response times with reliable processes that allow many customer-specific product and service enhancements. Logisticians have successfully applied various models to implement these new objectives. Some popular models are *ECR* (*efficient consumer response*), *JIT* (*just in time*) and *Lean* to mention a few. These models were developed in the 1950's, an era when efficient mass production was still the leading paradigm. Accordingly, the models have successfully eliminated a lot of the *waste* caused by mass production practices. In particular, on-hand inventories have shrunk from months or even years to only a few days or weeks.

In this context we may ask ourselves if the models are still valid. Should we continue to reduce the already shrunk inventories? Can it be that we have gone too far? The supply chain with the least inventory or the fewest process steps is not necessarily the winning supply chain (nor the cheapest supply chain for that matter). A lean configuration could seriously harm economies of scale in order processing, transportation and warehouse handling, not to mention the potential impact on customer service levels.

Consequently, it is no longer obvious in which direction we should explore further optimization. In fact, if we want to achieve a radical breakthrough, then we have to look beyond the options promoted by previous models. Whereas existing logistics models take it for granted that inventories should be reduced, response times should be shortened and activities should be eliminated, highly competitive warehouse management also considers the opposites as potential alternatives and makes an integral trade-off. We do not say that reducing inventories, rationalizing process steps or eliminating errors (as propagated by the popular *Six Sigma* model, e.g., Pyzdek, 2003) are bad practices. On the contrary, in many situations these are still the best options and highly competitive warehouse management will certainly recognize them as such. However, they are not the only options anymore. Accordingly, highly competitive warehouse management will continue to seek improvements where the current generation of logistics models falters.

We define *warehouse management* as the continuous effort to operate and improve the processes, organizational structure and use of information technology in the distribution center as well as collaboration with supply chain partners. Highly competitive warehouse management proposes an integral approach that examines all options for optimization. In accordance with the categories from the "clean socks experiment" in Section 1.3.5, we can state that *warehouse management* consists of the following four elements:
- People (persist in the old way)
- Process (change the process)
- Technology (introduce a tool)
- Business (redefine the problem).

We discuss these four elements in the following sections.

1.4.1 People

The manager has the responsibility to ensure that the *people* in the warehouse execute the processes well. This involves guiding and training people, addressing and motivating them and taking their feedback seriously. There are many books on management and leadership (e.g., Covey, 2004 or Kotter, 1996).

12. **Consider your capabilities with regard to the following.**
    a. *Training and guiding people*
    b. *Addressing and motivating personnel*
    c. *Taking feedback seriously*
    d. *What do you think of your strengths and weaknesses with regard to people management? Fill out the table below.*

    Table 1.3 Personal strengths and weaknesses.

Element	Strength (+)	Weakness (-)
Training and guiding people		
Addressing and motivating people		
Dealing with feedback		
Number of +'s or -'s		

Highly competitive warehouse management fosters continuous change. But oftentimes, we see that warehouse operators are reluctant to change: "We have been doing it this way for 10 years, why should we do it differently now?" The manager has the responsibility to guide his staff through these changes.

Change management includes training operators in new methods of working. However, there is more. We will also encounter changes that affect the culture in the warehouse. For instance, the introduction of a WMS requires that operators precisely follow the procedures of the system: No more working around the system. Also the introduction of performance indicators has an impact on the culture: Make decisions based on facts rather than feelings. In practice, these changes can be realized. However, they require considerable effort by the manager and his team. He constantly has to remind people of the new way of working and stress why it is so important. And he has to assess how people respond to change. In Chapter 2 we further discuss the aspects of change management.

13. **Think of a significant change that happened during your professional career.**
    a. *Describe the significant change*
    b. *What was your first emotional reaction to this change?*
    c. *What actions did you take as a response to this change?*
    d. *What was the result of your behavior?*
    e. *What happened after that?*
    f. *What do you think of that significant change now?*
    g. *What does this imply for your change management skills?*

1.4.2 Process

If there are no specified procedures in the warehouse, then each operator may perform a task in his own way. So, when there are 10 operators, one of them will have the best procedure. In fact, if we combine the best parts of each of those 10 procedures we could come up with a best practice that outperforms all others. Moreover, without specified procedures, the manager cannot tackle people on their conduct since there is no standard.

Hence, the key to managing processes is to make the warehouse operation *transparent*. By clearly defining processes, objectives, costs and performance measures, both the manager and operators obtain a better understanding of the operation. The transparency motivates operators to do their jobs in an efficient and precise manner. Moreover, it enables the people in the distribution center to autonomously make decisions based on facts rather than speculation, personal preferences or politics. In particular, transparency enables a continuous analysis and improvement of warehouse performance.

A great many software vendors have developed *warehouse management systems (WMSs)*. A WMS controls all activities in the distribution center, such as putaway, storage and order-picking. In particular, the system records all activities in detail. This considerable amount of data provides valuable input for more sophisticated performance indicators. In practice, managers rarely take advantage of this opportunity. Therefore, highly competitive warehouse management will show how detailed data can be used to compute valuable management information.

1.4.3 Technology

From the "clean socks experiment" in Section 1.3.2 we learned that tools and technology can create a major breakthrough in performance. The tools that we use in warehouses are automated material handling systems, such as conveyors and automated cranes, and information technology such as warehouse management systems.

Information technology has a major impact on warehouse performance. *Highly Competitive Warehouse Management* proposes the use of flexible and intelligent information systems. The systems should be able to support the desired method of working. Moreover, it should be easy to modify the software to accommodate any process redesign necessary to keep the distribution center up-to-date with ever-changing market requirements.

In particular, new technologies such as *radio frequency* (RF) scanning enable real-time communication between the WMS and the operators in the distribution center. The real-time and detailed information allows the WMS to control the warehouse operation in an intelligent manner. *Highly Competitive Warehouse Management* introduces a planning and control framework that exploits this abundance of data to make WMSs more intelligent. The framework helps to substantially improve the short-term and long-term performance of the distribution center.

14. **RF scanning is a technology that enhances the capabilities of a WMS.**
    a. Which other technologies do you know that could enhance the WMS?
    b. What will be the advantages of implementing these technologies?

1.4.4 Business

From the "clean socks experiment" in Section 1.3.3 we concluded that the ultimate solution may be to redefine the problem. Within a company, the warehouse typically plays the role of the service provider, while other departments such as sales or purchasing are its clients who decide what the warehouse should do. Thus if we could change the requirements imposed by others upon the warehouse operation, then we could achieve major benefits in the distribution center. The challenge is to *align* the various parties involved. This implies that their actions and decisions should be aimed at achieving the overall objective of the company or the supply chain rather than their individual objectives. *Supply chain management (SCM)* has been widely accepted in recent decades as industry's leading paradigm. SCM is defined as the management of upstream and downstream relationships with suppliers and customers with the objective of serving the customer as well as possible, whilst achieving the lowest possible costs for the entire supply chain (Christopher, 2005). Initiatives such as demand forecasting, synchronized planning, process redesign and electronic data interchange (EDI) have made business processes more efficient and reliable. Consequently, in the last few decades inventories and response times have been slashed, processes have become considerably more reliable and products and services can be tailored to the needs of individual customers.

Despite the apparent successes, progress in SCM is slow. In particular, the barriers between companies or even between internal departments are hard to overcome. Collaborating in joint efforts, developing mutual trust and sharing revenues are all challenges.

Which activities need to be performed by the distribution center follows directly from decisions made by other departments within the company and other members of the supply chain. The profiles, volumes and timeframes of the orders to be received, stored and shipped determine the workload in the distribution center and hence have an immediate impact on warehousing costs. However, the following questions arise:
- Did customers perceive the value added by the services?
- Did customers deliberately request the particular service?
- Would they have requested it if they understood the true costs?
- Did customers have another choice?
- Was it perhaps an old habit or an arbitrary computation by the ERP system?

Often, the parties involved are simply unaware of the cost effects of the service requested and many costs are wasted throughout the supply chain. Hence, requests for services from the distribution center should be based on a conscious trade-off between service levels and overall costs. As a typical example of poor alignment, think of a purchasing department that has awarded a contract for a product to the lowest cost supplier. However, the logistics performance of the supplier is poor and leads to extra demands upon the distribution center. The overall cost could have been considerably lower, had the purchasing department contracted a reliable supplier.

15. **As a customer, your preference in customer service may differ between products that you purchase.**
    a. *For which products would you prefer a distribution center with low prices and low customer service? And why?*
    b. *For which products would you prefer a distribution center with high prices and high customer service? And why?*

Achieving the optimal trade-off between service levels and overall costs requires close collaboration between departments and companies. *Highly Competitive Warehouse Management* introduces a framework for computing the optimal trade-offs and establishing a successful collaboration.

16. **Warehouse management consists of four elements: People, process, technology and business.**
    a. *Define each of these elements.*

1.5 Growth Path for Warehouse Optimization

Managers have been improving distribution centers haphazardly although effectively for decades. In this manner, logistics operations have been lifted to higher levels of performance. However, progress is difficult and slow. Many initiatives, in particular those involving either IT or supply chain integration, have only experienced minor successes or have failed completely. This probably has nothing to do with the initiatives or the systems themselves. They may have been excellent. The problem has been that they were introduced when the organization was not yet ready for them. Hence, if initiatives are introduced in the correct order, then they become more successful. This is comparable to building a house. First we lay the foundations, then we build the walls and the roof, and eventually we finish the interiors. If we do this in any other sequence, the result would be disastrous.

If we look at distribution centers, then we see three major implementation pitfalls:
- Being absorbed in a fire-fighting routine
- Introducing new technology before getting the processes right
- Deploying supply chain integration initiatives without proper information and systems.

Many managers are absorbed by their day-to-day routine. Ironically, they are so busy with everyday problem-solving that they rarely find time to solve problems. Subsequently, they attempt to solve their operational problems by introducing new software. However, if the new software is supposed to manage the old awkward processes, then the implementation will not bring any benefits. In fact, the requirement to fit the old processes to the new software compromises the project since it is likely to require an abundance of customizations. Hence, *Highly Competitive Warehouse Management* aims to get the processes right – improving, modifying, augmenting – whatever is required to clean up the mess created by years of minor changes and neglect. In other words, straighten out the operation before overlaying the new technology.

Furthermore, managers often struggle with supply chain integration initiatives. Supply chain management (SCM) advocates a close collaboration between businesses and business processes in order to optimize the overall added value in the supply chain. Necessary conditions for successful supply chain collaboration are:
- The parties involved commit to business and supply chain objectives and possess information to substantiate their actions accordingly.
- The parties involved are well organized internally. Collaboration increases mutual dependencies so that it becomes vital for the parties to perform according to the agreed standards.
- The parties involved have proper information technology to cope with the broad scope and the related complexity of decision making.

Under these conditions, supply chain integration initiatives will be significantly more successful.

So what is the proper implementation strategy for improving the distribution center? *Highly Competitive Warehouse Management* proposes a growth path that avoids the three implementation pitfalls. It guides managers from a poorly organized distribution center to a best-in-class operation. The growth path distinguishes four *maturity* stages as shown in the *maturity grid* (Figure 1.2):
- Reactive warehouse management
- Effective warehouse management
- Responsive warehouse management
- Collaborative warehouse management.

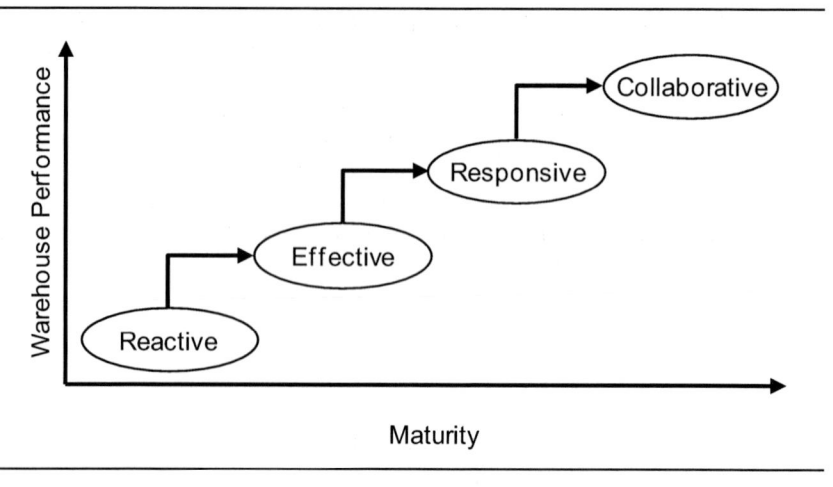

Figure 1.2 Warehouse management maturity grid.

The first stage of the maturity grid, *reactive warehouse management*, serves as the baseline. It is a distribution center where processes are unstructured and ill-defined. Performance is unreliable. The manager constantly needs to react to the same events that occur in the distribution center on a daily or even hourly basis. Individual heroics and "working around the system" are what make things happen in this type of distribution center.

The second stage is *effective warehouse management*. In this stage, we standardize the management of the distribution center. We systematically structure the organization, set goals and identify the cost and performance levels. These efforts not only simplify day-to-day management, they also facilitate a transparent analysis of the bottlenecks. The distribution center becomes an effective link in the supply chain.

The third stage is *responsive warehouse management*. In this stage we utilize information technology to increase performance. IT is a powerful enabler of logistical improvements. However, existing logistics models hardly address the use of intelligent information systems. We introduce new planning and control principles that respond in real-time to events.

The fourth and final stage is *collaborative warehouse management*. In this stage we reconsider the role of the distribution center in the supply chain. We look beyond the four walls of the distribution center. In other words, in the previous stages we sought to do things right in the distribution center, without considering if we were doing the right things. In this stage we demonstrate how to improve the performance of the entire supply chain through better collaboration.

Accordingly, highly competitive warehouse management is a growth model. The model guides the manager along the four stages in the maturity grid. Stage 2, effective warehouse management, structures the organization, then stage 3, responsive warehouse management, introduces intelligent controls and finally stage 4, collaborative warehouse management, realigns the supply chain. Each stage enables the distribution center to act successfully in the subsequent stage.

Is it a strict rule to obey the sequence of the maturity stages? In principle yes, but exceptions are possible. If a quick-win is observed in supply chain collaboration, i.e., a stage 4 optimization, while the distribution center is still muddling in stage 1, then the manager should not hesitate to implement it. Go ahead and pick the low hanging fruit! However, remember that the operation should be ready for it and realize that the project would be easier and more successful after mastering stage 3. In any case, be aware that you are dealing with a subsequent level.

17. **Highly competitive warehouse management considers the maturity of a distribution center: from a poorly organized distribution center to a best-in-class operation.**
    a. Think of your distribution center. On which level do you think it is operating?
        i. Poorly organized
        ii. Reasonably organized
        iii. Well organized
        iv. Best-in-class
    b. On which factors do you base this answer?
    c. How much money could be saved in your distribution center through better warehouse management? Express this as a percentage of current costs.
    d. How would you distribute the savings potential from question c. among the three maturity steps in Figure 1.3?

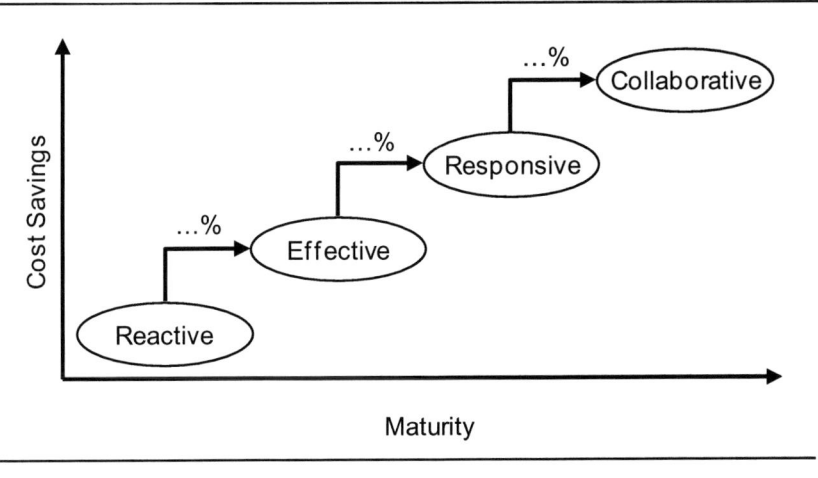

Figure 1.3 Estimate of possible cost savings.

1.6 Warehouse Maturity Scan

In Section 1.5 we introduced highly competitive warehouse management as an action plan that develops the operation along four maturity stages. The question arises as to how much we can realistically expect to save? Based on the international studies listed in Section 1.2 together with empirical evidence from a large number of warehousing projects, we assert that we can reduce overall costs by 10 percent as the organization moves to each successive maturity stage. Hence, highly competitive warehouse management could save as much as 30 percent, depending on the initial state of the distribution center (Figure 1.4). The savings potential applies to all distribution centers, big or small, simple or complex, across all industries and supply chains.

In addition, the changes in the distribution center may also lead to savings in transportation, production, order processing and holding inventories. In that case, the overall savings can be substantially higher than 30 percent of the warehousing costs. Moreover, many of the principles of highly competitive warehouse management may also be applied to other disciplines in the value chain, i.e., transparency to create efficient processes, intelligent IT for effective capacity utilization and collaboration for aligning services. These applications may be used to unleash the 30 percent savings potential on overall logistics costs (see Section 1.2).

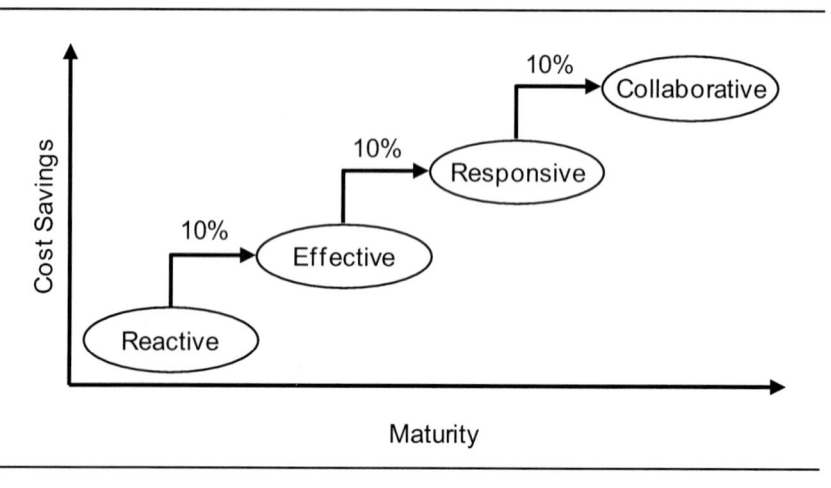

Figure 1.4 Anticipated cost savings from highly competitive warehouse management.

How can highly competitive warehouse management achieve such performance breakthroughs in each of these stages? Effective warehouse management, the second stage, makes the operation more transparent. The responsible staff can use the improved transparency to analyze bottlenecks in the distribution center and make processes more efficient. The subsequent stage, responsive warehouse management, introduces intelligent planning and control mechanisms, which help to improve the utilization of people and resources in the distribution center. Finally, collaborative warehouse management, the ultimate stage, re-evaluates the services provided by the distribution center and attempts to better align them with supply chain objectives. Table 1.4 characterizes the four maturity stages.

Table 1.4 Characterization of the maturity stages.

#	Maturity	Cost Level (%)	Key Element	Savings
1.	Reactive	100	Individual heroics	Baseline
2.	Effective	90	Transparency	Process efficiency
3.	Responsive	80	Planning and control	Resource utilization
4.	Collaborative	70	Collaboration	Service alignment

In Appendix A, we present the *warehouse maturity scan* that estimates the maturity of a distribution center[5]. The scan computes the facility's maturity level at the effective, responsive and collaborative stages and it estimates the savings potential. According to the previous discussion, the savings potential is between 0 and 30 percent. Another indicator computed by the scan is the *complexity* of the distribution center. This indicator relates to the size and variability of the distribution center operation.

For a better understanding of the following discussion, we suggest that you fill out the *warehouse maturity scan* for your distribution center before you continue reading.

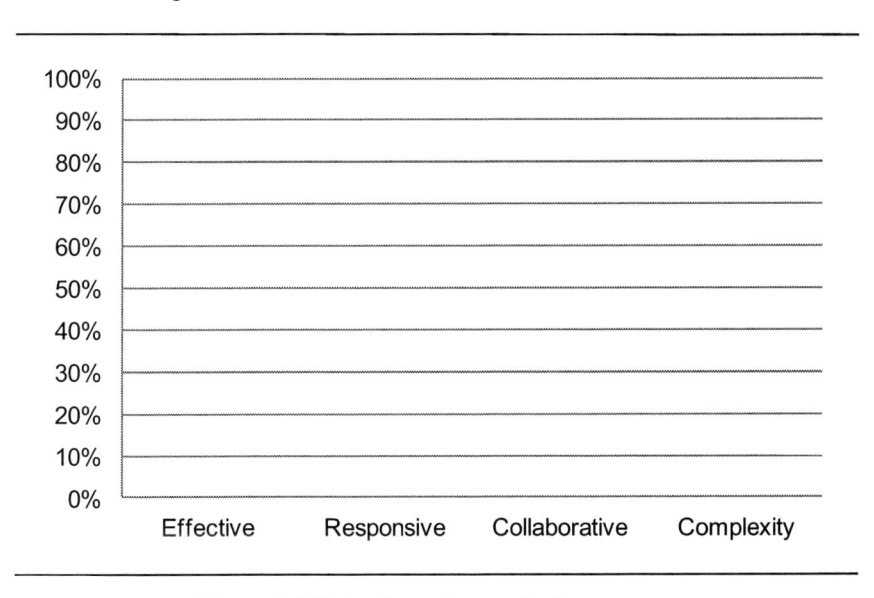

Figure 1.5 Maturity and complexity scores.

---

[5] The warehouse maturity scan can also be found online at www.hcwm.net.

18. Complete the warehouse maturity scan.
   a. Fill out the warehouse maturity scan for your distribution center in Appendix A or use the online scan at www.hcwm.net.
   b. Plot your maturity and complexity scores in the graph in Figure 1.5.

1.6.1 How Mature are Distribution Centers?

In total, 500 participants responded to the online warehouse maturity scan between 2008 and 2011. Most participants are based in The Netherlands. Table 1.5 shows the distribution of the participants across vertical markets.

Table 1.5 Survey breakdown by vertical market.

Vertical Market	Population Share (%)
Industrial products	18
Consumer goods (non-food)	16
Food	14
High-tech	11
Healthcare	8
Automotive	5
Fashion	5
Multi-media	5
Spare parts	4
Do-it-yourself	4
Chemicals	4
Cold storage	3
Office equipment	2

Table 1.6 shows the share of participants by position in the supply chain.

Table 1.6 Survey breakdown by supply chain position.

Company Type	Population Share (%)
Third party logistics provider	35
Wholesaler/distributor	34
Finished goods manufacturer	15
Retailer	7
Raw/semi-finished goods manufacturer	5
E-commerce	4

The black bars in Figure 1.6 show the average maturity scores of survey participants. We see a 36 percent compliance with the effective stage, 37 percent with the responsive stage and 30 percent with the collaborative stage. Note that there is no score for the reactive stage, since there are no practices associated with it. It only serves as a baseline.

HIGHLY COMPETITIVE WAREHOUSE MANAGEMENT 39

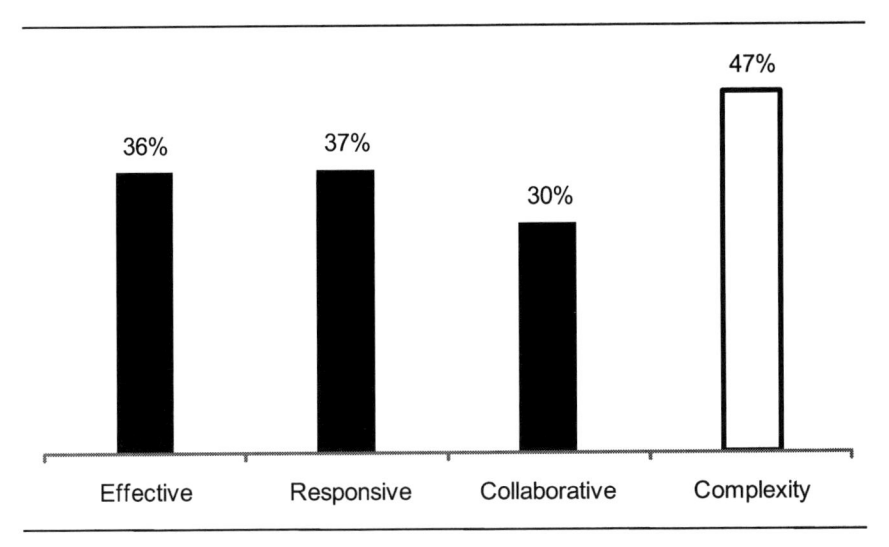

Figure 1.6 Average participant's score in online warehouse maturity scan.

The white bar in Figure 1.6 shows that the average complexity score of the survey participants is 47 percent. Thus, there is roughly an equal share of large/complex distribution centers and small/basic operations.

19. **Figure 1.6 shows the average participant's score in the online warehouse maturity scan.**
    a. Explain the graph in your own words.

1.6.2   Savings Potential

Based on the maturity scores, the warehouse maturity scan estimates the savings potential for distribution centers that can be attained by adopting the best practices used by leading practitioners.

20. **Calculate the savings potential.**
    a. Savings Potential $= (30\% - \dfrac{\text{Effective} + \text{Responsive} + \text{Collaborative}}{10})$
    b. Compare the calculated savings potential to your estimate in Figure 1.3. What do you notice?
    c. Are the scores in Figure 1.5 in accordance with your estimates in Figure 1.3? Do you agree with the warehouse maturity scan?

The online warehouse maturity scan reveals an average savings estimate among all participants of 20 percent – a substantial amount. The scan also asks participants how much they expect can be saved in their distribution centers by adopting best practices in processes, IT and collaboration. The participants expect that they can save 19 percent on average – nearly identical to the 20 percent average computed by the scan. Additionally, if we analyze the scores of individual participants, then we see a statistical correlation between estimates computed by the scan and participants' expectations. Therefore, we can conclude that despite the fact that the warehouse maturity scan has a limited set of questions, it gives a realistic estimate of the maturity and savings potential of a distribution center.

21. Take a look at the average participant's score in the online warehouse maturity scan.
   a. What do you think of the average scores? Are they as you would have expected?
   b. When you compare your own scores to the average scores in the scan, what do you notice?

1.6.3   Average Maturity Scores

If we interpret the average maturity scores in Figure 1.6, one striking observation is the relatively low score of the participants at the effective stage. Since the effective stage lays the foundation for subsequent stages, one might expect that the maturity score on the effective stage is higher than the maturity scores on the other two stages. However, this is not the case. The average effective score at 36 percent is slightly below the average responsive score at 37 percent. Besides, the initiatives required in the effective stage, such as creating transparency and streamlining processes, are relatively easy to achieve and less costly than those in subsequent stages. One expects that managers would be interested in this *low hanging fruit*. However, the outcome of the scan suggests otherwise. Instead, managers attempt to solve their operational problems through IT. Apparently, managers have heavily invested in IT systems in recent years, thereby neglecting the *basics* of warehouse management. Subsequently, they find out that new systems are ineffective due to the immaturity of the organization.

Another observation from the survey is that the absolute scores on all three maturity stages are relatively low. Although the practices which the scan addresses in each of the maturity stages are generally available, an average distribution center only adopts 30 to 40 percent of them. As a result, distribution centers could still attain an average savings potential of 20 percent. This is a substantial amount. Nonetheless, most managers struggle to close the performance gap. *Highly Competitive Warehouse Management* will show how to move forward successfully.

1.6.4 Maturity Scores by Vertical Market

Next, we look at the maturity scores of various vertical markets. Here we see that the most mature verticals (i.e., verticals with the lowest savings potential) are high-tech, fashion, consumer goods and office equipment (Table 1.7). What these four verticals have in common is that their products have relatively short lifecycles. Consequently, companies are forced to keep limited inventory levels to avoid the risk of obsolete stock. Satisfying customers with limited inventories imposes heavy demands on logistics operations. Thus companies in these verticals need mature logistics operations to remain competitive in their markets.

In particular, the high-tech industry outperforms all other verticals in warehouse maturity. This finding is in line with many international studies, which show that supply chain performance is essential for business success in the fast-paced high-tech market. For instance, the *2011 Supply Chain Top 25* by analyst firm Gartner (Hofman *et al.*, 2011) lists five high-tech companies in its Top 10: Apple, Dell, Research in Motion (Blackberry), Cisco Systems and Samsung. The analysts started publishing the list in 2004 and it has been dominated by high-tech companies ever since.

Table 1.7 Average savings potential by vertical market.

Vertical Market	Savings Potential (%)
High-tech	17.2
Fashion	18.6
Consumer goods (non-food)	18.7
Office equipment	18.8
Healthcare	19.1
Cold storage	19.4
Multi-media	19.6
Food	19.9
Automotive	20.1
Industrial products	21.1
Do-it-yourself	21.3
Chemicals	21.3
Spare parts	22.5

On the other end of the scale, we find the least mature verticals: do-it-yourself products, chemicals and spare parts. Contrary to the mature verticals, these businesses sell products with long lifecycles. As such, these companies experience less pressure on their logistics operations.

1.6.5 Maturity Scores by Supply Chain Position

Next, we look at the results by position in the supply chain. Table 1.8 shows the average savings potential for companies across the supply chain. Here we see that retail distribution centers are the most mature (i.e., they have the lowest savings potential), followed by e-commerce operations and third party logistics providers. The least mature distribution centers are typically found at manufacturers (of both components and finished goods).

Table 1.8 Average savings potential by supply chain position.

Position in Supply Chain	Savings Potential (%)
Retailer	16.9
E-commerce	18.3
Third party logistics provider	18.4
Wholesaler/distributor	20.8
Finished goods manufacturer	21.0
Components manufacturer	22.2

In fact, if we look at Table 1.8, we see that companies tend to have increasingly mature distribution centers once we move from upstream to downstream in the supply chain. At the end of the supply chain, where companies deliver to end-customers, logistics operations typically are more complex due to broad product ranges and small, frequent orders. Moreover, their *out-of-stock risks* are more serious. For example, if a retail distribution center cannot supply its stores, this rapidly leads to empty shelves and *lost sales*. For upstream companies this is less crucial. Their products are held by companies downstream in the supply chain, which serve as buffers for their supply interruptions. Hence, if supply is disrupted upstream, there may still be sufficient inventory in the supply chain to serve demand so that end-customers do not immediately have to face out-of-stocks.

Another reason for the maturity gap between upstream and downstream companies lies in the fact that manufacturers traditionally have higher profit margins than retailers. This implies that cost efficiency is more relevant at the end of the supply chain.

We can conclude that logistics complexity, out-of-stock risks and smaller profit margins mean that downstream companies in the supply chain need more mature distribution centers in order to be competitive in their markets.

22. **We distinguish six supply chain positions in Table 1.8.**
    a. What is the supply chain position of your company?
    b. Compare your calculated savings potential with the average savings potential in your supply chain position. What do you notice?

1.6.6 Leaders and Laggards

Next, we compare the leaders and laggards across all participants. Since the *warehouse maturity scan* computes a savings potential that lies between 0 and 30 percent, we distributed the participants into three segments:
- The *leaders* with mature operations who have a savings potential of 10 percent or less.
- The *followers* who have a savings potential between 10 and 20 percent.
- The *laggards* with immature operations who have a savings potential between 20 and 30 percent.

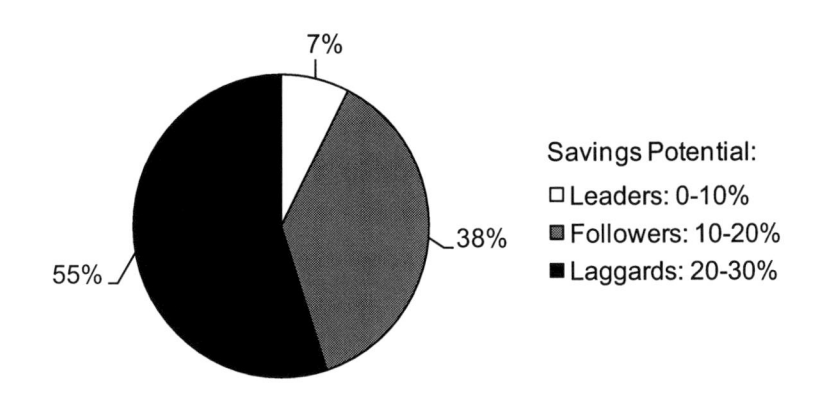

Savings Potential:
- ☐ Leaders: 0-10%
- ▨ Followers: 10-20%
- ■ Laggards: 20-30%

(7%, 38%, 55%)

Figure 1.7 Participants by savings potential.

Figure 1.7 shows the sizes of the three segments. Over 50 percent of the distribution centers are *laggards* according to our definitions. Warehouse operations in this segment are still struggling in the *Reactive* stage of the warehouse maturity model. Next, we see a large group of *followers* who constitute almost 40 percent of the total. These distribution centers achieve adequate performance levels and managers have a grip on the operation. Finally, there is a small group of *leaders* comprising just 7 percent of the distribution centers. These operations have outstanding performance levels and strongly contribute to the competitive strength of the company. Note that the international studies, which we discussed in Section 1.2 also identified small leader groups who were well ahead of the pack.

23. Look at your calculated savings potential again.
   a. How is your distribution center categorized: Leader, follower or laggard?

1.6.7 Balanced Growth

In Section 1.4, we argued that highly competitive warehouse management is a growth model that guides the manager through four maturity stages: reactive, effective, responsive and collaborative warehouse management. Each stage lays the foundation for subsequent stages. Hence, for balanced growth, it is preferable to achieve a reasonable level at one stage before attempting major initiatives in the next stage.

Figure 1.8 plots the maturity scores computed by the warehouse maturity scan for two arbitrary warehouses A and B. Warehouse A estimated an 80 percent compliance with the *effective* stage, 40 percent with the *responsive*

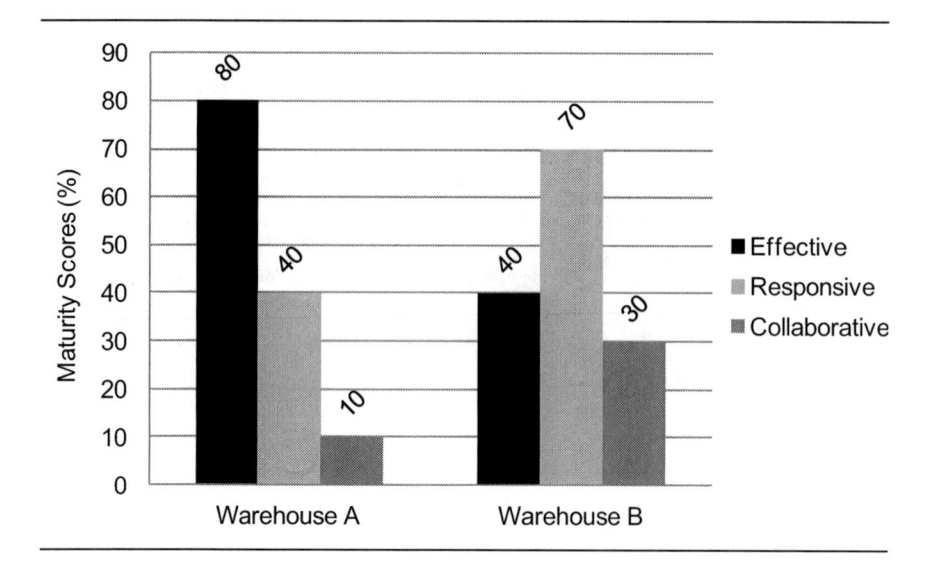

Figure 1.8 Maturity Score examples for two warehouses.

stage and 10 percent with the *collaborative* stage. This is a healthy pattern, since each stage has a lower maturity score than its predecessor. Conversely, Warehouse B heavily invested in stage 3, responsive warehouse management, without adequately mastering stage 2, effective warehouse management. This we regularly see in practice when managers attempt to solve their operational problems through IT. It turns out that the new systems are ineffective due to the immature nature of the organization.

Reviewing the survey results of the online warehouse maturity scan, we see that only 25 percent of participants have a balanced growth pattern. In other words, three quarters of the companies have an imbalance in their growth path. They have at least one stage (responsive or collaborative) with a maturity score that is higher than the score in a preceding stage. In such situations, we suggest that the manager focuses on re-establishing the balance. For instance, the manager of warehouse B in Figure 1.8 should invest in transparency and process optimization to increase the effective score before he continues with improvements in the subsequent stages.

24. **Look at the results of your maturity scan and check the growth pattern of your company.**
    a. *Is it a healthy pattern?*
    b. *If it is not a healthy pattern, what steps could you take to re-establish balance?*

1.7 Summary

Excellent warehouse performance helps companies to create competitive advantage by reducing logistics costs, by increasing internal and external customer service levels, and by aligning business activities. Research shows that best-in-class companies realize competitive customer service levels while achieving logistics costs advantages of 20 to 30 percent over their laggard peers. Moreover, these companies are financially more successful.

This book introduces an action plan called *Highly Competitive Warehouse Management* that helps to transform the distribution center into a best-in-class operation. It does not merely view the distribution center as a place where costs can be saved, it also explores how the distribution center may strengthen the competitive position of the whole company. In particular, we illustrate that *Highly Competitive Warehouse Management* does not only achieve competitive advantage for companies with private distribution centers, it also applies to third party logistics providers.

The methodology combines three principles: It goes back to basics in processes and people management, it uses intelligent IT systems and it strengthens the distribution center to become an equal partner with other departments within the company. *Highly Competitive Warehouse Management* follows a maturity grid with four consecutive stages: *Reactive, Effective, Responsive* and *Collaborative*.

The warehouse maturity scan, which can be found in Appendix A, estimates the maturity of a warehouse operation. A survey among 500 companies reveals a 20 percent average cost savings potential for distribution centers. There is a small group of leaders in warehouse management, while more than 50 percent of distribution centers are still laggards according to our definitions.

Chapter 2 discusses the change process that is involved in *Highly Competitive Warehouse Management*.

Chapter 3 explains the role and purpose of the distribution center in the supply chain. Moreover, it discusses the most common processes and control rules in the distribution center. This chapter provides the basic knowledge necessary for a warehousing study. Chapter 4 explores the state-of-the-art in warehouse management systems. The chapter gives more insight into the capabilities of the systems and the actions relevant to their implementation.

Chapter 5 introduces the models and techniques that create transparency in effective warehouse management. Chapter 6 discusses the actions that can be taken to use this transparency to optimize warehouse processes.

Chapter 7 introduces the planning and control framework of responsive warehouse management. Chapter 8 explains which actions can be taken to optimize resource utilization through the use of this planning and control framework.

Chapter 9 introduces the instruments for responsive warehouse management. These instruments help to improve collaboration in the supply chain. Finally, Chapter 10 talks about the actions that help to align warehouse services with the overall objectives of the company and the supply chain.

Chapter 2

The Challenge of Change

In the previous chapter we showed that most distribution centers can be improved considerably. In fact, we saw that over 50 percent of distribution centers are still in a stage that may best be described as continuous *fire-fighting*. Another 40 percent have adequate performance but still have ample opportunities for further improvement. Only a small group of less than 10 percent may be classified as leaders. How can it be that such a situation still exists today? Why are companies not making greater efforts to improve their distribution centers? In this chapter we examine the challenge of change and demonstrate that successful change needs the five *CDEFG*-ingredients:

- Culture
- Direction
- Evolution
- Fun
- Guidance.

Only a few underperforming distribution centers seem able to make progress. Most laggards stay in their backward position, even though there are many readily available practices that managers could easily adopt to advance their operations.

So, why are these distribution centers not making any progress? One important reason is that many people do not feel the need. They are involved in running the daily operation and change is not a priority. In addition, when someone suggests doing things differently, typically people fiercely oppose any changes. Hence, if we want to make progress, then we need a different *culture* where people feel the need and are open to change.

However, a change-oriented culture by itself is not enough. Change also needs *direction*, otherwise it is futile. The basic question of *Highly Competitive Warehouse Management* is this: How can the distribution center contribute most to overall company goals? Hence, any change in the distribution center should be aimed in this direction.

But again, *direction* itself is not sufficient. There are many roads that lead to Rome. Clearly, some roads are more easy-going than others. *Highly Competitive Warehouse Management* suggests a growth path that evolves along maturity stages. As discussed in Section 1.5, such a sequence creates fewer obstacles and more benefits. Hence, we have to design an effective plan for the *evolution* of the distribution center.

The fourth ingredient of successful change is *fun*. When successes have been achieved, this creates excitement and motivates people to continue. Hence, in addition to focusing on long-term results with plans, strategy and commitment, we also need to focus on short-term results with actions that actually improve the daily operation.

Finally, beside *culture, direction, evolution* and *fun,* the fifth ingredient of successful change is *guidance*. Without guidance, companies simply are not able to manage all the actions that are necessary for creating change.

25. With your distribution center in mind, think about the five ingredients for successful change.
   a. Which ingredients do you think are present in your distribution center?
   b. What does this mean for the process of making progress in your distribution center?

In this chapter, we are going to discuss how managers can tackle these five issues and create successful change in the distribution center. We discuss the following topics:

- *Change management* to facilitate a *change-oriented culture* (Section 2.1)
- *Warehouse strategy* to give *direction* (Section 2.2)
- *Warehouse action plan* to organize the *evolution* (Section 2.3)
- *Optimization actions* to create *fun* and successes (Section 2.4)
- *Project management* to give *guidance* (Section 2.5).

In Appendix C we present a set of *Do it* questions that help you to get started with these issues. We emphasize that successful change is the essence of implementing highly competitive warehouse management in your distribution center.

2.1 Change Management to Facilitate a Change-Oriented Culture

In the previous section, we argued that many distribution centers struggle to make progress. An important reason is that there is no *culture of change*. The majority of people in these operations actually feel comfortable with existing performance levels. They genuinely believe that they are doing a fine job. They do not sense the need to improve. These people are *unaware* of the mediocre performance of their operation and the significant improvement potential. Clearly, without *awareness* no one will make an effort to improve.

Then there is another substantial group of people who actually are *aware* that their distribution center performs poorly. However, these people lack the *motivation* to do something about it. They display a sense of fatalism: "We tried to change things before, but it just did not work." They blame others, other departments, senior management, colleagues, company culture or anything and anyone except themselves. Obviously, without motivation, no one will make an effort to improve.

Highly Competitive Warehouse Management presents many ideas and methodologies to improve distribution centers. However, they are likely to be fruitless unless people feel:
- Awareness of potential
- Motivation to change.

Having said this, there remains only a small group of people who are *aware of the potential* and do feel *motivation to change*. These people are our hope. Unfortunately, they are scarce in most organizations.

Now ask yourself: Am I such a person? Am I aware of the potential in our operation? Am I aware of any shortcomings in my personal role within the operation? Am I motivated to make a change? If you say "yes" to these questions, then, quite likely, you are such a person. You can make the difference! Make sure that you really believe in it, that you really think it is worth the effort, that you really want to make the difference[6].

2.1.1 Awareness of Potential

Why are so few people aware of the weaknesses in their own operation and the major potential to improve? Mostly, people feel comfortable with the status quo. Their company has been successful for so many years already: "Why should we change?" The successes from the past have made people smug and complacent. This is a major liability, since we live in an era of accelerated change. Technology, markets, competition – everything changes at a pace that we have never seen before in history. It requires that companies respond quickly to these developments. Companies that fail to make progress will sooner or later fall behind. We need to grasp opportunities and avert potential crises to stay competitive, to assure continuity and to keep up bottom-line results. It is necessary that people look to the future instead of the past. This creates awareness.

However, there are more reasons for the lack of awareness. For instance, most people are only familiar with their own operation. They do not frequently have the opportunity to look inside someone else's kitchen. This is the reason why benchmarking is a practical tool to create awareness, but visits to other distribution centers are a good alternative. For that matter, the warehouse maturity scan, discussed in Section 1.6, is a powerful tool to create awareness.

---

[6] Please refer to Appendix C.1 for *Do it* questions that help you to get started with the change initiative in your distribution center.

A final reason for people's lack of awareness is the limited view people have of daily business activities. For instance, they only see what happens inside the distribution center or inside their team. They do not see the consequences of their actions outside their scope. For this reason, we strongly advocate the use of performance indicators at all staff levels in the warehouse.

2.1.2 Motivation to Change

Kotter (2008) estimates, based on years of research, that more than 70 percent of change initiatives are unsuccessful. Either the necessary change does not occur despite the fact that everyone is convinced of the need, or it is not finalized despite the tremendous efforts of some people, or it ends eventually with overruns in time and costs without achieving the original goals. Clearly, a 70 percent failure rate is an enormous burden on the industry. The failure rate also inflicts a sense of fatalism among staff. They feel frustrated from previous experiences and they do not find the spirit and energy to try again. In particular, the sense of frustration among warehouse staff is often amplified by the comparatively low status of the distribution center compared to other departments such as sales and purchasing. These departments make decisions, which the distribution center has to follow. At the same time, other departments get priority, for instance, in investment budgets or IT support.

As stated in the previous section, modern times demand accelerated change. This implies that the amount of time we spend on projects vs. daily business is shifting. We will need to spend more and more time on projects to keep up with the pace of change. Also more people will be involved in these projects, from senior management to shop-floor operators. Projects will no longer be limited to project specialists. Everyone will be involved. This requires that we create a culture where people are open to change.

However, change means that people have to leave the present, a present where they feel comfortable, a present where they play an important role. In many companies we see people in various positions who, in a small way, rule their own kingdom. This may be a specific process or system where they have unique knowledge. For them, change is a threat since it may hurt their position. This is an important reason why a situation of constant *fire-fighting* may continue to exist for many years. People enjoy the fact that they are able to solve existing problems, despite the fact that these problems should not occur in the first place.

26. **Awareness of the potential and motivation to change are important factors to improve distribution centers.**
    a. *Why are awareness and motivation important for the improvement of distribution centers?*

27. Consider your own distribution center.
   a. What do you think about the levels of awareness and motivation?

2.1.3 Change-Oriented Culture

People will only become *aware of the potential* and develop *motivation to change* when they experience their own need for it and the personal benefit that they will derive from achieving it. For managers, this implies that they have to communicate the message of necessary change strongly and consistently. Often people will show resistance. They list many reasons why the change cannot or should not be implemented. They see threats rather than opportunities. Typically, people need time to contemplate and get accustomed to new ideas. Often, after some time the idea grows on them and they become more open to it. Managers should continue to communicate the message and explain how it provides benefits.

Preferably, managers start the change initiative with the people that are most susceptible to it. They commence with a small team and a limited scope to get people involved. Once the manager has proven that it works and people start seeing what is in it for them, then it is time to get more people involved. We refer to Gabriëls (2011) and Kotter (2008) for practical guides on this topic.

28. The management team of a distribution center could take several steps to create awareness of the potential and develop motivation to change.
   a. What steps could your management take to do this?

2.2 Warehouse Strategy to Give Direction

Section 2.1 showed that making progress requires a change-oriented culture. Awareness and motivation mobilize people towards achieving the desired change. In this section we are going to discuss how we can define a direction for change.

The ultimate goal of *Highly Competitive Warehouse Management* is to create competitive advantage for the entire company. Or, when the distribution center is operated by a logistics service provider, the goal is to create competitive advantage for its clients, and thus indirectly for itself. Accordingly, the goals and strategy for the distribution center should be derived from the *company strategy*. Hence, before we focus on warehouse strategy, we first discuss company strategy.

2.2.1 Company Strategy

Companies have different strategies for achieving long-term success in the market. The essence of the strategy is the choice of activities in which a company wants to excel and how it wants to perform these activities. Porter (1980) was the first to put the customer in the center of the strategy. Clearly, customers have different needs. Some only want the best quality products, others value great service and still others prefer a good bargain. Porter states that a company must focus its strategy on a specific customer group. On the other hand, Hamel & Prahalad (1994) worked out a strategy based on the strengths of the company. They recommend a continuous focus on core competencies to enable the company to outperform its competitors. Clearly, choosing a strategy is not an easy task. A successful strategy is a mix of existing company strengths, opportunities in the market, the choice of target markets and a vision of future developments. It is the task of the company's general management to define the vision and strategy.

The value disciplines model of Treacy & Wiersema (1995) is a practical model for defining a strategy. The model describes three distinct value disciplines.

- *Operational excellence.* Superb operations and execution often by providing a reasonable quality at a low price. The focus is on efficiency, streamlining operations, supply chain management, no-frills, volume discounts. Most large international companies use this discipline.
- *Product leadership.* Strong in innovation and brand marketing, operating in dynamic markets. The focus is on development, innovation, design, time-to-market and high margins in a short time frame after product introduction.
- *Customer intimacy.* Excel in customer attention and customer service. Tailor products and services to individual or almost individual customers. Focus is on customer relationship management, delivering products and services on time and above customer expectations, excellent after sales services, reliability, being close to the customer.

The authors argue that a company must choose to excel in one discipline, where it aims at class-leading performance. The other two disciplines should not be neglected, but rather the company should aim to be merely adequate at these. The chosen strategy must be deployed in a top-down manner to all levels of the company. Hence, the chosen strategy determines which customer segments should be targeted, how internal operations should create value and how intangible assets such as competencies, technology and culture combine to support the strategy.

Can a company only have one strategy? No, a company can have multiple strategies in different product-market combinations. For instance, the same mobile phone can be a commodity in one market (e.g., North America), while it is considered highly innovative in another market (e.g., Africa). Also, a company can realize product leadership in one product range and operational excellence in another. For instance, a food manufacturer may produce both exquisite delicacies (product leadership) as well as low-cost private-label brands on behalf of retailers. In general, companies use different brand names to distinguish between the varieties.

29. Treacy & Wiersema developed the value disciplines model.
   a. *What is the dominant strategy in your company, according to Treacy & Wiersema's model?*
   b. *Give an example that demonstrates the value discipline.*

2.2.2 Warehouse Strategy

Clearly, the strategy of the distribution center should support the company strategy. The manager of the distribution center should assess the company strategy and determine how the distribution center can best contribute to the success of the company. The popular *Balanced Scorecard* by Kaplan & Norton (1996, 2001) is an excellent approach for translating strategy into operational terms. The basic idea of the Balanced Scorecard is that performance should not just be measured in financial terms, but along multiple perspectives. In fact, the model distinguishes four perspectives:
- Financial perspective
- Customer perspective
- Operational perspective
- Learning and growth perspective.

Besides being a sophisticated model for performance measurement, the Balanced Scorecard also provides a framework for formalizing strategies in so-called *strategy maps* (Kaplan & Norton, 2004). In the following sections we demonstrate how to use the strategy map structure of the Balanced Scorecard to define a warehouse strategy[7] for the distribution center.

2.2.3 Financial Perspective

If we look at the distribution center from a financial perspective, then the overall objective is to realize the lowest warehousing costs relative to the *throughput value*. We define the throughput value as the value of the goods that pass through the distribution center. In Section 1.1 we referred to a study by Davis (2011), which reported average warehousing costs as 1.8 percent of sales, while the overall logistics costs amounted to 7.8 percent (Table 1.1 on page 16). We formulate the objective as follows:

$$\text{Minimize } \frac{\text{Warehousing costs}}{\text{Throughput value}}$$

---

[7] Please refer to Appendix C.2 for *Do it* questions that will help you to define a warehouse strategy.

How can the distribution center influence this objective? Clearly, it can attempt to lower warehousing costs. However, the formula tells us that there is another way. The distribution center may also attempt to raise its throughput capacity, which enables the company to increase throughput value.

Next we examine how the distribution center may contribute to these two goals? There are two ways to cut warehousing costs:
- Increase the productivity of the warehousing operation
- Improve the cost structure of the warehousing operation.

Productivity is defined as the output that is created relative to resource capacity (typically operator hours, machine hours or warehouse space) that is consumed, for example, the number of order lines picked per operator hour. In Section 5.4.2 we will demonstrate how to create productivity measures. In Section 5.3 we will use the activity-based costing methodology to define a cost structure that allocates fixed costs (e.g., building and equipment) and variable costs (e.g., salaries and materials) to available resource capacity.

Likewise, there are two ways the distribution center can contribute to raising throughput value:
- Increase the throughput capacity of the distribution center
- Increase the value of the goods by providing value-added services.

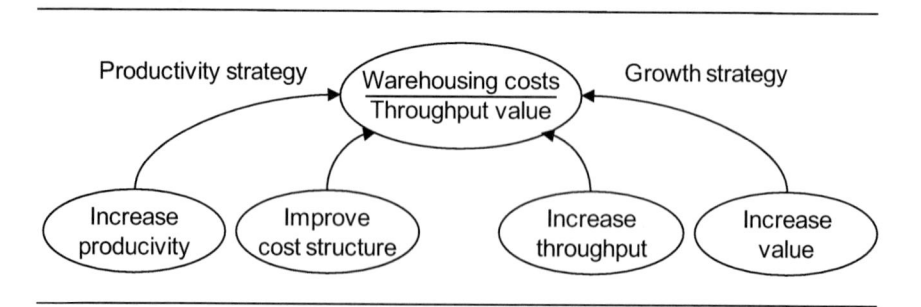

Figure 2.1 Financial perspective.

Figure 2.1 depicts how the distribution center can contribute to the overall objective of warehousing costs relative to throughput value. The figure distinguishes a *productivity strategy* focused on increasing productivity and improving the cost structure and a *growth strategy* focused on increasing throughput and value.

In fact, these four elements apply to all distribution centers. However, the emphasis that is placed on each element differs between operations. Companies that work from an *operational excellence* strategy, primarily focus on increasing productivity and improving the cost structure, i.e., a productivity strategy. The other two elements may still be relevant, but typically are of secondary importance. For instance, an operational excellence strategy accepts a higher rate of lost sales, which compromises the total sales volume.

Companies with a *product leadership* strategy typically have a primary focus on increasing sales volumes. These companies achieve high margins on products so that lost sales become a major loss. In particular in the introduction stage of a product, it is important that the distribution center is able to ramp up its throughput capacity. In summary, these companies accept higher operational cost levels that are necessary to reduce lost sales since the sizeable profit margins make up for it.

Finally, companies with a *customer intimacy* strategy typically focus on increasing value. These companies tailor their services to the needs of (individual) customers.

The relative importance of the elements of the financial perspective can be made specific by setting target levels for each element. Clearly, important elements get more ambitious targets. These target levels should be re-assessed each year in order to stay competitive in the market and to align with the company strategy.

> **Note: Financial Perspective for Logistics Service Providers**
> The above discussion clearly applies to private warehouses. However, we suggest that logistics service providers use the same formulation, since this objective creates the most value for its clients. Whether it makes the logistics service provider financially successful and profitable depends on the service fees which the logistics service provider negotiates with its clients. This is a different discussion. In this section we consider defining a warehouse strategy, not a company strategy. The definition of the company strategy was the topic of Section 2.2.1.

30. **Think of the financial perspective for your distribution center.**
    a. *How is your distribution center performing with regard to warehousing costs at the moment?*
    b. *Which of the two ways to cut warehousing costs (increasing productivity vs. improving the cost structure) is most applicable to your distribution center?*
    c. *Why?*
    d. *How could your distribution center contribute to raising throughput value?*
    e. *Are your answers on b and d aligned with company strategy?*

2.2.4 Customer Perspective

Now that we have clarified the financial perspective for the distribution center, we look at the *customer perspective* of the Balanced Scorecard. The customer perspective defines the *customer value proposition* for targeted customer segments. In fact, the customer value proposition is the essence of the chosen strategy. It explains how the company wants to be successful with targeted customers and drive financial performance. The warehouse strategy should be aligned with the customer value proposition.

Product Market Combinations

The customers of a company are usually not a homogeneous group. There are different market segments with different characteristics and different demands for products and services. For instance a manufacturer may supply wholesalers, retailers and consumers, each with different service requirements. Markets may also be segmented by geographic region.

Likewise, the company sells different products with different characteristics. We can classify products according to various criteria, such as consumer electronics, fashion and food. These segments may be further categorized as, innovative products vs. traditional products, fast movers vs. slow movers or frozen, chilled and ambient goods.

Typically, it is not *one-size-fits-all*. We may define a matrix with product segments on one axis and market segments on the other axis. For each *product/market combination* the distribution center could differentiate its services.

Customer Value Proposition

Kaplan & Norton (2001) consider nine elements of the customer value proposition:
- Price
- Quality
- Assortment
- Availability
- Responsiveness
- Product functionality
- Customer relationship
- Service
- Image.

Below we discuss how to define a customer value proposition for the distribution center along these nine elements.

Price

The sale price of a product is made up of the base price of the product plus the price for the support services provided to the customer. Clearly, the activities of the distribution center are part of the support services. The distribution center should charge fees that reflect the actual costs in an objective manner. In Section 5.1.3 we discuss how rates for warehouse services should be defined.

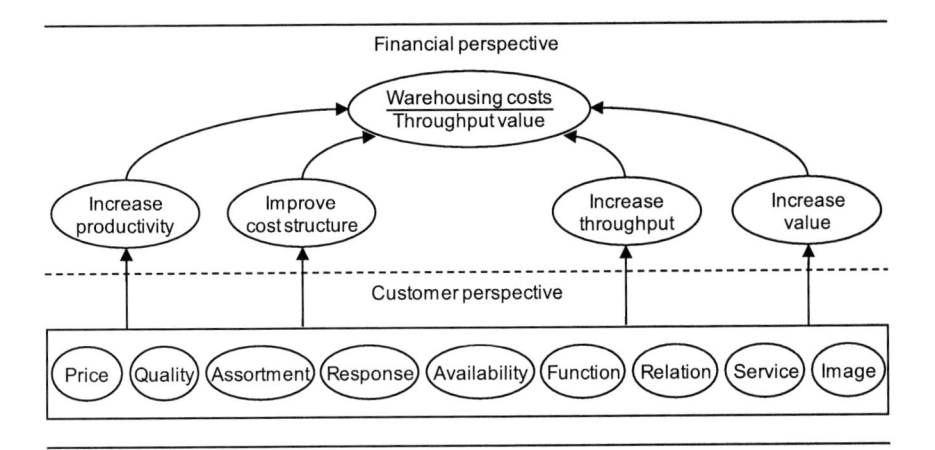

Figure 2.2 The customer perspective affects the financial perspective.

Quality

Quality relates both to the product and the support services. The distribution center should attempt to have its customers experience zero defects. The ideal customer experience is a product that meets customer specifications. This includes a correct delivery of the product, i.e., the right product in the right amount and condition and with proper documentation. In Section 5.1.2 we will define measures for accuracy.

Assortment

Some companies specialize in a narrow assortment of fast movers, while others sell a broad range with many product variants. Some companies have frequent new product introductions, while others have a steady assortment.

New product introductions are great opportunities for high sales volumes with lucrative profit margins. Think of the introduction of a new model of a game console or mobile phone. In such cases, it is essential that the distribution center is able to ramp up its capacity to meet the initial customer demand.

However, companies should manage their assortment. Unbridled product introductions may lead to unnecessary product proliferation, which creates waste in logistics and confuses marketing efforts. Hence, companies should develop strategies for phasing in new products and phasing out redundant products. For instance, set restrictions on *differentiation* (jam and fitness equipment *vs.* jam and marmalade) and *variation* (different types of jam).

Furthermore, we should track the product lifecycle. A product typically goes through various stages throughout its lifecycle: introduction, growth, maturity and decline. Products in the final phase hardly create turnover and profit margins. Such products are candidates for phase out. In particular, a new product introduction cannibalizes older products and accelerates the product lifecycle. For instance, if we introduce a new notebook model, then it renders the old model obsolete.

We see a similar effect with seasonal products. At the end of the season companies have to decide whether to keep the product until the next year or withdraw it from the mix.

After phasing out a certain product, it can be complicated to dispose of redundant stock. Accordingly, companies have to find strategies, e.g., selling redundant stock to other markets (selling food as cattle feed, for example) or different channels (outlet stores or junk dealers). In this way, storage space is freed for current products.

Availability

Availability relates to the customer order decoupling point (Van Goor *et al.*, 2003). A company does not necessarily supply its entire product range from stock. It may decide that some products are purchased from vendors only after customer orders arrive. Similarly, one may decide to only hold semi-finished goods or raw materials in stock. Then, after customer orders arrive, finished goods are assembled (assemble-to-order) or made (make-to-order). Clearly, the various *non-stock items* have longer response times than stock items.

The distribution center should have sufficient storage space to hold the stock items. Furthermore, the distribution of non-stock items through the distribution center should be organized via a process such as cross-docking.

Responsiveness

Responsiveness refers to speedy and timely delivery. Customers expect goods to arrive within the promised time frame. Responsiveness has several aspects.
- *Response time*. How soon after placing an order will the customer receive the goods, within 24 hours or 48 hours.
- *Frequency*. How often can a customer receive goods, each weekday or only on Tuesday and Friday.
- *Time frame*. What is the length of the time frame for delivery, in a specific week or on a set date between 8 AM and 10 AM.
- *Fill rate*. What percentage of orders are delivered on time, 95 percent or 98 percent of order lines.

In Section 5.1.2 we will define measures for responsiveness.

Product Functionality

Customers buy products to satisfy their needs. The distribution center may enhance the function of a product through value added logistics (VAL) services. These services customize the product to the needs of (individual) customers, e.g., configuring computer hardware or assembling kits of different products (such as a red, yellow and green pepper in one package).

Customer Relationship

Small customers may well be serviced through standard procedures. However, for large customers it may be beneficial to extend the relationship. Large customers are important to most companies. They are responsible for a large portion of the volume that goes through the distribution center. The distribution center can better service these customers, if they provide forecasts or announce large orders in advance. In return the company can reserve separate inventories for these customers or facilitate vendor managed inventories.

Service

It is highly efficient when a distribution center only provides standard services. Processes and IT systems can be designed to facilitate the standard procedures. On the contrary, if a customer desires different response times, documents, irregular product quantities or less strict return policies, this creates extra hassle for warehouse operators. Furthermore, it may well be that the warehouse management system does not support the procedures or that it creates exceptions that need to be handled separately and require special monitoring.

Hence, the distribution center should identify to what extent it needs to accommodate special services. Since the special requests disturb the regular processes, the distribution center should aim to have excellent standard services for all customers. At the same time, the company should carefully consider whether to grant specific customer privileges. Clearly, a company with a *customer intimacy* strategy will typically provide more special services than one with an *operational excellence* strategy.

Image

As we said before, the distribution center is an internal (private warehouse) or external service provider (third party warehouse). The distribution center provides its services to other departments like sales, production or purchasing. The decisions made in these departments strongly impact the work in the distribution center. Typical examples are unexpected fluctuations in order volumes or large amounts of dead stock. Hence, it is important that everyone understands the role of the warehouse operation within the company. This applies to people in the distribution center as well as in other departments.

We can make the distribution center more visible by creating an *image*. So far, we have defined the various elements of the financial perspective and customer perspective. Now we attempt to summarize our choices in a single slogan, i.e., a brief message that explains the intentions of the distribution center. Below are generic examples for each of the value disciplines discussed in Section 2.2.1:
- Low-cost reliable services (operational excellence)
- Customer-specific services (customer intimacy)
- Quick and flexible services (product leadership).

Customer Strategy

Strategy is about making choices. Now that we have identified how the distribution center supports each of the nine elements of the customer perspective, it is time to choose which elements are key. In other words, where should the distribution center excel and where does an average performance level suffice.

Operational Excellence:

(Price) (Quality) (Assortment) (Response) (Availability) (Function) (Relation) (Service) (Image)

Customer intimacy:

(Price) (Quality) (Assortment) (Response) (Availability) (Function) (Relation) (Service) (Image)

Product Leadership:

(Price) (Quality) (Assortment) (Response) (Availability) (Function) (Relation) (Service) (Image)

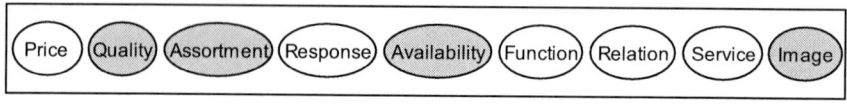

Figure 2.3 Key elements in customer perspective by value discipline.

Figure 2.3 shows the key elements for each of the three value disciplines in gray. For an *operational excellence* strategy, it is essential to provide low-cost service with a standard quality. The other elements should be adequate, but not necessarily outstanding. For instance, the assortment could be restricted to fast movers, response times could be standardized and special services may be limited. For a *customer intimacy* strategy the emphasis is on providing excellent services to customers. For instance, the distribution center supplies a broad assortment, with customer-specific response times, a high availability and various value added services. Finally, the *product leadership* strategy requires high quality services, a unique assortment and a high availability. In particular, the distribution center should be able to ramp up its capacity to ensure availability at new product introductions.

31. **Think of the customer perspective as it applies to your distribution center.**
    a. *How is your distribution center supporting each of the nine elements of the customer perspective?*
    b. *Which of these nine elements are key at the moment? Draw a figure like Figure 2.3.*
    c. *Based on these outcomes, which value discipline is dominant for your distribution center?*
    d. *Is this the value discipline that you prefer? If not, which one do you prefer and what would be your preferred key elements?*

2.2.5 Operational Perspective

Now that we have identified the key elements of the *customer perspective*, it is time to consider the *operational perspective* of the Balanced Scorecard. It is essential that the processes and activities in the distribution center are executed in such a way that they achieve the objectives of the customer perspective.

The warehouse strategy identifies how processes and activities in the distribution center contribute to the customer perspective. We distinguish four primary processes in the distribution center:
- Inbound handling[8]
- Storage
- Outbound handling
- Value added logistics.

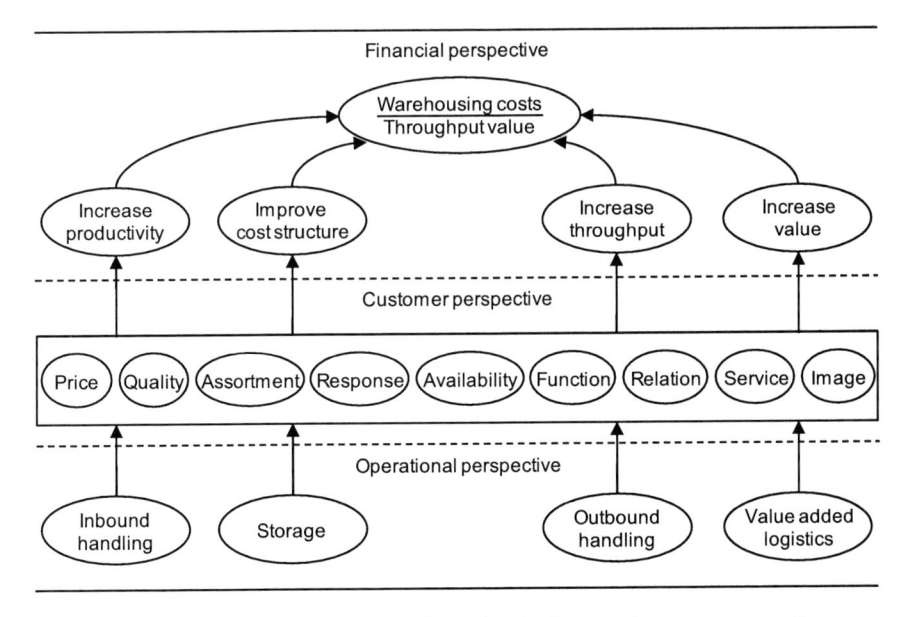

Figure 2.4 The internal perspective affects the customer perspective.

For each primary process we can identify how it supports the nine elements of the customer perspective: price, quality, assortment, responsiveness, availability, function, relationship, service and image. Below we give some examples.

Inbound handling:
- Balance inbound goods flow (price)
- Develop high quality supplier capability (quality)
- Create short dock-to-stock cycle times (responsiveness)

---

[8] Inbound handling refers to the activities in the flow of goods from the supplier into the distribution center.

Storage:
- Scrap obsolete stock (assortment)
- Register inventory levels accurately (quality)
- Enable overflow storage capacity in peak season (availability)

Outbound handling:
- Allow narrow time frames for delivery (responsiveness)
- Ban less-than-full-case order quantities (service)
- Provide information on delivery status via web portal (relationship)

Value added logistics:
- Enable specific services to individual customers (relationship)
- Customize products to meet country-specific requirements (assortment)
- Enhance value by kitting individual products (function).

It is not necessary to understand all possible effects of every process on each element of the customer perspective. Instead one should identify the key effects. A good approach is to list relevant effects per process and then choose key effects. Often we see that various key effects share similar characteristics. This allows us to further simplify the analysis by grouping similar effects. Typically, we find one or two communal principles that link together the key effects, for instance create flexible processes and IT support that can be tailored to meet changing customer requirements.

32. **Think of the operational perspective as it applies to your distribution center.**
    a. *Identify the key effects of each of the four processes (inbound handling, storage, outbound handling and value added logistics) as they are at the moment.*
    b. *How are the four processes supporting the nine elements of the customer perspective?*
    c. *Based on your outcomes, do you see common principles that link the key elements together?*
    d. *Are you satisfied with your current operational perspective? If not, what would you like to change?*

2.2.6 Learning and Growth Perspective

Linking down from the internal perspective to learning and growth objectives, we can identify the competencies, technologies and organizational climate that are essential for managing operations (Figure 2.5).

THE CHALLENGE OF CHANGE 63

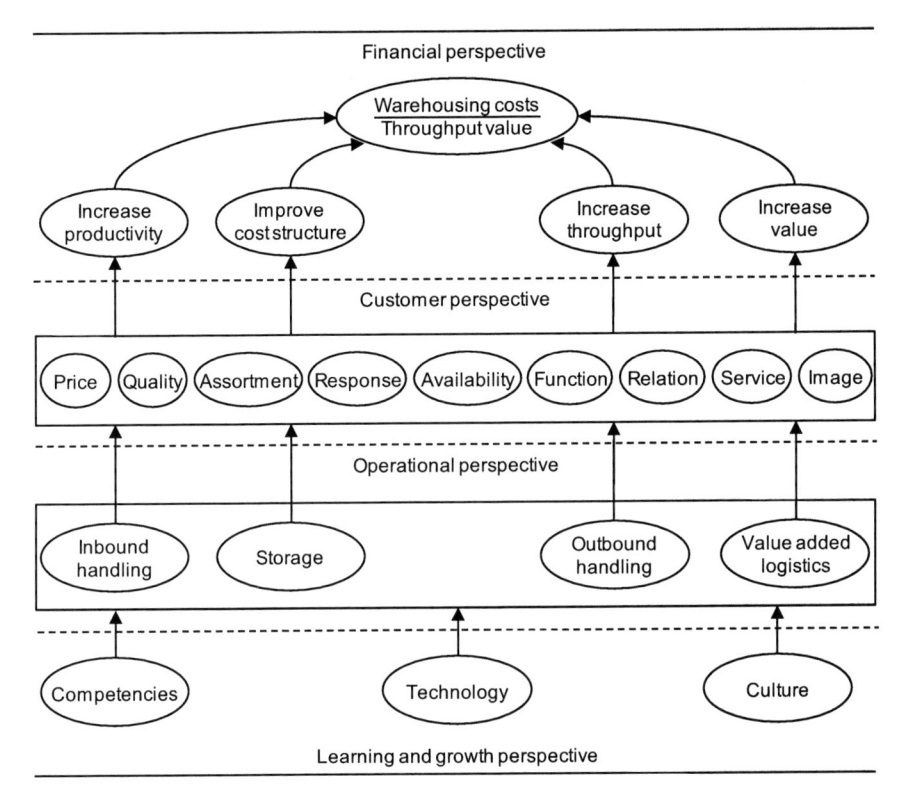

Figure 2.5 The learning and growth perspective affects the operational perspective.

Competencies

Employee competencies are key to improving operations. We must identify which skill sets and skill levels are needed by operators. Do we need operators who are capable of heavy physical labor or do we need operators who are accurate and can handle delicate materials? Also consider how broad the skill sets of operators have to be. Should an order-picker be able to handle the receipt of incoming goods? Which training courses should be available to operators, including refresher courses? What leadership and project skills would be useful?

Technology

Technology plays a critical role in distribution centers. Warehouse management systems, RF terminals, pick-to-light installations and automated material handling systems contribute to lower cost, more consistent quality and more rapid processing times. But technology also plays a role in continuous improvement. Operators need quick feedback on their performance including detailed and unbiased measurements on the output they produce. Technology also allows efficient and comprehensive interaction with other members of the supply chain.

Culture

People within the distribution center must have an intense focus on continuous process improvement and consistent service delivery to customers. As discussed in Section 2.1, awareness of the potential and a motivation to change are crucial qualities. The distribution center should grow a culture where people are open to change. The culture should encourage people to generate new ideas for process improvement. Innovations and best practices should be well documented and disseminated to all operators.

33. **Think of the learning and growth perspective as it applies to your distribution center.**
    a. *Define essential operational skills, leadership skills and project skills for your staff.*
    b. *How could technology play a role in improving operational performance in your distribution center?*
    c. *Describe the culture of your distribution center at the moment. In what way is your current culture focusing on continuous process improvement?*
    d. *What would you like to change with regard to skills, technology and culture?*

2.3 Warehouse Action Plan to Organize Evolution

The *warehouse strategy* gives *direction* to change in the distribution center. It defines *where* we want to be. However, we also need to decide along which path we want to travel. Which steps do we want to take, in which sequence and when?

In this section we show how to make an *action plan*[9] that defines timelines with milestones and concrete targets. In fact, a goal only becomes challenging and motivating when it has a timeframe, a deadline. A deadline makes people move.

Highly Competitive Warehouse Management recommends a three year plan for improving the distribution center. First, we evaluate the current state of the distribution center. We use the warehouse maturity scan to estimate the maturity of the distribution center. (We already did this exercise in Section 1.6.) Next, we list improvement actions that we want to roll out in each of the next three years. Finally, we fill out the warehouse maturity scan for each of the next three years under the assumption that we completed the projected actions. Let us look at an example.

---

[9] Please refer to Appendix C.3 for a set of *Do it* questions that help you to create an action plan for your distribution center.

2.3.1 Foodies' Warehouse Action Plan Example

Here we introduce a fictitious company called Foodies. We will encounter Foodies in various exercises throughout the remainder of this book.

> **Case Study: Foodies**
>
> *Foodies* is a fictitious company selling fresh food products. The company sells a range of healthy foods and beverages made from natural ingredients only. Foodies supplies its products to the national grocery retail chains and to the *out-of-home* channel[10]. The company has a single production plant on the east coast where it manufactures its products. The company's offices and distribution center are located adjacent to the production plant.
>
> The company was started five years ago by two former-employees of a large multinational food manufacturer. The two founders held positions in sales and operations. From the start, the company's offering was received enthusiastically by the market, which viewed their range as a healthy (and tasty) alternative to existing products. In particular, the remarkable back-to-basic packaging made the products stand out on the shelves of retailers and gave it a unique status. The company grew rapidly to an annual turnover of $60 million.

Figure 2.6 depicts the warehouse action plan for Foodies. It illustrates that the current maturity scores of the distribution center are relatively low (Year T). In particular the scores on the effective (10 percent) and collaborative stage (5 percent). By comparison, the score on the responsive stage is quite high. This suggests that in the past, management of the distribution center predominantly focused on using IT to solve its problems, rather than organizing the internal operation (effective stage) or claiming its place in the supply chain (collaborative stage).

After seeing the maturity scores, management realized that it could not continue in the current way. The IT projects were strenuous, expensive and created insufficient benefits. The management of the distribution center wanted to change this situation by first organizing its internal operations. The new organization would serve as a foundation for further improvement. Next, management decided which initiatives it wanted to roll out in each of the following three years.

For the first year (Year T+1), management plans to create transparency by introducing performance metrics, documenting processes and defining service level agreements for its services to other departments. The current WMS

---

[10] The out-of-home channel refers to the consumption of food and beverages by consumers outside their homes, either while *on the move* (e.g., gas stations) or *on premise* (e.g., cafeterias).

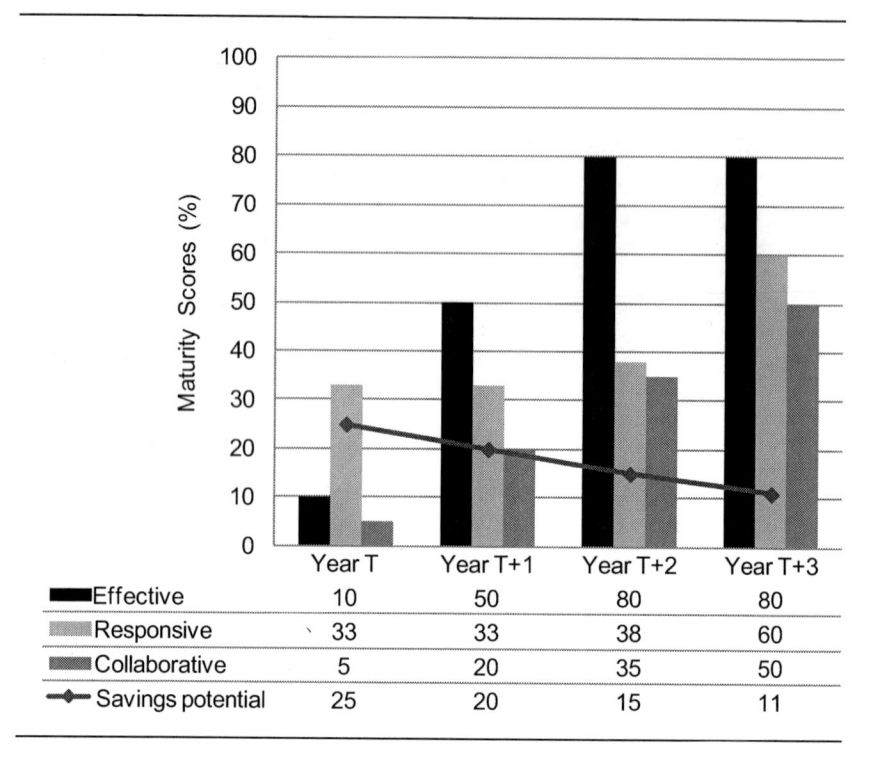

	Year T	Year T+1	Year T+2	Year T+3
■ Effective	10	50	80	80
▨ Responsive	33	33	38	60
▨ Collaborative	5	20	35	50
♦ Savings potential	25	20	15	11

Figure 2.6 Warehouse action plan for Foodies.

contains sufficient data to serve as input for the desired performance metrics. Management wants to use this transparency to create *awareness* and *motivation* among the people in the distribution center and improve performance (see Section 2.1). Management assesses that this will increase the effective score from 10 percent to 50 percent by the end of year T+1. They calculated the projected maturity scores by filling out the maturity scan with the planned actions in mind. At the same time, management wants to use transparency to create *awareness* and *motivation* among other departments and thereby increase the maturity score for the collaborative stage. The initiatives reduce the maximum savings potential from 25 percent to 20 percent after the first year. Management listed the expected savings and verified that the 5 percent cost reduction is realistic.

Note that the initiatives in the first year have restored the balance between the three maturity stages. As opposed to the scores in year T, the scores at the end of the year T+1 display a declining slope, i.e., the effective score is higher than the responsive score, which in turn is higher than the collaborative score. For improvement initiatives to be successful, it is important to maintain this balance.

In the second year T+2, management planned to extend transparency and introduce *activity-based costing* and a *continuous improvement cycle*. As a result of these initiatives, the effective score would rise to 80 percent. Management also wants to engage in a capacity planning initiative and create more flexibility in its workforce capacity. This initiative would raise the responsive score from 33 percent to 38 percent. Finally, management wants to use the cost transparency that comes from the activity-based costing model to create cost awareness among other departments. As a result of the initiatives, the maximum savings potential would go down in the second year from 20 percent to 15 percent. Equal to the first year, the projected cost reduction in the second year is 5 percent. Management verified that this cost reduction is reasonable.

Finally, Figure 2.6 shows that no new initiatives in the effective stage are planned for year T+3. Management primarily aims to consolidate its high effective score by that time. The focus in the third year shifts from transparency to IT. The profound effective score serves as a strong foundation for new IT initiatives. Management planned to upgrade its current, heavily customized, WMS to the latest standard version in the third year. The upgrade would eliminate most of the customizations and enable the use of intelligent planning and control rules. The enormous number of customizations in the current WMS often make it difficult to change processes, creating an obstacle for future improvements. The increased transparency and understanding of the operation would help to modify and streamline processes in the distribution center so that many of the existing WMS customizations become redundant. The actions in the third year further improve the maturity scores. As a result, the savings potential would further shrink to 11 percent, a 4 percent cost reduction for Foodies in the third year.

Figure 1.7 in Section 1.6.6 showed that only 7 percent of companies have a savings potential of 10 percent or less. We named this group the *leaders* in warehouse management. If Foodies is able to realize the projected plans, then its savings potential shrinks to 11 percent. Clearly, Foodies would have approached the *leader* group by then. Perhaps within subsequent years it could even join the group of leaders. This would be an impressive accomplishment considering that its current savings potential of 25 percent clearly puts the Foodies distribution center in the *laggards* segment.

Table 2.1 Foodies' planned actions for the next three years.

Stage	Year T+1	Year T+2	Year T+3
Effective	• Performance metrics • Standard operating procedures • Service level agreements	• Activity-based costing • Continuous Improvement	
Responsive		• Capacity planning	• WMS upgrade
Collaborative	• Awareness at other departments	• Cost awareness at other departments	• Alignment with other departments

2.3.2 Create a Warehouse Action Plan

The Foodies example illustrates how to create a warehouse action plan. We discuss the relevant elements here so that you can create your own action plan.

The action plan has a three year horizon. This is a period for which we can realistically plan. Since the future is uncertain, any longer planning period would likely be an illusion. On the other hand, it is necessary to know what we want in three years, since it may be necessary to start certain changes now if we want them to be implemented in three years. Typical examples are large-scale change programs or IT implementations.

We see three phases in the action plan:
1. Lay the foundation
2. Restore the balance
3. Create continuous improvement.

We discuss these phases in the following sections.

Lay the Foundation

It is impossible to build a house without first laying a good foundation. Likewise we need a good foundation of transparency for future improvements. Which actions should the distribution center take to lay a sufficient foundation? *Highly Competitive Warehouse Management* suggests building transparency with the following elements:

- A warehouse strategy derived from the company strategy (See Section 2.2)
- A WMS that is able to register warehouse activities, preferably in real-time via RF or *voice terminals*. We suggest using a standard WMS with limited customizations. (Chapter 4 discusses warehouse management systems.)
- Service level agreements with other departments on all warehouse services (See Section 5.1).
- Standard operating procedures for all warehouse processes (See Section 5.2).
- Performance indicators (See Section 5.4).

If your operation still lacks any of the foundation items, then put these on the action plan first. They create the minimum level of transparency to lay a foundation.

Restore the Balance

Next we want to restore the balance between the maturity scores. As we discussed in Section 1.6.7, improvement initiatives are more successful when maturity scores are balanced, i.e., the scores for the respective stages should be declining so that the effective score is higher than the responsive score, which in turn is higher than the collaborative score.

The actions which you planned to *lay the foundation* should have helped to restore the balance. Take the warehouse maturity scan and find out whether this

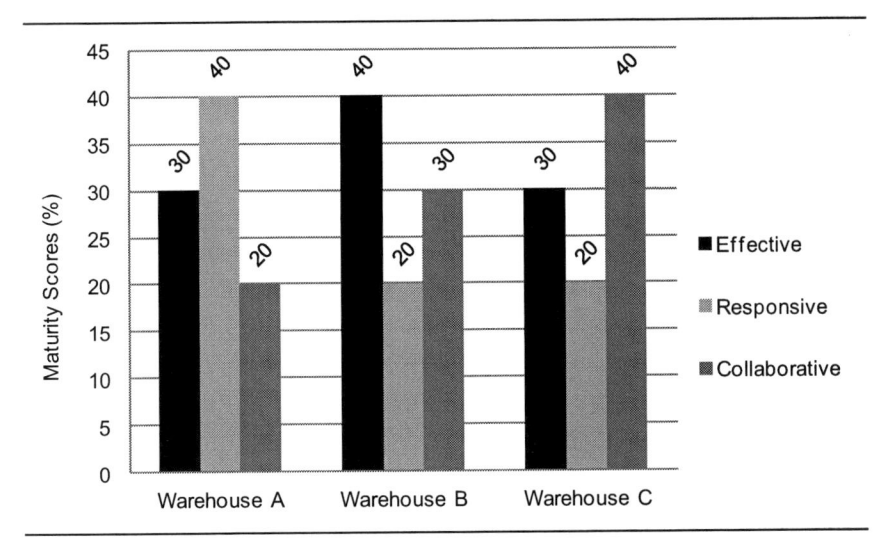

Figure 2.7 Maturity score examples for three warehouses.

is true. If your scores are still unbalanced, then put items on the action plan that restore the balance.

Consider the example in Figure 2.7. Here we see three warehouses: *Warehouse A*, *Warehouse B* and *Warehouse C*. None have balanced maturity scores. In *Warehouse A* the low effective score upsets the balance, in *Warehouse B* it is the responsive score and in *Warehouse C* it is both the effective and the responsive score.

Create Continuous Improvement

After laying the foundation in phase 1 and restoring the balance in phase 2, the time has come to commence the continuous improvement cycle. The continuous improvement cycle uses the transparency that we created to improve warehouse performance in a systematic manner. A well-known procedure that uses management information to drive performance is the *Deming circle* (Walton and Deming, 1986). The Deming circle (Figure 2.8) revolves around four cyclic stages:

- *Plan.* Define actions for improving the organization, systems, layout or processes.
- *Do.* Implement the initiatives, train the operators and view if the procedures are performed well.
- *Check.* Evaluate the performance against the goals.
- *Act.* Analyze bottlenecks and select possible improvements.

Hence, the Deming circle is a systematic procedure to establish continuous improvement. On a regular basis, the measured performance is reported and management and operators jointly look for possible improvements.

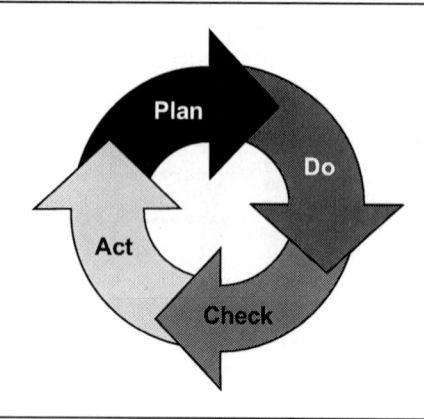

Figure 2.8 Deming circle.

The continuous improvement cycle probably is the most powerful instrument for improving warehouse performance. Unfortunately, only a few distribution centers use such a systematic approach. Table 2.2 shows that only 7 percent of participants in the warehouse maturity scan use a systematic procedure such as the *Deming circle*. Other examples of systematic procedures are *Lean* and *Six Sigma*. In fact, only a minority of one-third of the participants use performance indicators for finding improvement actions on a regular basis. Considering this outcome, it is not surprising that so many distribution centers are still struggling.

Table 2.2 Use of performance indicators for performance improvement by participants of the warehouse maturity scan.

Use Performance Indicators	Percentage
Not used	26
Irregularly, after experiencing problems	41
Regularly, but not systematically	26
Regularly and systematically	7

34. As discussed, we see three phases in the action plan.
    a. Explain the three phases in your own words.
        i. Lay the foundation
        ii. Restore the balance
        iii. Create continuous improvement

THE CHALLENGE OF CHANGE

CASE STUDY

35. Take a look at Foodies' action plan for the next three years (Table 2.1 on page 67) and the associated maturity scores in Figure 2.6 on page 66.
    a. Which actions in Table 2.1 "lay the foundation?"
    b. Do these actions create balance, or are additional actions necessary to "restore the balance?"
    c. Which actions in Table 2.1 "create continuous improvement?"

2.4 Optimization Actions to Create Fun and Successes

Highly Competitive Warehouse Management identifies a structure for improving the distribution center. For instance, it uses *performance indicators*, *standard operating procedures*, *WMSs* and many other tools and management instruments for improving operations. However, we should note that these tools do not create benefits *per se*. The benefits come from using the tools to streamline processes, to change the behavior of people or to make better decisions. The tools are merely *enablers*.

In fact, the actual benefits come, for instance, when we change the warehouse layout, modify the control rules in the WMS or make different arrangements with customers. Successful changes not only create benefits, they also motivate people to continue. Successes are *fun*. They need to be celebrated.

Hence, if we want to apply the methodology of *Highly Competitive Warehouse Management*, then we should not only focus on implementing tools and management instruments, but also on actions that create improvements[11].

Table 2.3 The nine optimization actions of *Highly Competitive Warehouse Management*.

Process efficiency	Benefit
1 Improve	Efficient activities
2 Combine	Economies of scale
3 Eliminate	Fewer activities
Resource utilization	Benefit
4 Cut	Exact capacity
5 Activate	Active resources
6 Postpone	Just in time deployment
Service alignment	Benefit
7 Balance	Balanced workload
8 Accelerate/decelerate	Perfect timing
9 Rationalize	Simplified services

---

[11] Please refer to Appendix C.4 for *Do it* questions that help you to define and implement these actions.

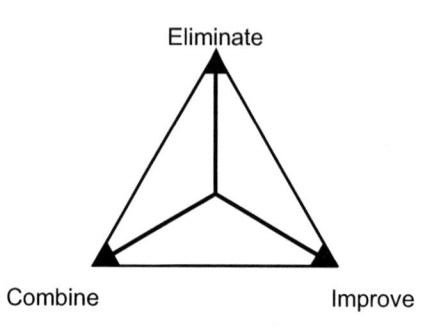

Which actions are implemented differs greatly between operations. *Highly Competitive Warehouse Management* distinguishes nine different types of actions for optimizing the distribution center (Table 2.3). Each action brings a specific benefit. Each maturity stage requires different actions. As a mnemonic aid, note the first letters of each action which spell ICE-CAP-BAR.

2.4.1 Process Efficiency

The most obvious approach for improving performance is to analyze the *processes* in the distribution center and find ways to make them more efficient. We define the *processes* as all the activities and procedures performed by humans, machines and equipment in the distribution center to facilitate the flow of goods. If we redesign the processes so that less time, space and materials are needed to complete the activities, then the operation becomes more *efficient*. Typical examples are eliminating redundant movements or reducing travel distances by means of an ABC classification (see example). Accordingly less warehouse staff, equipment, warehouse space and packing materials are needed. At the same time, the streamlining of the processes could reduce response times, increase throughput capacity, improve accuracy and increase the flexibility of the distribution center. Hence, it not only reduces costs but also improves service levels.

> **Example: Process Efficiency**
> A fork-lift driver requires on average 3 minutes for the putaway of a pallet to a storage location. We introduce an *ABC classification* (see Section 3.5.2) and store the fast moving A products in the front of the storage area, the medium moving B products in the middle and the slow moving C products in the back. Consequently, the average putaway time is reduced to 2.5 minutes. Instead of 20 putaways, the fork-lift driver could do 24 putaways per hour. Thus, the process efficiency has increased by 20 percent.

Figure 2.9 Actions for increasing process efficiency.

Highly Competitive Warehouse Management distinguishes three actions for streamlining processes (Figure 2.9). The first action is to *eliminate* activities. Sometimes activities are redundant or they occur due to improper or erroneous actions upstream. The second action is to *improve* activities. We perform the same activity, but we do it more efficiently. Finally, the third action is to *combine* activities thereby creating economies of scale, e.g., moving two pallets together instead of one at a time.

2.4.2 Resource Utilization

The *productivity* of an operator or a machine is defined as the output divided by the time spent, for example, an operator is present for 8 hours and performs 200 picks. Hence, his productivity is 25 picks per hour. Modern warehouse management systems, in combination with real-time communication systems, such as radio frequency (RF) terminals (see Section 4.2), enable us to measure warehouse productivity in detail. The WMS tracks in real-time which activities are performed by whom and how much time it took. From this detailed data we can derive a highly accurate breakdown of the time spent in the distribution center. Figure 2.10 gives an example of how this breakdown might look. The data not only tells us how much time the operators spend on the various activities, but also how much time they are not working on a task (idle time).

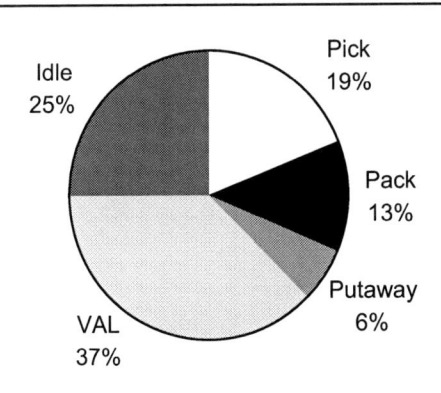

Figure 2.10 Example of the operator time breakdown.

In this book we strictly distinguish between *utilization* and *efficiency* in our quest to raise productivity because the mechanisms, characteristics, actions and instruments to influence these two factors differ greatly. *Efficiency* indicates how much is achieved when operators and machines are working, while *utilization* states the fraction of the available time that the operators and machines are actually involved in direct warehouse activities, such as picking and packing. In Figure 2.10 the utilization is 75 percent (and the remaining 25 percent of the time the operator was idle). This principle not only applies to operators, but also to other resources such as vehicles and machines.

> **Example: Resource Utilization**
> A fork-lift driver requires on average 2.5 minutes for the putaway of a pallet to a storage location. However, for various reasons he only has been busy for 67 percent of his time. Hence, the fork-lift driver performed 16 putaways per hour instead of the 24 putaways per hour from the previous example. The difference is not because he worked slowly, but because he did not work the entire time.

In the previous section we discussed three actions for increasing process efficiency. *Highly Competitive Warehouse Management* will also distinguish three actions for improving resource utilization. The first action is to *cut* excess capacity by tuning the resource capacity to the actual workload. The second action is to *activate* operators by resolving bottlenecks and deploying operators in a multifunctional manner. Finally, the third action is to *postpone* activities so that they are completed *just in time*. If activities are completed too early, then they might compromise the timely completion of other tasks or increase capacity requirements.

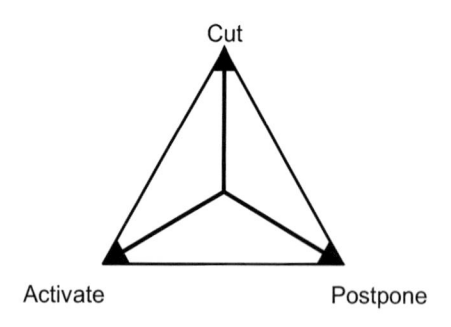

Figure 2.11 Actions for increasing resource utilization.

2.4.3 Service Alignment

The six optimization actions discussed so far can establish a strong warehouse operation. Through efficient processes and responsive capacity deployment, the distribution center can achieve reliable high-quality services balanced against competitive costs. After optimizing the internal operation, there are still opportunities to achieve savings in the wider supply chain.

Highly Competitive Warehouse Management re-evaluates the services provided by the distribution center. The activities that need to be performed by the distribution center are the direct result of decisions made by other departments within the company and other members of the supply chain. Therefore, the parties involved have to be aware of the cost effects of the requested services. Otherwise, many costs are wasted throughout the supply chain.

Departments within companies as well as companies in the supply chain have different objectives. *Highly Competitive Warehouse Management* aligns the objectives of the various parties so that they request logistics services based on a conscious trade-off between service levels and overall costs. There are many instances where a minor change in services can achieve major cost reductions. Accordingly, we achieve competitive service levels at lower costs for the supply chain as a whole.

Collaborative warehouse management, the fourth maturity stage of highly competitive warehouse management, looks beyond the boundaries of the distribution center. Integral optimization goes beyond the job of the traditional warehouse manager, logistics manager or distribution manager. At this stage, we need a *supply chain manager* who facilitates the trade-offs between the various departments.

Collaborative warehouse management distinguishes three actions for aligning services. The first action is to *rationalize* order profiles and thereby reduce the complexity of warehouse activities. Is it necessary that the distribution center holds such a large amount of inventory? Is it always necessary to receive and ship such small and frequent orders? Is it necessary to compensate for the inaccuracies upstream in the supply chain? The second action is to *balance* the fluctuations in the workload. Alternating high and low demand requires high flexibility in the availability of resources, with the associated costs. Finally, the third action is to *accelerate* or *decelerate* services. Quicker service helps to decrease inventories throughout the supply chain since safety stocks can be reduced. However, slower service allows for time to better plan the resource capacities and simplify the processes.

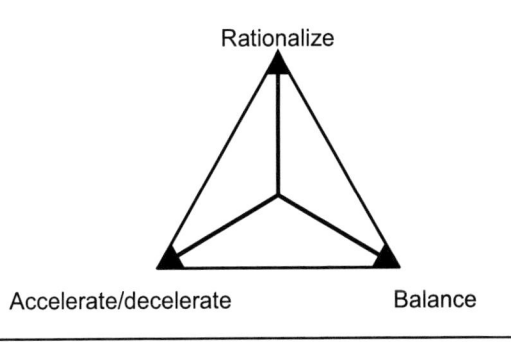

Figure 2.12 Actions for aligning services.

36. There are nine different actions for Highly Competitive Warehouse Management.
 a. List the nine actions including the benefit of each action.
   i.   I:
   ii. C:
   iii. E:
   iv. C:
   v.   A:
   vi. P:
   vii. B:
   viii. A:
   ix. R:

2.5 Project Management to Give Guidance

Highly competitive warehouse management will reveal various projects for improving the distribution center. In Section 1.5 we stated that an important condition for the success of a project is that the organization is ready for it. Nevertheless we see many organizations struggle and fail in their projects for reasons that seem obvious[12]. Therefore we emphasize the following crucial conditions:
- The project should bring sufficient benefits.
- The project should be well guided.

We discuss these conditions in Sections 2.5.1 and 2.5.2.

2.5.1 Costs and Benefits

Saving money can be expensive! Some projects require major investments to bring down the running costs. This might result in a *payback period* of many years. In practice, a payback period of three years (the project costs are no more than three times the annual savings) usually is considered to be acceptable. In fact, the projected savings from highly competitive warehouse management can likely be achieved through projects with a payback period of three years at the most.

> **Rule of Thumb: Payback Period**
> Projects should preferably provide a payback within three years.

Before the management team approves a project, it needs to know the prospective costs and benefits. This is the job of the project team. The check list below lists the main cost elements of a project. We distinguish between one-off

---

[12] Please refer to Appendix C.5 for *Do it* questions on defining a project plan.

> **Check List: Project Costs**
>
> One-off investments
> - Man hours (internal and external)
>   - Preparation and selection of vendors
>   - Implementation
>   - Software customizations
>   - Building interfaces
>   - Training and start-up
> - Software licenses
>   - Information systems, e.g., WMS
>   - Database systems
>   - Other software (e.g., for data communication)
> - Hardware
>   - Servers
>   - PCs
>   - RF terminals
>   - Printers
>   - Data network
>
> Annual operating costs
> - Software maintenance and support contracts
> - Hardware maintenance contracts
> - Man hours (internal and external) for maintenance and support
> - Depreciation and allowances for future software upgrades

investments and annual operating costs. Using quotations provided by vendors, the project team should be able to establish reasonable cost estimates.

The benefits are generally more difficult to estimate than the costs. Yet it is always possible to find a reasonable estimate. Arrange a meeting with the responsible staff, jointly compile a list of potential benefits and estimate the savings for each benefit. Finally, managers must commit to the realization of the benefits.

The benefits of a project can be diverse. Achieving higher productivity from the warehouse staff is a benefit that can be expressed in reduced personnel and equipment costs. Other benefits might be reduced response times, higher space utilization, better inventory accuracy or more effective space utilization. These improvements can be converted into reduced building and inventory costs or perhaps additional sales. Also savings on IT expenses could be achieved when a new information system is introduced with lower maintenance costs. Some benefits, such as improved customer service or improved staff morale, are important yet can be almost impossible to quantify in terms of cash savings. These can be included as *intangible benefits* instead.

We find that many benefits relate to personnel costs. For quantifying these benefits, we first identify which group of operators is involved. This could be, for example, the receipt operators, the forklift drivers, the order-pickers or the warehouse planners. By distinguishing the optimizations per operator group, we have a better sense of whether the savings are realistic and we prevent duplications.

Secondly, we identify how much time the operators spend on the activities and estimate which savings are possible. There is no general rule for this, but logical reasoning and some assumptions should bring us a long way. Sometimes benchmark figures can provide useful guidance. A practical technique is to deliberately estimate pessimistic and optimistic outcomes for each optimization. This provides a range for the expected savings with the average being the best guess. Do not hesitate to include small savings. Every little bit helps!

After estimating the costs and benefits, we compute the payback period. According to our rule of thumb, the payback period should be no more than three years. If the calculated payback period amounts to more than this, then we may have to re-evaluate our plan:
- Did we miss crucial optimizations?
- Should we first prepare the organization, so that we can take bigger steps at once?
- Have we been sufficiently creative and ambitious?

If we see no way to comply with the three year rule, then this might not be the right project for now. No doubt there are other projects with a better return on investment.

37. **Projects should preferably provide a payback within three years. Think of a project in your distribution center that started more than three years ago.**
    a. Were expected costs and benefits estimated at the beginning of the project?
    b. Compare the expected and actual costs and benefits. What do you see with regard to the payback period?
    c. If the calculated payback period amounted to more than three years, what caused it?

2.5.2 Project Management

So far we have discussed how to make realistic plans. Next, we need to implement them. A successful implementation often is hard work. There are many books on project management and it is beyond the scope of this book to discuss all of the issues involved. Nonetheless, we do want to give 10 practical guidelines:

1. The project has a sponsor who explicitly supports its goals.

2. The project has a project leader, who is responsible for the end result.

> **Example: Payback Calculation**
> The estimated costs for a project are between $1,200,000 and $1,300,000. The project team estimates the resulting cost savings between $500,000 and $550,000 per year. However, the annual operating costs are expected to increase by $70,000 due to additional software and hardware maintenance and support.
>
> A simple formula to compute the payback period is:
> $$\text{Payback period} = \frac{\text{Investment}}{\text{Annual cost savings} + \text{Operating cost savings}}$$
>
> Hence, the minimum payback period is:
> $$\frac{\$1,200,000}{\$550,000 - \$70,000} = 2.5 \text{ years}$$
>
> The maximum payback period is:
> $$\frac{\$1,300,000}{\$500,000 - \$70,000} = 3.0 \text{ years}$$
>
> Note: Your company may use more sophisticated financial formulas to compute the payback period.

3. The project has team members who execute the project jointly with the project leader.

4. The project leader creates a *project plan* that explains how he wants to achieve the project goals. The plan identifies the various stages of the project together with a feasible timeline.

5. The project leader and sponsor have to agree on the *project plan*.

6. The project starts with a *kick-off* meeting where the project leader discusses the project plan with the team members. This may lead to changes in the scope and approach. The project ends with a *closure* meeting, where the results are presented and the sponsor formally accepts the project.

7. During the project, the project leader and team members agree on tasks that need to be performed and specify deadlines upfront.

8. Each task has a single owner who is responsible for completing it on time. If a team member sees that he cannot complete the task on time, then he informs the project leader as soon as possible.

9. The project leader monitors time (*critical path*), budget and scope, follows up on tasks of team members and intervenes when project goals are at stake.

10. The project leader meets with the sponsor when necessary. This may either be when the original project goals in terms of time, budget or scope cannot be met or when project goals need further clarification.

Below is an example of the elements of the *project plan* mentioned in Step 4.

Project Plan
A project plan contains the following items:
- *Project name.* Find an inspiring name for the project.
- *Background.* Explain how this project creates a competitive advantage for the company.
- *Project goal.* Describe precisely what the end result should be.
- *Project team.* List project team members (including the project leader).
- *Resources.* Specify required budgets, time and facilities.
- *Benefits.* List expected benefits.
- *Kick-off date.* Set the date of the first meeting with *all* project members.
- *End date.* Find a deadline for the project that is both challenging and realistic.
- *Agreement.* Signatures by sponsor and project manager.

The project plan should typically be no longer than one page.

2.6 Summary

Although there is huge improvement potential in distribution centers, many companies fail to actually make progress. In this chapter we showed the five ingredients of successful change. The first ingredient is a *change-oriented culture*, with people who feel the need and who are motivated to make the change. The second ingredient is a *direction*, which we defined by the *warehouse strategy*, a strategy derived from the company strategy. The third ingredient is the path for the *evolution* of the distribution center, which we defined in the *warehouse action plan*. The fourth ingredient is *fun*, which arises from the successes that are achieved. In other words, it is not only important that we create structures for long-term improvement, but also implement short-term actions that actually show that we are making progress. Finally, the fifth ingredient is *guidance*, i.e., the project management that guides the project towards its goals.

Chapter 3

Warehousing

Redesigning a distribution center or implementing a new WMS requires a firm understanding of current warehousing practices. In this chapter we discuss the primary activities of a distribution center, introduce key definitions and pinpoint a number of best practices. This information is essential to anybody who ventures into a warehousing project.

Throughout the supply chain, we see various types of companies (Figure 3.1), each with different warehouses and distribution centers. Some supply chains contain many links, while others have only a few. The design of a proper *supply chain structure* (Figure 3.2) is a complex issue for a company and many questions relate to it:

- Where are the inventories stored, i.e., *centralized* vs. *decentralized* storage?
- Are the inventories *dedicated* to a certain customer group or are they *generally available*?
- Are the goods delivered from storage or are they driven through the supply chain using concepts such as *cross-docking*, *direct shipments* and *merge-in-transit*?
- Which goods are held in stock and which are sourced from suppliers or other distribution centers within the company as required, i.e., *buy-hold-sell* vs. *sell-source-ship*?

Other strategic questions relate to service providers, such as are the distribution centers operated by the company itself or are they outsourced to a third party logistics provider? Clearly, the supply chain structure strongly influences the warehouse operation and considerable improvements might be possible by changing the structure. For an elaborate discussion on supply chain design we refer to Gattorna (2010), Lee (2002, 2004) and Van Goor *et al.* (2003).

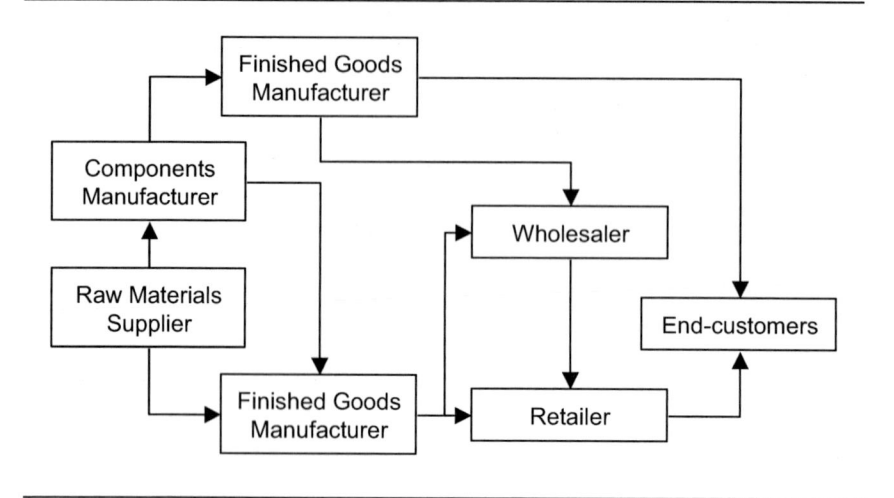

Figure 3.1 Example of a supply chain structure.

Throughout the supply chain we may find different types of warehouses. First, we distinguish between *production warehouses* and *distribution warehouses*.
- A *production warehouse* holds raw materials, semi-finished goods and finished goods. Goods are delivered to and received from a nearby production plant. Finished goods are delivered to customers or other warehouses.
- A *distribution warehouse* receives goods from various suppliers and ships these to customers.

38. **Give examples of the following warehouse types.**
    a. Production warehouse
    b. Distribution warehouse

Distribution warehouses can be further classified by the region that they serve.
- A *central warehouse* holds the centralized inventory for a large region. This centralization allows the region to be served while keeping total inventory low.
- A *local warehouse* serves a smaller geography, e.g., a city, region, or one or more (small) countries. Due to its close proximity to the local market, the local distribution center can quickly supply goods to customers. Sometimes the local warehouse only carries fast moving products in order to limit decentralized inventories.

Another warehouse classification relates to the proprietor.
- A *private warehouse* is operated by the owner of the goods.
- A *third party warehouse* is operated by a third party logistics provider on behalf of one or multiple clients.

Finally, third party warehouses can also be further classified.
- A *dedicated warehouse* holds the goods for one client.
- A *public warehouse* holds the goods for multiple clients.

39. **With Foodies' distribution center in mind (Section 2.3.1), consider the following:**
    a. What kind of warehouse is it? And why?
       i. Production or distribution warehouse?
       ii. Central or local warehouse?
       iii. Private or third party warehouse?
       iv. Dedicated or public warehouse?

Figure 3.2 shows the various warehouse types in a typical supply chain structure. We see a central warehouse that is supplied by several production warehouses. The central warehouse then distributes the goods to the local warehouses. The warehouses may belong to the same company or to different companies. Depending on order quantities and the customer's location, the customer might be supplied from the production warehouse, the central warehouse or the local warehouse.

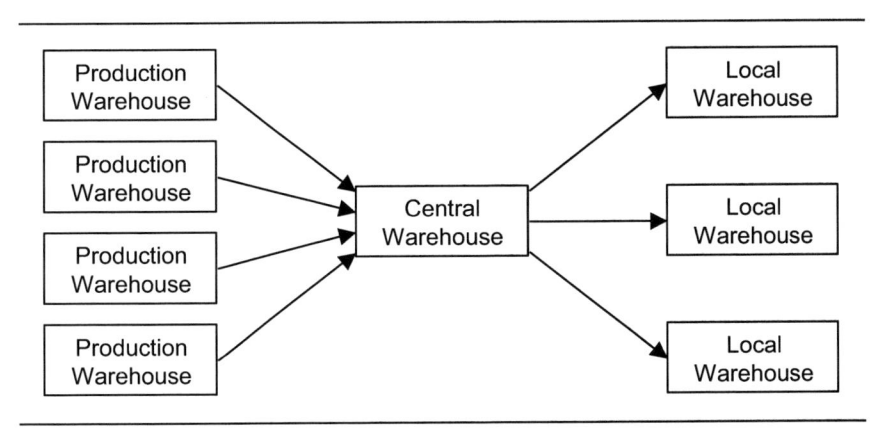

Figure 3.2 Warehouses in the supply chain.

3.1 Warehouse Justification

While goods move through the supply chain they are in one of the following three stages:
- Movement
- Transformation
- Storage.

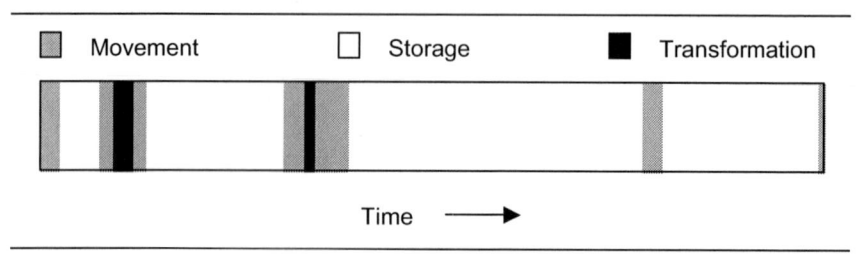

Figure 3.3 Supply chain life cycle of a typical product.

Movement refers to all external and internal transportation of goods, *transformation* to all production, assembly and value added logistics activities executed upon the goods and finally *storage* to all storage of raw materials, components, subassemblies and final products. Figure 3.3 gives an example of the *supply chain life cycle* of a product. We see that the goods spend a lot of time in storage and relatively little time in movement and transformation. It is often stated that transformation and movement add value in the supply chain and that storage, and hence warehousing, only adds cost.

Accordingly, warehousing is often regarded as a necessary evil that needs to be marginalized, if not eliminated. Although, we strongly disagree with this point of view in general, occasionally the value of warehousing might be redundant as demonstrated by the following case study.

> **Case Study: Office Supplies for Non-profit Organization**
> A non-profit organization held a central inventory of office supplies. A study revealed that it would be cheaper and quicker if the various branches ordered the office supplies directly from the wholesaler. Apparently, the distribution center only incurred costs and increased response times. The organization immediately decided to terminate the distribution center.

In most instances the distribution center does add value to the supply chain. Hence, it is important to understand the value of a distribution center. We distinguish four *basic warehouse functions* that add value:
- Break-bulk
- Storage
- Consolidation
- Customization.

Break-bulk
The break-bulk function allows for products to arrive in large quantities and then be shipped in small quantities. This enables economies of scale upstream in production, purchasing and inbound transportation. At the same time, it improves customer service since customers can order the specific quantity they want.

Storage
The storage of goods helps manage time delays between supply and demand. Having inventory serves various purposes:
- *Instant availability.* The available inventory furnishes customer demand within short response times. Clearly, this improves customer service.
- *Lot sizes.* Inventory due to large production runs or purchase quantities creates economies of scale in production, transportation and order processing.
- *Seasonal supply.* Storage of fresh produce (e.g., apples and potatoes) smoothes the level of supply throughout the year. Without distribution centers the prices and supply of seasonal products would fluctuate wildly.
- *Demand anticipation.* Storage allows availability of products during peak demand (e.g., toys in December). Without distribution centers an immense production capacity would be required.
- *Speculation.* Inventory, often raw materials, held because it is expected that prices will rise.
- *Strategic products.* Inventory of essential products with uncertain supply, e.g., rare metals.

Consolidation
The consolidation function implies that the distribution center holds products from various sources, so that customers can order a large product range from a single source. This improves customer service since the goods can be received in a single delivery. It also increases the efficiency of outbound transportation.

Customization
Customers may want products that are customized to their needs. Examples are customer or country specific labels, manuals or packaging. These, and other, value added services provide better service to customers. Furthermore, the *postponement* of customization services until the end of the supply chain reduces upstream inventories.

We should emphasize that a distribution center not only adds value through *physical* activities. The distribution center may also gather and maintain related information and then inform the supply chain partners as required. Hence, *information provision* is a prominent aspect of each of the four basic warehouse functions.

Notice that the distribution center in the previous *case study* did not support any of these four functions. Thus it only added costs, not value. The key message is this: before implementing highly competitive warehouse management, it is essential to first justify why the existing distribution center is needed. This may be done by evaluating the four warehouse functions. What would happen if we eliminated the distribution center? Would it negatively impact customer service? Would it increase the overall costs of the supply chain? In short, if a distribution center fails to support one or several of the warehouse functions, then one should consider the option of closing down the distribution center.

It may also be that there is a subset of the goods flow for which the distribution center does not add value. The following *case study* gives an example of a distribution center with a break-bulk function for only 50 percent of its volume.

> **Case Study: Distribution Center of Food Manufacturer**
> A central distribution center for a food manufacturer was supplied from two production plants. Approximately 50 percent of the product volume was delivered to customers in *full pallets*. A quantitative analysis showed that instead of routing these pallets through the central distribution center, it was cheaper to ship the full pallet loads directly from the production plants to the customers. This eliminated handling costs without increasing transportation costs.
>
> The direct shipments diminished the throughput of the central distribution center. Consequently, the manufacturer outsourced the remaining operation to a public warehouse, operated by a third party logistics provider, where less-than-pallet quantities were shipped. The 3PL could combine the small orders with orders from other clients to create better capacity utilization in warehousing and transportation.

3.2 Material Handling

Now that we have looked at the purpose of the distribution center in the supply chain, it is time to have a look inside the distribution center itself. A warehouse, or distribution center, is a building where products are stored. Typically, it is a sizable building with many dock doors around the various sides. Trucks arrive to unload and load goods. Inside we see a large number of parallel aisles with storage racks alongside. Forklift trucks drive by, moving the goods around. Warehouse operators are busy picking and packing goods with a quick peek at a computer terminal in-between. Possibly we see an area where operators are busy performing *value added logistics* (*VAL*) services to tailor goods to the customer's specific needs. We might also see automated material handling equipment such as roller conveyers, automated high-bay cranes or stacker robots. The layout of the distribution center strongly influences its performance, for instance:
- The position of storage racks
- The types of storage systems
- The level of mechanization.

As stated in Section 1.2, the warehouse layout and systems are beyond the scope of our analysis. However, in this section we give a brief introduction for a better understanding of the subsequent chapters. Readers familiar with warehousing systems may wish to skip this section. We shall discuss the following topics:
- Goods
- Storage systems
- Internal transport equipment.

3.2.1 Goods

A distribution center holds a number of different *products*. A finished goods warehouse of a manufacturer typically holds a limited assortment of between 20 and 200 different products. On the other end of the spectrum a spare-parts distribution center may hold 100,000 or more different products.

Each individual product, or *stock keeping unit (SKU)*, has unique features and is characterized by its unique product number. A computer with an English language manual is a different product from the same computer with a Spanish language manual. Two similar shirts that only differ by color, size or style are different products with their own unique product numbers. Product numbers allow the customer to specify the product with the exact features that he wants.

Many products are produced in *lots* or *batches*. A lot is a quantity of a product that is produced under essentially the same conditions. The products in a lot are of a single class, composition, model, size, type, expiry date or version and are intended to have uniform quality and characteristics within specified limits. Items from different lots can be present in the distribution center at the same time. The lot number is an important product attribute since it allows information on its history to be tracked. For example, food safety requires full *tracking and tracing* of food products and ingredients throughout the supply chain.

Products are often packed on pallets for easy storage and handling. Other product carriers include crates and roller containers. In this book we will generally refer to all product carriers as pallets.

Typically, we distinguish three packaging levels for a product. A *pallet* holds a number of *cases,* each holding a number of *individual pieces*. Similar to pallets, there are various alternatives to cases, such as trays, cartons, boxes, bags and bins. Sometimes, we see more than three packaging levels, such as when a case holds several *inner cases* (or inner packs) each with multiple individual pieces. For most products we can define a *standard pack configuration* that indicates the standard number of pieces in a case and the standard number of cases on a pallet. We refer to these packaging units as *full pallets*, *full cases* and *individual pieces,* respectively.

40. Many products are produced in lots.
   a. Give a definition of a lot.
   b. What is the importance of a lot number?

3.2.2 Storage Systems

The layout of a distribution center typically consists of a number of parallel aisles with goods stored on both sides of each aisle. A simple storage technique is *block stacking*. The goods are piled on top of each other without the support of a rack. A good example is the stacking of crates of beer or soft drinks.

A *shelving rack* is used for storing small parts. The rack consists of a number of wooden or metal shelves on which individual pieces or plastic bins can be placed. The height of the rack is limited by the reaching height of the operators (approximately 6.5 feet). An alternative to a shelving rack is a *drawer rack*. The drawers facilitate compact storage and good product protection.

A *mezzanine* is a level between the floor and the ceiling where operators can walk and access the goods. This makes it possible to utilize the space above the floor level.

Large products are mostly kept on pallets. A *pallet rack* consists of a metal frame with horizontal beams on which the pallets can rest. By storing multiple pallets behind each other (deep stacking), it is possible to increase the storage density. A difficulty is that the pallets at the back are difficult to access. Hence, the *last in first out* (LIFO) principle applies if this storage method is used. This principle increases the average inventory age and, thus, is not recommended for deteriorating products such as food.

A *gravity flow rack* facilitates deep stacking together with a *first in first out* (*FIFO*) policy. Consequently, the system avoids unwanted aging of inventories. The pallets or individual cases enter from the rear end on a roller conveyor. The rollers have been placed on a slope of three to four degrees, so that the goods automatically roll to the front. Other storage systems include movable racks, cantilever racks, drive-in racks and roll-back racks. For an elaborate discussion on warehousing systems, we refer to Frazelle (2002).

Case Study: Foodies' Storage Techniques
Foodies currently uses pallet racks with pick locations at the floor level and bulk locations at the elevated positions. Management is looking for alternative storage techniques and lists relevant characteristics of its assortment:
- Production runs typically consist of 10 to 80 pallets per lot.
- Foodies wants to keep track of its product lots.
- Its assortment consists of perishables.

41. **There are different storage techniques for warehouses: block stacking, shelving racks, mezzanines, pallet racks, gravity flow racks, etc.**
    a. Which storage techniques does your distribution center use?

42. **Consider Foodies' distribution center.**
    a. Which storage techniques could Foodies use in its distribution center? And why?

In the systems discussed so far, it is the order-picker who goes to the products. Horizontal and vertical carousels are *product-to-picker systems*. The storage locations rotate in a closed loop until the requested location is positioned in front of a central opening where the order-picker can access the goods. A vertical lift is similar to a vertical carousel, except that the shelves do not rotate in a closed loop. Instead the vertical lift is able to access shelves individually and position them in front of the operator.

An *automated storage/retrieval system (AS/RS)* also brings products to the picker. The AS/RS is a system with high-bay pallet racks where the putaway and retrieval are performed by automated cranes. The automated cranes drive along guided rails between an input/output (I/O) station and the storage locations. At the I/O station, an operator takes products from the pallet or puts products onto the pallet.

A *Miniload AS/RS* is an AS/RS for small products. The products are kept in bins or drawers that are moved in and out of the system by the automated crane. Each drawer or bin can be subdivided in several compartments, so that different products can be held together in the same container.

43. **Orders can be picked by product-to-picker systems, such as an AS/RS or Miniload.**
    a. In which situation should Foodies use a product-to-picker system?

3.2.3 Internal Transport Equipment

Seven types of equipment are commonly used in the distribution center for product movement.
- A *forklift truck* is used for moving pallet loads. The forklift truck can lift the goods to a height of up to 20 feet. The truck has a counterbalance in the rear to prevent it from tipping over when it carries a heavy load on its forks. Forklift trucks require an aisle width of between 10 and 11.5 feet.

- A *reach truck* is a variant with a telescopic mast that can reach up to approximately 32 feet. The reach truck tilts the mast backwards while lifting a load and moves it forward once again when arriving at the rack. The reach truck can operate in an aisle width of between 8 and 10 feet.
- A *narrow-aisle truck* can rotate its forks horizontally through 180 degrees and can pick up and deposit pallets at either side of the aisle without turning to face them. It can operate in aisles with a width of just 5 feet. Inside the aisle, the narrow-aisle truck travels quickly, while outside the aisle it is rather slow and difficult to maneuver. For that reason, the internal transport to and from the aisles is typically performed by forklift trucks or pallet trucks.
- An *order-pick cart* is a simple vehicle used for picking products from floor locations.
- An *order-pick truck* is a vehicle that moves the order-picker upwards to allow picking cases and pieces from locations at a higher level.
- A *combitruck* is a truck where the order-picker sits in a cabin that moves up and down along with the forks – this allows him to pick full pallets as well as cases and pieces from elevated positions.
- *Roller conveyors* are alternatives for moving goods around the distribution center. Conveyors have a high capacity and require limited labor. Conveyors can also be used for sorting products.

44. Examples of internal transport equipment are a forklift truck, a reach truck, a narrow-aisle truck, an order-pick cart, an order-pick truck, a combitruck and roller conveyors.
    a. Why is it important to use the right internal transport equipment?

3.3 Warehouse Services

The distribution center provides services that add value to the supply chain. *Service level agreements* (SLAs) define performance targets for these services. It is essential that the distribution center achieves these service levels so that the company can successfully execute its strategy. The following basic questions must be answered prior to creating SLAs:
- Which services should be provided?
- Who are the clients for these services?
- Which service levels should be achieved?

3.3.1 Services

Before we continue, we first define what we mean by a *service*. In particular, we make a strict distinction between activities and services. *Activities* are the actions performed by operators, equipment and machines to accommodate the goods flow. There are many activities in distribution centers, e.g., order-picking, storage, receiving, putaway, cycle counting and shipping. *Services* are the result of the activities as witnessed by the outside world, be it other departments within the company, clients of a logistics service provider, suppliers or customers. Although activities vary widely among distribution centers around the world, we consistently see four different services (Figure 3.4) in these operations. Three services support the primary goods flow in the distribution center: inbound handling, storage and outbound handling. We assume that all remaining services are *value added logistics* (VAL) services. VAL services can occur in the inbound flow, during storage, or in the outbound flow.

> **Example: Value Added Logistics**
> As an example of VAL, imagine an inbound handling process where most products are putaway directly into storage. However, some products require a special inspection, e.g., a laboratory test of chemical samples or a quality inspection of fresh product lots (vegetables, flowers). Here the inspection is regarded as a VAL service. If all receipts need the inspection, then it becomes part of the inbound handling service rather than a separate VAL service.

Cross-docking is a combination of inbound handling, perhaps a little storage in-between, and outbound handling. It combines the benefits of the three services. Sometimes cross-docking is treated as a separate service, when it has additional characteristics, e.g., different (tighter) planning constraints.

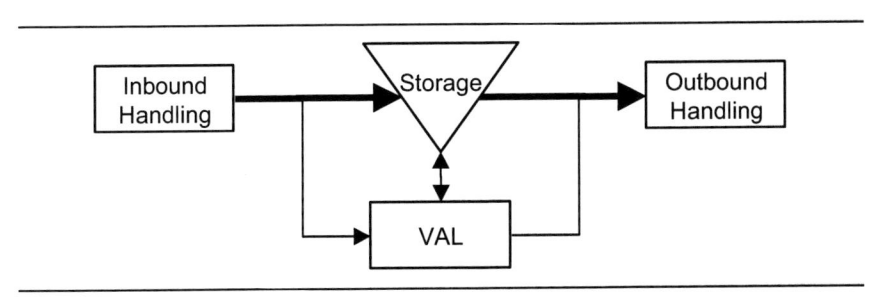

Figure 3.4 Warehouse services.

Let us briefly consider the benefits of the four main services to the supply chain.

Inbound handling

In the inbound handling process the goods are identified, sorted, labeled, registered in the information system, repacked and put away into storage. If these activities are well executed, then goods become available for customer orders, current inventory levels are updated in the information systems and the quality of the goods is safeguarded. Clearly, this service is valuable to other members of the supply chain.

Storage

Storage adds value since it allows larger quantities to be produced and transported, which is more efficient. It also enables orders to be quickly delivered to customers, which provides better service levels and prevents lost sales. In the case of whisky and wine, storage directly adds value.

Outbound handling

In the outbound handling process the goods are picked, packed, labeled, registered in the information system, consolidated into orders and loaded into the truck. This service determines how the goods are delivered to the customer. Moreover, customer specifications, such as special packing instructions, can be accommodated.

VAL

There can be various kinds of VAL services, such as labeling, sampling, *kitting* (assembling sets of different products into kits), testing, repacking, etc. These services transform or modify the product or ensure the product quality. VAL services customize the product to customer requirements. Furthermore, the postponement of these services may significantly reduce upstream inventories in the supply chain.

> **Example: Postponement**
> VAL services could be used to make products country-specific in the distribution center. These services eliminate the need for different lots to be produced for each country separately, thereby increasing production efficiency. Moreover, the overall inventory level drops. The company no longer has to hold separate inventories for each country. If countries are supplied from a single inventory of generic products, then the overall inventory level can be considerably lower since demand fluctuations between countries level out.

45. There is a difference between activities and services.
    a. Explain the difference between activities and services.
    b. Is cross-docking an activity or a service? Why?

3.3.2 Clients

Services by definition are provided to clients. Who are the clients of the distribution center? Here we see a major distinction between *private warehouses*, operated by the owner of the inventories, and *third party warehouses*, operated by *third party logistics providers*. Obviously, in a third party warehouse the various owners of the goods are the clients. The third party logistics provider

(3PL) delivers the services on behalf of these owners. They pay fees to the 3PL for these services.

Who are the clients of a private warehouse? Such a warehouse receives its orders from various departments within a company, e.g., sales, marketing, order desk, customer service, production planning, inventory control and purchasing. We can see on the one hand a variety of departments that are responsible for maintaining a sufficient inventory level in the distribution centers, i.e., production planning, inventory control and purchasing. We will refer to these departments jointly as the *source function*. On the other hand, there are several departments responsible for sales and customer interaction, such as sales, marketing, order desk and customer service. These departments are jointly responsible for selling the goods held in the distribution centers. We refer to these departments as the *sell function*. The private warehouse also deals with the *transportation planning function*, which is responsible for planning the trips to and from the distribution center.

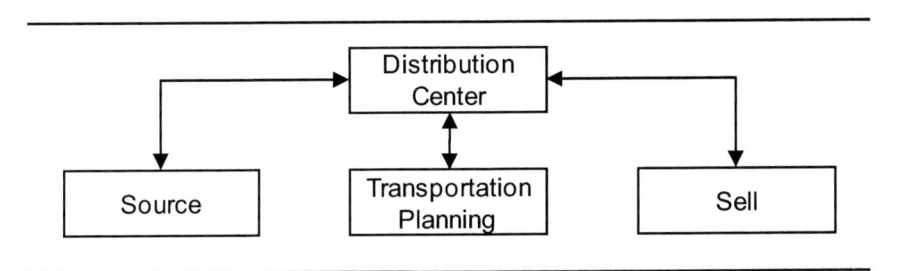

Figure 3.5 Clients of a private warehouse.

This simplification gives us the (internal) supply chain, also known as the *value chain*, depicted in Figure 3.5. Although overly simplified, we believe that it provides a realistic view for the discussions in this book.

In fact, the model may also be applied to third party warehouses. Here the *source function* represents the client's departments responsible for maintaining a sufficient inventory level. Likewise, the *sell function* represents the client's departments responsible for sales and customer contact. Finally, the third party warehouse deals with the client's *transportation planning function* (Figure 3.6). If the 3PL operates a dedicated warehouse, then there is only one client company, whereas in a public warehouse there are multiple clients. Throughout this book we consider the source, sell and transportation planning functions to be the clients of the distribution center irrespective of whether it is a private or third party warehouse.

> **Remark: Private and Third party Warehouses**
> Unless otherwise stated, all discussions in this book apply to *private warehouses* as well as *third party warehouses*.

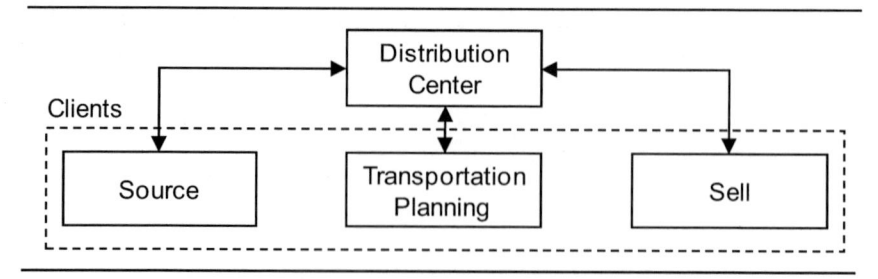

Figure 3.6 Clients of a third party warehouse.

The source function interacts with suppliers and the sell function with customers. We define the *supplier* as the party that supplies the goods, which are received in the distribution center. A supplier may be a manufacturer, a distributor or a wholesaler. Also some (of the client's) internal departments can be seen as suppliers, e.g., an internal manufacturing plant or another distribution center. As a result, for an internal manufacturing plant we separate the function responsible for production *planning and scheduling* from the function responsible for production *execution*. The former represents the source function while the latter is a supplier.

The *customer* is the party that receives the goods, which are shipped from the distribution center. The customer may be an external party, (e.g., a consumer or another company) but also an internal party, such as a retail store or local distribution center supplied from the central distribution center.

Finally, the *hauler* (also *haulage firm* or *carrier*) is the party that executes the transportation. The hauler may be part of the (client) company, the third party logistics provider or a separate transportation company.

As stated above, customers and suppliers are not the direct clients of the distribution center. The sell function closes the deal with the customer. A deal that includes both the goods and the accompanying services. Subsequently, the sell function asks the distribution center to pick the products and load them into the truck. In other words, the sell function is the *(internal) client* when goods are

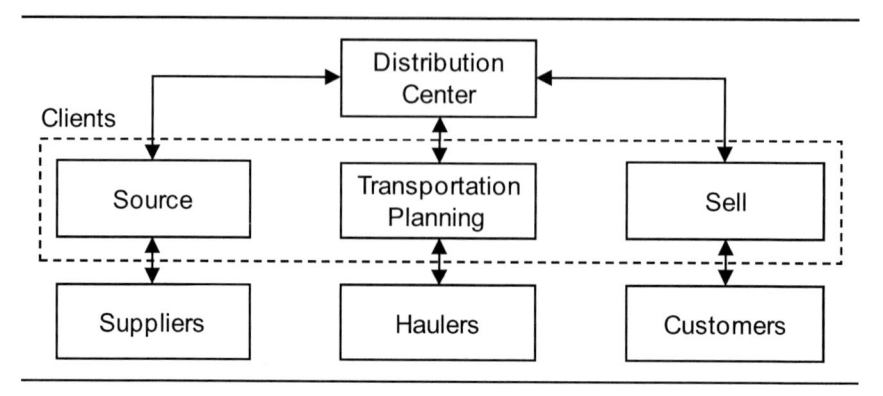

Figure 3.7 Distribution center clients and relationships.

shipped to customers. Likewise the source function is the client of the distribution center when goods are received from suppliers. It relies on the distribution center to receive and store goods.

> **Example: Clients and Relationships**
> We explain the definitions by giving two examples.
>
> **Automotive Manufacturer**
> - *Source function.* Production planning
> - *Sell function.* Sales department
> - *Suppliers.* Component manufacturers
> - *Customers.* Car dealers
>
> **Retail Company**
> - *Source function.* Purchasing department
> - *Sell function.* Store planning
> - *Suppliers.* Manufacturers
> - *Customers.* Stores

Although companies and distribution centers vary greatly between verticals and industry sectors, the above definitions illustrate how much distribution centers are also alike. They all have suppliers and customers and they all deal with functions that are responsible for what comes in and what goes out.

46. **With your operation in mind:**
    a. Define the clients of your distribution center.
    b. Define the function of each client.

3.3.3 Service Levels

Now that we have defined the services and clients, the question remains, which service levels should be achieved. The quality of the services is measured along three dimensions:
- Responsiveness
- Accuracy
- Flexibility.

Responsiveness specifies how soon after the request for a service it should be completed. *Accuracy* states the margin of error allowable in the services. Finally, *flexibility* indicates the degree to which fluctuations in the number of service requests can be accommodated. For example, the outbound handling service could require that 96 percent of the order lines are shipped to customers within 24 hours (responsiveness), 99 percent of the order lines are correct (accuracy) and the distribution center can process between 5,000 and 10,000 order lines per day (flexibility).

If the performance exceeds the target, then this could indicate that the distribution center has excessive running costs. Cost savings should be possible by reducing the service level. However, if the performance is insufficient, then we should focus first on service level compliance before searching for radical cost reductions. Poor performance is a major disadvantage in a competitive market.

3.4 Warehouse Processes

In the remainder of this chapter we explain the various warehouse activities. Figure 3.8 depicts the physical activities and flows in the distribution center.

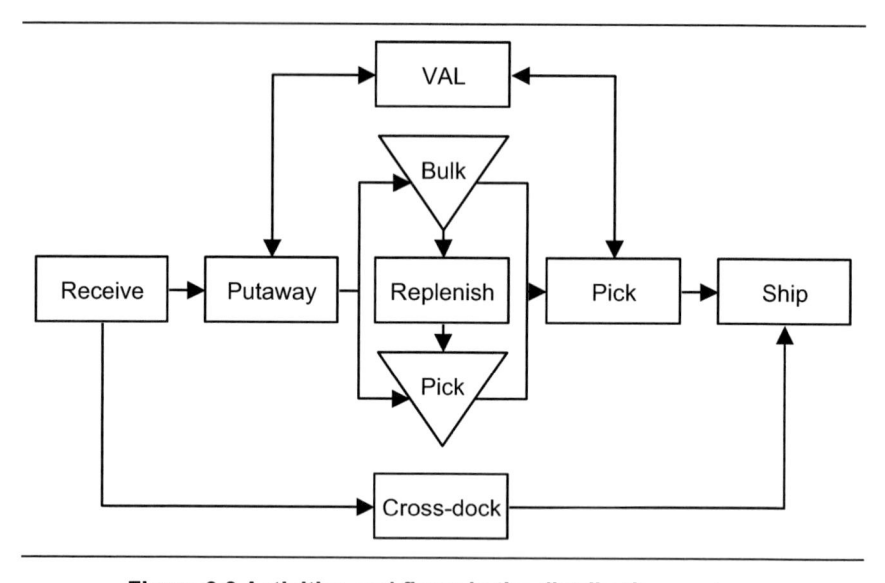

Figure 3.8 Activities and flows in the distribution center.

Receiving

Receiving is the process of unloading an incoming truck, identifying, registering and perhaps repacking the goods.

Putaway

The *putaway* process moves goods from the unloading dock to a storage location.

Storage (Bulk and Pick)

While the goods are in *storage*, activities may still take place which affect them, for example, the inventory is counted on a regular basis to verify quantities (*cycle counting*) or goods are moved to other locations, e.g., to optimize the space utilization (*internal movements*).

Replenish

If the inventory level of a product in the pick area runs low, it is *replenished* from the bulk area (provided there are separate pick and bulk areas).

Pick

Full pallets are picked from the bulk area. Smaller quantities are picked from the pick area.

Ship

After picking the product is packed, consolidated and staged for *shipping*. Once a shipment is complete, it is loaded into the truck and the truck departs.

Cross-dock

Some goods are not putaway into storage. After receipt the product is directly *cross-docked* to a shipping dock, possibly via a temporary staging location.

VAL (Value Added Logistics)

Some distribution centers perform special *value added logistics* services, such as customer-specific or country-specific packing and labeling.

In the subsequent sections we discuss the various warehouse processes in more detail.

47. **Consider the process flow diagram in Figure 3.8.**
    a. What do you think is the main activity in your distribution center?
    b. What percentage of labor time is spent on this activity?

3.5 Inbound Processes

The inbound processes are receiving and putaway.

3.5.1 Receiving

Receiving commences the goods flow through the distribution center. The goods are delivered by truck, or, in a few cases, by train, ship or airplane. Sometimes the goods are supplied by an adjacent production plant via a roller conveyor.

For our discussion, we assume that the goods arrive by truck. The truck drives to a *receipt dock* (or *unloading dock*). The goods are unloaded and a receipt operator quickly verifies whether the delivery appears complete and signs a transportation document after which the truck driver departs. Subsequently, the receipt operators identify and count the goods in detail and register the outcome in the WMS. If products are missing, damaged or otherwise do not meet the requirements, then the operators register the error. Some products such as fresh food, cut flowers or chemicals may require a quality inspection at every receipt. Sometimes the goods need to be repacked or restacked on pallets. Finally, a unique identification label (*license plate*) is attached to the goods for the purpose of tracking the movements of the pallet, e.g., a *barcode label* or an *RFID tag*.

> **Example: Goods Receiving**
> At the distribution center of Fender guitars in Rotterdam, The Netherlands, there are guitar players in the middle of the distribution hall to test the quality of the incoming goods.

Implementing a modern WMS increases the importance of the receipt process. Clearly, a WMS is only able to control the warehouse processes if it knows which goods are present. In fact, the introduction of a WMS might lead to extra time spent on the receipt process. However, the lost time can be gained back later in the process.

Dock Allocation

The truck driver arrives and the receipt operator allocates an empty dock. If no dock is available, then the truck driver has to wait. The operator can manually select a dock or the WMS can do this automatically. In large facilities, it is preferable to unload at a dock that is near the storage locations of the goods on the truck. We further discuss dock planning in Section 7.2.3.

First Carton Seen

By the time a new product arrives in the distribution center, the product attributes such as the product number, product group and pack configuration should already have been interfaced to the WMS (see Section 4.4.4). However, some attributes might not be included in the interface message. These must then be captured upon receipt via the so-called *first carton seen* procedure. For example, the receipt operators measure the weight and volume of a standard carton. The WMS requires these attributes to properly control the warehouse processes.

Goods Transfer

The receipt process is the formal transfer of the goods from the sender to the recipient. The receipt operator, representing the recipient, must verify whether the correct products and quantities have been delivered. The recipient is usually granted a certain period of time, such as a week, during which errors in the delivery can be claimed from the sender.

The WMS may receive information on the incoming goods via electronic interfaces. Therefore the WMS knows beforehand which orders and deliveries are expected. If this is the case, then the receipt operator compares the received quantities to the *purchase order* or *receipt advice* (*RECADV*, see Section 4.4.2). If goods arrive at the distribution center without any formal agreement, then we refer to the arrival as a *surprise receipt*.

LP Receiving

In some supply chains the sender attaches unique identification labels to pallets – which we refer to as *license plates* (LPs) – and sends an electronic *despatch advice* (DESADV). The DESADV includes the unique LP-numbers and the contents of the associated pallets. The unique LP-numbers are generally referred to as *SSCC*-numbers (Serial Shipping Container Code).

LP receiving is a highly efficient process. Instead of identifying, counting and registering the received goods, a single scan of the LP label suffices to receive a pallet or container. The WMS automatically links the pallet contents to the DESADV (note that the recipient refers to this message as the *receipt advice*, RECADV). Further verification may be limited to random checks, where the frequency of the checks is based on the delivery performance of the sender. Thus, a trusted supplier is rarely checked, while a supplier with delivery problems is checked at every receipt. Measuring the performance of suppliers is referred to as *vendor rating*.

Customer Returns

Many distribution centers receive returned goods from customers. The process of receiving returned goods is similar to the regular receipt process, but it requires two additional steps:
- Check if the customer is allowed to return the goods.
- Choose a destination for the goods.

The first additional step is to verify that the customer is authorized to return the goods. The return has to comply with the warranty terms and period. A general practice is to use a *return merchandise authorization* (RMA). The customer first has to apply for an RMA, before he can return the goods. After the request is granted, the customer receives an RMA number. The RMA is registered in the ERP and is communicated to the WMS. The interface message of a return order is similar to that of a purchase order (see Section 4.4.2).

Many distribution centers use the ERP to verify the RMA. If a lot of customer and order information is required, then the ERP is preferred over the WMS. Otherwise all this information would need to be communicated from the ERP to the WMS, which makes the interface unnecessarily complex. After the authorization, the goods follow the regular receipt process in the WMS.

The second step particular to returns receipt is the *disposition* of the returned goods. The operator has to check if everything is complete and must also assess the quality of the goods. Many returned goods can be put away into regular storage. However, some goods might be damaged or incomplete and need to be sent to a repair shop, sold to a junk dealer or simply thrown away. Also the packaging might be dented or scratched and in need of refurbishing. The operator has to decide which destination is most appropriate: regular storage, repair shop, junk dealer, waste disposal or refurbishing. This is called *disposition*. Based on this decision the returned goods follow a specific path.

48. Distribution centers receive returned goods.
   a. Explain what is meant by disposition in the customer returns process.

3.5.2 Putaway

Putaway is the second activity in the goods flow. The putaway process moves the goods from the receipt lane to the designated storage location, either in the *bulk area* or in the *pick area*. The bulk area (or *reserve area*) typically contains full pallet quantities. It is used for picking full pallets or for replenishing the pick area. The pick area (or *forward area*) contains individual cases and pieces. This area is used for picking small quantities. In some instances, the product is not putaway into storage, but *cross-docked* to an outbound truck (see Section 3.10).

Before the goods are putaway, the WMS allocates a storage location. Proper storage allocation rules optimize space utilization as well as the efficiency of the warehouse processes. After the goods are putaway, they become available for order-picking.

49. In the putaway process goods are moved to the *bulk area* or *pick area*.
   a. Explain the difference between the bulk area and the pick area.
   b. What is the function of the WMS in the putaway process?

Multi-step Move

The putaway can be performed in a *single-step move* or a *multi-step move*. In a single-step move, the forklift driver takes the goods from the receipt lane directly to the storage location. In a multi-step move, the forklift driver takes the goods from the receipt lane to an intermediate location, e.g., a *pick/drop (P/D) location* at the front-end of the aisle. Another vehicle, such as an automated crane or a narrow-aisle truck, brings the goods to their final destination or to a subsequent P/D location. The WMS guides the various moves. The multi-step move may also apply to the outbound goods flow.

Putaway Rules

The WMS selects a storage location for the incoming goods. The WMS may apply various control rules for selecting the location. First, the WMS decides whether the product should go to a bulk location or a pick location. Usually this is a bulk location, however when the product is out of stock, it might be efficient to move the goods directly to the pick location. In this way, we avoid the replenishment move. Below we list several control rules for selecting a bulk location.

- *Product Group.* We may designate *sections* in the distribution center for certain *product groups.* This may relate to the storage conditions, for example hazardous materials are in a specially protected section, expensive goods are in a secured section or chilled and frozen goods are in temperature-controlled sections. For logistical reasons, products with similar characteristics may also be grouped in a different sections, e.g., heavy and light-weight products, large and small products, etc.
- *ABC classification.* Some locations in the distribution center are more easily accessible than others, because they are in the front-end of the distribution center, or they are at reaching height. The *ABC classification* assigns popular products to these locations and thereby reduces travel and handling times. The classification distinguishes *fast moving A* products, *medium moving B* products and *slow moving C* products. Within every section we designate a specific *zone* for each *ABC class* or *velocity class.* The *ABC classes* are determined by the pick frequency of a product and can be derived from historical demand or from sales forecasts.
- *Separation.* We may want to physically separate certain products. Tobacco and cheese, for example, should not be stored closely together otherwise the fumes from each might affect the taste of the other. The best way to do this is by assigning the products to different product groups with distant sections.
- *Balancing.* We may want to balance the space utilization in the distribution center by assigning goods to the aisle that currently has the lowest space utilization.
- *Weight.* Heavy pallets are typically stored on floor locations rather than high up in a pallet rack. Other weight rules may apply, such as a maximum weight per horizontal beam or per vertical column.
- *Volume.* The WMS may select a storage location considering the height, width and depth of the pallet. The system looks for a best fit to optimize the space utilization.
- *Close to Pick Location.* The WMS may select a bulk location close to the pick location. This saves travel time when replenishing the pick location.
- *Lot Number.* If a location holds multiple pallets, e.g., a block stack location, then only product with the same lot number may be stored together in the same location. Some storage systems, such as a gravity flow rack, guarantee a first in first out sequence. In such a system it may be possible to add product to a location which already holds an older lot of the same product.

50. **The WMS plays an important role in the putaway process.**
    a. How does the WMS decide whether incoming goods have to go to a pick location or to a bulk location?

3.6 Storage

While goods are in storage, we can distinguish between the following activities:
- Cycle counts
- Internal movements.

3.6.1 Cycle Counts

Due to mistakes in the inbound and outbound processes, the actual product amount in stock may differ from the amount registered in the WMS. An inaccurate inventory leads to balance differences and *shortpicks* (see Section 3.8.2). In order to remedy this, the operators count the inventory to verify that the administrative quantity matches the physical quantity in the distribution center. This may be done via periodic *cycle counts*, where operators visit a number of locations and count the quantity in each location.

It is also possible to count inventory during other warehouse activities. For example, consider a situation where the WMS believes a location should be empty after a pick. The order-picker can easily confirm this. If there still are goods in the location after picking, then the picker has detected an inventory discrepancy. The same may be done when the pick location is replenished. Typically a location is replenished when it is empty or when a small amount remains. Before putting the new product in the pick location, the operator can confirm the quantity in the pick location.

> **Procedure: Blind Counts**
> It is a best practice not to show the expected quantity upfront to the operator. Otherwise the operator might be inclined to confirm the quantity without actually counting! This practice is referred to as a *blind count*. The operator enters the counted amount in the RF terminal and the WMS verifies if the quantity matches the quantity registered in the system.

Another alternative is that the order-picker counts the amount in the pick location when it is below a threshold level. Clearly, when fewer items remain, it is easier to count them. Furthermore, with little inventory in the location, the next pick may easily result in a shortpick if the true inventory is below the level held in the WMS. If the shortage is detected in time, then we may prevent the shortpick.

51. **Mistakes in the inbound and outbound processes could cause discrepancies between the product quantity in stock and the quantity registered in the WMS.**
    a. List possible mistakes that could cause inventory discrepancies.

3.6.2 Internal Movements

Another activity that may take place while goods are in storage is the *internal movement* of goods between locations. These are movements that are not driven by orders. One reason for doing this is when a small amount of a product resides in a large location. If we move the goods to a smaller location, then the large location becomes available for another product, and space utilization is improved.

Another reason for moving goods while in storage is when a slow moving product is filling a location in a fast mover zone. Perhaps the product used to be a fast mover, but demand has dropped lately. By moving the product to a slow mover zone, the fast mover location comes available for another product. Again, the movement improves warehouse efficiency.

52. Internal movements could be necessary for Foodies.
   a. Why?

3.7 Wave Planning

The outbound processes are initiated by the wave planning process. Here tasks for replenishing, picking and shipping are generated. Note that no separate process is needed to initiate the inbound process, since it immediately starts with the arrival of the truck.

Unlike the other processes in this chapter, *wave planning* is an administrative process, not a physical process. The ERP communicates the available orders to the WMS (see Section 4.4.1). Subsequently, wave planning initiates the outbound goods flow by releasing orders for picking, packing and shipping. The WMS identifies which tasks must be performed to fulfill the orders. We assume that the orders have been scheduled for trips (see Section 4.4.1). Therefore the WMS knows which orders go together on a trip and at what time the trips are scheduled to depart.

The *warehouse planner* selects a set of orders that are ready for picking and releases them. Subsequently, the WMS computes the tasks that need to be performed in the distribution center to fulfill the orders. Finally, the tasks become available for the warehouse operators and the automated material handling systems.

3.7.1 Wave Selection

The *warehouse planner* selects orders to be released to the warehouse operation. If he releases a high workload to the shop floor, then this gives the WMS more opportunities to combine tasks into efficient activities. For example, think of sequencing pallet moves for a forklift truck or picking multiple orders simultaneously in a batch-picking operation. However, a high workload also requires more intelligence from the WMS to adequately manage the operation so that all tasks are still completed in time. Unfortunately, many WMSs cannot cope with this challenge. As a *rule of thumb* a workload of two to four hours suffices.

> **Rule of thumb: Wave Release**
> A workload of two to four hours suffices to achieve an adequate efficiency level. Any further increase of the workload only has a marginal effect.

A *wave* consists of orders that are scheduled to depart during the same period. However, beside the departure time, we also have to consider the duration of the order-picking activities: the order-picking of individual pieces has a longer lead-time than the order-picking of full pallet loads. Hence, in some operations, separate waves are released for the case/piece picking and pallet picking sections.

3.7.2 Inventory Allocation

After the wave has been selected, the WMS determines from which storage locations the goods are picked or replenished. This is called *inventory allocation*. The WMS should know exactly which products and quantities are present in each location. If a product is available at multiple locations, then the WMS uses *inventory allocation rules* to choose between the locations. Below are some typical rules.

Package Units

For order line quantities that are greater than or equal to a full pallet load, pallet loads are picked directly from bulk locations. Any remaining quantities are taken from pick locations. Clearly, picking full pallet loads is more efficient than picking the same amount in individual pieces. If a distribution center has separate sections for case picking and piece picking, then an order line may even be split three ways between bulk locations, case pick locations and piece pick locations.

> **Example: Package Units**
> A product has a pack configuration of 10 pieces per case and 10 cases per pallet. An order line requests 234 pieces. The WMS splits the order line into two pallet picks from bulk locations (=200 pieces), one pick for 3 cases from the case pick area (=30 pieces) and one pick for 4 individual pieces from the piece pick area.

Variants

There may be multiple variants of a product in the distribution center, such as different qualities, versions or suppliers. Although all these goods have the same product number, the customer may request a specific variant. Typically, the requested variant is specified in the order line.

Substitution and Cannibalization

If a product is not available, then the WMS may substitute it with a different product. The substitute may be a similar product of a higher quality. Another alternative is to cannibalize a product. For instance, a customer orders a book that is out of stock. However, the distribution center holds specific sets of five books that contain the requested book. By breaking down a set into individual books, we can fulfill the customer's order. It goes without saying that substitution and cannibalization should be used with care, since they may incur considerable extra costs.

Age

Especially for deteriorating items, such as food and beverages, the WMS will allocate the product with the oldest expiry date first. A well-known allocation rule is *first expired first out* (*FEFO*). For non-deteriorating items it might also be preferred to allocate the oldest product first, in which case the *first in first out* (*FIFO*) rule may be used.

Age vs. Efficiency

There are instances where the FEFO and FIFO rules result in operational inefficiencies. Here, the *relaxed FEFO* and *relaxed FIFO* rules might be preferable. These rules allow for a newer product to be allocated whenever this is significantly more efficient. Typical examples are picking full pallets instead of individual pieces (see *example* below) or cross-docking instead of picking from storage. More sophisticated rules only allow the relaxation if the difference between the expiry dates is less than a maximum number of days or if the oldest batch is at least a minimum number of days from its *latest goods issue date*.

> **Example: Relaxed FEFO**
> An order line requests a full pallet. The goods in the pick location have an earlier expiry date than the goods in the bulk locations. According to the regular *FEFO rule*, the WMS should assign the (less-than-pallet) quantity in the pick location to the order line, supplemented by a quantity from another pallet that is replenished from a bulk location. Clearly, this is less efficient than picking a full pallet load directly from a bulk location as would be the case with the *relaxed FEFO rule*.

Distance

If a product is available at multiple (bulk) locations, then we save travel time by allocating the product in the closest location. Clearly, the rule should respect the FEFO or FIFO sequence.

Product Quantity

If there are multiple bulk locations holding different quantities of the same product, then the WMS can minimize the number of picks by selecting the locations with large quantities first. Conversely, the WMS could use another rule that selects the locations with the smallest quantities and clears as many locations as possible. In general, the latter rule is preferred since it improves the space utilization. Minimizing the number of picks achieves efficiency in the short term. However, in the long term this rule tends to build up many small quantities of a product spread all over the distribution center. This leads to inefficiencies and poor space utilization. *Clearing locations* is a policy that optimizes both efficiency and space utilization.

3.7.3 Task Generation

The inventory allocation process generates a set of replenishment tasks, pick tasks, sort tasks and pack tasks that need to be performed to fulfill the orders in the wave. We distinguish two types of tasks:
- Simple tasks
- Compound tasks.

Simple tasks are pallet moves, such as pallet picks and replenishments. The WMS does not determine the sequence of simple tasks upfront when planning the wave, but in real-time during the execution. We further discuss this topic in Section 7.4. *Compound tasks* consist of various individual tasks that belong together, for example, the WMS combines the pick tasks for the order lines in an order to create a pick tour. The WMS considers the following when designing a pick tour:
- Single-order picking or batch-picking
- Zone-picking
- Pick volume
- Pick sequence.

Single-order Picking or Batch-picking

Single-order picking and *batch-picking* are well-known policies. Single-order picking implies that only one order is picked in a tour, while multiple orders are picked simultaneously in a batch-pick tour. Clearly, batch-picking reduces the overall travel time compared to single-order picking. However, batch-picking requires that the orders are sorted before being shipped to customers. This may either be done during the pick tour (*sort-while-pick*) or afterwards (*pick-and-sort*). The sort-while-pick policy necessitates special order-pick carts with separate compartments for each order and the pick-and-sort policy requires an additional sorting procedure after the order-picking. In Figure 3.9 we compare the single-order picking of the gray order on the left vs. the batch-picking of the gray and black orders on the right.

53. Single-order picking and batch-picking are two well-known policies.
 a. Mention two advantages and two disadvantages of single-order picking vs. batch-picking.
 b. In which situations would you prefer single-order picking or batch-picking, respectively?

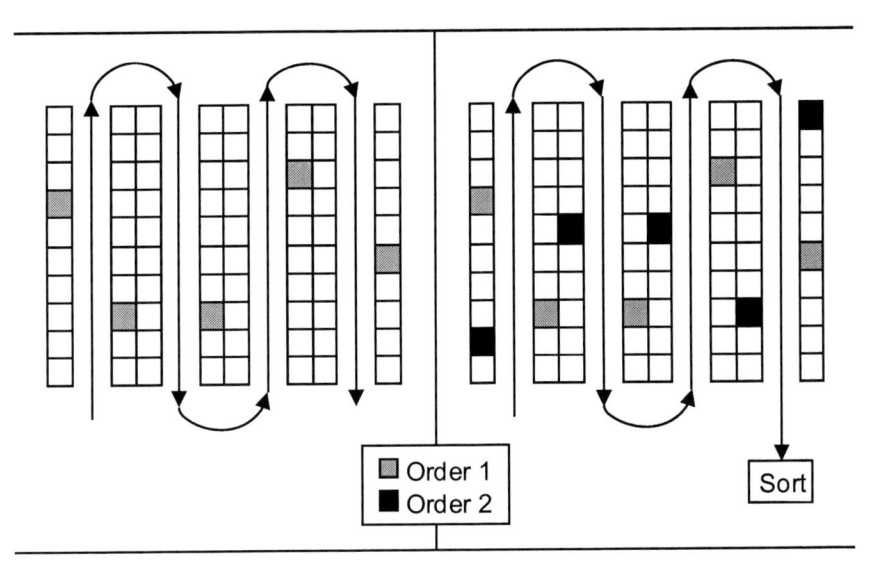

Figure 3.9 Single-order picking (left) vs. batch-picking (right).

Zone-picking

It is not necessary that the entire order is picked in one pick tour. *Zone-picking* divides the pick area into multiple zones and pick tours are restricted to one zone. Zone-picking is an effective method for reducing total travel distances. Additionally, it may be that some products cannot be picked onto the same pallet, e.g., heavy and light weight products, hazardous and non-hazardous products, chilled and ambient products, etc. Consequently, these products are stored in different zones and are picked separately. Zone-picking requires an additional handling step for consolidating the orders after order-picking. In

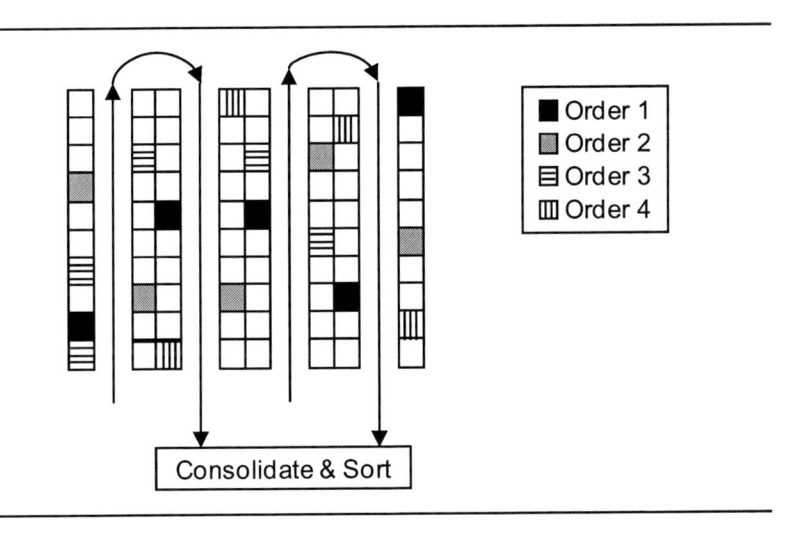

Figure 3.10 Zone-picking with four different orders in two tours.

Figure 3.10 we give an example where zone-picking and batch-picking are combined. We see that four orders are picked in two pick tours. The goods then need to be consolidated and sorted.

Pick Volume

An order-picker can bring one or multiple pallets or roller containers along on the pick cart. Of course, the total volume of the products that he can pick in a single tour is limited. The WMS knows the volume and weight of the individual products and can compute which products would fit together on the product carriers. Hence, the WMS can create pick tours consisting of picks whose total volume and weight meet the carrier restrictions. The assignment of picks to pick tours based on volume restrictions is called *cubing*. Simple cubing rules just add the individual volumes of the cases, while sophisticated cubing rules consider the dimensions and orientation of the individual cases. Obviously, a certain amount of air is being added when cases of different sizes are stacked together onto a pallet. The WMS estimates the required volume by computing a realistic stacking pattern. Figure 3.11 illustrates that there are six possible orientations for a case. Consequently, this is called *six dimensional (6D) cubing*.

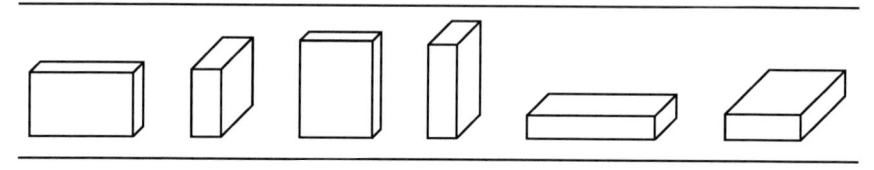

Figure 3.11 6D cubing.

For some products, the total volume of multiple pieces is not simply the sum of the individual volumes. A typical example is a pile of buckets. The combined volume of multiple pieces is less than the sum of the individual volumes. This is called *nesting*. The nested volume is calculated by adding a nesting fraction for each additional piece.

> **Example: Nesting**
> A bucket has a volume of 1 liter. The nesting fraction is 0.2, i.e., additional pieces increase the volume by 20 percent. Now five nested pieces have a volume of 1+0.2+0.2+0.2+0.2=1.8 liters.

Cubing has several advantages. First of all, it gives us a reliable estimate of the volume and weight that needs to be shipped with each order in advance. This is helpful input for transportation planning. Moreover, in situations where a single order is picked onto multiple pallets, cubing helps to split the work. Without cubing, one order-picker would have to pick the order until he finds that the first pallet is full, after which he continues with the next pallet. If we know in advance which order lines fit together on each pallet, then multiple order-pickers can work on the same order in parallel. This not only reduces response times, but may also increase the throughput capacity of the distribution center (see *case study* in Section 8.5).

Pick Sequence

After the WMS has decided which locations need to be visited on a pick tour, the system determines the sequence of the picks. A typical sequencing method among WMSs is to define an absolute ranking of the locations. Each location has a unique sequence number as shown in Figure 3.12.

The sequence on the left of Figure 3.12 represents one-sided picking. The order-picker first visits the locations on one side of the aisle and then returns to visit the locations on the other side. The location sequence on the right of Figure 3.12 amounts to two-sided picking. The order-picker traverses the aisle only once and picks from both sides. The latter sequence is also referred to as *S-shape*. Goedschalckx & Ratliff (1988) claim that one-sided picking is only preferable in very wide aisles or when a tour visits at least 50 percent of the locations in the aisles.

The rigid sequence of the locations does not necessarily lead to the shortest tour. Ratliff & Rosenthal (1983) developed a dynamic programming algorithm that computes the optimal sequence. Figure 3.13 shows the optimal sequence for the picks in Figure 3.12. Although it can reduce the travel time of the order-picker and its computation time is limited, hardly any WMS supports the optimal routing algorithm. An online comparison of sequencing routines can be found at Roodbergen (2001).

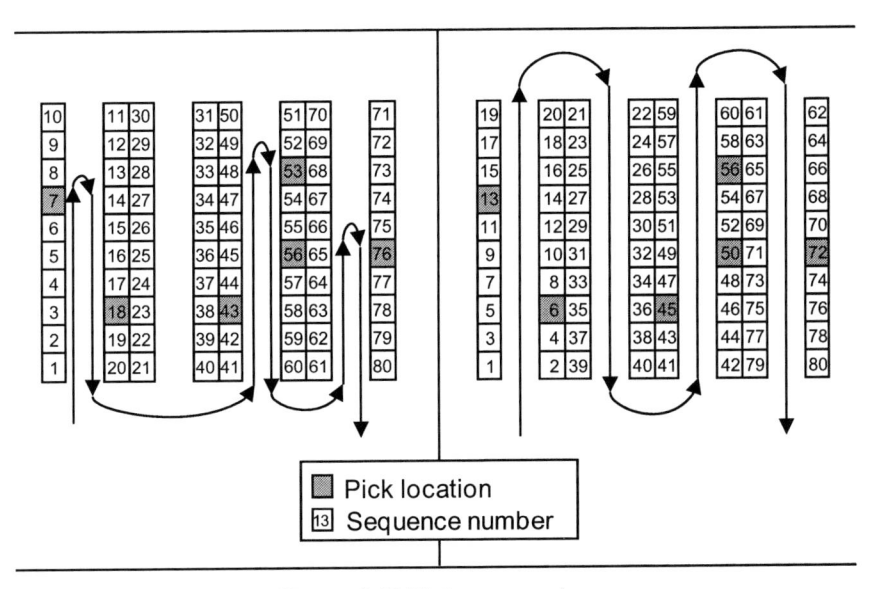

Figure 3.12 Pick sequencing.

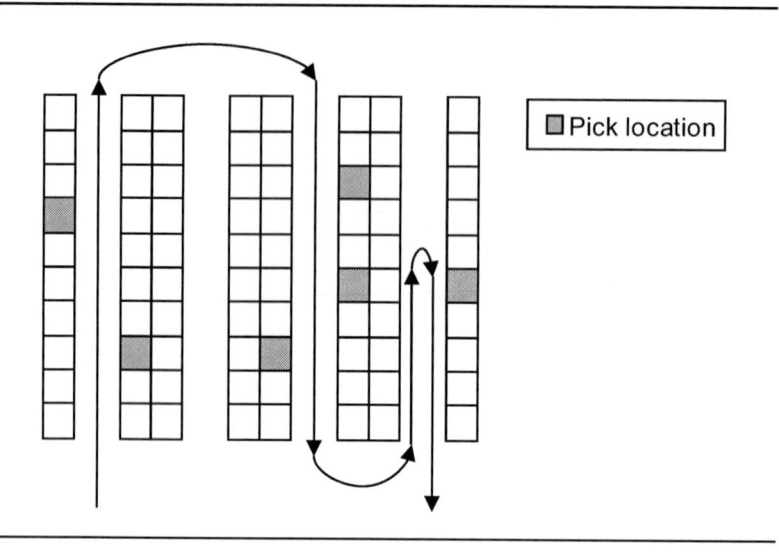

Figure 3.13 Optimal sequence.

> **Remark: Optimal Routing Algorithm**
> The optimal routing algorithm is especially successful when the *pick density* is low, i.e., long distances are traveled between each pick. If the pick density is high, i.e., a pick is performed every few feet, then the S-shape can rarely be beaten. Hence, when the optimal routing algorithm brings considerable benefits, this is a sign to the management that the pick density is low. In that case, we recommend investigating first whether it is possible to increase the pick density by introducing *batch-picking* or *ABC classes*, for example.

54. Tasks for replenishing, picking and shipping are generated during the wave planning process.
    a. Describe a possible wave planning process for Foodies. Think of:
        i. Wave selection
        ii. Inventory allocation
        iii. Task generation

3.8 Outbound Processes

The outbound process commences with the replenishment of the pick locations. Subsequent processes are order-picking and shipping.

3.8.1 Replenish

The replenishment process moves the goods from the bulk location to the pick location. The goods should arrive at the pick location in time, so that the order-picking is not delayed.

Replenishment Triggers

We distinguish two policies for initiating a replenishment task:
- Reactive replenishments
- Proactive replenishments.

The *reactive replenishment* policy triggers a replenishment when the quantity that has been allocated for a wave exceeds the amount in the pick location. Consequently, reactive replenishments are initiated during wave planning.

The *proactive replenishment* policy triggers a replenishment when the inventory level in the pick location drops below a certain threshold level. This typically occurs after an order-picker performs a pick. The threshold is configured in the WMS and should be chosen carefully. On the one hand, replenishments should occur well in advance, so that *shortpicks* are avoided. On the other hand, they should not occur too early, so that the amount in the pick location is low enough for large quantities to be replenished.

Reactive replenishments are created only when the goods are actually required for order-picking, i.e., they are *just in time*. The tight time constraints could result in late completions, which might delay the order-picking. Typically, proactive replenishments are created at an earlier stage, so that the time constraints are less stringent. However, proactive replenishments accumulate more goods in the pick locations so that a larger pick area would be necessary.

55. Reactive replenishments and proactive replenishments are two policies for initiating a replenishment task.
   a. Describe two advantages and two disadvantages of proactive replenishments vs. reactive replenishments.

Pick Location Assignment

Not all products are equally popular. Some are ordered more frequently than others. Typically 20 percent of the products amount to 80 percent of the picks. This phenomenon is generally known as *Pareto's law*. We can use the law to our advantage by assigning the *fast moving products* to easily accessible pick locations. These are the locations at the front of the distribution center and the locations at reaching height in the racks. *Slow movers* are stored in less accessible locations. Clearly, such a storage location assignment reduces the average travel times in the distribution center.

In addition to pick frequency we may have other considerations when assigning goods to a pick location, for example, some products are often ordered at the same time. We save travel time in order-picking by storing these *correlated products* close to each other. Obvious examples are components from the same supplier or products of the same size or color. Correlated products may also be revealed by analyzing historical data.

Another consideration may be to balance the activity in the distribution center. If we store all fast movers in a small area, then we reduce the travel time considerably but at the same time introduce heavy congestion among the order-pickers. The workload should also be balanced between zones. Likewise, if an AS/RS has multiple aisles with an automated crane in each aisle, then the workload should be balanced between the aisles.

For the assignment of pick locations we distinguish two policies:
- Static pick locations
- Dynamic pick locations.

The *static pick location* policy always assigns a product to the same pick location when it is replenished or putaway directly into the pick location. Moreover, if the product is not present in the distribution center, then the location is reserved for the product. The static pick location policy takes advantage of demand frequencies, by assigning popular products to easily accessible locations.

The *dynamic pick location* policy does not add the product to its current pick location, but assigns it to a new empty pick location when it is replenished or putaway. The dynamic pick location policy selects the empty pick location in a dedicated zone. In this way, the new pick location remains near the old location, for example to prevent long distances between the bulk locations of the product and its pick location. We can still take advantage of demand frequencies when using dynamic pick locations, by using *ABC classes* (the *A*-zone for fast movers, the *B*-zone for medium movers and the *C*-zone for slow movers). The *A*-zone is easily accessible and the *C*-zone is less accessible.

Dynamic pick locations have several advantages compared to static pick locations, for example, it is easier to put the new load into a location that is empty. This is especially true for products that are stocked on pallets in the pick locations. If product is replenished to a static pick location that is not empty, then the operator has to remove the existing product and the pallet underneath, deposit the new full pallet and finally add the old product onto the new load. This is quite labor intensive.

Another advantage is that we are able to replenish larger amounts at once to a pick location that is empty. This reduces the number of replenishments. Further, if a new lot is replenished to a dynamic pick location, then it is not mixed with the previous lot as would be the case with static pick locations. This eliminates the risk of the newer lot being accidentally shipped instead of the old lot, thus avoiding unnecessary inventory aging. A final advantage of dynamic pick locations is that they frequently become empty. At that time the inventory is easily counted by confirming that the location is empty – an inexpe.. of assessing inventory accuracy.

56. Dynamic pick locations have several advantages compared to static pick locations.
    a. What are four advantages of dynamic pick locations?
    b. A disadvantage of dynamic pick locations is that temporarily two pick locations are needed for a product. Consequently, which replenishment trigger would you prefer?
        i.   Reactive replenishments
        ii. Proactive replenishments

> **Case Study: Foodies' ABC Classification**
> Foodies' warehouse supervisor analyzed the demand frequencies of its juice range. Table 3.1 shows the number of picks per product over the previous three months. The pick area in the juice section contains three zones. The A-zone holds two locations, the B-zone holds three locations and the C-zone holds five locations.

57. Foodies' warehouse supervisor wants to optimize the ABC classification of the juice section.
    a. Assign the products in Table 3.1 to the A, B and C classes, respectively. Specify the zones in the right-hand column of the table.
    b. Calculate which percentage of the total pick activity has been generated by each class?
    c. Is historical data over a three month period a good basis for setting up an ABC classification?

Table 3.1 Picks per product over the past three months.

#	Product	Picks	ABC Class
1.	Apple juice	303	
2.	Pear juice	45	
3.	Strawberry juice	61	
4.	Tropical mix	13	
5.	Orange juice	512	
6.	Açaí juice	56	
7.	Forest fruit juice	25	
8.	Orange smoothie	121	
9.	Raspberry smoothie	216	
10.	Mango smoothie	648	

A complication of dynamic pick locations is that we temporarily need two pick locations for a product. If we are able to replenish the product just before the pick location becomes empty, then we need the two locations only for a short period of time. Hence, dynamic pick locations are often used in combination with reactive replenishments. Typically having 10 to 15 percent of pick locations empty is sufficient when using dynamic pick locations.

> **Case Study: Dynamic Pick Locations**
> A third party logistics provider wanted to combine static pick locations with efficient replenishments. They planned for the order-picker and the forklift driver with the replenishment pallet to arrive at the pick location at the same time. Their idea was that the order-picker would clear the pick location, then the forklift driver could immediately drop the new pallet.
>
> In practice, the order-pickers typically had to wait up to fifteen minutes until the forklift driver arrived. Moreover, the *just in time replenishments* disturbed the work of the forklift drivers who quite often had to come from another section within the distribution center.
>
> The 3PL changed from static pick locations to dynamic pick locations. *Reactive replenishments* delivered the goods to empty pick locations before the order-pickers arrived. Extra space was required, but this was found by turning some bulk locations at the second level of the racks into pick locations. At these locations, special man-up pick carts were used that could raise and lower the order-pickers between locations.

Replenishment Quantity
There are two rules for choosing the replenishment quantity:
- Fixed replenishment quantity
- Maximum replenishment quantity.

The *fixed replenishment quantity* usually is a full pallet or one or more full cases depending on the size of the pick location. The *maximum replenishment quantity* applies to the static pick location policy only. It considers how much is left in the pick location and calculates the maximum amount that can be added to the location.

3.8.2 Pick

The order-picking process is the main process in a distribution center. In this process, goods for the various orders are picked, consolidated and packed. Typically, some 50 to 60 percent of the time spent in the distribution center is used on order-picking (Frazelle, 2002).

We distinguish *pallet picking*, *case picking* and *piece picking*. Typically, a forklift driver picks *full pallets* from bulk locations and delivers them to the shipping dock, possibly via a multi-step move (see Section 3.5.2). Less-than pallet quantities (*cases* or *pieces*) are picked in pick tours where the order-picker visits a number of locations and picks the products onto a pallet or cart.

Pick Verification
Of course, it is important that the order-picker picks the correct products. When using RF terminals, the order-picker scans the barcode at the location, the license plate on the pallet or the barcode on the product before taking the goods. Which barcode is scanned varies between operations. Sometimes the order-picker is able to choose between the available barcodes since the WMS is able to recognize all of them. The WMS verifies the location and informs the order-picker via the RF terminal when it is incorrect. Clearly, this helps to reduce the number of order-picking errors.

An alternative to barcode scanning is the use of *check digits*. Check digits are random characters printed on each location (Figure 3.14). Instead of scanning the barcode, the order-picker enters the check digits in the RF terminal. Typically there are only two or three characters, so that they can be entered quickly. For the same reason check digits are highly popular with *voice-picking*.

> **Remark: Check Digits**
> Figure 3.14 shows a location with location code A-12-01-L. The location has random check digits, i.e., 51. The order-picker sees on his RF screen that he has to go to location A-12-01-L and confirm. The WMS can be configured to confirm by either scanning the location barcode (left-hand RF screen) or by typing in the check digits, i.e., 51 (right-hand RF screen).
>
> The use of check digits has one advantage over scanning location codes. Instead of scanning, the order-picker may also confirm the pick location by keying in the entire location code on the RF terminal while driving towards the location (the WMS cannot tell the difference between a code that is scanned or keyed in). This is a popular practice among order-pickers because it saves them time. However, it is an undesirable practice. The WMS is no longer able to check whether the order-picker is actually at the right location or whether he just typed the correct code and accidentally took the goods from the wrong location. Since the check digits are random throughout the distribution center, order-pickers do not know them before they actually arrive at the location.
>
> The check digits may also be included in the barcode, so that scanning the actual location barcode also identifies them.

Location code

```
A-12-01-L 51    |||||||||
```

Sample RF screens

```
Location: A-12-01-L
Confirm: _
```

```
Location: A-12-01-L
Check digit: _
```

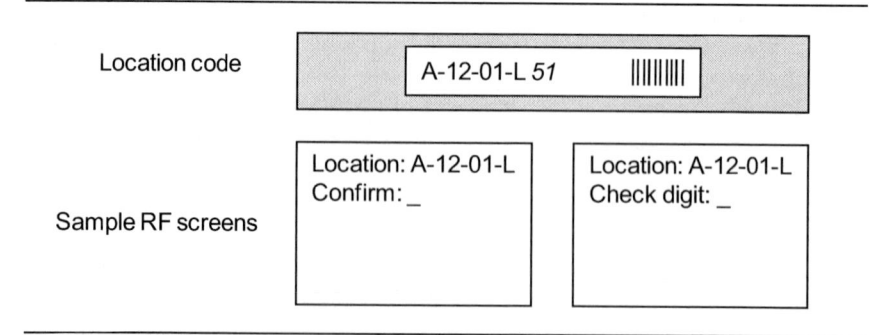

Figure 3.14 Location code with check digits and two different RF screens.

When using the *sort-while-pick* policy (see Section 3.7.3), the order-picker sorts the goods on the pick cart. Usually the pick cart has individual compartments for each order. Each compartment has a barcode (or check digits) and the order-picker has to confirm to the WMS in which compartment he places the goods. This allows the WMS to verify the sorting process. Due to the extra confirmation step, the sort-while-pick policy is particularly efficient when combined with voice-picking.

Shortpicks

As discussed in Section 3.7, the ERP and WMS verify if there is sufficient inventory before releasing the pick tasks. Consequently, there are only two reasons why an order-picker may still encounter insufficient inventory at the pick location:
- The replenishment is late.
- The quantity in the pick location is incorrect.

The first problem could be prevented by only releasing a pick tour after the replenishments have been completed. However, such a practice might increase the response times so that it cannot always be used. The second problem is difficult to overcome. The best way is to redesign processes and train order-pickers so that fewer errors are made (see Section 6.1). Modern technologies such as voice-picking, pick-to-light and RF scanning also help to reduce errors. Furthermore, regular inventory counts improve inventory accuracy (see Section 3.6.1).

When an order-picker encounters a shortpick, he corrects the inventory quantity in the WMS. Now there are two options. Either the WMS immediately adjusts the inventory levels or the WMS requests another operator to recount the inventory. The recount is performed by a clerk who is authorized to make inventory adjustments. Only after the clerk has ascertained that the inventory level is incorrect, is it modified in the WMS.

Sorting and Consolidation

After batch-picking and zone-picking, the orders need to be sorted and consolidated. This can be done manually or automatically with mechanized sorters. In a manual sorting operation, the operator puts the goods in a location designated for the customer. Put-to-light is a popular technique for manual sorting.

Packing

Individual pieces are packed together in a carton. Cases can be shipped individually or packed into larger cartons or plastic boxes. The WMS can compute how many containers and which container sizes are required for each order. The WMS may also provide special packing instructions, such as 'Add additional polystyrene foam' for fragile products. The operator attaches a shipping label to the carton with the customer address and other order details.

> **58. Analyze Foodies picking process in Appendix B.5.**
>   a. Which improvements with regard to this process would you recommend to Foodies?

3.8.3 Ship

The shipping process is the last process in the outbound goods flow. In the shipping process the goods are consolidated, shipping documents are generated and the goods are loaded into the truck.

Consolidate Truckload

After picking and packing, the goods are delivered to the shipping dock. At this point, pallets with few goods may be merged or high pallets may be split to create stability in the truck. The operators register the *restacking* in the WMS and new pallet labels are generated when necessary.

Shipping Documents

Due to shortpicks it could be that the shipped quantities differ from the ordered quantities. Hence, the shipping documents are typically printed only after all goods are picked and present at the *shipping dock* (or *loading dock*).

Loading Sequence

If a truck has to visit multiple destinations, then the goods for the customer who is visited first, should preferably be in the rear of the truck. This makes it easier for the truck driver to unload the goods. Therefore, the WMS ensures that the goods are loaded in the *reverse unloading sequence*.

There are two approaches for achieving this. The first approach is to stage the goods at the shipping dock in the preferred loading sequence. Hence, the WMS must arrange for the order-pickers to pick the goods strictly according to this sequence. This may impose tight constraints on the order-picking operation. It could result in severe efficiency losses, especially when the number of customers per truck is above two or three.

The second approach is to pick the goods in an arbitrary sequence and sort them in the preferred sequence while loading the truck. This approach introduces additional product handling and requires sufficient space at the shipping dock to randomly access each individual pallet.

59. At Foodies' distribution center, a warehouse operator is loading a truck. Goods will be delivered to various customers.
   a. In what way should the goods be loaded into the truck?
   b. How could this be organized?

Dock Allocation

Dock allocation for outbound trucks is similar to the inbound procedure (see Section 3.5.1). We further discuss dock planning in Section 7.2.3.

3.9 VAL

A distribution center may provide various value added logistics (VAL) services, such as customer-specific or country-specific assembly, packing, kitting or labeling. VAL services may be applied to goods in the inbound process, while in storage or in the outbound process.

For product assembly or kitting, the WMS determines which components are required for the final product. This is called the *bill of material (BOM)*. The WMS generates pick tasks for the components and makes sure that they are delivered to the VAL workstations. If the VAL services are executed as part of the inbound flow, then the WMS routes the goods from the receipt dock via the VAL workstations. Subsequently, the WMS provides the assembly instructions to the VAL operators. The operators confirm the completed activities in the WMS. In particular, the WMS registers which components have been used in each finished product to enable the tracking and tracing of the individual components.

After completing the VAL services, the goods are either returned to storage (*make-to-stock*) or they are consolidated with the outbound goods flow for shipping to the customer (*make-to-order*).

60. A distribution center may provide value added logistics (VAL) services.
   a. Which VAL services could be relevant for Foodies' products?
   b. When should the VAL services be applied (during the inbound process, while in storage or during the outbound process)?

3.10 Cross-dock

Cross-docking transfers the received goods directly, or via an intermediate buffer, to the shipping dock. Cross-docking saves handling steps, since the goods do not need to be putaway and picked. Moreover, the goods are available for shipping more quickly. If customers require less-than-pallet quantities, then the incoming full-pallet loads may be deposited in an intermediate buffer where the orders are picked. This is particularly popular for fast moving products. We distinguish two control rules for cross-docking:
- Opportunistic cross-dock
- Planned cross-dock.

Opportunistic cross-docking determines if the received goods are required for any outstanding sales orders once they come in. Opportunistic cross-docking can be applied in a putaway rule (see Section 3.5.2), i.e., can we putaway the received goods to the shipping dock? It can also be applied in an inventory allocation rule (see Section 3.7.2), i.e., can we pick the goods from the receipt dock? If the shipping dock is not yet available for the shipment, then we may divert to goods to an intermediate buffer.

Planned cross-docking requires that we know upfront which goods are to be received in a shipment. Prior to the arrival of the truck, the goods are allocated to outbound orders. Here we must ascertain that there is sufficient time between the arrival of the inbound truck and departure of the outbound trucks. Upon receipt the WMS guides the goods to the shipping docks.

61. **Some activities in the distribution center could be omitted when using cross-docking.**
    a. Explain which activities could be omitted.

3.11 Summary

Throughout the supply chain, warehouses have different roles. Upstream we see production warehouses with components, semi-finished goods and finished goods. A central warehouse or distribution center consolidates the goods from many sources and delivers to a large geographical market. A local warehouse supplies a small regional market, providing short response times.

Distribution centers provide several functions in the supply chain, i.e., break-bulk, storage, consolidation and customization. If the distribution center does not support these functions or only supports them to a limited degree, then we should question its purpose. Perhaps it can be eliminated.

There are various different types of equipment for storage and internal transport. Furthermore, we distinguished a number of standard activities that occur in the warehouse. We discussed the most popular ways to perform these activities as well as several variants. We also looked at the control rules in the WMS to guide the activities.

Chapter 4

Warehouse Management Systems

In this chapter we explain the fundamentals of warehouse management systems (WMSs). We discuss the functions and technology of the WMS as well as its integration within the IT architecture of a company. This information is essential for anyone embarking upon a WMS project.

A *warehouse management system* is a software system that controls the activities within the distribution center. The system knows which goods are to be received and shipped. It determines which tasks need to be performed to process the goods and sends commands to human operators and automated material handling systems to execute these tasks. Furthermore, the system captures relevant data on orders, shipments, inventory, warehouse layout, warehouse staff, vehicles, customers, suppliers and activities in the distribution center, to mention a few. This ensures the *tracking and tracing* and quality of warehouse activities.

If a company wants a new software system to operate its distribution center, then it can either decide to custom-build a system or to buy a standard WMS. In the 1980's and most of the 1990's companies predominantly used their own custom-built software to control their warehouse operations. The warehouse software was often part of a large monolithic business system that also supported sales, purchasing, production and finance. The capabilities of these so-called *legacy systems* were limited, but served the purpose of getting the goods in and out. Since then, a considerable number of software vendors have developed so-called *standard WMSs*. These *off-the-shelf systems* have dramatically changed the way in which the software is implemented. For custom-made systems, we first determine how we want to organize the warehouse processes, then we build the system accordingly. In the implementation of a standard WMS, as it is the case with any packaged software system, we configure the parameters in the WMS so that it supports the intended way of working.

Standard WMSs have been highly popular in the last decade. So what are the main advantages of standard WMSs compared to custom-made systems? We consider three advantages here:
- Quick implementation
- Ongoing development
- High flexibility.

An obvious benefit is that a standard WMS accelerates implementation time. Instead of writing customized software code from scratch, the user configures the options in a standard system, which saves a lot of time. Moreover, most standard packages have been installed numerous times before, so programming errors have generally been resolved. This also saves time in testing the new software prior to installation.

Standard systems also become better over time. Vendors provide new features in the form of software upgrades to their existing users. Furthermore, the vendors guarantee that old functions and configurations will continue to work in upgraded versions, meaning upgrades are reasonably easy to install without disrupting the current practices. Software upgrades not only provide new functions but they also keep the system up-to-date with the latest technological developments.

However, a standard WMS has one advantage that outweighs all others, namely its *flexibility*. If the manager decides to redesign the processes after some time, then this is achieved relatively easily by reconfiguring the parameters. For custom-built systems this is a much more complex challenge.

62. This chapter discusses the fundamentals of warehouse management systems.
   a. *What is a WMS?*
   b. *Give three advantages of a standard WMS compared to a custom-made WMS.*
   c. *Give one disadvantage.*

Nevertheless, standard software is not a panacea. If, after ample analysis, the desired method of working cannot be configured in the standard WMS, then it is necessary to amend the standard package software with customized enhancements prior to implementation. This introduces the many disadvantages of customized software. In fact, most failed package installation projects in recent years can be attributed to an abundance of custom enhancements. Related problems are encountered later on when the company wants to upgrade its system. The customizations have to be refitted to the standard software and the combination needs to be tested extensively once again. WMSs with many customizations can hardly be upgraded at all.

Product development in a WMS typically originates from enhancement requests. Users request new functions. The WMS vendor then considers whether the function is a useful asset to other users of the WMS. If this is the case, then the vendor might decide to include it in the next upgrade version of the WMS. For some WMSs, the user group jointly decides which new functions are included in the next version. There is a considerable advantage to the user if an enhancement is included in the standard WMS. Firstly, the function is automatically available in future upgrades. Secondly, the development costs for the new function are shared. Take advantage of this opportunity.

4.1 WMS Modules

The core function of a WMS is the control over the activities inside the distribution center, such as putaway, replenishing, order-picking and value added logistics. Moreover, the WMS records the locations and attributes of the goods in the distribution center. On top of these core functions WMS vendors usually offer complementary modules that can be purchased separately. Below are some examples of these so-called *add-on modules*.

Customs Management

Imported goods need to be cleared for customs. A *customs* module supports the customs declarations for goods in the distribution center and keeps an accurate view on the inventories under customs control.

Billing of Logistics Services

Third party warehouses charge their clients for services provided, e.g., a fee for receiving a pallet or a weekly fee for storing a pallet. Also private warehouses may charge their internal clients. The *billing* module registers which services have been provided to each individual client and generates periodic client invoices.

Web Portal

Clients, suppliers, customers and various other parties might be interested in the status of the warehouse activities, such as "Has the order already been shipped?" or "How much inventory is still available?" A *web portal* makes this information available via the internet. Users may also use the web portal to enter information, they may, for example, reserve a time-slot at the docks or pre-announce the contents of a delivery. Obviously, only authorized users can access the information.

Dock and Yard Management

The WMS may also control the truck movements in the yard. The *dock and yard management* module decides at which dock the truck should load or unload, or directs the truck to a parking spot to await its time window at the dock. Furthermore, the module may register the inventories held in trucks in the yard.

Slotting

A slotting module assigns products to pick locations (pick slots) based on product characteristics such as turnover velocity, weight, volume, etc. Since assortments and demand patterns change, the slotting module does a periodic update of the preferred pick locations of products.

Management Information

Throughout the day, the WMS registers detailed information on the activities that are performed. Useful management information can be extracted from this detail. The *management information* module analyzes and reports such information.

Labor Management

The workload in the distribution center fluctuates from day to day. A *labor management* module computes the number of man hours for a given set of orders. This estimate is used to plan the required number of operators in advance. The computations use detailed standard times for activities, so-called *engineered labor standards*.

Case Study: Foodies' WMS

Four years ago, Foodies implemented a WMS in its distribution center together with a customs add-on module. Foodies needed the customs module because it imports various fruits and juices from Latin America.

Now the manager is considering which other add-on modules might be helpful for Foodies.

---

63. Consider Foodies' action plan in Table 2.1 on page 67.
    a. Which add-on module would you recommend to Foodies in year T+1?
    b. And which one in year T+2?

With these add-on modules, the scope of a WMS can be extensive. However, there are certain functions that are usually considered to be outside the domain of the WMS. Below are some typical examples.

Inventory Management

Ironically inventory management is not a WMS function. Although the distribution center is constantly amending the inventory levels, it does not decide how much inventory should be present. This is decided by the inventory control department. Often the inventory management module is contained in the *ERP system*. There also are specialized inventory management systems.

Order Management
Order management entails various order-related activities such as order-entry, order processing and order acceptance. Order management modules are typically contained in the ERP system, but there also are specialized order management systems (OMSs).

Finance
The WMS records the goods that have been received and shipped as well as the associated logistics services that have been provided to each client. However, after listing the goods and services provided, the WMS leaves the actual invoicing and accounting to a separate financial system or the financial module of the ERP.

Transportation Planning
A WMS is capable of planning the external transportation when the routes are *fixed*, e.g., the truck to New Yotk departs each day at 3 PM. If routes are *variable*, then the transportation is planned by a *transportation management system* (*TMS*) or *vehicle routing and scheduling system* (*VRS*).

Nevertheless, WMS vendors often broaden their portfolio with these non-warehousing functions. This provides good opportunities for cross-selling and the vendor is not solely dependent on WMS revenues.

4.1.1 Integrated vs. Best-of-Breed Systems

As WMS vendors extend their systems with non-warehousing functions, we see that vendors of ERP, TMS and material handling control systems (MHCSs) expand their systems with WMS functions.

An *ERP (Enterprise Resource Planning)* is an integrated system that facilitates finance, production planning, order management and inventory management to name a few functions. A *TMS* is a system that supports the planning of external transportation. Finally, the *MHCS* is a system that controls the automated material handling devices within the distribution center, such as automated stacker cranes, conveyors, sorters or stacker robots.

The question arises as to whether we should opt for an *integrated system* that provides many different functions, or for a combination of so-called *best-of-breed systems* that are each specialized in a single function, such as a WMS or a TMS. If a company chooses best-of-breed systems, then the separate systems must be integrated via interfaces, which can be a complex and expensive task.

The obvious advantage of an integrated system is that no interfaces are required. In general, best-of-breed WMSs offer more sophisticated functions, although some ERP vendors have almost caught up in recent years. We recommend that users base their choice between a best-of-breed WMS and an integrated WM-module on logistical considerations rather than IT considerations. In other words, if the WM-module of the ERP seriously compromises the logistics performance of the distribution center, then the advantages of a uniform IT standard should not prevail.

> **Case Study: Foodies' WMS Selection**
> Foodies implemented an ERP system for finance, order processing, customer relationship management (CRM) and production planning. The ERP system also contained a simple warehouse management module, but the logistics manager believed that it did not meet Foodies' requirements. Hence, the manager decided to buy a separate WMS from a different vendor, which was linked to the ERP via interfaces.

64. Consider Foodies' WMS selection in the case study above.
    a. Did Foodies decide on an *integrated system* or a so-called *best-of-breed system*?
    b. What are the advantages and disadvantages of this choice?
    c. Do you agree with this choice?

4.2 Real-time Communication

A WMS organizes the warehouse operation by assigning tasks to human operators and machines. In Section 4.3 we will discuss the assignment of tasks to machines. First, we focus on the communication with human operators. We distinguish two methods for communicating tasks to operators:
- Batch communication
- Real-time communication.

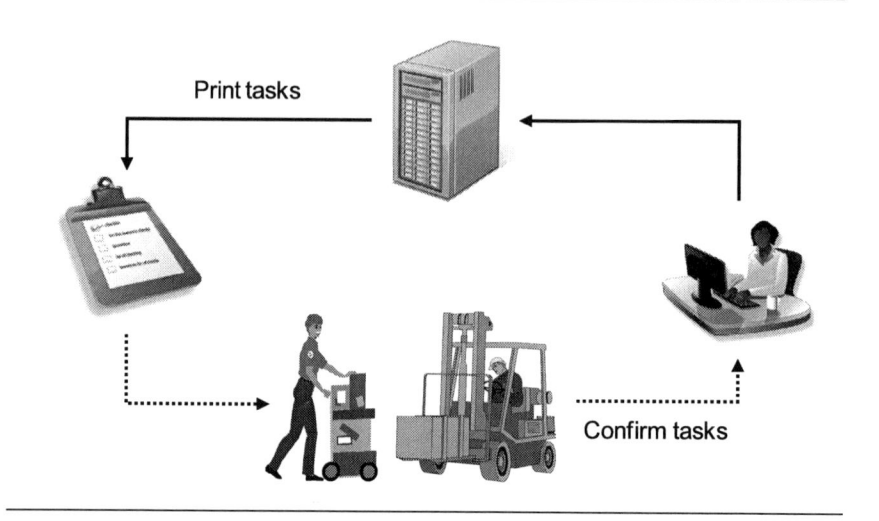

Figure 4.1 Task assignment via paper lists.

Figure 4.1 shows a WMS that prints paper lists to guide the operators, e.g., a *pick list*. After the operator has completed the tasks, he returns to a PC to confirm this with the WMS. Only at that time is the information in the WMS updated. Hence, there always is a time delay. We refer to this process where tasks are communicated group by group with a certain time delay as *batch communication*.

A popular alternative is to use *radio frequency* (*RF*) *terminals*. The RF terminal is a device with a key pad, a small screen, an antenna and a barcode scanner. The RF terminal has a radio connection with the WMS. The WMS displays commands on the screen of the RF terminal and the operator replies by typing a response or scanning a barcode. For this purpose warehouse locations and products carry barcode labels. Furthermore, pallets carry unique barcode labels which we refer to as *license plates* (LPs). The application of RF gives the WMS a real-time view of the progress in the distribution center.

Other *real-time communication* devices are voice terminals and pick-to-light. *Voice terminals* are devices where the operator listens to commands through a headset and replies via commands spoken into a microphone. The advantage of voice terminals over RF terminals is that it is hands free. The actions of the operator are not interrupted by scanning or typing on the RF terminal. This saves time and reduces errors. *Pick-to-light* applies when only one operator works in a section. Each location has a display that can show the pick quantity. The operator picks the displayed quantity and pushes a button next to the display to confirm the pick. The technique is also popular for sorting products among customer orders, in which case it is called *put-to-light*. With put-to-light, each location represents a customer. The operator scans a product and the put-to-light system displays which quantity is designated for the various customer locations.

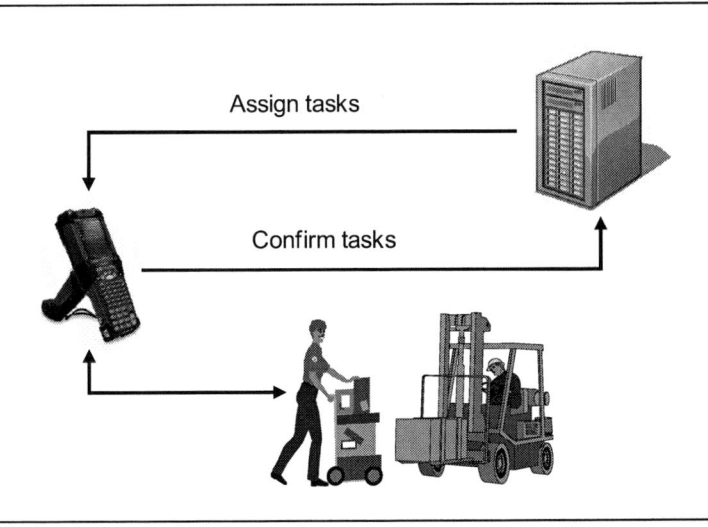

Figure 4.2 Paperless warehousing.

Figure 4.2 shows a WMS that uses real-time communication, also referred to as *paperless warehousing*. Real-time communication has been a breakthrough in the field of warehousing. It enables the WMS to assign tasks to operators, taking into consideration the current location of the operator and the urgency of the tasks. For instance, the WMS can decide to assign a pallet move to a forklift driver who has just completed a nearby task, thereby minimizing the empty travel time, or to assign a task that is at a further distance but more urgent. Clearly, this is not possible with a system that prints paper slips to guide operators. Furthermore, the WMS verifies every task in real-time, so that RF communication reduces errors compared to paper lists. Finally, administrative tasks such as confirming receipts, orders and pick tasks, are performed directly on the warehouse floor. This makes several administrative functions redundant.

Real-time communication makes it possible to control more effectively, verify more accurately and register more efficiently. We distinguish three real-time operating modes:

- *System-directed.* The WMS decides which task the operator should perform next and to which location the product must be moved.
- *System-guided.* The operator chooses which task he performs next and the WMS decides to which location the product must be moved.
- *System-assisted.* The operator chooses which task he performs next and to which location the product must be moved. The system's only purpose is to record the tasks.

> **Rule of Thumb: Warehouse Complexity**
> Warehouse management systems can deliver substantial cost savings, but the question arises as to the level of return on investment that can be achieved. Different distribution centers may require different degrees of automation. Table 4.1 shows the criteria to characterize the *complexity* of a distribution center as *low*, *medium* or *high*. Based on the complexity, the appropriate degree of automation should be selected:
> - *Low complexity.* Basic WMS with RF or paper.
> - *Medium complexity.* Regular WMS with RF and standard wave, task and performance management.
> - *High complexity.* Advanced WMS with RF, capacity planning and advanced wave, task and performance management.

CASE STUDY

65. **Analyze the complexity of Foodies' distribution center using Table 4.1.**
    a. How would you characterize its complexity (low, medium or high)?
    b. Based on the complexity, what is the appropriate degree of automation for Foodies?

> **Case Study: Foodies' Warehouse Complexity**
> Foodies' distribution center has a surface area of 130,000 ft^2. Here are some averages over the past year:
> - *Staff.* 25 warehouse operators in a single shift schedule.
> - *Volume.* 15 outgoing trucks per day.
> - *Orders.* 5.5 sales orders per truckload.
> - *Order lines.* 17 order lines per sales order.
>
> The departure times of the trucks are spread over the day. Cases and individual pieces are picked from pallet locations on the floor positions in a pallet rack, while full pallet loads are picked directly from bulk locations. On peak days the total workload of the warehouse may increase by 30 percent.

Table 4.1 Warehouse complexity.

Complexity	Low	Medium	High
Number of operators	≤ 15	15-45	≥ 45
Warehouse area (ft^2)	≤ 50,000	50,000-150,000	≥ 150,000
Order lines shipped per day	≤ 1,000	1,000-5,000	≥ 5,000
Separate picking processes[13]	1-2	3-4	≥ 5
Shipping pattern[14]	1 wave	2-3 waves	Individual
Fluctuations in workload[15]	≤ 150%	150%-250%	≥ 250%

4.3 Material Handling Control

A distribution center might use various automated *material handling systems*, such as roller conveyors, sorters, robots, carousels and automated storage/retrieval systems. As they are part of the warehouse operation, the WMS needs to control their activities.

Figure 4.3 shows a typical configuration for controlling automated material handling systems. The WMS communicates with the material handling control system (MHCS), which in turn communicates with the *PLCs (programmable logic controllers)*.

---

[13] Whether orders are picked in a single process, or picked from multiple areas using different methods, then consolidated afterwards, e.g., a pick-to-belt area for fast movers and a shelving area for slow movers.
[14] Whether orders are picked in one wave for the entire day, in multiple waves or each individual shipment is planned separately.
[15] Maximum daily workload relative to the average daily workload.

```
        ┌─────────┐
        │   WMS   │
        └────┬────┘
             ↕
        ┌─────────┐
        │  MHCS   │
        └────┬────┘
             ↕
        ┌─────────┐
        │  PLC's  │
        └─────────┘
```

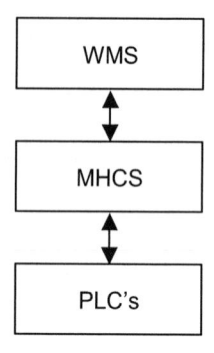

Figure 4.3 Material handling control.

The MHCS is an information system that controls and monitors the overall material handling system, e.g., a conveyor system or an automated storage/retrieval system. A PLC is a simple rugged computer device that reads input signals, runs control logic and then writes output signals. A PLC can, for example, control the engine of an automated crane, a section of a roller conveyor or a sorter device. Thus, a material handling system is controlled by a number of PLCs each controlling a segment of the system. The PLC receives its input signals from sensors, such as optical sensors or barcode readers or from the material handling control system. The output signals control the engines in the material handling system or provide feedback to the material handling control system. Some WMSs contain an integrated MHCS. In that case, the WMS directly communicates with the PLCs.

Consider the following example. Figure 4.4 shows the configuration of a conveyor system. Pallets enter the conveyor system at input station X to be transported to output stations A through F. The conveyor system contains five sorter devices, depicted by the black squares. The conveyor system has to sort the pallets to the correct output station. The WMS, responsible for the overall management of the warehouse processes, decides to which output station a pallet needs to go. For each pallet, the WMS communicates the license plate, together with the origin and destination, to the MHCS, which then controls the PLCs accordingly.

The intelligence in the MHCS varies between systems. Since the WMS manages the entire warehouse operation, it is important that the WMS has adequate control over the material handling systems.

66. **Figure 4.3 shows a configuration for material handling control.**
    a. *Explain the relationship between WMS, MHCS and PLCs.*
    b. *Which material handling systems would be suitable for Foodies? And why?*

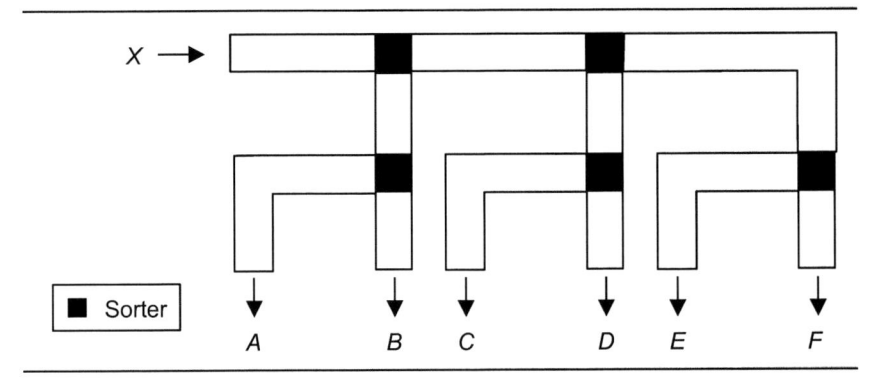

Figure 4.4 Conveyor system.

4.4 Interfaces

Various departments within a company need to know how much inventory is available in the distribution center. The inventory levels are important inputs for production, purchasing, sales and marketing plans. Likewise, the departments may need to know which orders have arrived from suppliers and which have been shipped to customers. It is the responsibility of the distribution center to keep the inventory and order information up-to-date. Thus, the WMS records all inventory transactions and shares the information with related information systems.

If the WMS is an integral part of a corporate business system, such as an ERP or a legacy system, then the information is instantly available to all departments. However, if the departments use different systems, then the information must be synchronized between the various systems. This could be done manually, but electronic interface messages are obviously preferable as the data volume increases. Accordingly, the WMS may share information not only with the ERP, but also with some other information systems within the company such as the TMS, the MHCS and various other systems from customs management systems to data warehouses. The WMS might even be connected to systems outside the company, such as systems of suppliers, customers and transportation service providers.

Modern communication protocols and technology, such as *XML* and *enterprise application integration* (*EAI*) platforms, make it easier to connect systems. However, the challenge remains to decide which data is shared between the systems. It is important that the logistics staff does not leave it to the IT department to come up with the definitions. An improper interface definition could result in major inefficiencies in the logistics operation. Moreover, the interface definitions are a prominent element of a WMS project, which could cause considerable delays and budget overruns if specified incorrectly.

The following information is communicated between the ERP and the WMS:
- Incoming goods
- Stock adjustments
- Outgoing goods
- Product attributes.

For our discussion, we consider the generic IT architecture depicted in Figure 4.5. The ERP system supports finance, inventory management, purchasing, order management and production. The ERP is the central information system that holds all data on inventories, orders, products, customers, suppliers, etc. Since the data is kept in only one system instead of multiple systems, the consistency of the data is guaranteed. In other words, everyone in the company finds the same product characteristics, inventory levels and supplier/customer attributes. Furthermore, the WMS communicates with the TMS as well as the ERP systems of suppliers and customers.

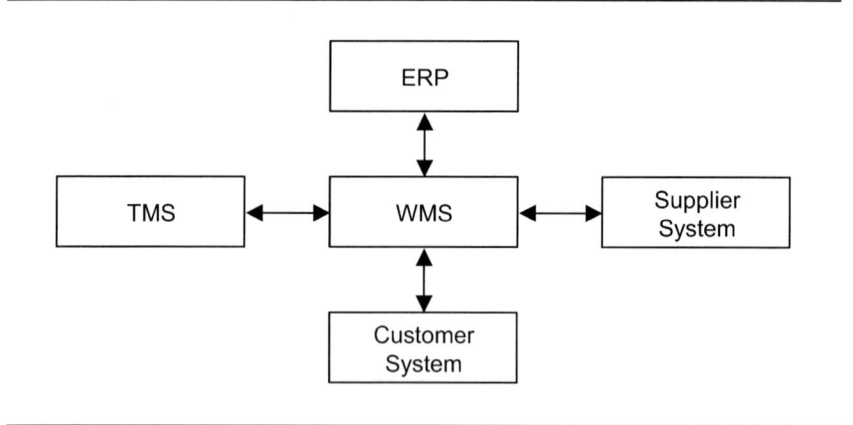

Figure 4.5 Sample IT configuration.

The architecture applies both to companies with private warehouses as well as third party warehouses. The source and sell functions use the ERP, while the transportation planning function uses the TMS. In practice, we encounter many different configurations, with legacy systems and with several best-of-breed systems instead of the ERP. Also there might not be a TMS if the delivery routes are fixed. Nevertheless, most of what is discussed here can be applied to various different configurations.

67. The WMS communicates with other systems.
   a. Which systems may communicate with the WMS?

4.4.1 Outgoing Goods

We start our analysis by examining the outbound goods flow. The goods flow is driven by orders. An *order* is a contract between a supplier and a customer for the transfer of goods. The parties agree where and when the goods will be delivered (by the supplier) or picked up (by the customer). The order contains one or more *order lines*, where each order line specifies the quantity ordered of a single product.

Figure 4.6 shows the typical order process, which contains four steps. Sometimes we see that companies combine certain steps or use a different sequence. The process in Figure 4.6 starts with the customer who places an order at the sell function by phone, fax, email, internet or automatically via *electronic data interchange (EDI)*. We refer to the associated record as a *customer order*.

Function	System	Record
Customer	Customer ERP	Customer order
Sell	ERP	Sales order
Transportation Planning	TMS	Transport order
Distribution Center	WMS	Delivery

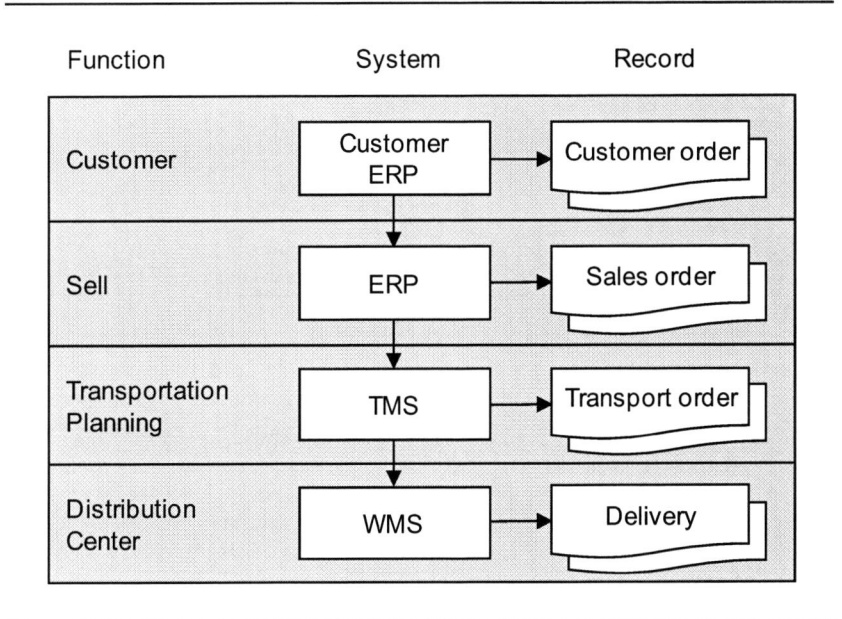

Figure 4.6 Order process.

The sell function evaluates the customer order in the ERP. This is called *order acceptance*. Usually this is done automatically by the ERP, but certain parts of the process might be performed by a sales representative in person. The orders can be reviewed one by one as they arrive (*real-time processing*) or collected together and reviewed periodically (*batch processing*).

Which verifications occur in the order acceptance process varies between companies. A typical first check is to verify if the information in the order is valid, for example, there should not be alphabetic characters in a numerical field. Furthermore, some companies check whether the customer is allowed to order the product or product quantity, e.g., certain products are restricted to particular markets only, quotas on products apply per customer or a financial check determines the remaining credit of the customer. Also some companies round the ordered amounts to full case or full pallet quantities, for example, if a customer orders over 85 percent of a full pallet, then the order line is rounded to a full pallet quantity.

In any case, the most important step in order acceptance is the inventory check. Does the distribution center hold enough stock to fill the orders? If the orders require more than the available inventory, then the system decides which customers may receive the available product. This is called *order disposition*. Typical disposition rules are:
- First come first served
- Even allocation
- Even allocation relative to the ordered quantities
- Important customers served first.

If the order cannot be fulfilled, then the customer might (implicitly or explicitly) agree to wait for the remaining quantities and a *backorder* is created. The company has to purchase or manufacture new amounts or acquire product from other warehouse facilities to fulfill the backorders. The order lines that are currently available in the distribution center are either shipped immediately or they wait until the goods in backorder become available. Consequently, order acceptance converts a customer order into one or multiple *sales orders*. It may even occur that multiple customer orders from the same customer are combined into a single sales order.

A more sophisticated variant of order acceptance is *order promising*. In the previous example, orders with insufficient stock were put in backorder with unknown response times. In contrast, order promising considers the options for fulfilling backorders and promises a response time. Is the requested product available at another distribution center within the company? Can it be purchased from a supplier or does the production plant still have to manufacture the product? Based on these options, the ERP can calculate and thereby promise a response time for the order. If the decision is limited to the inventory available within the company, then it is referred to as *available to promise*. If the decision also includes the purchase or manufacture of goods, then it is referred to as *capable to promise*.

68. Foodies has insufficient stock for today's orders.
a. Which order disposition rule would you prefer for Foodies? And why?

The ERP transfers the sales orders to the TMS. The TMS plans the routes of the trucks and supports administration and invoicing relating to the transportation fleet. The system helps to consolidate less-than-truckload orders into multi-stop full truckload routes. The system might also decide which carriers to use. Most

TMSs are not sophisticated enough to consider street-level routing. They use point-to-point distances for making their decisions.

A vehicle routing and scheduling system (VRS) is an alternative for companies that offer local deliveries. The VRS calculates efficient routes using a detailed roadmap and complex constraints on the volume and weight capacity of the trucks, the duration of the route and the limited time windows for customer visits. Whether a company uses a TMS, a VRS or both systems has no impact on the specification of the interface with the WMS. Therefore we limit our discussion to the interface with the TMS.

> **Remark: Factory Gate Pricing**
> Most companies only plan *outbound* routes for the delivery of goods to customers, since *inbound* trips are organized by suppliers. Recently we have seen that several organizations (retailers in particular) have started to plan the inbound routes as well. Their trucks deliver goods to the various stores and instead of returning empty, the trucks pick up goods at a supplier on the return trip (backhauling). By combining the pick-up and delivery routes, the transportation becomes more efficient. A concept that capitalizes on this idea is *factory gate pricing*. The customers buy the goods with the transportation costs deducted (also referred to as *ex works*).

The TMS plans the transport and decides which sales orders go together on a route. As a consequence, a sales order could be split among multiple routes, or multiple sales orders from the same customer could be combined in the same route. The order lines from a sales order that go together on the same route are referred to as a *transport order*. The transport order also specifies the scheduled departure date and time.

Many WMSs are able to assign deliveries to fixed routes, taking into account simple weight and volume constraints for the truckload. So, companies with fixed routes do not usually require an additional TMS or VRS to plan the routes and, hence, no interface is needed.

Finally, the transport orders are communicated to the WMS. As discussed, the sell function has already checked if there is sufficient inventory and the transportation planning department has ascertained that the ordered goods fit into the truck. Now, the distribution center should be able to ship the requested quantities. However, it may be that not all goods specified in the *transport order* can actually be shipped, e.g., the cubic volume of the picked goods exceeds the volume calculated by the TMS and the goods do not fit in the truck. We refer to the goods that are actually shipped as the *delivery*.

Goods that leave the distribution center may go to various categories of destination. Table 4.2 shows the order type associated with each destination type. A *bill of material order* lists all components (or ingredients) and semi-finished goods that are needed by a production plant for a production order. A *transfer order* lists the goods that need to be shipped to another distribution center within the same company. Finally, a *return merchandise authorization* (RMA) is an agreement with a supplier to return goods.

Table 4.2 Order types per destination.

Destination	Order type
Customer	Sales order
Production plant	Bill of material order
Distribution center	Transfer order
Supplier	Return merchandise authorization

We shall restrict our discussions to sales orders since the interfaces for the other order types contain the same elements. The WMS may exchange three different interface messages with the other systems:
- Transport order (TO)
- Transport order confirmation (TOC)
- Despatch advice (DESADV).

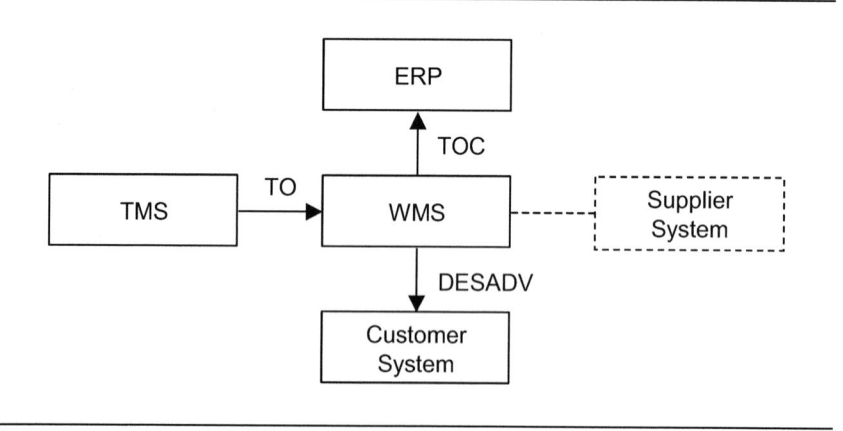

Figure 4.7 Interfaces for the outbound goods flow.

We observed in Figure 4.6 that the order acceptance process converted the customer orders into transport orders. Likewise, the other order types specified in Table 4.2 will be transformed into transport orders. The ERP or TMS interfaces the transport orders to the WMS well before the planned departure time of the truck, so that the warehouse operators have sufficient time to pick the goods. Note that in Figure 4.7 the transport orders are created by the TMS (instead of the ERP). Transport orders can be communicated daily, hourly or even more frequently. Updates and cancellations of previously communicated transport orders can also be included.

Once the goods leave the distribution center, the WMS matches the shipped quantities against the transport orders. Subsequently, the WMS confirms to the

ERP how much was shipped against each transport order. We refer to this message as the *transport order confirmation*. The ERP updates its inventory levels which in turn impacts other processes, for example, the finance department can then send an invoice to the customer.

> **Example: Orders and Deliveries**
> As explained in Figure 4.6 an order is transformed into one or multiple deliveries. Figure 4.8 illustrates how orders may be split among deliveries. The customer places three orders, numbered 1000, 1001 and 1002. The distribution center ships two deliveries to the customer, numbered 500 and 501.

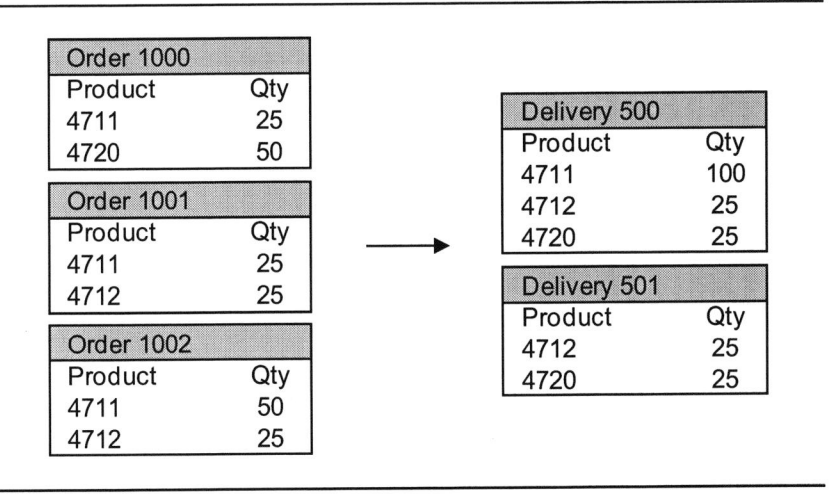

Order 1000	
Product	Qty
4711	25
4720	50

Order 1001	
Product	Qty
4711	25
4712	25

Order 1002	
Product	Qty
4711	50
4712	25

Delivery 500	
Product	Qty
4711	100
4712	25
4720	25

Delivery 501	
Product	Qty
4712	25
4720	25

Figure 4.8 Orders and deliveries.

The customer checks if the delivery is complete. If the supplier ships each order separately, then the customer can compare the received goods to the orders. However, when orders may be split across deliveries (or deliveries split across orders), then the customer cannot determine from the purchase orders whether the delivered quantities were short or in back order. Usually, the truck driver brings a paper document, called the *bill of lading*, that specifies the contents of the delivery. The customer can use the paper document to receive against. However, this is inefficient and might easily lead to errors.

A better practice is to set up an interface. The WMS sends an interface message, called a *despatch advice* (*DESADV*) to the WMS of the customer, which specifies the contents of the deliveries. Alternative names for the despatch advice are *advance shipment notification* (*ASN*) or *advance notice of receipt* (*ANR*).

69. **The WMS may exchange three different interface messages: PO, POC and DESADV.**
    a. Consider Figure 4.8, and explain how many times each interface message is sent.
    b. Explain for each message, which system is the sender and which system is the recipient.

An electronic DESADV offers many advantages. Clearly, it considerably reduces the administrative efforts as well as the potential for errors in the receipt process since the WMS verifies each entry in real-time. Moreover, the data can be sent in much more detail, e.g., serial numbers, lot numbers, expiry dates, etc. We already discussed the benefits of the DESADV in Section 3.5.1. Although all modern WMSs support it, we do not see a wide scale implementation of the DESADV. The fact that companies, manufacturers in particular, still use old-fashioned software in their distribution centers is a major obstacle. Additionally, the cost of linking two companies' WMSs can be substantial, so that the investments only pay back where there is a high order volume.

70. **There are a lot of concepts in the order process that are relevant.**
    a. Define the following concepts of the outgoing goods process:
       i. Order
       ii. Order line
       iii. EDI
       iv. Customer order
       v. Order acceptance
       vi. Back order
       vii. Delivery
       viii. RMA

4.4.2 Incoming Goods

Next we look at the incoming goods. A distribution center receives goods from various sources. Table 4.3 lists the sources and the associated order types. The inbound goods flow is the mirror image of the outbound goods flow. The *purchase order* specifies the goods which we ordered from the supplier, i.e., it is the supplier's sales order. A *production order* specifies a *lot* of (finished) goods produced at the production plant. A *transfer order* lists the goods that are to be received from another distribution center within the same company. Finally, a *return merchandise authorization* (RMA) is an agreement that specifies which goods a customer may return.

Table 4.3 Order types per source.

Source	Order type
Supplier	Purchase order
Production plant	Production order
Distribution center	Transfer order
Customer	Return merchandise authorization

71. **There are differences between a purchase order, a production order and a transfer order.**
    a. Explain the differences.

In this section we investigate the interface messages associated with inbound orders. Like in the previous section, we restrict our discussion to purchase orders, since the interfaces for the other order types contain the same elements. However, there may be a few specifics to customer returns, which we discussed in Section 3.5.1. We distinguish the following three interface messages:
- Purchase order (PO)
- Receipt advice (RECADV)
- Purchase order confirmation (POC).

The ERP communicates the *purchase orders* (POs) to the WMS (Figure 4.9), after the supplier has accepted the order. The PO tells the WMS which goods are to be expected. The WMS can also receive a *receipt advice* (RECADV) from the supplier (note that the supplier refers to this message as a *despatch advice*). The receipt advice specifies the contents of a delivery and is the same message as the despatch advice discussed in the previous section.

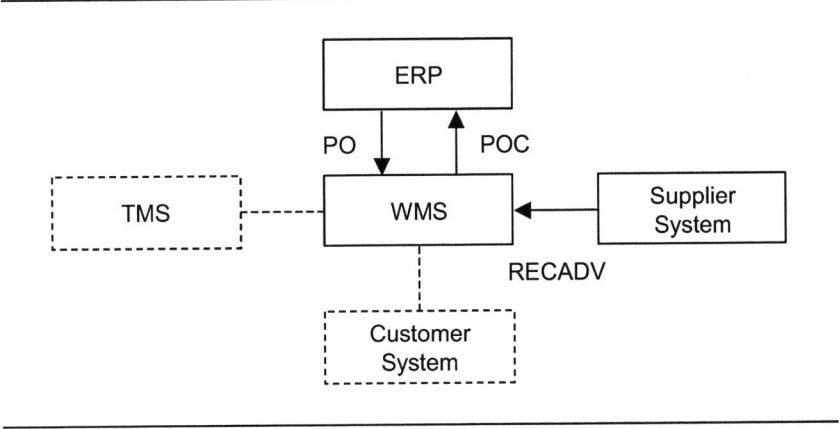

Figure 4.9 Interfaces in the inbound goods flow.

When the goods arrive in the distribution center, the warehouse operators register how much of each product has been received as well as any shortages, overages or damages. The WMS supports this process by comparing the received quantities to the purchase order (and, if available, the receipt advice). Subsequently, the WMS sends an interface message to the ERP to confirm how much was received against the purchase order. We refer to this message as the *purchase order confirmation*.

72. Analyze Foodies' incoming goods process in Appendix B.1.
   a. Which parts of the process are well organized?
   b. Which could be improved?

4.4.3 Stock Adjustments

Inventory levels are kept in the ERP to support the activities of various departments within a company. The ERP typically registers the overall inventory level of a product in the distribution center, whereas the WMS registers the inventory levels per storage location, the packaging type of the products in the location (full pallet, full case or individual pieces) as well as many inventory attributes such as serial numbers, lot numbers, expiry dates, quality status, etc. The ERP might also hold some of these attributes if this is of use to departments outside the distribution center.

Each time goods are received or shipped, the WMS updates the inventory levels in the ERP. However, there are other events that affect the inventory levels. Consider the following.

Inventory Discrepancies

Due to receiving and picking errors or theft, for example, the inventory levels registered in the WMS may differ from the actual inventories. Therefore, in every distribution center the inventory is counted regularly (*cycle counts,* see Section 3.6.1). If the counted quantity differs from the registered quantity of a product, then the inventory level is adjusted accordingly.

Damage

When product is damaged, it cannot be shipped to customers. The product is thrown away, shipped to a repair center or sent to a junk dealer.

Expiration

Perishable products have a *latest goods issue date*, e.g., the goods should leave the distribution center at least eight weeks prior to the best-before date. If the product cannot be shipped by the latest goods issue date, then it is disposed of or shipped to an alternate destination, e.g., food sold as cattle feed.

Blocking

Product may be blocked for various reasons, for example, because the quality of the product still needs to be tested. Only when the test results are positive, is the blocking lifted and the product available to be shipped to customers.

Of these four events, only the first, *inventory discrepancies,* immediately affects the inventory level. In the latter three instances, the inventory receives a special *status* in the information systems, i.e., damaged, expired or blocked. Product with a special status is not generally available to customers. It remains in the distribution center until the special status is lifted or it is assigned to an alternative destination.

If the inventory level or status changes due to an event other than receiving or shipping, then the WMS sends a message to the ERP with the *stock adjustment* (SA).

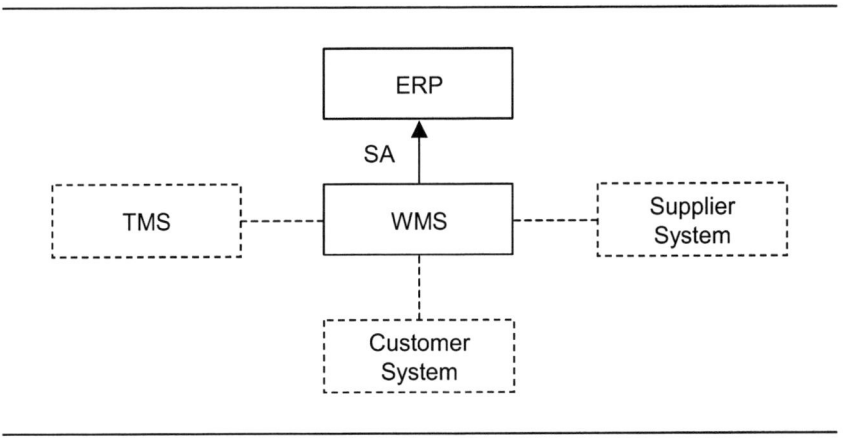

Figure 4.10 Interface for stock adjustments.

73. **The WMS is responsible for keeping the inventory levels up-to-date.**
    a. Which events affect the inventory levels?
    b. Which events affect the status of inventories?

It is a strict rule that the WMS updates the inventory in the ERP instead of vice versa. Obviously, if a company would choose to modify the inventory level in the ERP first, then this change might not be represented by a physical inventory change in the distribution center. Companies that violate this rule find it hard to keep their inventory levels accurate. We give an example in the *case study* below.

> **Case Study: Retailer Updated Inventories in ERP**
> A retail organization updated its inventory levels when one of its stores claimed that it had received too little or too much. The company always assumed that the distribution center had shipped the wrong quantity and updated the inventory in the ERP system accordingly. This immediately affected the WMS where the quantity in the pick location was updated via the ERP after each store complaint. However, in many instances the store had in fact miscounted the products or the product was accidentally shipped to a different store. Thus the update of the WMS inventory via the ERP caused many inventory errors.

The example in this *case study* is clearly a bad practice. A better practice is to first check the inventory levels in the distribution center after a complaint. If there appears to be an inventory discrepancy, then the inventory level is adjusted in the WMS and subsequently in the ERP via the interface.

74. **There is an interface for stock adjustments between the WMS and the ERP.**
    a. Explain this interface.
    b. Which system is leading, WMS or ERP?

4.4.4 Product Attributes

A product (or SKU) has certain attributes. We also refer to these product attributes as *product master data* or *product definitions*. Here are some examples:

1. Product number
2. Product description
3. Product group
4. Price
5. (Preferred) supplier
6. Temperature class, e.g., ambient, chilled, frozen
7. Hazardous material classification
8. Dimensions (length, width, height) of an individual item, a case or a pallet
9. Weight
10. Pack configuration, i.e., pieces per pallet, pieces per case, etc.

A company registers its master data in a central database. The central database can be part of the ERP or it can be a dedicated system. Beside product master data, the central database also contains other master data, such as supplier or customer information. It is a best practice that all information systems within the company obtain their master data via interfaces from the central database. This ensures consistency between the systems.

Before a new product arrives in the distribution center, the *product attributes* (PA) are interfaced from the central database to the WMS. Also, when the product attributes change, the updated product master data are sent to the WMS.

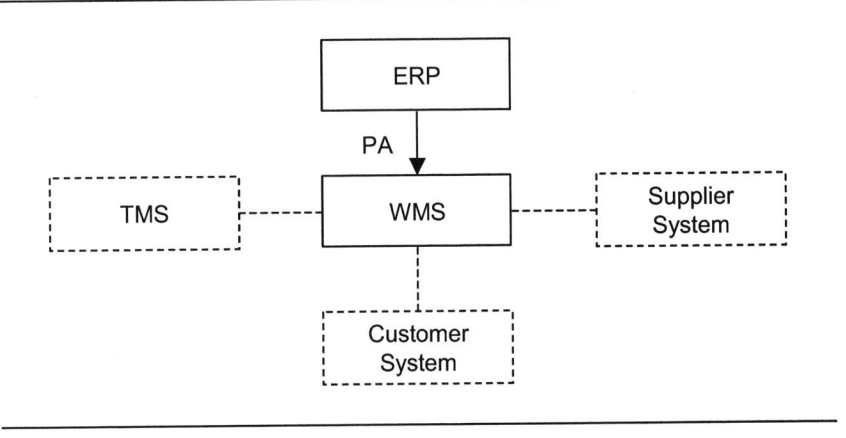

Figure 4.11 Interface for the product attributes.

Some product attributes are specific to the distribution center and are not necessarily kept in the central database. If we look at the above list of product attributes, then we see that the first five are general attributes while the others are typical logistic product attributes. If the central database does not hold all of the logistic product attributes, then these are gathered when the product is first received. This is called the *first carton seen* procedure (see Section 3.5.1). During this procedure, attributes such as the dimensions and weight of a case and a single piece are measured and registered as additional master data in the WMS.

It is important to emphasize the difference between *product attributes* and *inventory attributes*. Product attributes define the product. These attributes apply to every unit of a product. Inventory attributes relate to the goods that are physically present in the distribution center. Typical inventory attributes are the lot numbers, serial numbers and expiry dates of the goods. In short, inventory attributes may differ between units of the same product, whereas product attributes stay the same.

75. Mango smoothie in a 1 liter carton is one of Foodies' products.
   a. Specify its possible attributes.
      i.   Product number
      ii. Product description
      iii. Product group
      iv. Price
      v.   (Preferred) supplier
      vi. Temperature class
      vii. Hazardous material classification
      viii. Dimensions
      ix. Weight
      x.   Pack configuration

4.4.5 Rules of Thumb

We end our discussion on interfaces with 10 *rules of thumb* for defining the interface between ERP and WMS.

Rules of Thumb: Interface between ERP and WMS

1. When defining new interfaces, describe for the ERP and WMS which functions they have to support, and determine which data are needed by each system.
2. To guarantee consistency in the corporate data, every data element should be maintained in a single information system only. This system feeds all other systems.
3. The ERP registers the inventory levels. However, it does not need to know the precise pick location where the goods are held. This is covered by the WMS.
4. Stock adjustments can only be initiated by the WMS, never by the ERP.
5. The WMS notifies the ERP of all changes in the inventory levels.
6. Master data for products (product description, color, price, etc.) is kept in the ERP. Before a product arrives for the first time in the distribution center, the master data is communicated to the WMS.
7. Some master data is only relevant to the WMS, not to the ERP. This often holds for volume and weight measures. This data is maintained by the WMS.
8. The ERP communicates orders to the WMS. The WMS confirms the receipt of purchase orders and the despatch of sales orders to the ERP. This is a trigger for the ERP to update the inventory levels and to commence other tasks, such as invoice processing.

9. A delivery to a customer can be a partial order, an entire order or multiple orders. The conversion of sales orders into transport orders can be managed in the ERP, the TMS or the WMS. In the first case, customer arrangements prevail, in the second case transportation efficiency and in the third case warehouse efficiency.
10. The receipt of customer returns requires several administrative steps. The operator has to check whether the customer was authorized to return the goods, whether the goods were on time, whether the customer has the right to a refund, etc. Although these processes are performed by operators in the distribution center, they may well be performed directly in the ERP. If they were performed in the WMS, then a complicated and elaborate interface would be required. Moreover, only a few WMSs offer support for these steps.

4.5 Summary

A considerable number of software vendors have developed so-called *standard* warehouse management systems (WMSs). These systems enable relatively fast implementation. Also the vendors are constantly improving their systems and users are able to take advantage of the latest features. However, customizations to the software to accommodate specific process flows make the software inflexible for future changes. Therefore customizations to the WMS should be minimized.

In addition to the core function of managing the warehouse, WMSs offer various add-on modules, such as customs management, dock and yard management, labor management, etc. A key technology is the real-time communication between the WMS and the operators and machines in the distribution center. Real-time communication gives the WMS an immediate view of the status of the various activities. This enables the WMS to better control these activities.

Finally, a WMS is not a stand-alone system. It is linked to other information systems, such as the ERP or the TMS. The systems communicate via interface messages. The most important messages concern orders, deliveries, stock adjustments and product attributes.

Chapter 5

Effective Warehouse Management

Effective warehouse management is the second maturity stage in the model (Figure 5.1). It introduces a number of methodologies and techniques that establish *transparency* in a distribution center. These are generally considered to be best practices that help the manager to evaluate and improve the performance of the distribution center.

Modern warehouse management systems have the capability to capture highly detailed data on the activities in the distribution center. These systems track in real-time the activities being performed, the level of available inventory and the orders being fulfilled. In the future the amount of available information is expected to grow even further with the use of *RFID*. In this chapter, we show how this data can help us to achieve *transparency*. In Chapter 6, we explain how to systematically improve the efficiency of warehouse processes.

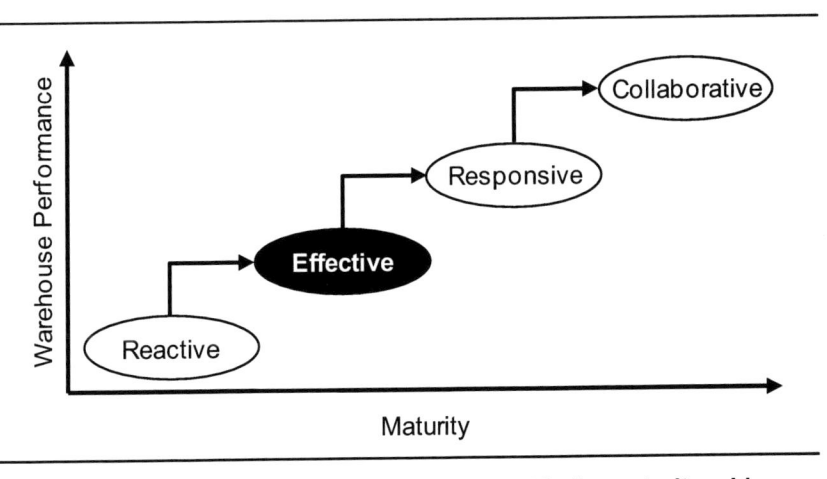

Figure 5.1 Effective warehouse management in the maturity grid.

The first maturity stage of *Highly Competitive Warehouse Management* is reactive warehouse management. This stage serves as a baseline and represents a collection of unstructured processes and behaviors, some of which are still present in many distribution centers. Listed below are some typical characteristics of these reactive distribution centers:
- Managers and team leaders are constantly engaged in fire-fighting activities and do not have time to analyze and permanently solve problems, thus the same problems continue to occur on a frequent basis.
- There are no formal targets or performance measures.
- Interfaces between systems are missing.
- Processes are inefficient and unreliable.
- There is no mutual understanding between departments.

Effective warehouse management is the second stage in the maturity grid (Figure 5.1). In this stage we formalize the objectives and activities of the distribution center. This in turn establishes a more *transparent* warehouse operation. *Transparency* helps to better understand and manage the distribution center. The importance of transparency is captured in the old adage: *You manage what you measure*. The unstated corollary is: *You mismanage what you do not measure*. *Highly Competitive Warehouse Management* creates transparency through the following:
- Warehouse strategy
- Service level agreements
- Standard operating procedures
- Activity-based costing
- Performance indicators.

76. Effective warehouse management is the second stage in the maturity grid.
a. What is the goal of this second stage?

5.1 Service Level Agreements

Logistics is the art of balancing service levels against cost levels. Clearly, if we want higher service levels in terms of quick response times, perfect order fulfillment and high flexibility in order volumes, then this results in higher costs. Poor service levels or exorbitant cost levels can be deadly in a competitive market. Here a dilemma arises. How good should the services be and what cost levels are acceptable? Should it be impeccable and fulfill all the customer's wishes or may we put some restrictions on the service levels?

In Section 2.2 we defined the warehouse strategy. How do we translate the warehouse strategy into service and cost objectives? Highly competitive warehouse management first sets service level targets derived from the company strategy. If quick delivery is an important aspect of the strategy, then this is reflected in the response time targets. If heavy fluctuations in demand must be accommodated, then this is defined in flexibility targets. The desired target levels are formalized in *service level agreements* (*SLAs*). The SLAs are defined for a period of at least one year. After that period the SLAs are reviewed and possibly modified to accommodate changes in the company strategy and market developments.

The objective of this exercise is not to drastically increase the service levels, although this may seem tempting. Rather it is an attempt to formalize the current standard as a starting point for gradual improvement. Unless some aspect of your service is a major source of dissatisfaction and is harming customer relationships, maintaining the current service levels is the best choice. A sudden increase in service levels would create unnecessary stress and higher cost levels. Highly competitive warehouse management aims to achieve gradual growth of service levels without increasing cost levels.

Many companies successfully apply SLAs. It is generally considered to be a best practice. Yet there are still a lot of companies without formal service level targets or only implicit targets. It goes without saying that this seriously complicates the management of the distribution center as well as collaboration with other departments and parties in the supply chain.

As said, logistics searches for the optimal mix of costs and service levels. However, with the use of SLAs the desired service levels become fixed and managing costs remains the only variable for the manager of the distribution center. In other words, the manager's goal is to continuously look for ways to cut costs while achieving or maintaining the chosen service levels. Service levels are typically updated in an annual review. The new service levels are based on outside forces such as competitive analysis, market standards or strategic choices. It should not be a decision made solely by the manager of the distribution center.

Before tackling how to develop SLAs, we take a step back and consider the distribution center in a more abstract sense. How does it add value to the supply chain? In other words, which services does the distribution center provide to the supply chain? Or even better, which services *should* the distribution center provide? In Section 3.3.1 we distinguished four services provided by the distribution center (Figure 5.2):

- Inbound handling
- Storage
- Outbound handling
- Value added logistics (VAL).

It is essential to formalize the services of a distribution center, since they give a purpose to its activities. Services, by definition, are provided to clients. In Section 3.3.2 we reasoned that the clients of the distribution center are the source function (i.e., purchasing, production and inventory control) and the sell function (i.e., sales, marketing, order desk and customer service). The source and sell functions interact with the suppliers and customers to create orders. These orders include both the goods and the (logistics) services. It is the task of the

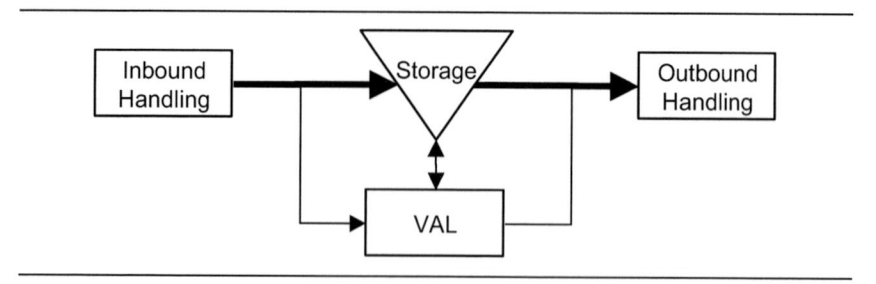

Figure 5.2 Warehouse Services.

distribution center, together with the transportation planning function, to provide the logistics services.

It is essential to formalize the services of a distribution center, since they give a purpose to its activities. Services, by definition, are provided to clients. In Section 3.3.2 we reasoned that the clients of the distribution center are the source function (i.e., purchasing, production and inventory control) and the sell function (i.e., sales, marketing, order desk and customer service). The source and sell functions interact with the suppliers and customers to create orders. These orders include both the goods and the (logistics) services. It is the task of the distribution center, together with the transportation planning function, to provide the logistics services.

A precondition for a successful collaboration between the distribution center, its clients and the other members of the supply chain is the use of a *service portfolio*. The portfolio lists the services that the distribution center provides together with the service levels and rates, similar to a menu in a restaurant. The use of a service portfolio is a best practice, both for third party warehouses as well as private warehouses. The portfolio tells all parties involved what they can expect from the distribution center. At the same time, it tells the warehouse staff what the distribution center is expected to achieve.

For each of the four services there may be several variants with different service level requirements, for example, for the inbound handling service, the distribution center may distinguish between frozen goods that need to be in storage within 30 minutes and ambient goods that can wait as long as 3 hours.

77. **A service portfolio list the services of a distribution center.**
    a. *Explain the function of a service portfolio.*

The following information should be included in the SLA:
- Service definition and purpose
- Performance targets, tracking and reporting
- Service fees
- Control rules and exceptions
- Client duties and responsibilities.

EFFECTIVE WAREHOUSE MANAGEMENT

78. **Search the Internet for an example of an SLA. Compare this SLA with the above information on what should be included in the SLA.**
    a. What do you notice?

We discuss each of the elements in an SLA in more detail below.

5.1.1   Service Definition and Purpose

Why should the distribution center provide the service? How does the service add value for the client? In Section 3.1 we identified that the services of a distribution center may add value in four ways:
- Break-bulk
- Storage
- Consolidation
- Customization.

These added values relate both to the *goods flow* and the *information flow*. Consider the following: the inbound handling service moves the goods from the truck into a storage location, so that they become available for sales orders. In addition to handling the physical flow of goods, the distribution center collects information on the quantity and quality of the goods that arrive. Both the physical handling as well as the information provision contribute to the break-bulk function of the inbound handling service, i.e., they make the incoming goods available to be distributed in smaller quantities to customers.

It is essential that we recognize which elements of a service provide value to the client, e.g., if we sort the goods before putaway, this may provide a valuable service element if it saves a sorting step upstream in the supply chain. However, if the only purpose of the sorting is a more convenient warehouse procedure, then it has no direct value to the client. Accordingly, the service definition helps the clients to understand what they can (and cannot) expect from the service.

79. **A service definition is important for an SLA.**
    a. Why is a service definition important for an SLA?

80. **Foodies wants to develop an SLA for its inbound handling service.**
    a. Write down the service definition and purpose for the SLA.

5.1.2 Performance Targets, Tracking and Reporting

After defining the service, we set the performance targets. We can measure performance along three dimensions:
- Responsiveness
- Accuracy
- Flexibility.

The distribution center not only has to meet the performance targets. It must also track its performance levels and report this information to the clients.

Responsiveness

Responsiveness tells the clients how soon they may expect a service. Responsiveness applies to inbound handling, outbound handling and VAL services, not to storage. Responsiveness has four parameters:
- Response time
- Frequency
- Time frame
- Fill rate.

The *response time* is the most important parameter of responsiveness. It defines how long a client has to wait. We define a *cut-off time* for a service. This is the latest moment at which the client can order the service. If a client orders before the cut-off time of 2 PM, for example, then the distribution center ships the goods on the next day. If the order arrives after the cut-off time, then it is shipped one day later. Until the cut-off time, customers are usually entitled to modify or cancel their orders without many consequences. After the cut-off time the order is committed.

The distribution center guarantees a maximum response time and sometimes also a minimum response time. The latter applies to situations where customers do not want the service before a certain time, e.g., because they have limited storage space.

We discuss two practices for defining response times:
- Prearranged response time
- Negotiated response time.

Prearranged response times define upfront for each individual service request how soon it should be completed, for example, all sales orders are shipped within 24 hours. Clearly, the distribution center may have different prearranged response times for their various clients, customers, suppliers or order types. Prearranged response times may be defined for all customers as part of the sales conditions or by agreement with individual customers.

The parties involved may also negotiate a response time for individual service requests. *Negotiated response times* are determined separately for each request. These response times apply when there are no formal agreements or when the customer does not want the goods as soon as possible, but rather at a specific moment when he has the resources to receive the goods.

EFFECTIVE WAREHOUSE MANAGEMENT

If a company sees that it cannot deliver within the standard, prearranged response time, then it may instead offer a negotiated response time to the customer. Thus, the customer knows that the goods will arrive later and can decide whether to accept the offer. Sometimes suppliers use this practice as an 'escape route' to enhance their performance measures. They measure how well they keep their adjusted promises, rather than measuring their original objectives. Since these promises are easy to keep, the measures do not say much about the actual performance, let alone the level of customer satisfaction.

The second parameter is the *frequency*. The frequency states how often the client can order a service. Some examples are: every weekday; twice per day; on Tuesday's and Friday's only. The latter example is frequently seen in retail operations where outlets are supplied on specific weekdays only. The outlet may order every day, but the goods depart with the next scheduled delivery.

The third parameter is the *time frame*. The time frame defines the length of the period in which the delivery will take place. A wide time frame gives the party that ships the goods more flexibility to plan its activities. A narrow time frame helps the recipient to plan its resources.

> **Example: Web-grocer**
> Customers of a typical e-commerce grocery retailer, can choose a two-hour time frame for the home delivery of their purchases, see Table 5.1. This is an example of a negotiated response time and time frame. Note that the delivery fee varies based on the popularity of the time frame. This variation helps to balance the workload.

Table 5.1 Time frames for home delivery.

Time frame	Mon	Tue	Wed	Thu	Fri	Sat	Sun
8 - 10 AM	$7.95	$6.95	$6.95	$6.95	$6.95	$7.95	
12 - 2 PM	$6.95	$4.95	$4.95	$4.95	$5.95	$6.95	
4 - 6 PM	$5.95	$4.95	$4.95	$5.95	$7.95		
7 - 9 PM	$6.95	$5.95	$5.95	$6.95	$7.95		

81. There is a difference between prearranged response times and negotiated response times.
    a. Explain the difference.

Finally, the fourth parameter is the *fill rate*, i.e., the percentage of service requests that should be completed within the response time, e.g., 98 percent of the order lines must be shipped within 24 hours from the cut-off time.

For the outbound handling service (and perhaps some types of VAL service) there are three reasons why a service might be late:
- There is insufficient stock.
- The goods are delivered too late to the loading dock.
- Transportation to the customer takes too long.

The first reason falls under the responsibility of the source function, the second under the responsibility of the distribution center and the third under the responsibility of the transportation planning function. However, it is the combined performance of these three parties that determine the availability to the customer. Each has separate fill rate targets, which combine to create an overall target for the customer.

> **Example: Fill Rate Targets**
> A company has SLAs, which specify that the source function has to guarantee an inventory availability of 96 percent of the order lines, the distribution center has to guarantee a fill rate (timely departure) of 99 percent of the order lines and the transportation operation has to guarantee a fill rate (timely delivery) of 98 percent of the order lines. If all three departments meet their performance targets, the customer will experience a timely availability on only 96% x 99% x 98% = 93% of the order lines.

82. There are various reasons why a service might be late.
    a. Mention three reasons.
    b. Explain which departments are responsible in each case.

Accuracy

Accuracy is the next performance dimension to consider. The *accuracy rate* defines for each service the minimum percentage of service requests which should be performed accurately. Accuracy rates for inbound handling, outbound handling and VAL services are typically measured as the percentage of order lines that are correctly processed. The following dimensions are considered:
- Product
- Quantity
- Condition
- Information.

Accuracy for the storage service is typically measured through *cycle counts* (see Section 3.6.1), i.e., the number of counts that revealed a correct inventory as a percentage of the total number of counts. Inventory discrepancies may be caused by picking errors, damage, etc. The financial value of the inventory discrepancies is also an important indicator.

> **Example: Accuracy**
> An order consists of one or more order lines and each order line of one or more handling units (e.g., pallets). As an example, assume that every order has five order lines and each order line contains two handling units. With these characteristics, 99 percent accuracy by handling unit equals 98 percent (=0.99^2) accuracy by order line and only 90 percent (=0.99^{10}) accuracy by order!

83. **The accuracy rate sets a target for the percentage of service requests that should be performed accurately.**
    a. *Set the accuracy rate for two services in your distribution center.*
    b. *Describe the four dimensions (product, quantity, condition and information) for each service.*

Flexibility

The third performance dimension is *flexibility*. A distribution center is designed to accommodate a certain workload. If the distribution center has to process significantly higher volumes, then it might not be able to complete all service requests in time or only against considerably higher costs for overtime and temporary staff. If the volume is significantly lower, then this might lead to underutilization of staff and resources. For the inbound handling service, for example, we may state that the distribution center can receive between 100 and 400 pallets per day. A higher or lower workload could significantly increase costs.

The flexibility targets do not apply to individual customers. Instead they are arranged per client. In a private warehouse, the flexibility targets explain to the source and sell functions which daily order volumes they can pass on to the distribution center. In a *public warehouse,* each client has separate flexibility targets. However, fluctuations differ between clients and peaks may level out. These synergies stretch the flexibility ranges of public warehouses.

We define the *flexibility* by the volume range that the distribution center can accommodate per client and service. By including the flexibility in the SLAs, the distribution center guarantees its clients that it can fulfill any volume within the range against the prescribed conditions. If volumes go outside the range, then the distribution center cannot guarantee the performance targets (or, it will still meet them, but at a higher cost per unit).

The amount of flexibility required from a distribution center differs between companies. Some companies experience high fluctuations in order volume, due to seasonality, volatile product life cycles, etc. Such a company demands a high flexibility from its distribution center. The distribution center should have flexible contracts with its staff members, close arrangements with employment agencies and excess capacity within the operation.

84. **The level of flexibility required from a distribution center varies between companies.**
    a. How is this possible?

85. **Foodies wants to develop an SLA for its inbound handling service.**
    a. Define possible performance targets for the responsiveness, accuracy and flexibility of this service.

5.1.3 Service Fee

Charging *service fees* is a powerful instrument for optimizing the activities in the supply chain. A necessary condition is that the fees are realistic. Then, they make clients aware of the actual costs involved in the logistics services. With this information, clients automatically start to look for ways to adjust their order and delivery patterns so that excessive demands on logistics resources are avoided.

In practice, we see many private warehouses operate under a fixed annual budget. In this situation, the source and sell functions do not realize their impact on the distribution center and take it for granted. Companies might find it odd to charge internal fees between departments and believe that it only causes administrative overhead. However, the benefits that can be realized from a well designed system of service fees far outweighs any concerns about such an approach.

In third party warehouses we see a different effect. 3PLs have to make a profit with the distribution center. A popular practice among 3PLs is to design obscure pricing schemes that give the clients no transparency in the actual costs. Actual examples are: the client pays storage charges for the entire week (Monday to Sunday) even when the goods arrive midweek, or no inbound handling fee is charged when goods remain in the distribution center for at least two weeks. Beside the fact that these schemes are difficult to administer, they may lead to undesired behavior from the clients. In the short-term, these pricing schemes might seem attractive to the 3PL. However, for the long-term they threaten the relationship between the client and the 3PL. Since the pricing scheme does not reveal the *hidden costs*, clients cannot search for efficient service patterns – this makes the distribution center unnecessarily expensive.

Service fees should be realistic. This requires that:
- The fees are unbiased.
- The fees reflect the actual cost levels.

If products are processed inside the distribution center, then they are typically handled by pallet, by case or by individual piece. Accordingly, the services should be charged per physical unit, e.g., service fees per pallet, case and piece. The pallet fee is charged when full pallets are ordered. The fee per case applies when a customer requests a less-than-pallet quantity, which consists of full cases only. Finally, if the customer wants a broken case quantity, then the fee per individual piece applies. Administrative services, however, such as order-entry and complaint handling should be charged per administrative unit, such as per order or order line. We refer to these fees as *unbiased*, since they give a fair representation of the actual efforts, as opposed to biased fees (see *example*).

> **Example: Biased Fees**
>
> Numerous distribution centers charge fees by order line, by weight or by volume. Note that an order line can be, for example, one blue pen or five truck loads of the same blue pen. Clearly the effort, and hence the costs involved, differ greatly. However, if the distribution center charges a fee per order line, then both would cost the same amount.
>
> The same holds for fees that are based on weight or volume. For example, if seven cases of one item or 500 individual pieces of a different item both have the same total weight, then the charge will be the same while the workload is very different.
>
> We refer to fees for physical services based on order line, weight or volume as biased fees, since they do not represent the actual efforts.

A biased fee assumes an underlying order profile. For the outbound handling service it assumes a *fixed proportion* of pallet picks, case picks and piece picks. However, as soon as the order profile changes, this immediately affects the warehousing costs.

In the last decade, we have seen a strong tendency towards smaller order quantities. This increased the handling costs in the distribution center, however the change was not always represented in the fees. For example, if a biased fee per weight or volume was invoiced, then the actual handling costs would increase relative to the fees. Conversely, if a fee per order line was charged, then the true costs would decrease relative to the fees. In practice, we see that managers revise the fees once they observe that the order profiles have changed. Clients often do not understand why fees are modified and are reluctant to pay elevated charges.

The service fees should reflect the actual cost level. In Section 5.3 we will determine accurate cost estimates through *activity-based costing*. Clearly, 3PLs add a profit margin, but it is dangerous to substantially overcharge or subsidize some services. One should realize that the clients are choosing from available service options based on what they are charged. If there is no direct relationship between service fees and the actual cost levels, then the client's decisions will not optimize overall costs. Remember that optimizing overall costs is a primary objective of *Highly Competitive Warehouse Management*.

86. **There is a difference between biased and unbiased fees.**
    a. Explain the difference.

5.1.4 Control Rules and Exceptions

Control rules are needed in order to deliver consistent service, e.g., for food products the distribution center ships the oldest products first, to prevent the expiration of stock. A popular control rule for allocating fresh produce to sales orders is the *first expired first out* (FEFO) rule. There are several other control rules that may apply. They can either be managed via the WMS or can be incorporated in the procedures for the operators. Other decisions relate to exceptions:
- What to do when the supplier arrives late?
- What if he arrives without prior notification?
- What if a customer orders after the cut-off time?

Control rules and exceptions differ between operations. The relevant issues are identified in the SLAs and define how the distribution center performs its activities.

87. **Foodies wants to develop an SLA for its inbound handling service.**
    a. Define possible control rules and exceptions for the inbound handling service.
    b. What purpose do control rules serve in the SLA?

5.1.5 Client Duties and Responsibilities

Clients also have certain responsibilities to help ensure a smooth logistics process. For example, the transportation planning function has the duty to plan the outbound trips and inform the distribution center in time. Likewise, it is the responsibility of the source function that deliveries are pre-notified and well documented. For some of these duties we can also define target service levels for the client, such as 95 percent of the deliveries are pre-notified.

88. **Clients of the distribution center have different duties and responsibilities.**
    a. What are some of the duties and responsibilities of each client?
        i. Source function
        ii. Sell function
        iii. Transportation planning function

89. Foodies wants to develop an SLA for its inbound handling service.
   a. Define possible duties and responsibilities for clients.
   b. Which clients are involved?

5.2 Standard Operating Procedures

In a distribution center with reactive warehouse management, standard operating procedures are often absent. And if they do exist, then they might be outdated, overly superficial or impossible to perform in practice. The documents are typically somewhere in a drawer gathering dust, not on the work floor.

However, clear standard operating procedures are an essential element of *Highly Competitive Warehouse Management*. First of all, they help the management and staff to understand the processes. Discussions on process optimization are futile when the participants do not share the same view. Second, the specifications help the manager to look at the processes in an integral manner. Instead of solving the individual problems that arise, he can look at the overall impact. Third, during the exercise of documenting the processes, most managers discover that different operators use different procedures for the same activity. One approach might be better than another. Thus the manager should adopt the best approach during the process specification exercise, thereby getting all the operators working in the most efficient way.

Beside the fact that standard operating procedures create transparency, they also are a powerful technique for improving processes. The success factors for achieving good results are:
- Operators understand and follow the specified procedures.
- Inappropriate conduct is actively challenged.
- Standard operating procedures are kept up-to-date.

Having standard operating procedures is not enough. It is essential that the operators understand and follow the procedures. The manager has to introduce and actively promote the specified processes on the work floor. The specifications also serve as training material for new employees. Often, operators receive a compact booklet with the most important guidelines. At convenient spots throughout the distribution center, signs on the wall remind the operators of the proper procedures. The manager must also link the job descriptions with the tasks, authorities and responsibilities of the operators.

The specifications also present the best procedures for safeguarding safety, ergonomics, hygiene, efficiency and quality. If operators fail to perform the procedures, then the manager or the responsible team leader has to address this behavior. A best practice is to highlight the *issue of the month*. Each month a procedure or rule is selected that is ill performed by the operators while it has a significant effect on the warehouse performance. Posters are placed on the walls illustrating the bad practice and promoting the preferred behavior. During the month the manager and team leaders explain the importance of the issue and remind the "offenders." Afterwards, the manager reports the achieved improvements and the resulting benefits for the company.

It is vital that the standard operating procedures are kept up-to-date. In Chapter 6 we will demonstrate how the acquired transparency can be used to continuously streamline the warehouse processes. Each change in the procedures, systems or product flow should immediately be incorporated in the standard operating procedures. Also the manager has to inform the operators and manage the implementation of the changes. There are two reasons for changing processes:
- Improve the processes.
- Accommodate new services.

If a new service is requested from the distribution center, either structural or ad hoc, then the service should preferably be mapped onto the existing procedures. The existing process steps can be seen as building blocks for any services that the distribution center provides. Using such *modular procedures* has many advantages:
- The use of efficient procedures is guaranteed.
- The accumulation of different procedures is prevented. This would increase complexity and destroy scale economies.
- Customizations to the warehouse management system are minimized.

> **Example: Modular Procedures**
> A distribution center introduces a variant to the regular inbound handling service, where special RFID-labels are attached to incoming pallets for a certain product group.
>
> One option is to set up a new workstation where the RFID-labels are attached. This process is not mapped onto the existing procedures and requires many changes in the procedures and information systems.
>
> An alternative is to re-use the existing procedures. Perhaps the RFID-labels can be attached as part of the receipt procedure, i.e., operators apply an RFID-label instead of a barcode label. If this is inefficient or simply not possible, then perhaps the application of the RFID-labels can be integrated in an existing VAL process. The pallets that need an RFID-label follow the same procedure as other pallets that need special handling after receipt at a VAL station.

In Appendix B we provide an example of Foodies' standard operating procedures. This example may serve as a starting point for your own specifications. We suggest that you go through the example line by line and rewrite it to fit your own processes.

90. Standard operating procedures are an essential element of *Highly Competitive Warehouse Management*.
    a. What is specified in standard operating procedures?

91. Study Foodies' standard operating procedures in Appendix B.
    a. What do you notice?

> **Remark: Standard Operating Procedures**
>
> If you look at the standard operating procedures in Appendix B, then you will see that it uses the active voice of a verb to describe activities, rather than the passive voice. For example, the specification states: "The receipt operator assigns the truck to a receipt dock in the WMS" instead of "A receipt dock is assigned." Clearly, the former formulation leaves less room for misinterpretation. In particular, it clarifies whether the selection of the dock is made by the WMS or by the operator.
>
> Often, people use graphical schemes to describe processes, e.g., value stream mapping (Womack and Jones, 2003), or abstract wording. Using the *active voice* in standard operating procedures automatically forces the designer to clearly specify the action. Accordingly, this approach is not only simple to perform, it also delivers easy-to-understand procedures and more complete specifications.

5.3 Activity-Based Costing

So far we have described the services and activities in the typical distribution center. Now we want to identify how expensive they are. An excellent methodology for estimating costs is *activity-based costing* (Kaplan & Cooper, 1998). Activity-based costing (ABC) considers all costs in the warehouse budget, i.e., building, fixtures, equipment, materials, staff, IT, inventory and overhead, and assigns these costs to activities. Consequently, the costs of activities become significantly higher than just the *time and material costs*. ABC provides interesting insights into the cost structure. Straightforward activities that are performed in large homogeneous volumes will typically appear substantially cheaper than expected, while similar activities with customer specific enhancements can be surprisingly expensive.

These insights can be used for various purposes. Clearly, activity-based costing creates awareness. Managers and staff realize the costs of inefficiency, rework, redundant activities, dead stock, etc. Another obvious application is the analysis of processes. Often, managers decide to change the processes based on their gut feeling. An ABC analysis reveals the true facts. The insight also facilitates discussions between the distribution center and other departments. By quantifying the costs of rush orders, frequent deliveries, poor supplier performance and high inventories, other departments might change their behavior in order to reduce overall costs.

5.3.1 Strategic Model

Organizations contract most of their resources, especially those other than materials, energy and other services purchased from external vendors, before they are actually used (Kaplan & Cooper, 1998). We refer to these resources as *committed resources*. Examples of committed resources are buildings and equipment. These resources incur an expense in each period of their useful life. Also, workforce and IT contracts usually are committed for a certain period of time.

The ABC model treats committed and *flexible resources* alike. Hence, if the ABC model estimates a cost saving, it includes both savings on committed as well as flexible resources. Clearly, it is not always possible to immediately capitalize on the committed resources. The initial result may be that the efficiency improvement only produces more excess capacity. The unused capacity can eventually be eliminated by reducing the supply of resources (cost reduction) or by increasing the demand for the resource (revenue increase). Activity-based costing helps to reveal the unused capacities. It is the challenge of the manager to exploit these capacities.

Since activity-based costing turns committed costs into variables (for instance, building costs being spread among individual transactions), it typically applies to long-term decisions. Thus, activity-based costing is considered to be a strategic model, rather than an operational model. This corresponds to the objective of *Highly Competitive Warehouse Management* to create long-term improvements.

92. **One method for estimating costs is activity-based costing.**
    a. What is the main goal of activity-based costing?
    b. Activity-based costing is a strategic model, not an operational model. Explain why.

5.3.2 Time-Driven Activity-Based Costing

The traditional ABC model has been difficult for many organizations to implement (Kaplan & Anderson, 2007). The authors mention several problems:
- It is time-consuming and costly to identify the time that operators spend on activities through interviews, observation and surveys.
- The model is difficult to scale. Adding a new activity requires re-estimating the amount of cost that should be assigned to the new activity.
- When the size of the model increases, the number of variables escalate. Accordingly, the model's computation time increases dramatically.
- When operators distribute their spent time between activities, invariably they report percentages that add up to 100 percent. Idle or unused time is not reported.

Time-driven activity-based costing (TDABC) is an alternative approach that addresses all the above limitations. It is an excellent procedure for creating a cost model with limited efforts. In the subsequent sections we discuss the design of a TDABC model for a distribution center.

93. There is a difference between time-driven activity-based costing and activity-based costing.
   a. What is the advantage of time-driven activity-based costing compared to traditional activity-based costing?

5.3.3 Cost Factors

TDABC starts by gathering the cost items from the warehouse budget. The costs for the various items may be the rent, lease, mortgage, fees, salaries, depreciation and/or interest on the capital employed. The checklist on page 164 lists typical cost factors in a distribution center.

Check List: Cost Factors

Building costs
- Ground and building
- Utilities
- Maintenance
- Security
- Insurance
- Property taxes

Fixture costs
- Racking and other storage devices
- Labels and signs

Equipment costs
- Forklift trucks and other vehicles including automated cranes
- Roller conveyors and other internal transportation devices
- Sorting devices
- Other stationary equipment such as waste disposal machines, shrink-wrap machines, etc.

Materials costs
- Pallets, roller cages or other product carriers
- Packaging materials
- Packaging labels

Staff costs
- Salaries for warehouse staff
- Outsourced services such as catering or cleaning
- Other staff related costs, such as training and celebrations

IT costs
- Information systems such as a WMS
- Data communication
- Hardware such as servers, PCs, printers, RF terminals, etc.
- Maintenance, support and upgrade services

Inventory holding costs
- Write-downs on damaged or missing products

Overhead costs
- Partial charges for (senior) management (note that certain managers are only partly involved in the distribution center)
- Partial charges for financial services, human resource management and other support functions

> **Remark: Inventory Holding Costs**
> The costs for having inventories are referred to as the *inventory holding costs*. Some inventory holding costs can be attributed to warehouse activities:
> - Storage
> - Damages
> - Inventory discrepancies.
>
> These costs can be incorporated in the ABC model. Other inventory holding costs are not directly linked to warehouse activities. Usually, these factors are charged to the budget of the source and sell functions. These include:
> - Interest on the invested capital
> - Insurance
> - Write-downs due to expiration, depreciation and obsolescence.
>
> The latter factors can be estimated as a percentage of the average value of the inventory on hand, typically between 10 to 30 percent (Wild, 2002). A factor that requires special attention is the interest rate. While commercial interest rates in the Western world are around 5 percent, companies often use artificial rates of 12 to 18 percent in their calculations to reflect the opportunity costs or the anticipated return on investment. These overestimates amplify the cost savings from inventory reductions. Consequently, companies might be enticed to overly reduce their inventories at the expense of more frequent deliveries. This does not necessarily result in the lowest integral costs.

5.3.4 Cost Allocation

After identifying the cost items, TDABC allocates the items to processes. Table 5.2 gives an example of a warehouse budget that totals $5.0 million. The cost items in the budget are allocated to four processes: inbound handling, storage, outbound handling and VAL. Typically, these four processes together constitute a comprehensive model. However, if some activities or transactions performed within these processes use a different mix of resources, then the process breakdown should be further refined. For example, if pallet picking is executed automatically by an automated storage/retrieval system (AS/RS) and case picking is performed manually, then the outbound handling process should be separated into pallet picking and case picking processes. Conversely, if the inbound and outbound handling processes use the same resources, then these processes may be merged into a single process in the TDABC model.

Table 5.2 Cost allocation example.

Item	Annual Budget ($)	Inbound handling (%)	Storage (%)	Outbound handling (%)	VAL (%)
Building	900,000	20	50	25	5
Fixtures	500,000	6	84	7	3
Equipment	450,000	30	3	60	7
Materials	50,000	40	0	40	20
Staff	2,000,000	40	10	47	3
IT	700,000	23	20	53	4
Inventory	300,000	25	25	45	5
Overhead	100,000	25	25	25	25
Total ($)	5,000,000	1,426,000	1,323,500	2,021,000	229,500

Subsequently, costs are allocated by estimating the fraction of each cost item that is used by each process (Figure 5.3). For example, the building costs are distributed among the processes relative to the amount of warehouse space consumed by each process. Similarly, the staff costs are distributed according to the number of hours they spend per process. Allocating the overhead costs of head office staff and support services can sometimes be difficult. However, with some logical reasoning, one can estimate how much of each resource should be

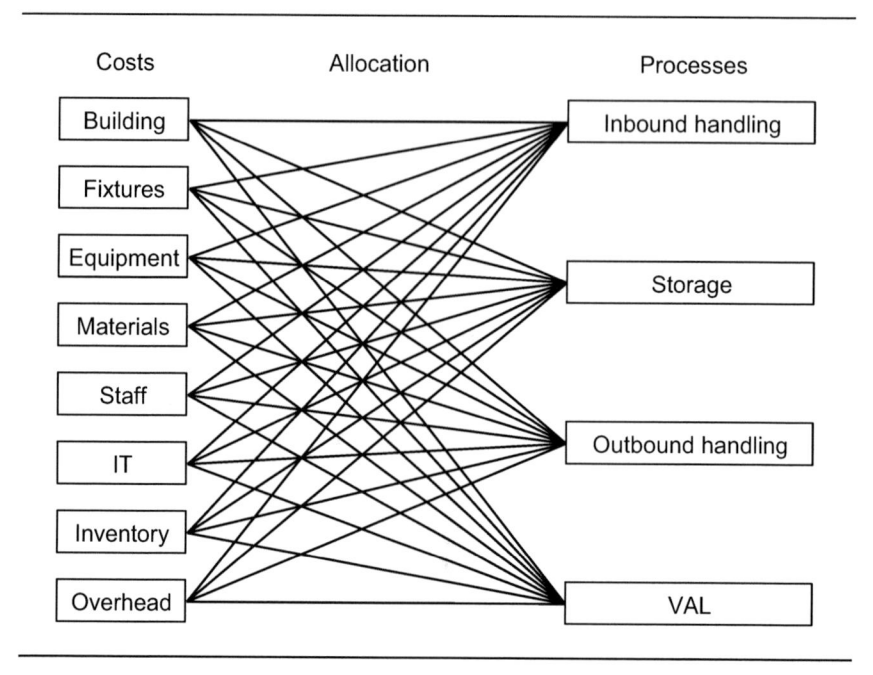

Figure 5.3 Cost allocation.

allocated to each process. Activity-based costing is not greatly sensitive to small errors in estimating parameters. The goal is to be approximately right, say within 5 to 10 percent of the actual number.

> **Example: Cost Allocation**
> In the example in Table 5.2 we see that the outbound handling process has an annual cost of $2,021,000. The cost consists of:
>   25% of the building costs
> + 7% of the fixture costs
> + 60% of the equipment costs
> + 40% of the materials costs
> + 47% of the staff costs
> + 53% of the IT costs
> + 45% of the inventory costs
> + 25% of the overhead costs.

94. Table 5.3 below shows the cost allocation for Foodies' distribution center.
    a. Calculate the annual costs of the inbound handling process.

Table 5.3 Cost allocation for Foodies.

Item	Annual Budget ($)	Inbound handling (%)	Storage (%)	Outbound handling (%)	VAL (%)
Building	400.000	15	60	15	10
Fixtures	200.000	6	84	7	3
Equipment	200.000	20	5	65	10
Materials	25.000	20	0	60	20
Staff	800.000	12	8	60	20
IT	250.000	20	25	50	5
Inventory	25.000	25	25	45	5
Overhead	100.000	25	25	25	25
Total ($)					

5.3.5 Capacity Measures

TDABC drives the costs in each process to individual transactions, products, orders, services or customers based on the amount of capacity that is used. Typically, the model measures the capacity of a process in terms of the available *time* from staff or devices. This explains the name *time-driven* ABC. In a distribution center the capacities in inbound handling, outbound handling and

VAL are measured in seconds of operator time (or machine time for unmanned processes).

Storage is measured in cubic feet. As such, warehouse space is one of the exceptions in TDABC where the capacity is not *time-driven*, but *volume-driven*. Nevertheless, Kaplan & Anderson (2007) refer to the model as *time-driven* ABC, since time is the most common capacity driver.

5.3.6 Standard Times

The exercise in Table 5.2 identified the annual costs of processes, which may provide valuable insight to the management. However, if we want to analyze the commercial service fees or the profitability of specific products or customers, then we have to assign costs to individual transactions.

In order to do this, we need to know how much time is consumed. We focus our discussion on capacities measured in time, although the approach can also be applied to space usage (measured in cubic feet). TDABC uses an estimate of the time to perform a transactional activity, i.e., the *standard time*. Determining standard times is not a trivial task, nor is it an insurmountable challenge. The standard times can either be obtained by direct observation or, preferably, through the analysis of historical transaction data from the WMS. This exercise replaces the process of interviewing people to learn what percentage of their time is spent on all the activities involved (Kaplan & Anderson, 2007).

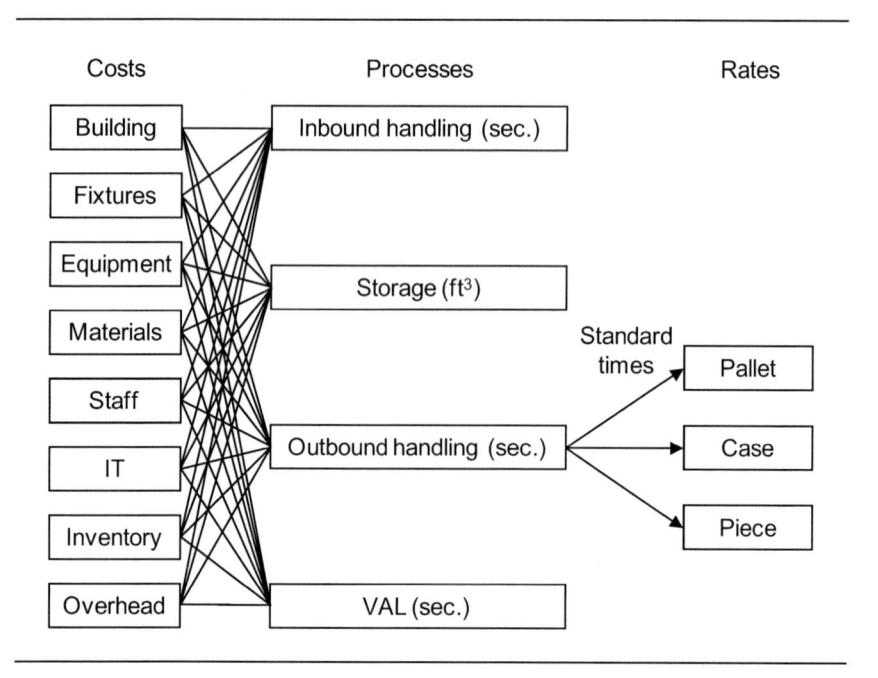

Figure 5.4 Time-driven activity-based costing.

EFFECTIVE WAREHOUSE MANAGEMENT

We can use the standard times to determine rates for services (Figure 5.4). In Section 5.1.3 we reasoned that physical warehouse activities are preferably charged by physical units, i.e., by pallet, case or piece. Storage is typically charged by volume consumed (ft^3). Any administrative services, such as order-entry, are charged per order or order line.

> **Example: Calculating Activity Costs**
>
> We continue with the previous example, and now estimate the standard times for the *outbound handling* of full pallet loads, full cases and individual pieces. Table 5.4 shows that the standard times are 5.0 minutes, 0.5 minutes and 0.15 minutes, respectively. If we multiply these standard times by the number of transactions, then we find that in total 1,500,000 minutes have been spent this year on outbound handling.
>
> In Table 5.2 we calculated that the annual outbound handling costs were $2,021,000, so that the cost per minute for outbound handling becomes $1.35.
>
> $$\text{Cost per minute} = \frac{\$2,021,000}{1,500,000} = \$1.35$$
>
> Finally, we may compute the service fees by multiplying the cost per minute by the standard times: $6.74 for a pallet, $0.67 for a case and $0.20 for an individual piece.

Table 5.4 Calculation of the activity costs.

Outbound handling	Estimate (minutes)	Number of transactions	Total time (minutes)	Cost per minute ($)	Service fee ($)	Total cost ($)
Pallet	5.00	120,000	600,000	1.35	6.74	808,400
Case	0.50	1,500,000	750,000	1.35	0.67	1,010,500
Piece	0.15	1,000,000	150,000	1.35	0.20	202,100
Total			1,500,000			2,021,000

CASE STUDY

95. shows the time estimates and number of transactions for Foodies' inbound handling process.
    a. Calculate the answers and fill out the remaining columns of Table 5.5.
    b. What are the service fees for pallets and cases, respectively?

Table 5.5 Foodies' inbound handling activity costs.

Inbound handling	Estimate (minutes)	Number of transactions	Total time (minutes)	Cost per minute ($)	Service fee ($)	Total cost ($)
Pallet	4.00	25,000				
Case	0.40	50,000				
Total						

> **Example: Calculating Storage Costs**
> There are 450,000 ft³ of storage space in the distribution center. On average 80 percent of the locations are occupied, i.e., 360,000 ft³. Hence, we see in Table 5.6 that the unit cost per ft³ equals $3.68 per year.

Table 5.6 Calculation of the unit costs for storage.

Activity	Activity cost ($)	Effective capacity (ft³)	Unit cost ($/ft³)
Storage	1,323,500	360,000	3.68

5.3.7 Resource Utilization

All estimates in the activity-based costing model are based on the standard times. The standard times are easy to validate. The calculated total process time, based on standard times for all transactions in the period, can be reconciled to head count (resources supplied during the period). The *resource utilization* shows the amount of the available time that was spent on the activities.

$$\text{Resource utilization} = \frac{\text{Calculated process time}}{\text{Capacity}} \times 100\%$$

> **Example: Calculating Resource Utilization**
> We continue with the example. The distribution center has 40 operators, each with a contractual capacity of 1,600 hours per year. In Table 5.2 we see that 47 percent of the staff costs have been allocated to outbound handling. This implies that the 40 warehouse operators spent on average 47 percent of their time on outbound handling, i.e., 47% × 40 × 1,600 hours = 30,080 hours = 1,804,800 minutes of available capacity per year. In Table 5.4 we identified that the calculated process time equals 1,500,000 minutes. Now we may calculate the resource utilization.
>
> $$\text{Resource utilization} = \frac{1,500,000}{1,804,800} \times 100\% = 83\%$$

EFFECTIVE WAREHOUSE MANAGEMENT

If the calculated process time exceeds the available capacity of the resources supplied, i.e., the *resource utilization* is more than 100 percent, then the manager receives a signal that some of the standard times are likely too high. If the resource utilization is considerably below, say, 70 to 80 percent, but operators feel they are working at capacity, then managers learn that their standard times are too low or operators are working less efficiently than anticipated.

96. Foodies has two full-time operators for the inbound handling process. Both operators are employed for 1,600 hours per year.
   a. Calculate the resource utilization for the inbound operators?
   b. What do you think of their performance level?
   c. Can you give an explanation for their performance level?

5.3.8 Time Equations

Of course, not all deliveries are the same or require the same amount of time to process. For instance, some products require a quality inspection upon receipt or need to be restacked on pallets. Rather than defining a separate activity for every possible combination of handling characteristics, time-driven activity-based costing estimates the resource demand by building a modular equation. For example:

Inbound handling time (minutes) = 4.5
+ 3 (if inspection is required)
+ 3.5 (if restacking is required)

An additional benefit of this approach is that the extra costs become visible. Managers often are surprised by how much time it takes to process a special order.

5.4 Performance Indicators

Service level agreements (SLAs) set the goals for the distribution center. In Section 5.1 we reasoned that the SLAs set operational goals that are aligned with the company's strategic and tactical objectives. Subsequently, the *performance indicators* (PIs) measure if the distribution center achieves these goals.

By definition, PIs translate historical achievements of the distribution center into transparent metrics. Clearly, transparency is not a goal in itself. The objective is to use the transparency to improve warehouse performance.

A study by De Leeuw & Van den Berg (2011) that incorporated 100+ logistics operations showed that successful application of performance indicators influenced the behavior of shop floor operators. In fact, the research identified three separate behavioral effects, which the authors show contribute to higher overall performance of the distribution center:
- Understanding
- Motivation
- Focus on improvement.

Companies should pursue these three behavioral effects when applying PIs. Successful companies report an increase of 5 percent or more in productivity and accuracy as well as inventory turnover.

Understanding
- Staff members (i.e., management and shop-floor operators) have an accurate and up-to-date view on the achieved performance.
- Staff members know the company's objectives and values and understand how their performance contributes to these objectives.
- Operational bottlenecks and the underlying causes are quickly identified.

Motivation
- Operators experience the PIs as a tool to improve performance rather than to control their activities.
- The PIs are a vivid element of the day-to-day operation. The operators are motivated to realize good scores on the performance indicators.
- Operators are able to see that good performance actually contributes to better company results (although the objectives of the various departments must be clearly aligned).

Focus on improvement
- Operators understand the relationship between PIs and company results. Hence, they can make decisions that positively influence the overall company results.
- Operators are encouraged to interpret PIs, consider the results and suggest improvements.
- The PIs become anchored in a continuous optimization cycle (e.g., Deming circle, see Section 5.4.5).

97. **Performance indicators translate historical achievements into transparent metrics.**
    a. Which behavioral effects of PIs on shop floor operators have been shown to actually improve logistics performance?

Next, we consider how companies can achieve these behavioral effects and thereby improve their logistics performance. The study suggests the use of a number of proven best practices for each of the following four stages:
- Defining performance indicators
- Introducing performance indicators
- Reporting management information
- Performance management.

The four stages serve as a chronological framework for the application of PIs. We discuss best practices in each of these stages in the subsequent sections.

5.4.1 Defining Performance Indicators

The first stage in the framework is to define a set of performance indicators. Managers often struggle to find the right metrics. They compile a set of PIs based on their own experience and recent incidents. Then, after the reports have been developed, they come to the conclusion that they need more indicators, different indicators or additional management information on details that substantiate the outcome of the PIs. Accordingly, more and more reports need to be built and the exercise of developing a set of performance indicators never ends. The result is an inconsistent concoction of PIs. In some companies, indicators are still regularly reported even though they have not been used by anyone for years.

How can the manager define a proper set of indicators? In the literature we find various models that help managers to develop a well-defined set of PIs. Popular examples are the Balanced Scorecard (Kaplan & Norton, 2001), the EFQM Excellence Model (Hardjono & Bakker, 2002) or the SCOR-model (Supply Chain Council, 2004). The advantage of these models is that they help to find a set of PIs that give relevant information in all important areas. We will not discuss these models here, but certainly recommend their use.

98. There are various models that can be used for defining PIs.
   a. Which models are you familiar with?
   b. Which one do you prefer? And why?

The performance indicators should provide an instant reflection of warehouse performance. At the highest level, we use a set of *key performance indicators (KPIs)*. The KPIs are supplemented by regular PIs and detailed management information. Where the KPI highlights a problem, the detailed information helps to explain the causes.

> **Example: Performance Indicators**
>
> It is important to note the difference between key performance indicators, performance indicators and detailed management information.
>
> An example of a *key performance indicator* is the *order line fill rate*, i.e., the percentage of order lines that were shipped on time.
>
> Associated *performance indicators* are, for example, the average lead-time of order lines or the average number of back order lines.
>
> Associated *detailed management information* is, for example, the number of order lines per day, lists of order lines that were too late, lists of open back orders, etc. These lists provide details on the clients, products and customers involved.

99. We distinguish KPIs, PIs and detailed management information.
    a. Explain the difference between a KPI, a PI and detailed management information.

Highly Competitive Warehouse Management states that key performance indicators should provide a *complete, up-to-date* and *unbiased* view of the performance.
- *Complete.* All relevant aspects are captured in the KPIs.
- *Up-to-date.* The KPIs are reported no later than the next day.
- *Unbiased.* The KPIs give a fair view of the actual performance.

If a set of KPIs meets the above conditions, then it gives clear and objective signals on the performance. It should not happen that operators perform well while the performance indicators suggest differently, or vice versa. Obviously, that would undermine the commitment among operators and managers to the use of PIs.

Complete

The KPIs give a *complete view* of the warehouse performance if they measure all dimensions specified in the SLAs. Thus, they should include:
- Productivity (representing the costs)
- Availability
- Accuracy
- Flexibility.

The KPIs may reflect these dimensions separately for different processes, i.e., inbound handling, storage, outbound handling and VAL. A practical number of

KPIs is between 8 and 16. This mix enables the manager to make educated trade-offs. If only a few aspects are covered in the KPIs, then this may result in a myopic view of the operation. Operators (and managers) will focus on these issues only and neglect the rest.

Individual operators are involved in three to five KPIs only. Nevertheless, they learn that their behavior affects the performance of the distribution center in many different ways. For example, it is not only important to work at a sufficient pace to achieve high productivity, but also to work carefully to prevent damage and mistakes.

Furthermore, it is best to avoid overlap between KPIs. This can unnecessarily increase the number of KPIs. Managers and operators will suffer from information overload and lose sight of the "big picture." Consider: a KPI that measures the *order line fill rate* (the percentage of order lines shipped on time) and a KPI that measures the *average response time of order lines* have a high correlation. If the average response times rise, then it is likely that more order lines are late, and vice versa. In this situation it is best to remove one of these KPIs and use it as a regular PI.

Up-to-date

Another important condition is that KPIs are *up-to-date*. It is a best practice that performance indicators be provided to operators within one day. Then the operators have a fresh recollection of the events and they are able to interpret the results. Consequently, they learn from their errors and performance will continuously improve. If the performance indicators are reported, say, after a week, a lot of the benefit is lost. It is even possible to report the PIs during the day for instant feedback, for example, via large central computer screens in the distribution center or via RF terminals.

Unbiased

Finally, the KPIs have to provide an *unbiased view* of the performance. Traditional performance indicators measure productivity by the number of picks, volume or weight per man hour, etc. Such indicators have an obvious bias. Some picks are clearly more labor-intensive than others. Managers expect that these variances will cancel out over the entire operation, however, the indicators do not give an objective view of the performance for individual operators, clients or product groups. More importantly, if the order profiles change over a number of years, the performance indicators will no longer give an accurate account of the achievements.

100. **KPIs should provide a complete, up-to-date and unbiased view of performance.**
    a. Define these three concepts.
    b. Think of a KPI of your warehouse and write down its definition.
    c. Is the KPI about productivity, availability, accuracy or flexibility?

HIGHLY COMPETITIVE WAREHOUSE MANAGEMENT

Unbiased Performance Indicators

In this section we discuss how we may prevent bias in the KPIs. We examine measures for:
- Productivity
- Availability
- Accuracy
- Flexibility.

Productivity

The service fees, defined in the SLAs, are based on assumptions regarding the productivity of resources. If operators achieve higher productivity than expected, then the actual costs are lower and the margin on the service fees increases. However, if their productivity is lower, then the margin drops or becomes negative.

> **Case Study: Productivity Measures for Manufacturer**
> The operators in the central distribution center of a food manufacturer worked in three shifts. The productivity of each shift was measured by the number of inbound and outbound shipments completed per man hour. There was a fierce competition between the three shifts to achieve the highest productivity score. However, in the last hour of the shift, the operators were reluctant to commence a new shipment, since they knew that it would take longer than one hour to process. If they did not finish the shipment, then it would be rapidly completed by the next shift and count towards their productivity score. Thus, to avoid being 'robbed', the operators dramatically reduced their efforts in the final hour – the opposite effect to that which managers intended when they introduced the KPI.

How can we define unbiased productivity KPIs? Many third party logistics providers, in particular, measure the productivity of their warehouse operation by comparing the accumulated service fees to the actual costs, in other words, they observe the profit margins. Clearly, these margins give an immediate insight into the profitability of the warehouse operation, which makes them excellent financial indicators. However, they are biased productivity PIs. Typically, the profit margins vary between clients and services. Consequently, inefficiencies in services with a high margin become less visible than inefficiencies in services with a low margin. Highly competitive warehouse management defines the productivity KPI as follows:

$$\text{Productivity} = \frac{\text{Standard performance}}{\text{Capacity} \times \text{Utilization target}} \times 100\%$$

The *capacity* is the amount of time that the resources are available. For operators, the capacity is the number of labor hours specified in their contract, e.g., 40 hours per week. For machines and vehicles, the capacity is usually equal to the opening hours of the distribution center.

The *utilization target* is the percentage of their capacity during which resources are supposed to be involved in direct activities. In fact, this definition breaks down resource time into three segments (Figure 5.5):
- Time spent on direct activities, such as order-picking and putaway
- Time spent on indirect activities, including management supervision or sweeping the floor (or idle time for machines and vehicles)
- Time absent (or downtime for machines and vehicles).

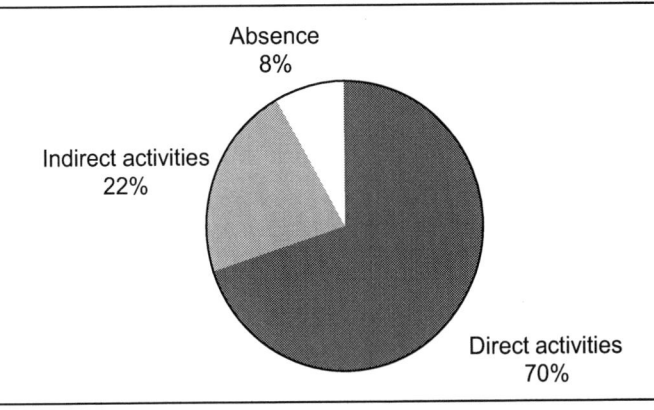

Figure 5.5 Example of the resource time breakdown.

Finally, the *standard performance* is computed by adding up the standard times of the direct activities performed by the resources. In Section 5.3.6 we introduced the standard times for various warehouse activities. The standard times for individual tasks may be further refined by incorporating travel distances, product quantities, warehouse sections, etc.

> **Example: Calculating Productivity**
> An operator has a capacity of 8 hours per day, i.e., 480 minutes, with a utilization target of 80 percent. The WMS registers which activities he performs. Table 5.7 shows the performed activities together with the standard times per activity. If we multiply the standard times by the number of activities, then we find that the operator achieved 400 minutes of standard time in total.
>
> Now we may compute the productivity as follows:
>
> $$\text{Productivity} = \frac{400}{480 \times 80\%} \times 100\% = 104\%$$
>
> Thus, the operator performed 4 percent above the productivity target.

Table 5.7 Example activities and standard times.

Activity	Number of activities	Standard time (min)	Total standard time (min)
Pallet pick	50	3.5	175
Case pick	250	0.5	125
Pallet receipt	40	2.5	100
Total			**400**

101. Service fees in SLAs are based on assumptions regarding the productivity of resources. Therefore we need unbiased productivity KPIs.
    a. How can we compute an unbiased productivity KPI?
    b. What does it mean if the operator in the above example has a productivity rate of 87 percent.

> **Example: Productivity of John vs. Pete**
> John is a sedate order-picker and Pete is his highly active colleague who seems to be busy all the time. The distribution center used the traditional productivity measure of the number of picks per man hour.
>
> Table 5.8 showed that Pete did 19 picks per hour and John 10 picks per hour. However, if we used unbiased productivity measures, then we would see the reason for this difference. It appears that John primarily works in the TV-section and Pete in the DVD-section. After adding up the standard times of the activities performed by both pickers, we see that John was expected to do 12 picks per hour and Pete 23 picks per hour. Accordingly, the unbiased productivity rates are 83 percent for each picker (actual picks per hour / standard picks per hour). Surprisingly, both pickers have the same productivity and more importantly both score 17 percent below the target.

Table 5.8 Productivity of John vs. Pete.

Indicator	John	Pete
Traditional productivity (picks/hour)	10	19
Analysis	TV-section	DVD-section
Standard performance (picks/hour)	12	23
Unbiased productivity	83%	83%

The productivity formula can be reformulated as follows:

$$\text{Productivity} = \text{Efficiency} \times \frac{\text{Utilization}}{\text{Utilization target}}$$

This formula breaks down the *productivity* indicator into two indicators for *efficiency* and *utilization*. The *utilization* is the percentage of resource time used for direct activities:

$$\text{Utilization} = \frac{\text{Capacity spent on direct activities}}{\text{Capacity}} \times 100\%$$

The *efficiency* is the performance of resources relative to the standard performance:

$$\text{Efficiency} = \frac{\text{Standard performance}}{\text{Capacity spent on direct activities}} \times 100\%$$

Example: Calculating Utilization and Efficiency

The WMS reported that the operator in the previous example spent 350 minutes on direct activities during his 8 hour workday (480 minutes).

$$\text{Utilization} = \frac{350}{480} \times 100\% = 73\%$$

His utilization is below the *utilization target* of 80 percent. Table 5.7 showed that the operator achieved 400 minutes of standard time in total. Since the operator completed these activities in 350 minutes, his efficiency equaled:

$$\text{Efficiency} = \frac{400}{350} \times 100\% = 114\%$$

His efficiency was well above the 100 percent target. Now we may recalculate *productivity*:

$$\text{Productivity} = 114\% \times \frac{73\%}{80\%} = 104\%$$

In addition to the *utilization* and *efficiency* of operators and machines, we can also measure these indicators for the resource *space*. The *utilization* of space is measured by the fraction of the volume that is occupied. A suitable *efficiency* measure is the *inventory turnover rate* (outbound volume relative to inventory volume).

> **Example: Utilization and Efficiency of John vs. Pete**
>
> Let us measure the *efficiency* and *utilization* of John and Pete according to the definitions in the section. Table 5.9 shows that John's efficiency rate is 80 percent, which is well below the target, but his utilization rate is above the target. Accordingly, he is a slow but consistent worker. Pete, however, works highly efficiently with a 110 percent score, but only works on direct activities for 60 percent of his time. Although Pete is a skilled order-picker, it seems that he loses a lot of time talking to others.
>
> Now we can improve performance by helping John to work more efficiently and Pete to work more consistently. In this way, both operators should be able to increase their performance by 17 percent.

Table 5.9 Utilization and Efficiency of John vs. Pete.

Indicator	John	Pete
Efficiency (target = 100%)	80%	110%
Utilization (target = 80%)	83%	60%

CASE STUDY

102. George and Paula are two operators at Foodies. The warehouse supervisor computed their individual efficiency and utilization indicators in Table 5.10.
    a. In what way can George's performance be improved?
    b. In what way can Paula's performance be improved?
    c. Who has the highest productivity?

Table 5.10 Utilization and Efficiency of George vs. Paula.

Indicator	George	Paula
Efficiency (target = 100%)	105%	90%
Utilization (target = 85%)	70%	80%

Availability

The fill rate measures whether services are available on time:

$$\text{Fill rate} = \frac{\text{On time services}}{\text{Provided services}} \times 100\%$$

We can measure the fill rate of inbound handling, VAL and outbound handling services by the on time percentage of orders, order lines, deliveries, delivery lines or handling units. If we want to measure the fill rate of the inbound handling service, then we must define the maximum allowed *dock-to-stock time*, i.e., the time between the arrival of a truck and the placement of the goods in the storage location. Thus, the availability is the percentage of orders that are passed from dock to stock within the target time.

In the SLAs, we not only set performance targets for the distribution center, but also for clients and other parties in the supply chain (see Section 5.1.5). Their performance may also be measured in the KPIs. Some typical examples of availability KPIs are the suppliers' *fill rate performance* (on time deliveries) or the *inventory fill rate* achieved by the source function (percentage of order lines directly delivered from stock).

103. Fill rate is an important KPI.
   a. What does fill rate mean?
   b. Define a fill rate KPI for the outbound handling service.

Accuracy

Accuracy measures the accurate services provided as a percentage of the total services provided:

$$\text{Accuracy} = \frac{\text{Accurate services}}{\text{Provided services}} \times 100\%$$

We can measure the accuracy of inbound handling, VAL and outbound handling services as the percentage of orders, order lines, deliveries, delivery lines or handling units that are accurate. Furthermore, the accuracy of the storage process (or *inventory accuracy*) is measured by the number of storage locations with the correct contents as a percentage of the total number of locations. The inventory accuracy is determined through *cycle counting*.

Note that a service is *perfect* only if it is both on time (availability) and correct (accuracy). This performance indicator is often referred to as the *perfect order (line) rate* or the *on time in full* (OTIF) rate.

104. Accuracy measures accurate services vs. provided services.
   a. What does the accuracy KPI mean?
   b. For which services of the distribution center can we measure accuracy?
   c. Define an accuracy KPI for the outbound handling service.

Flexibility

In Section 5.1.2 we defined *flexibility* as the degree to which fluctuations in the number of service requests can be accommodated. Figure 5.6 depicts the number of requests per day for an arbitrary service over a period of 22 days. The dotted

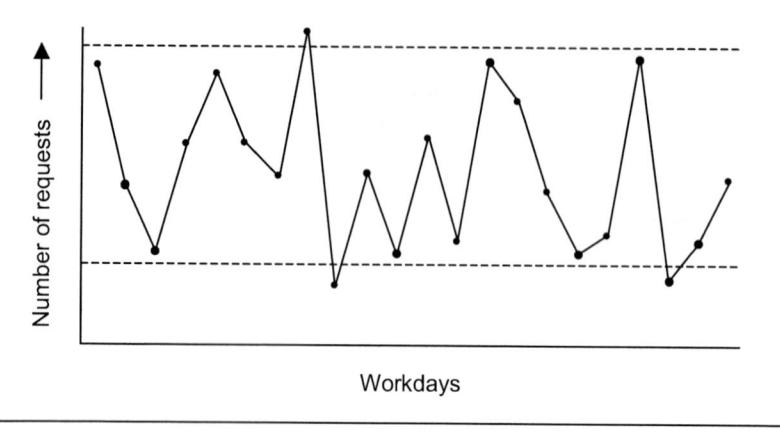

Figure 5.6 Workload fluctuations over a time period.

horizontal lines show the lower and upper limit to the number of requests. On most days the number of requests, i.e., the workload, is within the specified range. However, we see a few days outside the *flexibility range*. The service level agreements define flexibility ranges for services. We may use these ranges to assess two flexibility indicators:
- Does the distribution center satisfy its flexibility target?
- Does the distribution center provide sufficient flexibility?

First, we determine whether the distribution center satisfies the flexibility target specified in the SLAs. We restrict ourselves to those days with a workload within the flexibility range and examine the previously defined KPIs on productivity, accuracy and availability. If the KPIs meet their targets on those days, then the distribution center satisfies its flexibility target. If the distribution center does not meet its flexibility targets, then either the combined productivity, accuracy and availability levels are insufficient or the flexibility range is too broad.

Secondly, we examine whether the distribution center provides sufficient flexibility. A narrow range limits the flexibility in the supply chain, whereas a broad range demands excess capacities in the distribution center. To determine if the distribution center provides adequate flexibility, we calculate the percentage of workdays in the period that service requests were inside the flexibility range. If more than, say, 10 percent of the workdays fall outside the flexibility range, then this suggests that the supply chain demands a broader range. Either the distribution center should take measures to increase its flexibility range or it should attempt, in collaboration with clients, to smooth the fluctuations.

It is interesting to see what happens on days that lie above or below the range. If service levels are still satisfactory, then this indicates that the range may easily be extended thereby offering a higher flexibility to the clients. An alternative conclusion might be that there is too much excess capacity available and costs could be reduced.

105. Workload could exceed the flexibility range.
   a. What does it mean when workload exceeds the flexibility range?
   b. Which actions are needed when workload exceeds the flexibility range?
   c. Define a flexibility KPI for the outbound handling service.

> **Example: Calculating the Flexibility Range**
> Figure 5.6 shows the number of requests for an arbitrary service over a period of 22 workdays. The dotted lines indicate the range for the permitted number of service requests per working day. We see that the number of requests exceed the flexibility range on three days. Consequently, the workload is within the flexibility range on 19/22 = 86% of the workdays.

5.4.3 Introducing Performance Indicators to the Distribution Center

In the previous sections we discussed how to define meaningful performance indicators. Subsequently, they must be introduced in the distribution center. Together with the other techniques and methodologies discussed in this chapter, i.e., service level agreements, standard operating procedures and activity-based costing, the performance indicators create transparency. Clearly, transparency is not a goal by itself. We need to *exploit* it to increase warehouse performance.

Transparency will change the operation fundamentally. Operators and management are confronted with metrics more frequently and they have to learn how to interpret them. Operators start to understand how their behavior affects the overall company results. Instructions and regulations are defined (more) explicitly and management monitors whether the objectives are met. We list several best practices for guiding this *change process*.

Management Commitment

An essential success factor is commitment from senior management. Without this support the implementation will remain the personal toy of the manager. Management commitment empowers the endeavor, in particular when it involves other departments. Moreover, since the SLAs are derived from strategic and tactical company objectives, input from senior management is essential.

Cross-Departmental Involvement

The introduction of performance indicators also has an effect on other departments in the company such as the source, sell and transportation planning functions. Hence, it is a best practice to involve the relevant departments in the definition of procedures, targets and performance indicators. Companies have better results if they introduce performance management as part of a company-wide initiative. This ensures the commitment of other departments as well as the management team.

Operator Involvement

Managers might be afraid of encountering operator resistance. We do not deny that strong resistance may occur. However, the survey by De Leeuw & Van den Berg (2011) showed no difference in the eventual success between those companies that did meet resistance, and those that did not. Apparently, managers are able to overcome resistance through proper *change management*.

It is essential that operators consider the introduction of PIs as an initiative to improve warehouse performance rather than to control their behavior. Clearly, this requires a careful introduction with sufficient communication. For example, operators must understand the importance of their activities. They should be trained in the new instructions and regulations. And finally they must be taught how to interpret the PIs.

Hence, it is essential to involve the operators and team leaders in the implementation process. This will increase their understanding and commitment. They should help to develop the new plans and be encouraged to share their ideas. They should receive feedback about what has been done with their input and if their ideas were adopted.

106. There are several best practices for guiding the introduction of performance indicators.
   a. List these best practices.

107. With your distribution center in mind.
   a. Which best practices were taken into account when performance indicators were introduced?

5.4.4 Reporting Performance Indicators

Modern warehouse management systems (WMSs) capture a lot of detailed data, such as the tasks performed by operators, orders and deliveries shipped, inventory levels and space utilization. How can we convert these data into useful management information? Following are some best practices.

Management Information Systems

WMS and ERP systems have insufficient capabilities to compute management information. However, it is a best practice to use a separate management information system that extracts the data from the WMS and transforms it into management information. The system may be built in Excel or in a *business intelligence system*.

Dashboard and Drill-Downs

Another best practice for reporting performance indicators is the use of a dashboard with the KPIs. The dashboard tells the manager and responsible team leaders at a glance which indicators need attention.

The system should also give access to the details underlying the KPIs. It is a best practice that this information is available electronically, so that after observing an inadequate KPI-score, the manager can immediately drill down into the details.

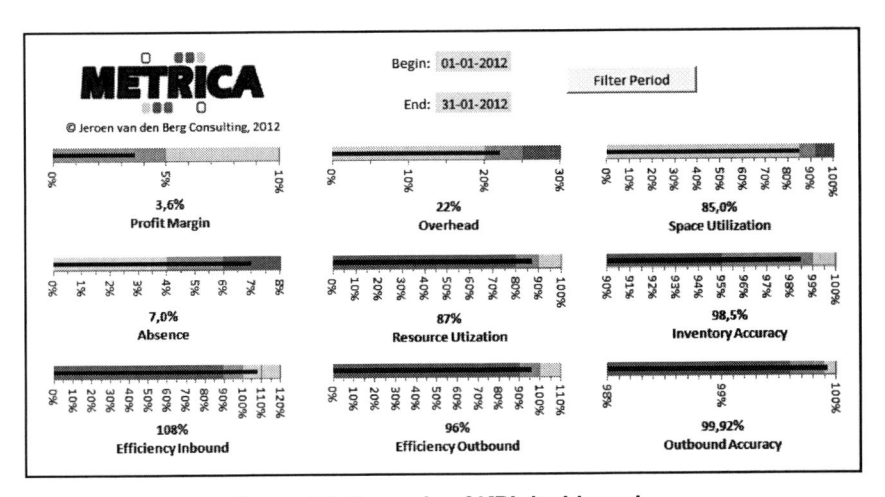

Figure 5.7 Example of KPI dashboard.

108. Think about management information systems.
   a. Which management information systems do you know?
   b. Which one do you prefer? And why?

5.4.5 Performance Management

Performance management is the use of performance indicators to manage and optimize an operation. The PIs should become an inseparable element of the day-to-day operation. Here are some best practices.

Individual Performance Reports

Regularly, we find that managers are reluctant to measure the performance of individual operators. They do not wish to be accused of running an Orwellian Big Brother operation. However, in reality, it appears that operators often appreciate the individual feedback on their performance. A necessary condition is that they experience the performance indicators as a technique to improve warehouse performance rather than to control their behavior.

Operator Incentives

In addition to reporting individual scores, should management also judge the operators by their individual PIs, during periodic performance reviews or via the use of financial incentives? The survey identified that a best practice is to evaluate operators by their *team performance*. We consider a team to be a group of approximately 10 operators who work closely together. On the one hand, if operators are assessed on the departmental or company performance, then they regard this as too abstract, i.e., the impact of their actions on the PIs is not clear. On the other hand, if they are evaluated on their *individual performance*, then they tend to focus primarily on their own activities and forget to look at the big picture.

A related question is whether we should give a financial reward for outstanding performance. As surprising as it may seem, the survey did not reveal any difference between companies with or without incentives. Apparently, *intrinsic motivation*, such as encouraging the operators' own drive to perform well, is more important than *extrinsic motivation*, such as encouraging staff through rewards. In particular, companies that do want to introduce financial rewards should not commence immediately after the introduction of performance indicators. It is better to wait until the PIs have been well accepted in the operation.

Continuous Optimization

PIs should be used to improve warehouse performance. An effective procedure that uses management information to drive performance is the *Deming circle* (see Section 2.3.2).

109. Performance management is the use of performance indicators to manage and optimize an operation.
  a. How does performance management work in your distribution center?
  b. Are there any best practices in performance management practices that you could introduce?

5.5 Summary

Highly Competitive Warehouse Management introduces several techniques and methodologies that provide transparency in a distribution center. These instruments define objectives, processes, costs and performance metrics. They are proven best practices that help the manager to evaluate and improve the performance of the distribution center.

Modern warehouse management systems have the capability to capture highly detailed data on the activities in the distribution center. We illustrated how this data can help us to define powerful performance indicators.

Chapter 6

Process Efficiency

Effective warehouse management is the second stage in the maturity grid (Figure 6.1). In the previous chapter we introduced several techniques and methodologies that create transparency in the distribution center. *Highly Competitive Warehouse Management* claims that in each stage a 10 percent cost reduction can be established relative to the initial costs. At the same time, competitive service levels can be achieved and maintained.

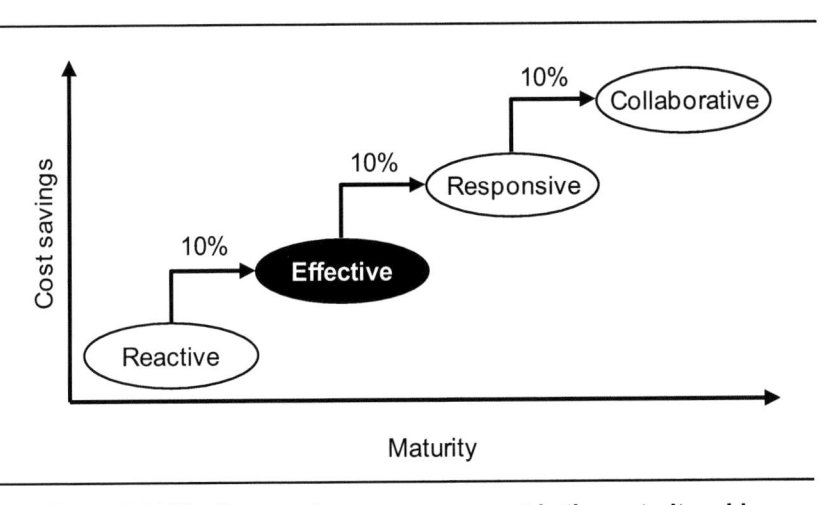

Figure 6.1 Effective warehouse management in the maturity grid.

The cost savings in effective warehouse management do not come from transparency itself, but because we redesign the warehouse processes. As stated in Section 1.2, the aim of the redesign is to make the processes more efficient, so that operators (and machines) need less time to perform the activities. It is also possible to use resource *space* more efficiently, by using it more compactly.

Additionally, we seek ways to improve the service levels of the distribution center. In Section 5.1 we defined the *service level agreements* that specify the service level targets for the distribution center. The targets indicate for all services which levels of accuracy, responsiveness and flexibility must be accommodated by the distribution center. If the current service levels are below the targets, then highly competitive warehouse management favors service improvement over cost reduction. This does not mean that cost reductions are completely ignored before service level compliance is achieved. Cost reductions that do not negatively impact service levels could be introduced.

In this chapter we give examples to illustrate how improved transparency may help to achieve cost reductions as well as higher service levels. The examples can be applied to many different distribution centers, but not necessarily to all. The idea behind this chapter is to inspire managers to examine the bottlenecks in their own distribution centers and develop appropriate solutions. After identifying the possible optimizations, the manager can plot the projects in the action plan discussed in Section 2.3 and design a logical implementation plan.

110. Effective warehouse management is the second stage in the maturity grid.
   a. *Where do cost savings in effective warehouse management come from?*

6.1 Service Level Improvement

First, we look at improving service levels. We give examples for:
- Reducing response times
- Increasing availability
- Improving accuracy
- Increasing flexibility.

Response Time

Figure 6.2 shows a three day response time for sales orders. Before the cut-off time on day zero, the sell function enters the orders. We do not consider the time elapsed before the cut-off time as part of the response time, since only then are the orders committed. Prior to the cut-off time, customers typically are entitled to cancel or modify their orders without consequences. Subsequently, one day is used for inventory allocation, and planning both transportation and warehouse staff capacity. The second day is used for order-picking and the third day for transport to the customers.

PROCESS EFFICIENCY

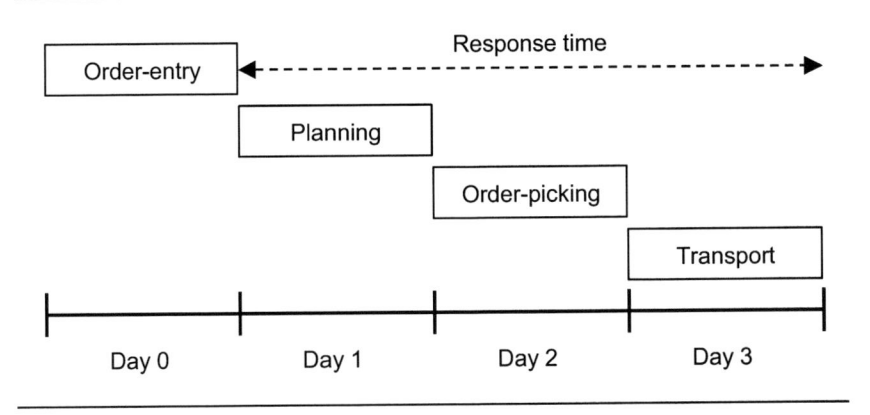

Figure 6.2 Response time of sales orders.

In many cases, the planning stage can be accelerated. Often, orders are held for many hours or even days in the various information systems, i.e., ERP and TMS, before they are communicated to the WMS.

It is problematic to start order-picking before the planning stage has been completed, because we do not yet know which orders are assigned to which trips. However, once the distribution center has received the orders, the operators are able to start the replenishment of pick locations. Then, when the planning is complete, the pick locations have already been replenished so that the warehouse operators can immediately start the order-picking (Figure 6.3).

Furthermore, trucks do not have to wait until all orders for that day are complete before they can depart. If a full truckload is ready prior to day 3, then a truck can come and pick it up. This requires that the orders are picked in accordance with the sequence of the departure schedule. Consequently, orders are picked in a certain time sequence and there might be fewer opportunities to combine activities, such as *batch-picking* or *dual-command cycles*. As a rule of

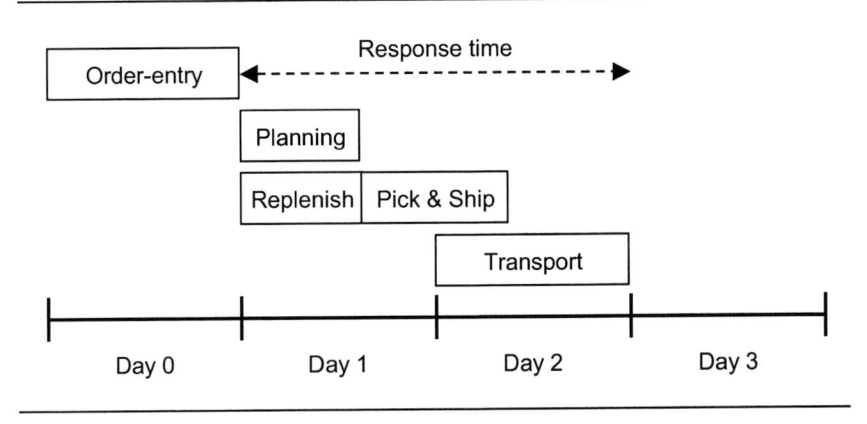

Figure 6.3 Reduced response time.

t hours work on hand suffices to achieve a satisfactory efficiency ion 3.7.1). Figure 6.3 shows the resulting response time reduction.

Availability

To ship goods on time, they must be present in sufficient quantities in the distribution center. It is the responsibility of the source function to ensure adequate stock levels. A numerical analysis of the number of days worth of inventory on hand (inventory level divided by the average daily sales) can be an effective way to identify products with insufficient inventory.

> **Case Study: Savings from Response Time Reduction**
> A retailer with an annual turnover of $250 million supplied its stores from a central distribution center. The operation was open for 250 days per year and held an average inventory level of twenty working days' stock, i.e., $20 million. The annual inventory holding costs were estimated at 20 percent of the average inventory value. This covered the interest on capital employed, the use of warehousing space and the inventory risks (damage, theft, expiration, obsolescence).
>
> The company introduced a new ERP system that reduced the order processing time (planning stage) by 24 hours. Due to technical limitations, the old system held the orders for one day before they could be processed. With the new ERP the goods could leave the distribution center one day sooner, so that the distribution center held one day less on hand. Hence, the inventory level was reduced by $1 million.
>
> Another advantage of the new ERP was that the inventory levels were updated immediately after the receipt of the goods in the distribution center. Previously, this was done overnight, so that the received goods only became available for sales orders the next day. Consequently, the distribution center held on average one half day of inventory on hand which could not be shipped. Once this inventory became available immediately, the distribution center needed half a day less safety stock. Hence, the inventory level was reduced by another $0.5 million.
>
> The total savings from the response time reduction can be estimated at: 20% × $1.5 million = $300,000.

It may also be the case that goods are not available due to inventory discrepancies. By improving inventory accuracy, availability also increases. Accuracy can be increased by improving the procedures so that fewer errors occur (*preventive measures*) or by more frequent cycle counting (*corrective measures*).

Goods may also be late due to a high workload, in particular when the workload exceeds the volume ranges in the *service level agreements*. We further discuss how to anticipate volume fluctuations in Section 10.3.

111. Availability of goods is essential in a distribution center.
   a. List five reasons why goods may not be available in your distribution center.
   b. How could these availability problems be resolved?

Accuracy

Improving accuracy involves identifying the causes of errors and using preventive or corrective measures. *Preventive measures* enhance the procedures so that fewer errors occur. In particular, the *Six Sigma* method (Pyzdek, 2003) is a useful approach for eliminating errors. *Corrective measures* check the activities afterwards. For example, cycle counting checks the inventory levels (see Section 3.6.1) and inspections at the shipping dock check the work of the order-pickers. A *weight-check* automatically inspects the orders after picking, i.e., a scale determines the weight and the WMS compares it to the calculated weight of the picked goods. If the weight deviation is more than a pre-specified margin, then the goods are passed to a human operator for further examination.

Unlike preventive measures, corrective measures have an immediate effect. However, corrective measures usually are more expensive. Therefore, we suggest it is best to start with corrective measures to comply with the accuracy targets, and then gradually reduce the efforts once fewer errors occur due to the preventive measures.

Errors do not necessarily originate in the distribution center. Suppliers and internal departments may also cause mistakes. In this case we can also take preventive and corrective measures. We further elaborate on collaboration with other parties in the supply chain in Chapter 9.

112. Preventive and corrective measures could be taken to improve accuracy.
   a. Give an example of a preventive measure and a corrective measure to overcome order-picking errors.

Flexibility

If volume fluctuations are known in advance, then we can anticipate them by either hiring temporary staff or by planning a day off for some operators. We can also balance the workload by shifting orders to a previous or subsequent day. We further discuss these measures in Section 7.2.3.

6.2 Efficiency Improvement

Highly Competitive Warehouse Management introduces a systematic procedure that seeks integral optimization. In Section 2.4.1 we distinguished three actions for improving the efficiency of the processes. Step by step, we evaluate all the individual activities in the standard operating procedures (see Section 5.2). We question each activity and ask ourselves how it can be optimized. For each step we consider three possible actions for optimization: *elimination, combination* or *improvement* (see Figure 6.4).

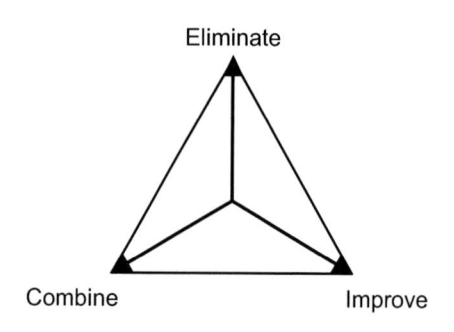

Figure 6.4 Optimization actions for effective warehouse management.

Sometimes we can *eliminate* activities because they are redundant or they occur due to improper or erroneous activities upstream. Another action is to *combine* activities thereby creating economies of scale. The third action is to *improve* activities. We continue doing the same activity, but do it more efficiently.

113. **Effective warehouse management distinguishes three optimization actions.**
    a. *Name the three actions.*
    b. *Explain them.*

The following *procedure* helps to analyze the processes objectively. Since we are looking for integral optimizations, it is essential that we consider the entire process. Often, a saving in one process step requires additional handling in another step. This should not be a reason for putting off the optimization. If we calculate the overall cost effect, the idea might still be worthwhile.

> **Procedure: Process Optimization**
> *Highly Competitive Warehouse Management* suggests the following procedure for finding optimizations:
> 1. Compose standard operating procedures (Section 5.2). The specifications list step by step which activities take place.
> 2. Estimate the standard time for each process step. It does not have to be exact, but should be approximately correct.
> 3. Calculate the costs associated with each process step using the time-driven activity-based costing model (Section 5.3).
> 4. Determine how often each process step occurs per year and calculate the annual costs.
> 5. Examine how process steps may be eliminated, combined or improved.
> 6. Calculate the resulting savings from each optimization.

It is important to consider the details, since they might reveal many opportunities. However, to focus excessively on details is dangerous. Instead of improving the individual steps in an activity, it might sometimes be possible to eliminate the entire activity. Hence, *Highly Competitive Warehouse Management* recommends that practitioners take an abstract view of the current processes and consider completely new ways of working. This is a creative process, which involves brainstorming for new ideas. During a *brainstorm session,* ideas may not be rejected on subjective grounds. The transparency that has been created will enable every idea to be examined objectively. People may often suggest reasons why a particular idea might not work. Challenge them to find ways to make it work instead. We emphasize that, as long as it is legal, anything should be open for discussion! Before you start your discussions, we suggest that you share the *remark* on page 194 among team members.

114. Foodies' logistics manager would like to optimize the VAL process in the distribution center.
    a. Which six steps should he follow to find optimizations?

115. Consider the *remark* on page 194 and think of your own role in discussions.
    a. When are you a "yes-but-er" and when a "why-not-er"?

> **Remark: Yes-but, What if it all Works Out? (Gunster, 2007)**
> Yes-but-ers have all the answers:
> - Yes-but sales won't listen to our plans
> - Yes-but we couldn't sell it to our staff
> - Yes-but we can't explain it to our management
> - Yes-but the WMS doesn't support that
> - Yes-but it already didn't seem like a good idea last week either.
>
> Yes-but-ers don't just kill ideas. They kill companies. Why-not-ers move companies. The next time that you are in a brainstorm session, apply the following rules:
> 1. Why-not-ers welcome, yes-but-ers out
> 2. Say why-not to every little idea: let your heart and imagination speak
> 3. Silence is allowed
> 4. It is okay to take time for a good idea, when necessary we can sleep on it.
>
> Why-not-ers dare to dream and to act. By acting, they achieve what others see as unachievable. Why not, indeed?

6.2.1 Eliminate

Various activities in the distribution center, such as checks and rework, often occur due to unreliable or erroneous upstream actions. Other activities may be due to a lack of information, e.g., the inspection and identification of received goods. Hence, with more reliable processes and improved data interchange we may be able to *eliminate* many activities.

Besides savings on the physical activities, we can also eliminate certain administrative and managerial activities. For example, the inventory levels and order status need to be updated in the WMS after order-picking. However, if the order-pickers use *RF terminals*, then the WMS updates the status automatically, thereby eliminating the need for manual confirmation. Moreover, if the RF terminals tell the operators which tasks to perform, then this reduces the workload of the team leaders. With a modern WMS, the team leaders will primarily manage the operation through the system thereby increasing their span of control. Consequently, fewer team leaders are necessary to manage the operation.

116. Think of your own distribution center.
   a. What kind of activities could be eliminated?
   b. How can this be achieved?

PROCESS EFFICIENCY

> **Case Study: Redesign Receiving Process**
> A logistics service provider re-examined its receiving process. The goods stayed at the warehouse docking area for a considerable period of time. This congested the area and pallets needed to be moved aside several times to make way. Moreover, various activities took place at different locations, which required several moves – and sometimes goods were even counted twice. Finally, the products were taken manually from the pallet and put on a table at a workstation where they were counted and sorted.
>
> The project manager invited the operators to reinvent their process. He challenged them to think of new ways to make the process more efficient. The operators designed a new process where the pallets were moved from the receipt dock to the workstation as soon as possible. Since the pallets stayed only briefly at the docking area, congestion issues were resolved. Additionally, the pallets only needed to be moved once. Finally, lift tables were introduced at the workstations. So instead of having to move the products from the pallet onto the table, pallets were mounted on an adjustable-height lift table so that the operators could count and sort the goods immediately from the pallet.
>
> The process redesign eliminated various pallet moves and product handling routines and reduced the number of required operators from 13.5 to 12.5. Moreover, it shortened the *dock-to-stock time*.

GET IT

117. A modern WMS makes it possible to reduce the number of team leaders.
    a. How?

Receiving
This example illustrates how process steps can be eliminated in the receiving process. We first consider the traditional manner of delivering goods to the distribution center. Figure 6.5 depicts the process flow. The supplier registers the relevant information in his information system and prints the freight documents. The documents are faxed or the truck driver hands the papers to the receipt clerk in the distribution center, where the information is entered in the WMS.

Meanwhile the truck arrives at the distribution center to deliver the goods. They are unloaded and the receipt operator checks them, and enters the received product quantities in the WMS via an RF terminal. Finally, the goods are ready for putaway into the storage locations.

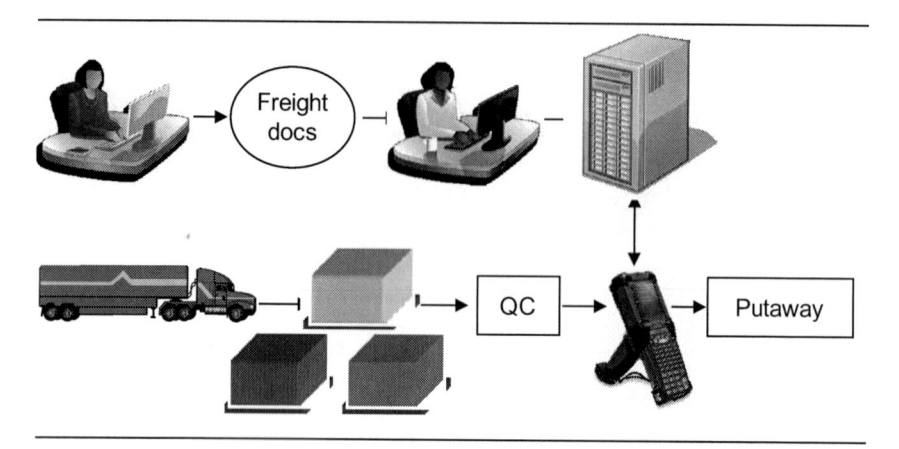

Figure 6.5 Traditional receiving process.

Figure 6.6 shows a receipt process where the delivery information is electronically communicated in a *despatch advice* (DESADV, see Section 3.5.1). If we compare this situation to Figure 6.5, then we see that the electronic message eliminates many administrative tasks. Moreover, the supplier has attached labels to the pallets with unique license plate numbers, generally referred to as *SSCC*-numbers (Serial Shipping Container Code). The contents of each pallet have been communicated in the electronic despatch advice with a reference to its unique SSCC number. Accordingly, one scan of the SSCC barcode suffices to recognize the contents of the pallet. Therefore we eliminate the processes of identifying, checking and registering the received goods. Or perhaps operators may perform random checks where the frequency of the checks is based on the delivery performance of the supplier (*vendor rating*).

After scanning we can immediately putaway the goods, or alternatively, we could cross-dock the goods to an outbound truck. Since we know upfront which goods will arrive, we can match incoming goods against sales orders. Hence, orders can be allocated to goods that are still in transit, i.e., the goods in the truck become *rolling stock*. Note that cross-docking *eliminates* many process steps.

If we do not have the electronic DESADV, then cross-docking becomes difficult. In particular, if deliveries do not necessarily correspond to individual purchase orders (POs), then it is hard to predict which goods will arrive. The PO and the delivery may differ because, for example, some goods are in backorder at the supplier. Additionally, upon receipt we have to determine whether the goods are required for any open sales orders. If that is the case, then the amounts that are requested by the various orders may exceed the incoming quantities. Thus, we have to decide who gets the goods (*order disposition*, see Section 4.4.1) within a short time frame. Moreover, we have to reschedule the trips, so that the cross-docked goods can be included. All-in-all, there are many decisions that complicate the process. Thus, without DESADV, cross-docking is only possible in exceptional circumstances. We refer to such events as *opportunistic cross-docking*, as opposed to the *planned cross-docking* described above.

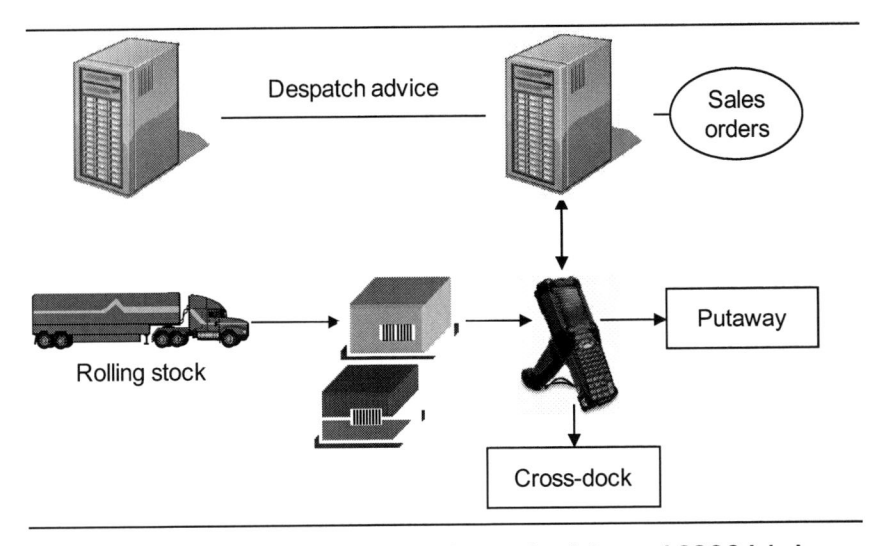

Figure 6.6 Receiving process with despatch advice and SSCC-labels.

> 💡 **GET IT**

118. There are several cross-docking variants.
  a. *Define the cross-docking concept.*
  b. *In your own words, explain the difference between the processes in Figure 6.5 and Figure 6.6.*
  c. *Explain the difference between opportunistic cross-docking and planned cross-docking.*

Dynamic Pick Locations

This example considers the replenishment of pick locations. Figure 6.7 shows a forklift driver who arrives at the aisle to replenish pallet X to the pick location. There are two policies for selecting the pick location for a product (see Section 3.8):
- Static pick locations
- Dynamic pick locations.

Under the first policy, the forklift driver merges the new pallet X with the remaining cases in the pick location. Or alternatively, the order-picker removes the remaining cases from the pick location and waits (or comes back later) to pick the remainder of the order line after the replenishment has been completed. Thus, we see that static pick locations lead to inefficiencies in the replenishment and order-picking processes.

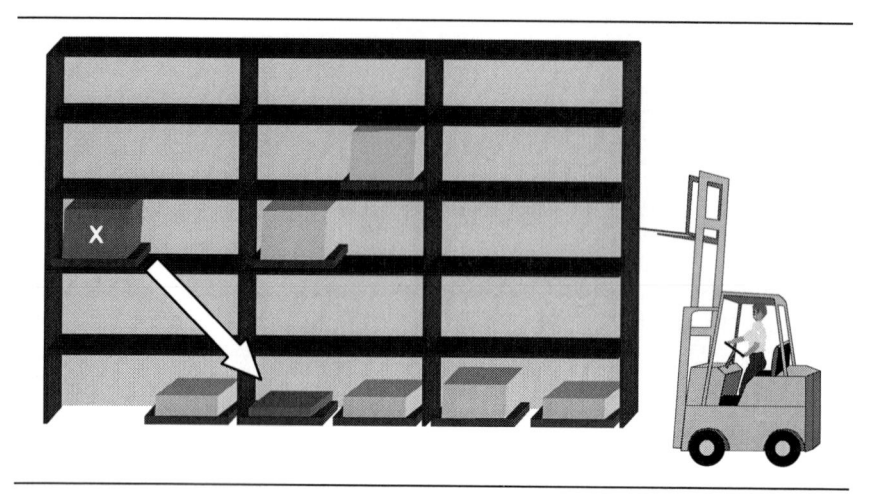

Figure 6.7 Static pick locations.

Preferably, the replenishment of the pick location happens *just in time*, i.e., less than one hour before the order-picker arrives at the pick location. In this way, we avoid having two pick locations for the same product for a long time. That would significantly increase the need for space in the picking area. With just in time replenishments, dynamic pick locations are typically possible with 10 to 15 percent open pick locations.

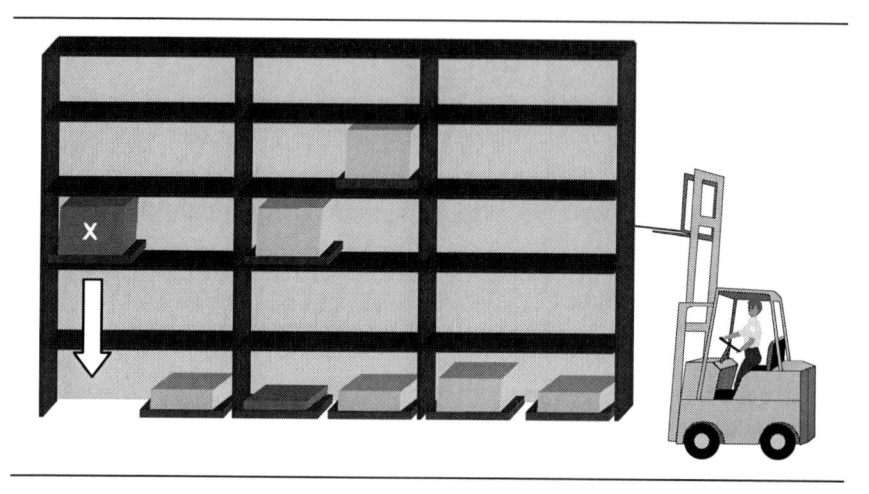

Figure 6.8 Dynamic pick locations.

6.2.2 Combine

The second action that we consider for streamlining processes in effective warehouse management is to *combine* activities. If operators handle larger amounts at the same time, then they achieve economies of scale.

Batch-picking

A popular method to combine activities is *batch-picking*. Instead of only picking a single order in a pick tour (*single-order picking*), the operator picks multiple orders simultaneously (see Figure 6.9). Since the travel distance does not (significantly) increase compared to single-order picking, combining multiple orders in a single tour reduces the overall travel time. The order-picker either sorts the orders during the pick tour (*sort-while-pick*) or afterwards (*pick-and-sort*). Batch-picking is only practical when the travel time saving offsets the additional handling time.

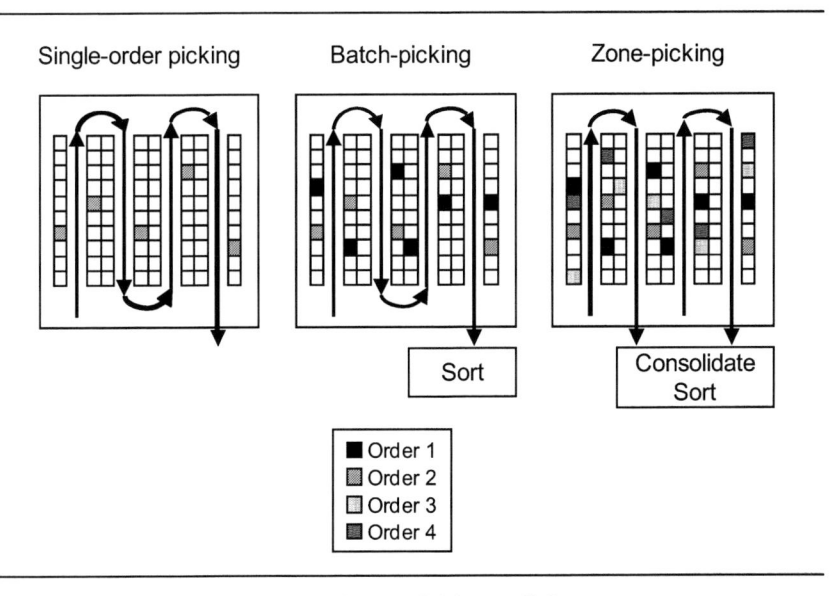

Figure 6.9 Order-picking policies.

The number of orders that can be picked in one tour is limited by the volume capacity of the pick cart. Therefore, we could further raise the number of batched orders by picking the orders in parallel zones (see Figure 6.9). *Zone-picking* requires that the order lines from the various zones are *sorted* as well as *consolidated* after picking. Once again the travel time saving should make up for the additional handling time.

119. Batch-picking is a method to combine activities.
  a. Explain how batch-picking is related to effective warehouse management.

Dual-command Cycles

A WMS with *real-time communication* can *combine* pallet moves for putaway and pallet picking into *dual-command cycles*. Dual-command cycles reduce the empty travel time compared to *single-command cycles*. We further discuss this topic in Section 7.4.

120. Think of your own distribution center.
  a. Which of the existing activities could be combined?
  b. How?

6.2.3 Improve

The third and final action for optimizing process efficiency is to *improve* existing activities. In other words, we continue doing the same thing, only we do it more efficiently. Modern technologies such as voice-picking and pick-to-light help to improve efficiency. Other examples are the use of an *ABC classification* (see Section 3.5.2) to reduce travel and handling times, or *pick sequencing* routines (see Section 3.7.3) that reduce travel distances or limit the number of aisle changes of the forklift trucks (changing aisles usually takes a considerable amount of time, especially for narrow-aisle trucks).

121. Consider Foodies' standard operating procedures in Appendix B.
  a. Find an activity that could be improved.
  b. How can it be improved?

6.3 Compact Storage

In the previous section, we showed how transparency helps to create efficient activities. Transparency may also be used to optimize space requirements. If we are able to store goods more compactly, then we need less storage space.

A storage location typically contains only one product. It may be that a large location is occupied by a small amount of a product. If the product is a *fast mover*, then we may expect the location to be cleared soon. However, for *slow movers* this is often not the case. Therefore, we monitor space utilization. If more than 85 to 90 percent of the locations are occupied, then we can start to relocate these small amounts into smaller locations.

It may also be that there are many locations with small quantities. In that case, it could be a solution to subdivide large locations into smaller locations. This may be done, for example, by inserting an additional horizontal beam in a pallet rack. While moving products between locations is an operational measure, increasing the number of locations is a more structural tactical measure.

Other options to improve space utilization include putaway rules that select the storage location that best fits the product volume (see Section 3.5.2) or inventory allocation rules that clear locations (see Section 3.7.2).

6.4 Summary

Transparency is a powerful tool for increasing warehouse performance. *Highly Competitive Warehouse Management* proposes a systematic procedure that uses improvements in transparency to optimize processes, service levels and space usage in the distribution center. The model distinguishes three possible actions: *eliminate*, *improve* and *combine*. The first action reduces the number of process steps, the second action makes the existing activities more efficient and the third action combines activities, thereby exploiting the scale economies.

Chapter 7

Responsive Warehouse Management

Responsive warehouse management is the third stage in the maturity grid (Figure 7.1). In the previous stage, effective warehouse management, we introduced several instruments that created transparency in the distribution center. We used this transparency to increase the efficiency of the processes. Thus, in our further analysis we assume that the efficiency of the *processes* can no longer be improved. However, there are still other ways to increase warehouse productivity. Responsive warehouse management optimizes productivity through better *utilization* of resources, i.e., people, machines, vehicles and warehouse space.

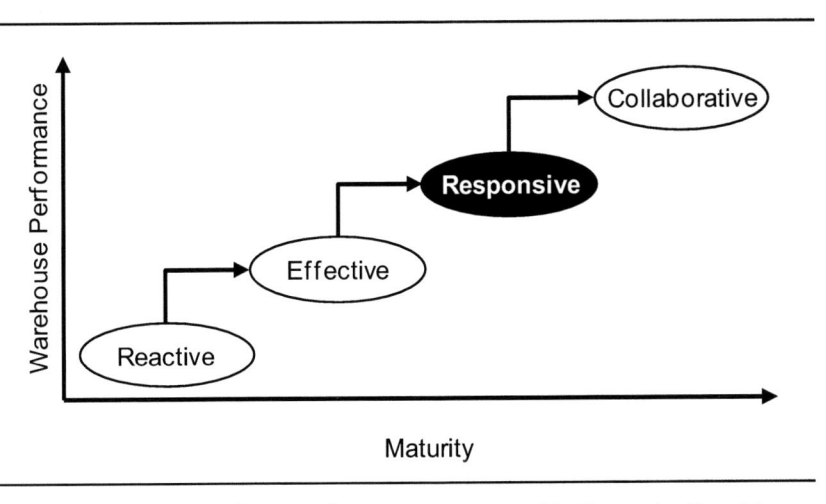

Figure 7.1 Responsive warehouse management in the maturity grid.

We improve resource utilization primarily through the use of software with intelligent planning and control rules. Therefore, *Highly Competitive Warehouse Management* introduces a planning and control framework. Not every modern WMS may be able to support all concepts in the framework. The manager who wants software tools to support these concepts must either ask the WMS vendor to build these tools into the WMS or arrange for the tools to be built separately (either by an internal IT department or external development organization).

122. Responsive warehouse management is the third stage in the maturity grid.
   a. What is the difference between effective warehouse management and responsive warehouse management?

Figure 7.2 shows the planning and control framework represented as a *warehouse management cycle*. It integrates strategic, tactical and operational management into a closed loop decision process. Strategic choices, formalized in *service level agreements* (see Section 5.1), identify which services the distribution center has to provide and how well they must be performed. *Capacity planning*, at the tactical level, determines the necessary warehouse capacity, e.g., labor capacity, dock capacity, storage capacity and inventories. *Wave management* refers to the operational control during the day and *task management* to the actual assignment of tasks to both operators and automated material handling devices. Finally, *performance management* (see Section 5.4) closes the feedback loop. It measures the performance of the execution and reports performance indicators to the operational, tactical and strategic levels.

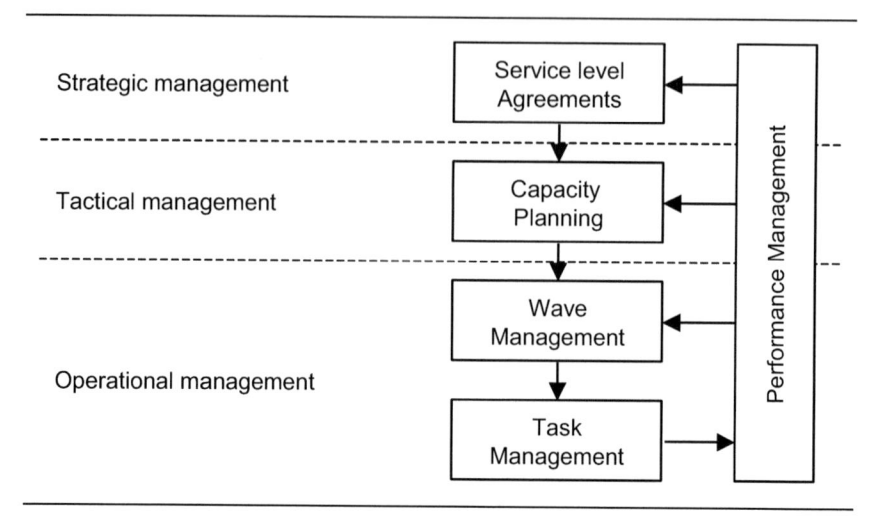

Figure 7.2 Warehouse management cycle.

In Section 5.1 we defined *service level agreements* (SLAs) for the distribution center. The SLAs state which services the warehouse should provide, how well they must be performed and how much they cost. The performance targets in the SLAs serve as the objectives for planning and control in the warehouse.

In Section 5.4 we discussed the role of performance management in the distribution center. In the warehouse management cycle we use the PIs as a feedback mechanism for the other management levels. In Sections 7.2, 7.3 and 7.4, we will further discuss *capacity planning*, *wave management* and *task management*.

However, before a manager decides to implement these systems, he has to answer two important questions:
- Will the benefits repay the investments?
- Is it preferable to outsource the distribution center to a third party logistics provider and avoid the need for major investment?

We first answer these questions in Section 7.1.

123. Foodies' logistics manager wants to implement a WMS module for capacity planning in year T+2 (Table 2.1 on page 67).
   a. What is the popular name for a WMS module that supports capacity planning?
   b. Which two important questions should the logistics manager answer before he decides to implement the module?

7.1 Justification

The planning and control policies described in this chapter require substantial IT support. Hence, the question arises as to whether the benefits are sufficient to repay the investments in these systems. In Section 4.2 we introduced the criteria in Table 4.1 to characterize the complexity of a distribution center. The advanced intelligence for capacity planning, wave management, task management and performance management primarily applies to distribution centers with a *high complexity*. A distribution center of *medium complexity* requires a WMS with standard wave, task and performance management. Perhaps, the manager could consider using some of the advanced tools. Finally, a distribution center with mainly *low complexity* characteristics should find a basic WMS sufficient.

Nevertheless, managers of distribution centers of basic and medium complexity should still attempt to apply the principles behind the planning and control framework. Due to the limited complexity of the operation, many of the results can be achieved without the use of advanced IT support. Most importantly, the projected 10 percent savings for responsive warehouse management are also still achievable.

7.1.1 Outsourcing

The planning and control instruments for responsive warehouse management require significant investments in software and hardware. Before a company decides to implement these tools, it should consider the alternative option of outsourcing the distribution center to a *third party logistics provider*. The transparency that we created in the previous stage, effective warehouse management, provides valuable information for the bid process. The objectives, processes and performance indicators can be used to clearly explain to the 3PLs what is expected from the operation. Moreover the transparent costs make it possible to benchmark the current operation against the quotations of the 3PLs.

124. **Search for a company that outsourced its distribution center to a third party logistics provider.**
    a. Why did the company outsource its distribution center?
    b. What were the obstacles in the outsourcing process?
    c. How are they performing now?
    d. Was it the right choice to outsource the distribution center?

Outsourcing a distribution center can have several advantages:
- More focus on core business
- Reduced costs
- Lower capital investment
- More flexible capacities.

The third party logistics provider has expertise in designing and managing a distribution center. Consequently, outsourcing relieves the company from a lot of operational issues. This allows the company to focus on its core business.

Moreover, the 3PL has experience with a WMS and can configure it to meet the requirements of a specific operation. They can create economies of scale, by sharing resources among the operations of multiple clients or between different distribution centers. Therefore, despite the fact that they require a profit on their services, 3PLs may be able to run the warehouse operation at a lower overall cost.

Furthermore, fixed capital costs become variable operational costs for the client, for example, upfront investments in the building, equipment, software and hardware are no longer required. Instead the 3PL charges a fee per service transaction.

Finally, if a distribution center experiences strong fluctuations in the workload, then a logistics service provider might be better equipped to accommodate these fluctuations. By combining clients with countercyclical assortments, such as ice creams in the summer and frozen vegetables in the winter, the 3PL is able to accommodate peak demands efficiently.

However, there are also some disadvantages to outsourcing:
- Rates are not necessarily cheaper
- Dependency on third party logistics provider
- Less control over the operation.

The productivity of a logistics service provider is not necessarily higher. If the client has a sizable operation, then the economies of scale may already be optimized. Moreover, it is often the case that 3PLs are reluctant to invest in automated material handling systems. These systems can be highly efficient but they are not flexible to changes in product or demand characteristics. Hence, these investments require a long-term commitment from the client, since the 3PL may not be able to use the devices for other clients.

After outsourcing the distribution center, the client has to rely heavily on the 3PL. If the outsourced operation delivers poor service levels or cannot process the required volumes, then the client cannot simply move to another 3PL on short notice. Starting up a new operation is a complex, labor-intensive and risky operation.

Finally, outsourcing introduces an additional link in the supply chain. Where the collaboration between departments within a company may be complex, the collaboration between the client and the service provider can be even more complicated. Clients are at a distance from the distribution center and cannot see directly into the WMS. Hence, it is essential that the client remains involved in the logistics operation. We often see in practice that clients withdraw from logistics and let the 3PL cope with the consequences of late order communication, poor forecasting, high workload fluctuations and inefficient order profiles. A client with logistics expertise could adequately plan the logistics activities and effectively run the operation jointly with the 3PL. This benefits both the client and the logistics service provider.

Looking at the disadvantages, we see that the success of an outsourced distribution center is not just the responsibility of the 3PL. It requires close collaboration between the client and the 3PL. We further discuss this topic in Chapter 9.

125. Outsourcing a distribution center could have several advantages, but also some disadvantages.
  a. List the advantages and disadvantages.

7.2 Capacity Planning

The workload in the distribution center usually fluctuates. In practically every market, we see daily, weekly, monthly and seasonal patterns. Some fluctuations are predictable from historical behavior, e.g., Monday is always busier than Friday. Others can be explained by external influences, such as sales promotions, the weather, a rich or poor harvest, or special events (e.g., the soccer world championship boosts sales of many products, from drinks and snacks to consumer electronics and sportswear). Finally, there remain fluctuations that are totally unpredictable.

The manager can use an estimate of the workload to determine how many resources are required (people, machines, vehicles and warehouse space). On a daily basis, the quantities of machines, vehicles and space do not change. A medium-term plan should guarantee that sufficient capacity is available. However, the number of operators working in the distribution center can change every day. If the manager tunes the number of operators to match the expected workload, then an excellent utilization rate can be achieved.

Capacity planning is a technique that matches the resource capacity with the expected workload. Typically, capacity planning in distribution centers distinguishes a weekly and a daily horizon. The weekly planning provides a rough estimate of the workload. It helps to plan variables such as days off or maintenance. It can also be used for *workload balancing*, for example, if we expect a busy day on Wednesday, we could start shipping some orders in advance on Monday and Tuesday.

The weekly plan solidifies into a daily plan. The daily plan is established at least one day in advance. By then we have the latest information on the expected workload, which we can use to make a reliable capacity plan. The daily planning is used, for example, to hire temporary staff or to plan overtime for operators.

We may optimize capacity utilization by either adjusting the number of resources to the workload or by tuning the workload to the available resources. We refer to these two techniques as:
- Resource planning
- Workload balancing.

Next, in Section 7.2.1 we scrutinize the capabilities of the systems for capacity planning that are currently available. Then in Sections 7.2.2 and 7.2.3 we discuss how the instruments of resource planning and workload balancing can best be designed.

126. **Since the workload in distribution centers fluctuates, capacity planning is important.**
    a. Explain what capacity planning is.

127. **There are two ways to optimize the capacity utilization in distribution centers.**
    a. Describe each method.
    b. Which techniques are associated with these two methods?

7.2.1 Labor Management Systems

Several WMS vendors offer *labor management systems* (LMSs). An LMS is an add-on module to a WMS for resource planning. The system calculates how much labor time is required to fulfill a given set of orders. The LMS first determines which tasks need to be performed to fulfill the orders. It then considers the actual inventory locations of the products in the distribution center and uses the same putaway and inventory allocation rules as the WMS (see Sections 3.5.2 and 3.7.2) to compute which tasks need to be performed. Subsequently, the system applies engineered labor standards, i.e., detailed standard times for the tasks, to calculate the labor time estimates. As such, the estimates of the workload are highly accurate.

A sophisticated LMS should support the following functions:
- Workload forecasting
- Workload fluctuations during the day
- Operator skills
- Workload balancing.

Workload Forecasting

The systems do not provide a forecast of the workload, instead they assume that all orders are known in advance. This requires that the orders arrive at least one day in advance. However, in many distribution centers the orders arrive on the night before or even during the day that they are shipped. Within such short response times, it is not possible to modify the labor capacity. Accordingly, we need a *forecast* of the workload rather than the actual orders to plan the labor capacity in operations with short response times.

Workload Fluctuations During the Day

Systems should consider fluctuations in the workload *during the day*. If there is a peak workload in the morning, then several part-time operators are required only in the morning. Thus, the systems have to consider the timing of the activities.

Operator Skills

Not every operator is capable of performing all activities. For instance, only a few operators are certified to drive a narrow-aisle truck. In particular, temporary staff usually have had only basic training and as such are limited to straightforward tasks. Therefore it is important to be able to link the *skills* of the available operators to the required activities. The system then has to make a schedule and decide which activities each operator works on during the day.

Workload Balancing

Not all orders need to be performed on the indicated day. By advancing or postponing orders, we may be able to balance the workload. This helps to prevent expensive overtime on busy days or underutilization of resources on quiet days. Hence, the systems should understand which orders *must* be and which can *optionally* be fulfilled on any particular day. We further discuss this topic in Section 7.2.3.

128. A sophisticated LMS should support several critical functions.
   a. Which functions?
   b. Why are these functions important for adequate resource planning?

7.2.2   Resource Planning

Resource planning is a function that calculates the necessary resources for all warehouse processes in a given time period, such as a day or a week. This prevents underutilization, which occurs when there are more operators than necessary. Likewise, it reduces expensive overtime or late orders which may be the case when there are too few members of staff. *Highly Competitive Warehouse Management* introduces a four step procedure for computing the required number of resources for a certain time period:
1. Estimate the expected order volume
2. Convert orders into tasks
3. Compute the required process time
4. Compute the required resources.

Estimate the Expected Order Volume

The first step is to estimate the expected order volume. We may estimate the expected number of inbound, outbound and VAL orders and order lines from actual orders, historical demand patterns, estimates from the source and sell functions or a mix of these. Clearly, which inputs prevail will vary between distribution centers. For example, operations with lengthy response times could use actual orders, while operations with intensive market promotions may have an emphasis on the inputs from the source and sell functions.

If we know all orders well in advance, then these may serve as the input for resource planning (see Section 7.2.1). If this is not the case, a practical approach might be to first determine a *forecast* based on historical data and actual orders, using inventory control techniques (Makridakis *et al.*, 1998). These techniques extrapolate historical order patterns. Subsequently, the source and sell functions can evaluate the calculated forecast and modify it with regard to anticipated orders, special promotions, etc. In particular, we should decide which level of detail is required for the forecast. Generally it is not necessary to forecast each individual product, but rather to determine an estimate per relevant product group and order type.

Convert Orders into Tasks

The second step is to convert the orders into tasks. If we receive the exact orders upfront, then we know precisely which products and quantities need to be processed. If, however, we base the capacity plan on a calculated forecast per product group, then we must derive the necessary tasks from historical data. The WMS records which tasks were performed to fulfill the orders in the past. We may derive how often the various tasks were performed on average to fulfill an order line in the product group. We may use these parameters to compute the number of tasks to be performed.

> **Example: Calculating the Number of Tasks**
> We expect 200 purchase order lines and 3,000 sales order lines for a day. From the historical analysis, we determined the number of tasks per order line as shown in the center column of Table 7.1. If we multiply these parameters by the number of order lines, then we find the resulting number of tasks as shown in the right hand column of Table 7.1.

Table 7.1 Computation of the number of tasks.

Task type	Order lines	Tasks / order line	Tasks
Receipt	200	2.40	480
Putaway	200	2.85	570
Replenishment	3,000	0.11	330
Case pick	3,000	1.03	3,090
Pallet pick	3,000	0.08	240
Pack	3,000	1.24	3,720
Ship	3,000	0.25	750

Compute the Required Process Time

The third step is to compute the required process time. For each type of task we determined a standard time in Section 5.3.6. If we multiply the calculated number of tasks by these standard times, then we obtain the total process time.

> **Example: Calculating the Total Process Time**
> Table 7.2 shows the total process times for the tasks in the previous example. This is calculated as number of tasks x standard time. Hence, we estimate the total process time for the 200 purchase order lines and the 3,000 sales order lines at 158 hours and 15 minutes.

Table 7.2 Computation of process times.

Task type	Tasks	Standard time (sec.)	Process time (hrs)
Receipt	480	80	10:40:00
Putaway	570	180	28:30:00
Replenishment	330	120	11:00:00
Case pick	3,090	30	25:45:00
Pallet pick	240	180	12:00:00
Pack	3,720	60	62:00:00
Ship	750	40	8:20:00
Total			158:15:00

Compute the Required Resources

The final step is to compute the resources required to perform the tasks. We find the number of resources by dividing the calculated process times by the capacity per resource (see *example* below).

> **Example: Required Resources**
>
> We continue with the previous example and assume that a (full-time) operator can effectively work 6 hours per day. The center column in Table 7.3 shows that we need 26.4 operators to fulfill the orders. However, there are certain other factors that we must consider. One assumption is that the 26.4 operators switch between the various tasks. This may not always be possible. Operators have certain skills. Not everyone is capable of driving a forklift truck or has the authority to receive incoming goods. If operators only work on dedicated tasks, then the required number of operators would rise to 29 as can be seen in the right hand column of Table 7.3, a 10 percent increase. This illustrates the importance of *job rotation* or cross-training.
>
> Apart from the operators, we can also compute the required number of machines or vehicles. If we use forklift trucks only for putaways, replenishments and pallet picks, then we can calculate from the center column of Table 7.3 that we need 8.6 (=4.8+1.8+2.0) forklift trucks.
>
> Furthermore, we have to consider when activities take place. For example, we have two separate shifts and we plan to perform the receipts, putaways and replenishments in the morning shift (6 AM-3 PM) and the other activities in the afternoon shift (3 PM-12 AM). Then we can compute from the center column of Table 7.3 that we need 8.4 operators in the morning shift and 18.0 operators in the afternoon shift. Some operations might even see fluctuations during the shifts due to the arrival and departure schedules of the trucks.

Table 7.3 Estimated number of operators.

Task type	Process time (hrs)	Operators	Dedicated Operators
Receipt	10:40:00	1.8	2.0
Putaway	28:30:00	4.8	5.0
Replenishment	11:00:00	1.8	2.0
Case pick	25:45:00	4.3	5.0
Pallet pick	12:00:00	2.0	2.0
Pack	62:00:00	10.3	11.0
Ship	8:20:00	1.4	2.0
Total	158:15:00	26.4	29.0

RESPONSIVE WAREHOUSE MANAGEMENT

CASE STUDY

129. Foodies' warehouse supervisor wants to compute the required number of operators for a day with the four step procedure on page 210.
   a. Note that he estimated the expected number of order lines in the first column of Table 7.4 (step 1).
   b. Compute the expected number of tasks per task type and specify your answers in the third column of Table 7.4 (step 2).
   c. Compute the required process time per task type and specify your answers in the fifth column of Table 7.4 (step 3).
   d. Every operator can work effectively for six hours per day. Compute the required number of operators per task type and specify your answers in the sixth column of Table 7.4 (step 4).
   e. How many operators are required in total?

Table 7.4 Required resources for Foodies.

Task type	Order lines	Tasks / order line	Tasks	Standard time (sec.)	Process time (hrs)	Operators
Receipt	25	7.4	___	60	___	___
Putaway	25	9.85	___	180	___	___
Replenishment	1,500	0.23	___	120	___	___
Case pick	1,500	0.73	___	40	___	___
Pallet pick	1,500	0.52	___	180	___	___
VAL	70	22.24	___	60	___	___
Pack	1,500	0.85	___	30	___	___
Ship	1,500	0.12	___	40	___	___
Total						

7.2.3 Workload Balancing

In the previous section we estimated the workload for the distribution center and calculated the required number of operators. However, this number may change dramatically between days and even during the same day. In this section we investigate whether we can balance these fluctuations by shifting the workload between periods. In busy periods some orders can be postponed, thereby reducing the need for expensive overtime and temporary staff. In quiet periods we advance a number of orders to prevent underutilization of resources.

The inbound process of a distribution center is initiated by the arrival of a truck, while the outbound and VAL processes are initiated by the warehouse planner (see Section 3.7). Hence, the distribution center may influence the workload of the latter processes through its own planning. Workload manipulation in the inbound process mostly requires the participation of external parties, such as the source function, suppliers and haulers (transportation companies).

In Section 9.3 we will discuss how better collaboration between parties in the supply chain may smooth the fluctuations. In this section, we examine the initiatives which the distribution center may take by itself to balance the workload.

Balancing the Inbound Process

In the order acceptance process, the source function and the supplier agree on a time frame for the delivery of an order, such as the following Wednesday. Subsequently, the transportation planning function and the hauler plan the trips and thereby further refine the time frames (Wednesday between 2 PM and 4 PM). Consequently, order acceptance and transportation planning determine when the inbound trucks arrive at the distribution center. Often these decisions are taken without considering the impact on warehouse capacities.

Dock planning is an excellent technique for incorporating these capacity restrictions in the overall planning. Dock planning assigns time slots to incoming trucks. The distribution center guarantees that a dock will be available during the time slot. This avoids waiting times for the truck drivers as long as they arrive on time. The advantage for the distribution center is that the workload of the inbound process is known in advance and spread smoothly across the day.

We can distinguish *fixed routes* and *variable routes* for the incoming trucks. A fixed route implies that the truck always arrives on the same day at the same time. Variable routes are planned based on actual delivery requirements, and as such the arrival times of trucks may vary. For fixed routes we could renegotiate the delivery days and time slots with the suppliers/haulers in cases where the workload is not spread evenly, as demonstrated by the following *case study*.

> **Case Study: Smoothing Inbound Fluctuations**
> A wholesale distribution center primarily used the morning hours for receiving and putaway and the afternoon hours for picking and shipping. The distribution center opened at 8.30 AM, but few trucks arrived this early. The bulk of the trucks came between 10 AM and 11 AM. Thus, before that time there was little work, while the putaways for the later arrivals could not be completed by 2 PM. At that time the order-picking would start. Hence, the putaways interfered with the order-picking, which caused considerable congestion.
>
> Subsequently, the warehouse manager had a meeting with the inventory control department and explained the issue. The inventory manager made a single phone call to a large supplier to ask whether several of his trucks could deliver earlier. This was not a problem for the supplier, and thus the peak in inbound trucks was effectively smoothed.

For variable routes it is necessary to determine a time slot for each individual arrival. Some WMS vendors offer *dock and yard management* modules that help the warehouse planner to plan the arrivals and departures of the trucks in advance as well as their stay at the yard. Several of these systems allow suppliers and carriers to access the plans via the internet. They can view online when the docks are available and make a reservation for a time slot.

Even with dock and yard management, there may still be fluctuations during the day. The distribution center could further manipulate the workload by increasing or decreasing the number of available docks at certain periods. For example, if many trucks arrive in the morning and few in the afternoon, then the distribution center could open all docks in the morning and only a few docks in the afternoon. This smoothes any sudden arrival peaks in the afternoon, so that the receipt process can be handled in the afternoon by a smaller crew with a steady workload.

130. A dock and yard management module could balance the inbound flow.
a. Explain which functions of the module help to smooth the inbound flow.

Balancing the Outbound Process

The outbound processes (including any VAL processes) are planned by the warehouse planner. Clearly, the plan has to satisfy existing agreements with clients and customers regarding response times. Nevertheless, there may be some opportunities for balancing the workload by distinguishing between activities which *must* be performed and others which *can* be performed over a certain time period. The latter activities may be used for workload balancing.

In Section 7.2.2 we calculated the workload and the required number of operators. This number might be considerably higher or lower than the regularly available workforce. In such cases, the warehouse planner may consider advancing or postponing orders. Advancing orders might mean that those orders are actually shipped earlier or that they are staged in advance and shipped on a subsequent day. The latter requires that there is enough space available in the staging area. Before shifting the orders, the planner should have a rough estimate of the workload in the forthcoming week. This estimate may be determined from historical patterns and existing orders.

Postponing orders, where the expected workload is still high on subsequent days, is not a good idea (Figure 7.3). Neither is it desirable for orders to be advanced when there is little work expected on subsequent days (Figure 7.4). In these circumstances it is preferable to adjust the number of operators, rather than shifting the workload. Figure 7.3 shows a scenario where the workforce should be increased, while in Figure 7.4 we seek to decrease the workforce.

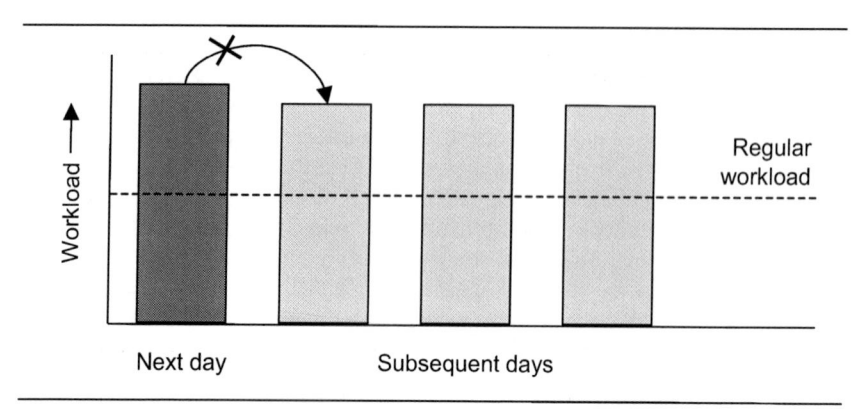

Figure 7.3 Increase the workforce in a busy period.

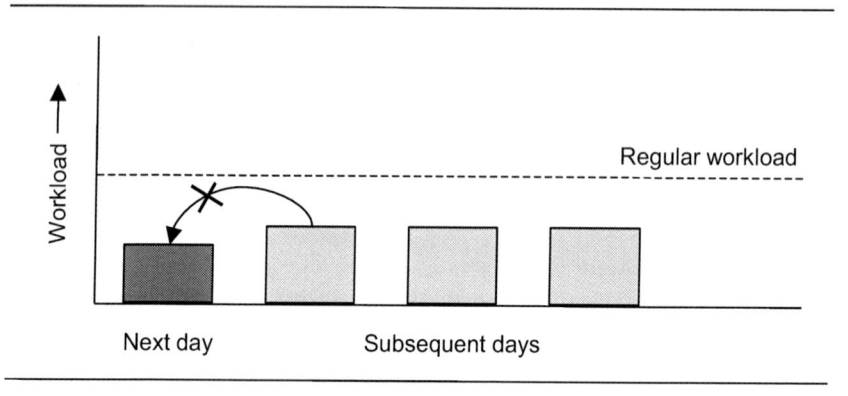

Figure 7.4 Decrease the workforce in a quiet period.

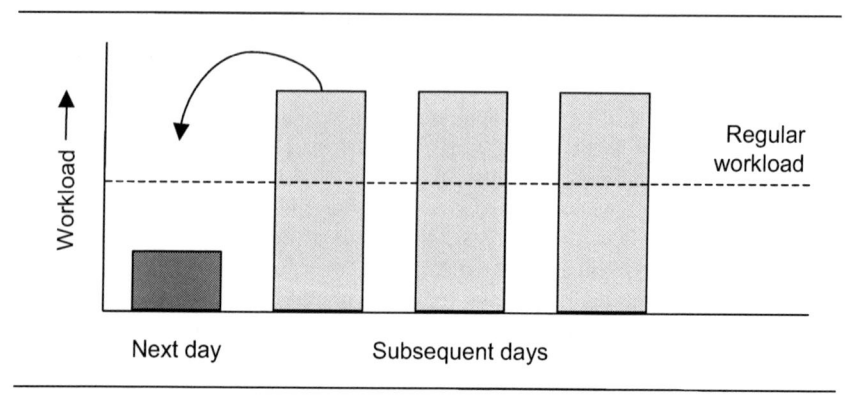

Figure 7.5 Advance orders on a quiet day.

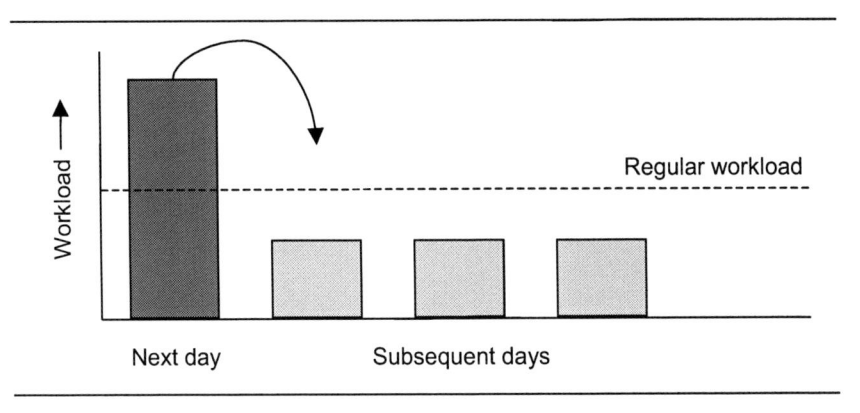

Figure 7.6 Postpone orders on a busy day.

Where the overall workload fluctuates, it should be balanced by shifting orders between days. Figure 7.5 illustrates a situation where the next day seems quiet, although there is a considerable workload for the subsequent days. In this situation orders should be advanced. Figure 7.6 shows the opposite situation where a high workload is anticipated on the next day, while the subsequent days seem quiet. Here, orders should be postponed.

Furthermore, we can consider the costs associated with the workforce required for the various volumes. Figure 7.7 shows three workload levels:
- The level that can be fulfilled by the regular staff.
- The level that can be fulfilled by the regular staff with the aid of temporary staff.
- The level that can be achieved by the regular and temporary staff with maximum overtime.

Temporary staff usually have relatively low productivity due to their limited training and experience. Consequently, their output is more costly. Overtime can be even more expensive, since hourly labor rates may increase by 50 to 100 percent.

Hence, when balancing the workload, we should attempt to avoid the need for temporary staff or overtime. The example in Figure 7.7 shows a situation where the next day requires overtime, while the subsequent days only need additional temporary staff to complete the work. In that situation, we may avoid overtime by balancing the workload at a level below the combined workforce capacity of regular and temporary staff. In other situations, we could try to avoid the need for temporary staff by balancing the workload below the level of the regular workforce. If the workload exceeds the maximum overtime level, then the distribution center cannot possibly fulfill the orders in time. In fact, this should be captured in the service level agreements as being the maximum workload in the *flexibility range* (see Section 5.1.2).

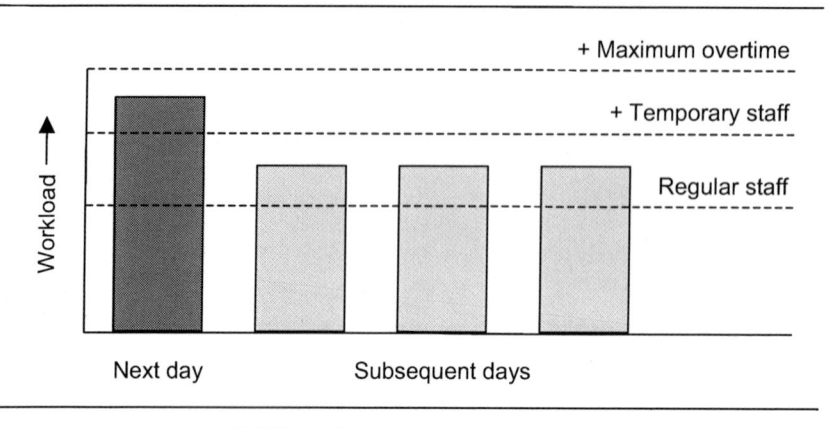

Figure 7.7 Workload vs. workforce capacities.

131. An increase in the workload may be anticipated by hiring temporary staff or working overtime.
    a. Why should one attempt to avoid the need for temporary staff or overtime?

7.3 Wave Management

Once the orders have been accepted and transportation has been planned, it is time for the distribution center to plan and execute its internal activities within the time constraints set by the earlier processes. When managing the workload, there is a difference between inbound and outbound goods flow. The inbound goods flow begins automatically after an inbound truck arrives. The outbound goods flow does not start automatically. Instead it is driven by the warehouse planner, who decides which orders are released for picking (*wave planning*). He also monitors the progress of the inbound and outbound activities in the distribution center (*wave monitoring*).

7.3.1 Wave Planning (Outbound)

In Section 3.7 we talked about *wave planning*. It is the process where *waves* are formed from (outbound) orders with similar deadlines. The WMS generates tasks for replenishing, picking and shipping the orders.

Wave planning is usually performed manually by a warehouse planner, who manages the workload. If the warehouse planner releases many orders, then this increases the efficiency of the distribution center since the WMS has more opportunities to combine tasks for *batch-picking* and *dual-command cycles*. As a rule of thumb, a workload of 2 to 4 hours achieves satisfactory efficiency (see

Section 3.7.1). If the workload is more than that, then modern WMSs may have trouble setting priorities. For example, systems may assign low priority tasks before urgent tasks.

7.3.2   Wave Monitoring (Inbound and Outbound)

The warehouse planner monitors the progress of the tasks relative to their deadline. If progress in certain activities lags behind the plan and deadlines become critical, then the planner can decide to shift operators between activities.

Unfortunately, many WMSs still have only basic screens for monitoring. These show the number of open orders and lack indications of the workload or deadlines, let alone graphical representations.

A *wave monitoring screen*, such as the sample in Figure 7.8, gives a graphical representation of the workload and deadlines. The workload shown, is based on the *standard times* of the activities. Furthermore, the screens allow the warehouse planner to shift operators between activities without leaving his office.

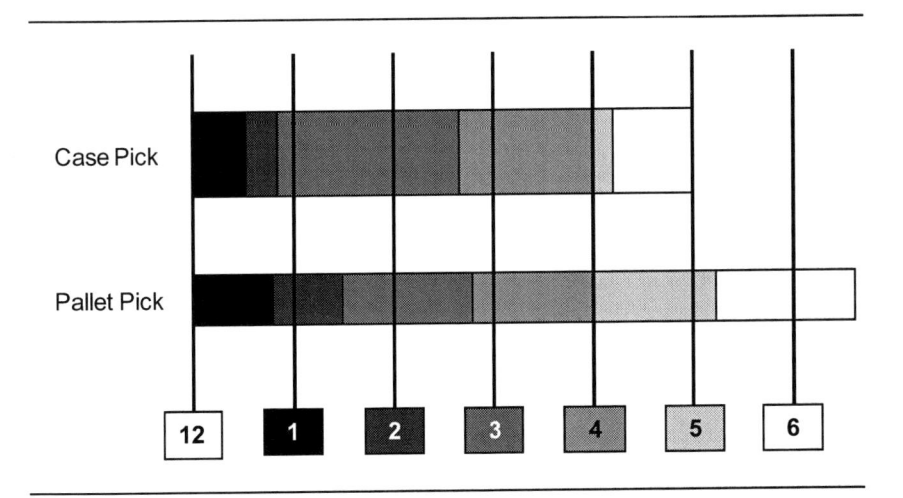

Figure 7.8 Wave monitoring screen.

Figure 7.8 shows an example of an operation with two activities, *case picking* and *pallet picking*. In practice, more than two activities will typically be monitored on the screen (including the inbound processes). On the horizontal axis we see the remaining hours of the day divided into *time buckets* of one hour. On the vertical axis we see the activities. The figure portrays the situation at 12 noon. The screen shows the workload of the released orders in the horizontal bars. The workload for the two activities is computed according to the *standard times* defined for the various tasks. The different shades indicate the time buckets with specific deadlines. For instance, the tasks that need to be completed before 1 PM are black, 2 PM are dark gray, etc. The height of the bars represents the number of operators. Clearly, if more operators work on an activity, then it will be completed sooner.

If we examine the situation in Figure 7.8, then we see that the operation encounters a problem with those tasks that need to be completed by 5 PM and 6 PM. According to the capacity calculations, pallet picking will be late. At the same time, we see that the operators in the case picking area run out of work after 4 PM. Hence, the warehouse planner may decide to shift some operators from case picking to pallet picking at 4 PM (assuming that there are sufficient forklift trucks). Figure 7.9 shows the resulting schedule with all activities completed on time.

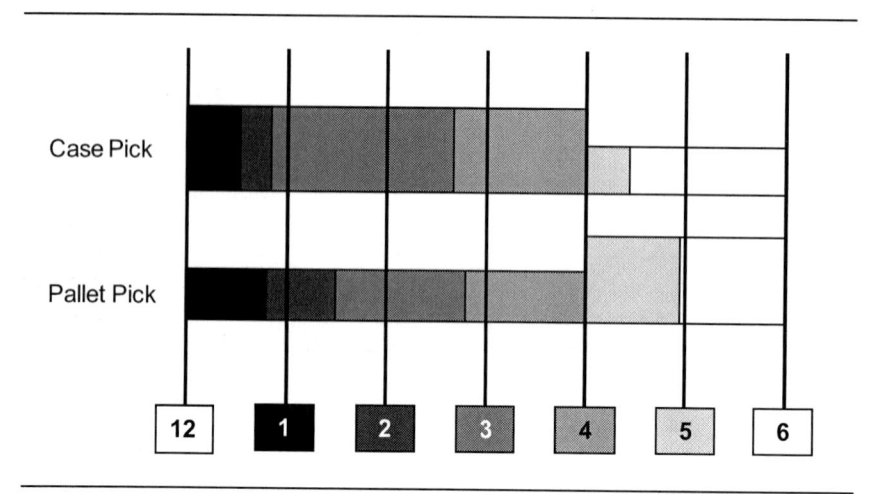

Figure 7.9 Operators transferred from case picking to pallet picking.

7.4 Task Management

In the previous section we discussed *wave management*, where waves were released, tasks determined and operators allocated to activities. In this section we discuss *task management*. A WMS with *real-time communication* (see Section 4.2) can assign tasks directly to operators. In contrast, if the operators read their tasks from paper lists, then the WMS must assign the tasks well in advance and cannot optimize during the execution (*batch communication*). Task management primarily applies to operations with real-time communication, i.e., the operators communicate with the WMS via RF terminals, voice terminals or pick-to-light.

Similar to *capacity planning* and *wave management*, the intelligence in most modern WMSs for *task management* is limited. In this section we describe sophisticated routines for real-time management of the operation.

7.4.1 Constraints

As argued in Section 3.7.3, we distinguish between *simple tasks* and *compound tasks*. A simple task is a pallet move such as a putaway, a replenishment, a pallet relocation or a pallet pick. A compound task is, for example, a pick tour. The WMS assigns tasks to operators one by one in real-time. This applies both to simple tasks and compound tasks.

The WMS needs to comply with various *constraints* when assigning tasks to operators. For instance, tasks can only be assigned to an operator for the activity to which he has been allocated by the warehouse planner (see Section 7.3.2). Shifting operators between activities is an element of *wave management*, not task management.

Moreover, it must be physically possible for the operator to perform the task, e.g., the WMS cannot assign an operator using a forklift truck with a maximum height of 20 feet to pick a pallet from a location at a height of 30 feet.

Similarly, if many operators work in a small zone, then this may lead to a considerable efficiency drop, due to the increased waiting times caused by congestion. This can be prevented by setting a constraint on the number of operators in a zone. Once the upper limit has been reached, no more tasks for this zone can be assigned to operators outside the zone. A well-known example applies to *narrow-aisle trucks*. If a truck is in an aisle, no further operators are allowed in this aisle. This not only prevents congestion, it also improves safety since the narrow-aisle truck driver has a limited view of his surroundings. Of course, there can be many more constraints. Constraints usually are obvious, but they need to be configured in the WMS in order for it to work effectively.

132. We discussed wave management and task management.
  a. How does wave management affect task management?
  b. How does task management affect wave management?

7.4.2 Objectives

The WMS optimizes task assignment within the given constraints. Each time an operator completes a task, the WMS assigns a new one, either a simple task or a compound task. If it assigns a compound task, then the order-picker has to complete the entire tour before the WMS assigns the next task. With simple tasks, for example pallet moves, the WMS continuously assigns new tasks. *Highly Competitive Warehouse Management* stresses that task management should make a trade-off between two objectives: *efficiency* and *urgency*.

Efficiency

If the WMS assigns a task to an operator that is close to his current position, then it minimizes the empty travel (*interleaving*) distance between the tasks. Since the loaded travel distance and the handling time cannot be influenced by the task sequence, minimizing empty travel optimizes overall *efficiency*.

In distribution centers, we often see that a forklift driver performs only putaways, only replenishments or only pallet picks. After completing a task, the driver returns empty to go to the next task. These tours are generally known as *single-command cycles*, with approximately 50 percent empty travel time. If the forklift truck combines a putaway task and a pallet pick task, then it is referred to as a *dual-command cycle*. It is also possible to include one or multiple replenishments into the cycle.

In a typical operation, dual-command cycles reduce *travel* time by approximately 30 percent compared to single-command cycles (Graves et al., 1977). If we consider that the travel time represents approximately 50 percent of the total labor time of the forklift driver, then dual-command cycles generate a labor reduction of approximately 15 percent.

133. Foodies has separate forklift drivers for putaways, replenishments and for pallet picking.
   a. What happens if the forklift drivers transform their activities into dual-command cycles?
   b. How much travel time could be saved compared to single-command cycles?

Urgency

In addition to travel distances, the WMS also has to consider the urgency of tasks. Examples of urgent tasks are a pallet pick for a truck that is scheduled to depart soon or a replenishment to a pick location where an order-picker is waiting for stock. By considering the urgency of tasks, the WMS prevents waiting times in the process or late departures of trucks. Inbound activities may also be urgent. If we define maximum *dock-to-stock times* for inbound handling (see Section 5.4.2), then these deadlines determine whether receipt and putaway tasks are urgent.

Urgency is not only caused by deadlines that need to be met. It may also be due to critical *bottlenecks*. These bottlenecks typically occur in the staging areas behind the docks and the *pick/drop (P/D) locations* (see Section 3.5.2) at the end of the aisles. If these locations are occupied, then this may disrupt the goods flow. In such situations, the tasks required to move goods from these locations become urgent even though their deadlines may still be remote.

Some WMSs are able to relate the urgency of tasks directly to deadlines, other WMSs represent the urgency by a *priority* number. The priority may be fixed, e.g., a replenishment task is always more urgent than a pick task, or the initial priority may automatically increase over the course of time. In any case, we believe that priorities should relate to deadlines rather than start times. Hence, users should be creative and attempt to configure priority numbers in the WMS so that they are linked to deadlines.

RESPONSIVE WAREHOUSE MANAGEMENT 223

> **Example: Congestion of Pick/Drop locations**
> The P/D location at the end of an aisle may hold four pallets. As long as there are no more than three pallets, there is no congestion. However, if there are four pallets, then it becomes impossible to deliver more pallets to the location. Thus the WMS may increase the urgency of tasks that move pallets from the P/D location. This translates congestion into an 'urgency' objective.

CASE STUDY

134. Foodies' warehouse supervisor identified the following elements that might affect the urgency of tasks:
   - The space in the staging area behind the receiving docks is limited.
   - Frozen goods need to be putaway quickly to a storage location in the frozen food section.
   - All pallet moves are direct, i.e., there are no P/D locations.
   - Outbound trucks depart according to a fixed transportation plan.

   a. Explain which elements affect the urgency of tasks.
   b. How could the urgency be configured in the WMS?

> **Example: Increasing Priorities**
> Figure 7.10 gives an example of a WMS that automatically increases the priority of tasks without considering deadlines. At 8 AM, a pick task and a replenishment task are released for a truck that departs by 11 AM. Subsequently, at 10 AM an additional pick task is released for the same departure. Since the initial priority of pick tasks is fixed, the added pick task still has a low priority by the time the truck is scheduled to depart. This example illustrates that the priority of tasks should not be based on the time of release, but rather on the anticipated deadline.
>
> Figure 7.11 shows the priorities when they are driven by deadlines. The initial priorities have been increased compared to Figure 7.10, so that the tasks attain a high priority prior to the scheduled departure time. Moreover, the added pick task receives the same priority as the original pick task since they both have the same deadline.

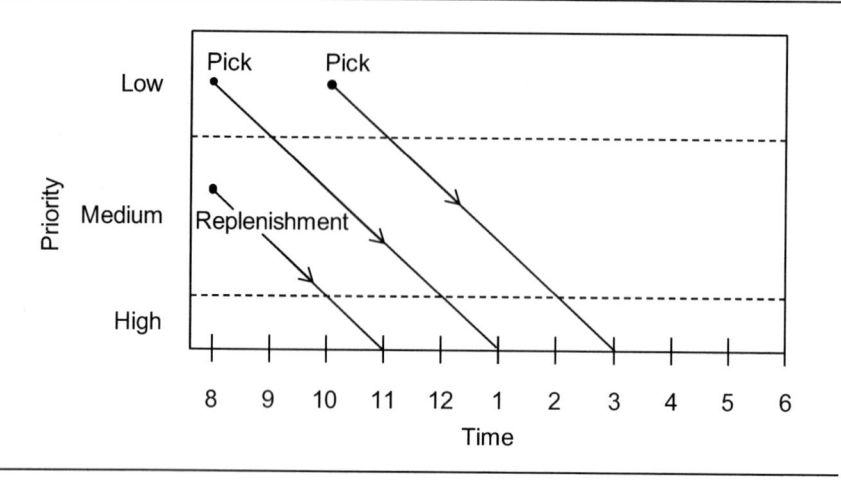

Figure 7.10 Automatically increasing task priorities.

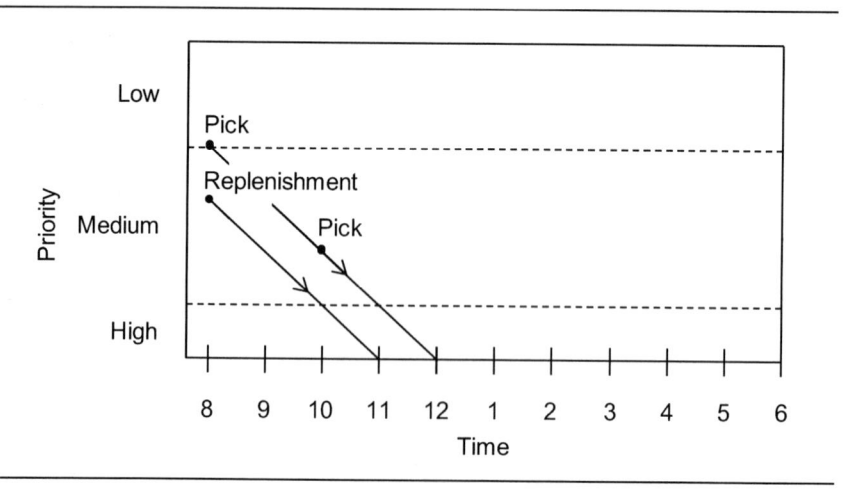

Figure 7.11 Priorities driven by deadlines.

Example: Output Station of AS/RS

A distribution center used a multi-aisle *automated storage/ retrieval system* (AS/RS). The pallets left the AS/RS via an accumulation conveyor which was able to hold 15 pallets. However, it was often full, which hindered throughput. One option considered was to extend the conveyor. However, it was concluded that this would only take extra space and the conveyor could still become full. Instead the WMS rules were changed so that the pallets were removed from the conveyor more quickly.

7.4.3 Optimizing Two Objectives

The WMS considers the current situation when assigning a new task to an operator or machine. What is his/its present position and how urgent are the various open tasks? The following *example* shows that it is necessary to make a trade-off between the urgency and efficiency objectives. A focus on one objective only may turn out to be counterproductive.

> **Example: Efficiency vs. Urgency**
> A third party logistics provider had a distribution center where forklift trucks replenished the pick locations while the order-pickers were picking (*reactive replenishments*, see Section 3.8.1). The order-pickers regularly arrived at a pick location before the replenishment was completed. They then found insufficient product for their order. Since the client of the 3PL insisted on a specific stacking sequence of the products, the order-pickers could not continue with the next pick, but had to wait for the replenishment instead.
>
> When an order-picker arrived at a location with insufficient inventory, the WMS called a forklift driver to come and perform the replenishment, irrespective of his location. Since the forklift driver first had to complete his present task and because the forklift truck drove slowly outside the aisle, the order-picker sometimes had to wait up to twenty minutes.
>
> How did this happen? For general tasks, the control rules of the WMS always assigned the closest task to the forklift driver (*nearest neighbor rule*), thereby minimizing the *interleaving* travel time. However, when always selecting the closest tasks, it may be that some tasks, such as the replenishment task for the order-picker mentioned earlier, are not dealt with for a considerable period of time. Eventually, the task becomes critical and an emergency replenishment is required. This is highly inefficient. Hence, the operation may gain 2 percent efficiency by minimizing the empty travel times, but at the same time it loses 10 percent due to emergency replenishments. In such a situation, efficiency and urgency are poorly balanced.

7.4.4 Control Rules

How do WMSs make the trade-off between efficiency and urgency? In fact, many systems do not consider these competing requirements. These systems simply sequence the tasks based on either urgency or proximity. This may be acceptable for some operations, but is highly inefficient for others.

Other WMSs use a sophisticated, yet highly ineffective method. These systems assign *scores* for travel distance and urgency to the tasks and compute the weighted sum of these scores. Subsequently, the WMS selects the task with the highest overall score. Calculating a weighted sum means that the system appraises the travel distance of one task against the urgency of another task. This is a complicated trade-off which makes it difficult to configure the parameters in these WMSs so that they take the right decisions. A better approach is to use a *hierarchical control rule* as explained by the following *example*.

> **Example: Hierarchical Control Rule**
> Figure 7.12 shows a top view of the warehouse floor. The forklift driver has just completed a task. Now there are six pallet moves that he could perform next, represented by the black pointers. Alongside the pointers are the deadlines for the tasks. In the previous example we saw that a control rule (*nearest neighbor rule*) that continuously selects the closest task, i.e., task *e* in Figure 7.12, can be counterproductive since it might skip urgent tasks. Another option could be to continuously select the most urgent task (*earliest deadline rule*), i.e., task *a*. However, this might considerably increase the interleaving travel distances as shown in the diagram.
>
> We suggest the following alternative control rule. We first divide the distribution center into zones, represented by the gridlines. A zone can be multiple aisles, one aisle or even a segment of an aisle. When the forklift driver completes a task, the WMS searches for the most urgent task within the zone where the forklift is situated, i.e., task *d*. The forklift driver picks up the pallet and delivers it to its destination. Subsequently, the WMS again selects the next task *within the zone where the forklift driver dropped the pallet*. Consequently, the urgent tasks are not endlessly skipped while the empty travel distances remain acceptable. This control rule is *hierarchical* because it considers the two objectives successively rather than simultaneously. It first considers the travel distance objective (available tasks *within the zone*) and then the urgency objective (*most urgent* task in zone). As a final tie-breaker, if there are multiple tasks in the zone with the highest urgency, then select the closest.

The *example* introduces an alternative control rule that makes a hierarchical trade-off between urgency and efficiency. The rule is intuitive and easy to explain. Unfortunately, there are few WMSs that support this control rule. Where this functionality is available, the warehouse area should be divided into zones and configured accordingly. For a narrow-aisle truck a zone could be a single aisle. Since aisle changes take a lot of time for a narrow-aisle truck, we prefer that the next task is found within the same aisle. For forklift trucks a zone could extend multiple aisles, which further minimizes the number of *emergency tasks*.

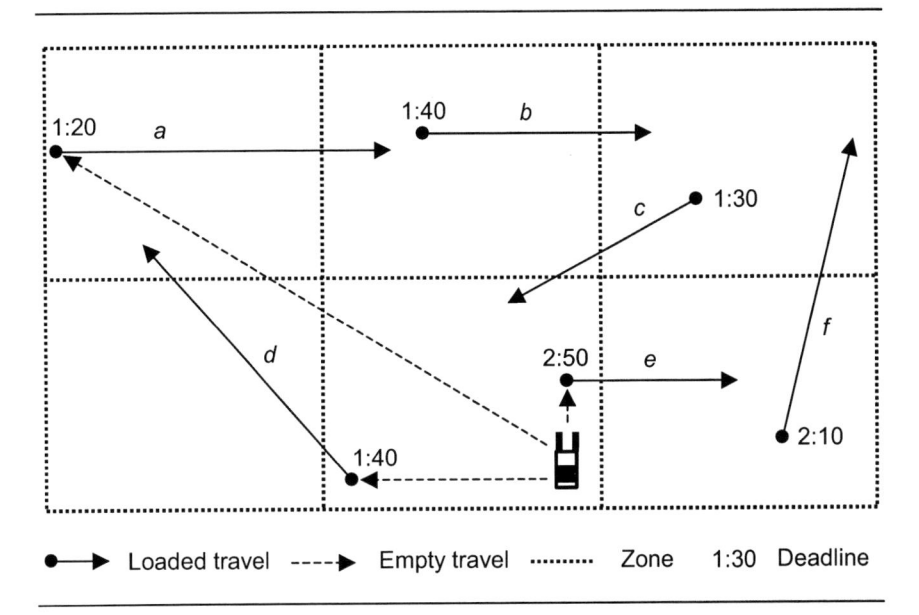

Figure 7.12 Hierarchical task assignment rules.

The control rule works well when the pallet moves bring the operators to different zones. If they remain in one zone, then the tasks in other zones may be ignored by operators even though they are urgent. In the next section we incorporate the control rule in an integral framework to overcome this problem.

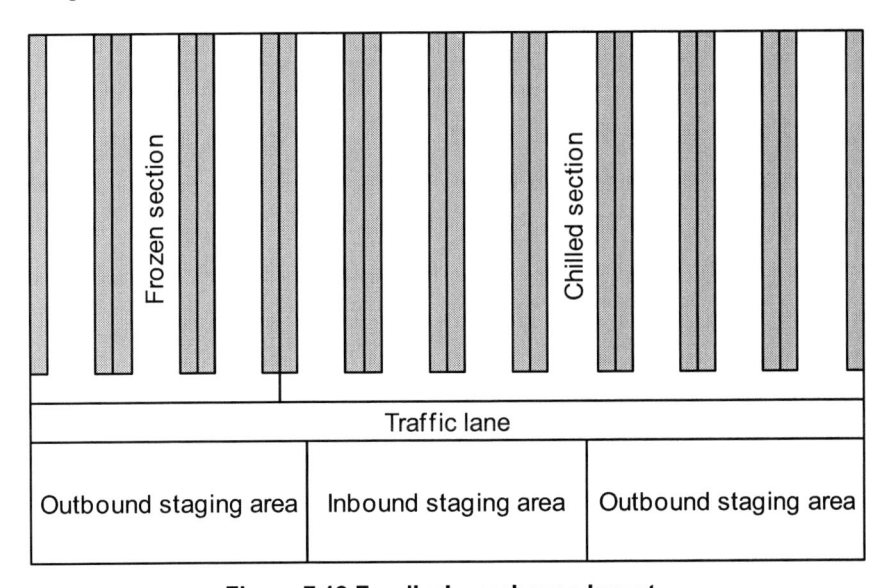

Figure 7.13 Foodies' warehouse layout.

135. **Foodies wants to develop sophisticated control rules for assigning pallet moves to forklift drivers.**
   a. Consider Foodies' warehouse layout in Figure 7.13. It contains separate inbound and outbound staging areas. There are three aisles on the left-hand side in the frozen section; the remaining aisles are in the chilled section.
   b. Define zones in Figure 7.13 that could be used in a hierarchical control rule.
   c. Define hierarchical control rules for assigning pallet moves to forklift drivers that consider both efficiency and urgency.

7.4.5 Integral Control Framework

The hierarchical control rule defined in the previous section can be highly effective, but it needs to be amended to operate well in extreme circumstances. These extremes are:
- Tasks reach a high urgency
- All tasks have low urgency.

With the hierarchical control rule, tasks may become *highly urgent* when forklift drivers do not visit a particular zone for a while. Clearly, this occurs less often with the hierarchical rule than with the *nearest neighbor rule*. Nevertheless, we need a safety net. A highly urgent task should be assigned to a forklift driver as soon as possible despite the additional travel distance. We arrange this by augmenting the control rule with a *threshold level*. If the urgency of a task surpasses the threshold level, then it may also be assigned to forklift drivers outside the zone. The forklift driver will have to travel a considerable distance which is inefficient, but this is acceptable as long as it occurs only as an exception.

Another extreme is when all tasks have low urgency. For example, it is 9 AM and the warehouse operators are working on trips that depart at 6 PM and 7 PM. In this situation, the WMS could disregard the urgencies and purely focus on efficiency, i.e., minimize the empty travel distances.

Table 7.5 illustrates how the above considerations can be combined in an integral control framework. The WMS should distinguish three statuses. If all tasks that could be assigned to the operator have a low urgency, then the WMS selects the nearest task thereby optimizing the *efficiency*. If there are tasks available for the operator that have a medium urgency, then the WMS selects the most urgent task within the zone. Finally, if there are tasks available with a high urgency, then the WMS assigns the most urgent task which disregards the travel distances but makes sure that the tasks are completed on time. This rule achieves efficient travel sequences and at the same time prevents emergency tasks. If we want to configure this in the WMS, the system should distinguish two thresholds: one between low and medium urgency and one between medium and high urgency, e.g., high urgency is less than 30 minutes before the deadline and medium urgency is less than 4 hours before the deadline.

Table 7.5 Rules in integral control framework.

Urgency	Rule
Low	Nearest task
Medium	Most urgent task in zone
High	Most urgent task

136. **Consider the hierarchical control rules that you designed for Foodies in the previous question.**
    a. Amend the control rules so that they also operate well in the following circumstances.
        i. Tasks reach a high urgency
        ii. All tasks have low urgency

Although these control rules have proven to be highly effective in practice (Van den Berg, 2002), few WMSs support them. We suggest that users encourage their WMS vendors to include these rules in their system. Until then, users could attempt to translate the philosophy explained in this section as well as possible into the functions available in the WMS.

137. **Consider the control rules for assigning tasks to operators in your own WMS.**
    a. How do they compare to the integral control framework in Table 7.5?

7.5 Summary

The warehouse management cycle is a closed-loop framework for the planning and control of a distribution center. It integrates strategic objectives with tactical planning and operational control and execution. The execution data is transformed into management information and fed back to the operational, tactical and strategic levels.

We have introduced several planning and control rules that are not generally supported by modern warehouse management systems. Yet they are easy to understand and highly effective. Managers who want to apply these functions should either ask their software vendors to integrate the functions in the WMS or consider developing custom-built software to support these functions.

Chapter 8

Resource Utilization

Responsive warehouse management is the third stage of the maturity grid (Figure 8.1). The objective of this stage is to achieve desired service levels and reduce overall costs by another 10 percent through better utilization of available resources. In Chapter 7 we introduced innovative planning and control rules to achieve this goal.

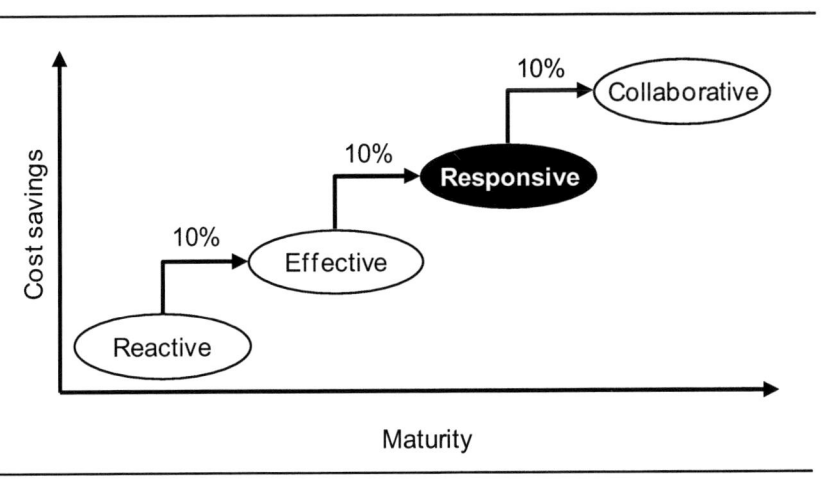

Figure 8.1 Responsive warehouse management in the maturity grid.

In this chapter we discuss examples that illustrate how intelligent planning and control may achieve cost reductions as well as increase service levels. In addition to IT systems, organizational changes are also necessary. These changes may include cross-training of the warehouse operators, flexible contracts with permanent members of staff and reliable arrangements with employment agencies for temporary staff. The examples in this chapter can be applied to many different operations, but not necessarily to every distribution center. However, we hope to inspire managers to consider the examples presented and to develop ways to implement similar ideas in their own operations.

8.1 Utilization Improvement

The *warehouse management cycle*, introduced in Chapter 7, provides a powerful framework for optimizing the deployment of resources using advanced IT support. Operators are usually the most prominent and expensive resources in the distribution center. Therefore, we first analyze operator utilization.

Figure 8.2 illustrates an example of operator capacity utilization throughout the day. The horizontal axis represents time and the vertical axis shows the available capacity. We see that total capacity is fixed. The gray segment represents the time that operators are *active*. The white segment represents the time that there is work for the operators but they are unable to do it (*idle* time). Finally, the black segment represents the *excess* capacity. This spare capacity is not needed for processing the day's workload.

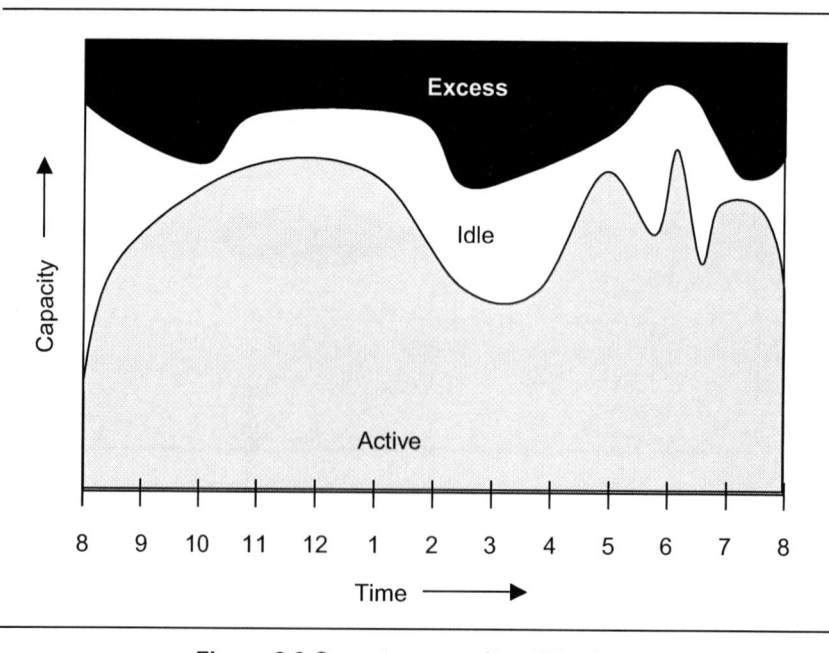

Figure 8.2 Operator capacity utilization.

Excess capacity may be due to an improper estimate of the workload or an inflexible workforce. We may *cut* excess capacity through better capacity planning.

The *idle capacity* could be due to operational bottlenecks or to the fact that operators are authorized to work on a few activities only. Hence, we may *activate* the operators by resolving the bottlenecks and deploying the operators in a multifunctional manner.

Finally, the *active capacity* cannot be reduced, since we assume that the operators perform the activities in an efficient way. This we established in the previous phase, effective warehouse management. However, it might be that activities are performed too early, thereby compromising the timely completion of other tasks or increasing the capacity requirements. By *postponing* activities these negative effects may be resolved. We therefore distinguish three actions for improving resource utilization. These are shown in Figure 8.3.

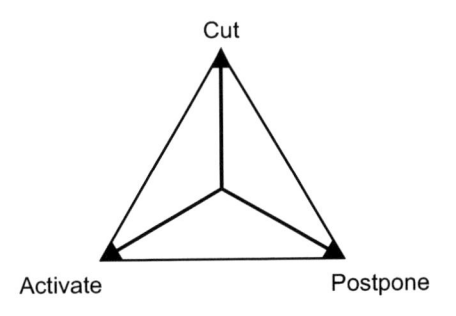

Figure 8.3 Optimization actions for responsive warehouse management.

138. Cut, activate and postpone are three actions for improving resource utilization.
    a. Explain the three actions in relation to the concepts of active, idle and excess capacity.

8.2 Cut

The first action in responsive warehouse management is to *cut* excess capacity. In Section 7.2 we explained how capacity planning can compute the required capacity in advance and balance the workload between days. The former option tunes the number of operators to the workload, while the latter adjusts the workload to the number of operators. In fact, we could apply the two approaches simultaneously to further tune the resources to the workload. Thus, we distinguish the following two options:
- Flexible capacity deployment
- Workload balancing.

Flexible Capacity Deployment

If we want to respond effectively to fluctuations in the workload, then we need a flexible workforce. For instance, we can set up flexible contracts with permanent members of staff. On busy days, the operators work some extra time, while on quiet days they leave early or stay home entirely.

Engaging temporary staff is also a popular way to manage busy days. However, this requires that the employment agency is able to deliver employees on short notice. In a distribution center, it is difficult to predict far in advance how many workers will be required. Typically, the distribution center contacts the employment agency in the afternoon to say how many people are needed for the next day. Consequently, the distribution center needs reliable arrangements with the employment agency. They have to provide qualified operators who are committed to work regularly in the distribution center. Many distribution centers deliberately operate with substantial excess capacity among their permanent staff, since they cannot rely on temporary staff being available at the right time.

Furthermore, the temporary operators should be well trained. Untrained operators have low productivity and may require essential training from the warehouse's existing staff, which results in both operators being temporarily unproductive. Nevertheless, good quality training material must be developed to expedite the training process.

139. A flexible workforce helps to respond to workload fluctuations.
   a. *Which advantages and disadvantages of temporary staff do you experience in your own distribution center?*

It is important to analyze the fluctuations in the workload. If it fluctuates heavily, then we may prefer a small dedicated workforce complemented with a large flexible crew. Conversely, if fluctuations are limited, then a relatively large

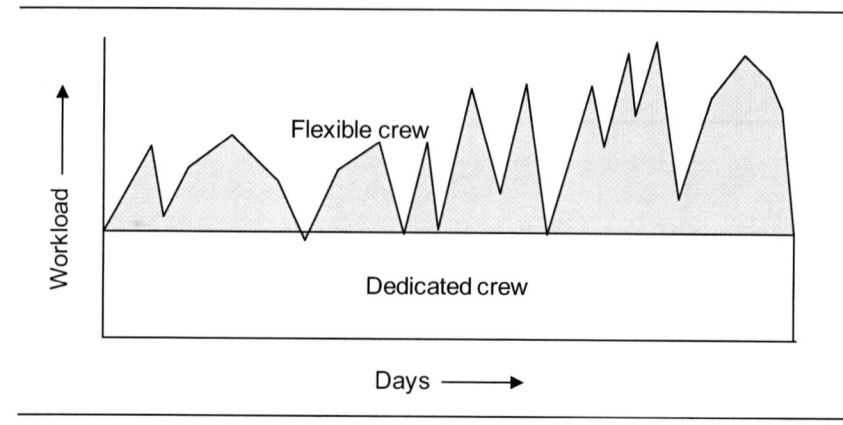

Figure 8.4 Dedicated vs. flexible workforce.

dedicated crew might be the best option. Figure 8.4 shows an example of workload fluctuations over a number of days. In this example, the distribution center should try to establish a dedicated workforce for the basic workload and arrange a flexible workforce for the additional resource demands.

Another angle for examining the composition of the workforce is to look at the *age mix*. Young people tend to earn lower wages and might have better stamina. Older people earn higher salaries, are more experienced and may be better suited to responsible tasks. It is advisable to seek a balanced age mix. We may not be able to modify the age mix on short notice. However, if the workforce consists primarily of older people, then we should realize that competitors may have lower salary costs. Conversely, with mainly young staff the distribution center may turn out to be less reliable.

140. Analyze the workload fluctuations in your distribution center.
   a. Based on your analysis, what do you think of the size of the flexible workforce relative to the dedicated workforce?
   b. What do you think of the age mix of the warehouse staff?
   c. How could you cut excess capacity in your distribution center?

Workload Balancing in the Distribution Center

As discussed in Section 7.2.3, it may be useful to see whether the workload can be balanced when calculating the required capacity. The distribution center could distinguish orders that must be shipped and orders that can be shipped. Subsequently, while the *must-ship orders* are processed during the day, the *can-ship orders* are processed whenever there is sufficient capacity. Depending on the productivity of the operators, a greater or lesser number of the optional tasks are completed.

8.3 Activate

The second optimization action is to activate idle resources. Idle time arises when operators do not perform tasks even though there is work to be done. We emphasize that an operator who works slowly loses for instance 5 to 10 percent productivity, while an operator who stops working loses 100 percent productivity. Thus we should be highly conscious of idle time. Some common causes of idle time follow.

Absenteeism

Obviously, operators who report in sick are inactive. A good policy towards fighting absenteeism can be an effective tool. Such a policy promotes safety and ergonomics, it improves operator morale and actively monitors sick operators. With proper measures, absenteeism in a distribution center should be no more than 4 to 6 percent on average.

Starting and Ending

In addition to a lunch break, most operators are granted fifteen minute breaks in the morning and afternoon. Without monitoring, they might linger in the break room which adds to the idle time. We see a similar effect at the end of a shift. With only fifteen minutes remaining, operators are reluctant to commence work on a new order. Perhaps it is possible to pick the order halfway and continue the next day, thereby avoiding the time loss.

Organizational Silos

Operators may also be idle due to organizational silos. For instance, an operator is assigned to receiving. When all receipts have been completed, he has no work to do and waits for another truck to arrive. However, if he were also allowed to work on other activities, such as loading or order-picking, then he could move on to those activities.

The multifunctional deployment of operators requires that they are trained to perform various activities. This strategy allows operators to perform non-urgent activities once they become idle. This could be, for example, a VAL operation where products are assembled to stock. It is the responsibility of the warehouse planner to transfer operators between activities with the *wave monitoring* function in the WMS, see Section 7.3.2.

In some situations it is mandatory that an operator remains present at a workstation, e.g., at an inspection or packing station. However, the operator is only active when there are goods to be processed. It may be possible to tune the *task management* rules in the WMS, so that the workload of the workstation is balanced over the day. An alternative may be to eliminate these dedicated activities. For instance, rearranging the processes so that the forklift driver who picks up the pallet performs the inspection instead of a dedicated operator. Naturally, it takes the forklift driver more time to inspect the pallet than it would take the dedicated operator. However, we save a considerable amount of idle time, which outweighs these inefficiencies. Another alternative is to have non-urgent work available for the operator at the workstation, as discussed above.

Workload Fluctuations

Idle time may also occur due to workload fluctuations during the day. For example, if the order-picking activity is concentrated within a short time period in the afternoon, then the WMS could release *advance replenishments* in the morning for all products that are below a threshold level. This is an alternative use of *proactive replenishments* (see Section 3.8.1).

Bottlenecks

Task management can also reduce idle time. We saw in Section 7.4.1 and 7.4.2 that it can effectively reduce congestion and bottlenecks and thereby prevent idle times.

GET IT

141. There are various options for reducing idle time.
   a. List several options for reducing idle time.

EXPLORE IT

142. Consider your own distribution center.
   a. Which measures to reduce idle time do you use?

8.4 Postpone

The third action in responsive warehouse management is to *postpone* activities. In the previous two sections we have *cut* excess capacity and *activated* the idle time of operators and resources. Hence, available capacities are used actively and efficiently. The remaining question is whether the capacities are used for the right activities at the right time. To this end, *Highly Competitive Warehouse Management* stresses that activities should be completed just in time to prevent the following effects:
- Poor space utilization, because the goods wait considerable times at staging locations.
- Late completion of urgent activities due to the fact that operators complete less urgent activities first.
- Increased capacity requirements, since operators perform activities that could wait until later.

Figure 8.5 gives an example of the workload for the combined activities in a typical distribution center. On the horizontal axis we see the hours of the day. Currently it is 12 noon and the horizontal bar shows the workload for the entire distribution center. The workload is computed according to the *standard times* defined for the various tasks. We distinguish *one-hour time buckets* with a workload that needs to be completed before the deadline. The segments

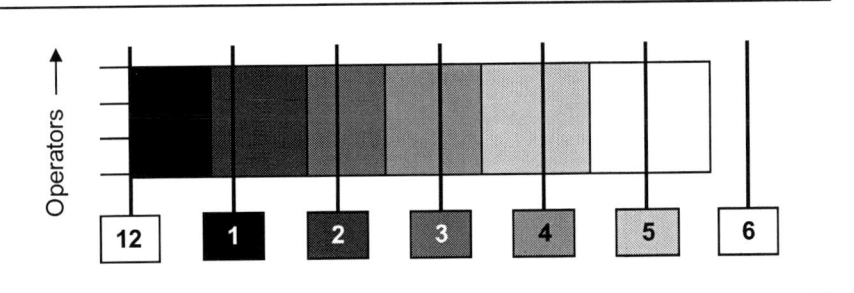

Figure 8.5 Workload by deadline.

correspond with the deadlines: tasks that need to be completed before 1 PM are in the black segment, before 2 PM in the dark gray segment, etc. The height of the horizontal bar represents the number of operators.

We see in Figure 8.5 that all activities are expected to be completed well before their deadline. Moreover, there is some excess capacity remaining at the end of the day. This capacity could be used to work ahead. However, we could also reduce the number of operators and still complete the activities in time, as shown in Figure 8.6.

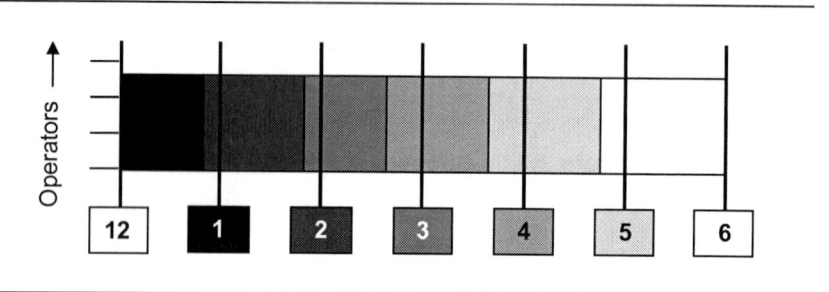

Figure 8.6 Complete the activities with fewer operators.

We see in Figure 8.6 that the activities with a deadline at 6 PM will be completed just in time. All other activities will be completed some time before the anticipated deadlines. We could postpone these activities if the available capacity in the distribution center were completely flexible (Figure 8.7). In practice, part-time workers can create some variation in capacity, but the uneven pattern in Figure 8.7 is unrealistic. In fact, the schedules for part-time workers could be the outcome of this analysis.

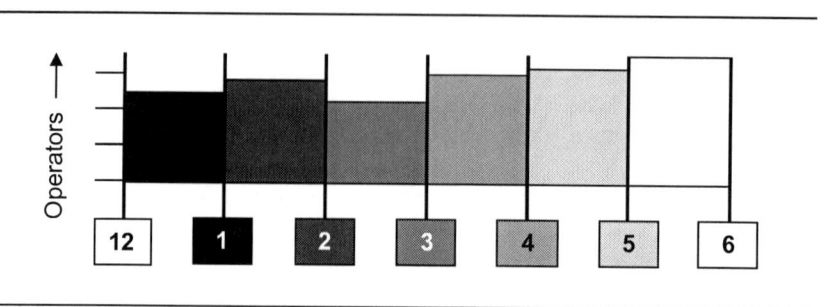

Figure 8.7 Workload planning with flexible capacity.

For now, we shall assume that the number of available warehouse operators during the day is fixed and that their capacity is well-tuned to the workload. Notice in Figure 8.6 that between 12 PM and 1 PM, the warehouse operators have to complete the activities in the black segment with a deadline of 1 PM but also some activities in the dark gray segment which need to be completed by 2 PM. However, operators may be able to perform these activities simultaneously, as shown in Figure 8.8. This could benefit the efficiency of the warehouse operation, since the combined workloads provide better opportunities for time-saving activities such as *batch-picking* and *dual-command cycles*.

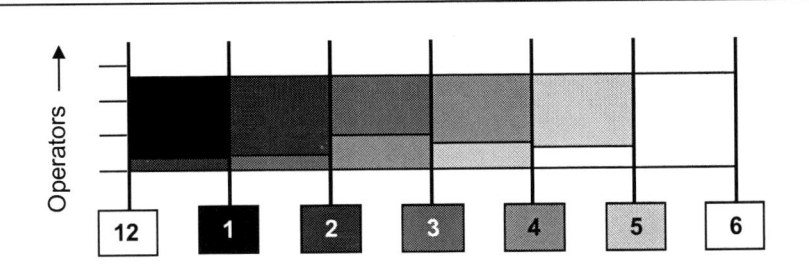

Figure 8.8 Simultaneous activities.

> **Remark: Earliest Starting Time**
> Few WMSs provide the planning function described in this section. However, there are several systems that can compute the *latest starting time* for an activity so that it still can be completed in time. Considering the previous discussion, this information is not helpful to the management of the operation. Instead of the latest starting time, we would like to know the *earliest starting time*. How soon can we commence an activity while still ensuring existing activities meet their deadlines?

143. Warehouse activities should preferably be completed just in time.
   a. What can happen when activities are not completed just in time?

8.5 Space Utilization

In the previous stage, effective warehouse management, we attempted to reduce space requirements by storing goods more compactly. In this stage, responsive warehouse management, we attempt to expedite the goods flow so that we require the storage space for a shorter period of time, and can thereby use it more often. This applies particularly to warehouse space that may become a bottleneck in the goods flow, such as docks and pick/drop (P/D) locations. Consequently, expediting the goods flow may relieve bottlenecks and reduce space requirements. The following *case study* illustrates how intelligent task management rules can accelerate the goods flow.

> **Case Study: Bottleneck in the Docking Area**
> A food manufacturer had a central distribution center which shipped goods to retailers and wholesalers. The distribution center had an old-fashioned WMS that printed the pick tasks on paper slips. This made it difficult to split the activities among order-pickers. Consequently, one or two operators had to pick the goods for an entire truckload, which included both pallet picking and case picking. This could take three or four hours to complete and the shipping dock was occupied the entire time. The distribution center had eighteen docks for loading and unloading. Due to the long cycle times at the docks, the dock capacity became a critical bottleneck.
>
> The lack of dock capacity made it impossible to increase the throughput of the distribution center. Raising the number of operators in the distribution center would not help due to the bottleneck. Consequently, management decided to extend their hours of operation to three shifts – 24 hours per day – five days per week. The nightshift received a 50 percent salary supplement, which dramatically increased labor costs.
>
> Eventually, a new WMS with intelligent task management rules effectively solved the bottleneck. Instead of one or two operators, all operators could work simultaneously on a shipment, thereby completing it within a shorter time-span. Consequently, it was no longer necessary to start the shipments well in advance. Instead they were assembled *just in time*. The shorter cycle times at the docks eliminated the bottleneck, so that more operators could work simultaneously in the distribution center. This increased the throughput capacity of the distribution center which made the nightshift unnecessary.

The *case study* not only illustrates how space can be utilized more effectively. It also shows how task management can be a helpful tool for dividing the work among operators. By assigning more operators to a single shipment, it is possible to start the activity later while retaining the same end time. Thus, tasks can effectively be *postponed* (see Section 8.4).

8.6 Summary

Responsive warehouse management proposes a systematic procedure that uses intelligent planning and control policies and flexible capacities to optimize resource utilization. The model distinguishes three possible actions: *cut*, *activate* and *postpone*. The first action matches the number of operators to the workload, the second action reduces the idle time of resources and the third action postpones activities, so that they are performed just in time. The model improves space utilization in the distribution center by expediting the flow of goods. This particularly applies to warehouse space that may become a bottleneck in the goods flow, such as docks and pick/drop (P/D) locations.

Chapter 9

Collaborative Warehouse Management

Collaborative warehouse management is the fourth and final stage in the maturity grid (Figure 9.1). In the previous stages of *Highly Competitive Warehouse Management*, we established a well-organized warehouse operation. Through effective processes and responsive capacity deployment, the distribution center provides reliable services at competitive prices. Now we turn our attention to optimization in the wider supply chain. This is the ultimate objective of collaborative warehouse management.

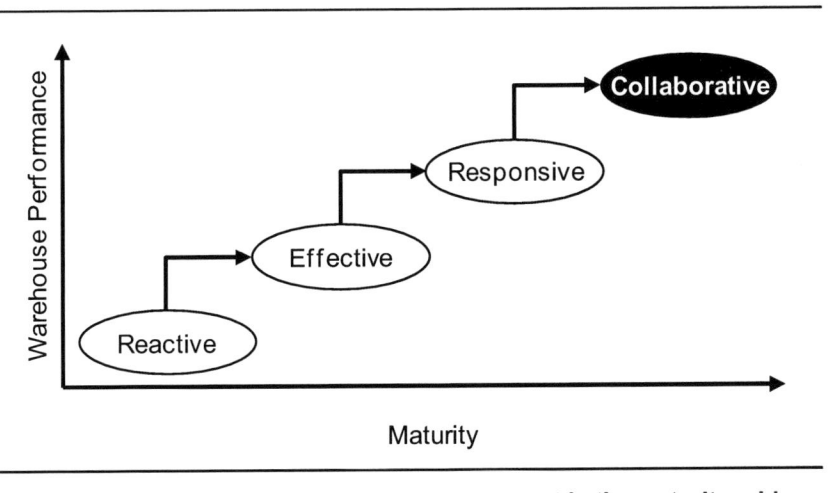

Figure 9.1 Collaborative warehouse management in the maturity grid.

Supply chain management advocates close *collaboration* between members of the supply chain. However, the distribution center has a noteworthy position in the supply chain due to the fact that it is highly dependent on the decisions made by others. In fact, the source, sell and transportation planning functions together with suppliers and customers determine which services the distribution center has to provide and when, not the distribution center itself. They would like it if the distribution center provided instant response times, an unlimited capability to accommodate demand fluctuations and the ability to handle all order specifications. In fact, in the previous stages, effective and responsive warehouse management, we have made significant advances to accommodate small order sizes, varieties and customizations in a cost-effective manner. Nevertheless, these fierce demands may have dramatic cost impacts and they need be treated cautiously.

Consequently, we have to look at the *big picture*. On the one hand, the internal functions and external parties should be aware of their impact on warehousing costs and capacities. On the other hand, the distribution center must devise cost-effective services with reliable service levels. If the activities of all internal and external players are properly aligned, then competitive services may be achieved against low overall costs. This will positively impact company performance and customer satisfaction.

By definition, collaboration involves multiple parties. Preferably, we find optimizations that provide better service and lower costs for all parties in the supply chain. Such optimizations will encounter little opposition. However, it may occur that some parties benefit from an optimization while others see their cost levels go up. Nevertheless, the supply chain as a whole might benefit and a financial arrangement could be designed. Another option is that cost reductions for some parties lead to a service decline for other parties. In that situation, we should ask ourselves whether the original service level was worth the extra cost.

Hence, the question arises as to exactly which services the distribution center should provide. In this chapter we attempt to align the services of the distribution center to the supply chain by redesigning:
- The warehouse services
- The service fee structure
- The collaboration between departments and companies
- The supply chain structure.

We present the following tools to accomplish these redesigns, respectively:
- Discontinuities
- Activity-based pricing
- Synchronized planning
- Virtual warehousing.

144. Collaboration involves multiple parties.
a. List the internal and external parties in Foodies' supply chain.

9.1 Discontinuities

Decisions by various parties in the supply chain affect the activities in the distribution center. Some decisions have a minor impact, while others may have a dramatic effect. A *discontinuity* occurs when a party outside of the distribution center makes a decision that has a minor effect outside of the distribution center, but a disproportionately large effect on warehouse costs. Highly competitive warehouse management aims to find discontinuities and correct them. Typically, we look at discontinuities where at least a 50 percent saving in the associated warehousing costs is possible. Changes that result in lower savings in the distribution center can easily raise costs elsewhere and eliminate overall savings.

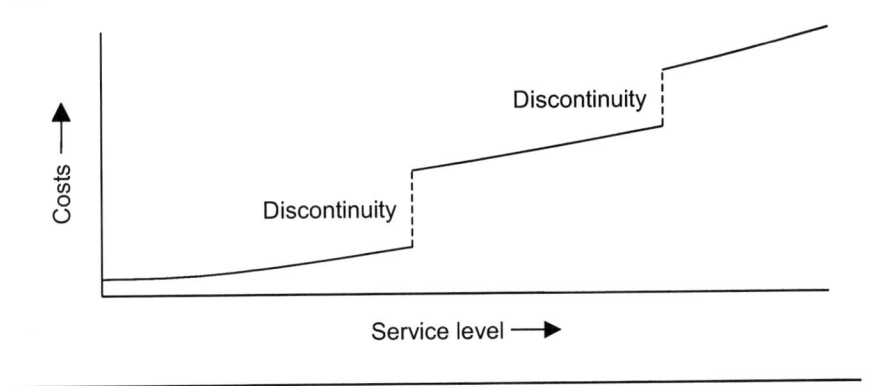

Figure 9.2 Discontinuities in services.

Example: Order Size Discontinuities

Order sizes and order frequencies have a significant impact on warehousing costs. Figure 9.3 illustrates this effect. The graph shows the results of an activity-based costing analysis applied to a single product. The product is packed with twenty pieces per case and twenty cases per pallet. The graph compares the warehousing costs per 400 delivered pieces for various order quantities. For instance, the customer could order 400 pieces by placing one order for 400 pieces, two orders for 200 pieces, up to 400 orders for 1 piece or any number in between.

The saw-tooth pattern in Figure 9.3 is caused by the cost drop when the order quantity is a multiple of a *full case*. The final drop at the right of the graph relates to the order quantity equal to a *full pallet*. If we look at the cost model behind Figure 9.3, then we see that shipping a full pallet is up to 80 times less expensive than shipping the same amount in less-than-case quantities. Note that these costs exclude the transportation costs, which would further magnify the cost differences.

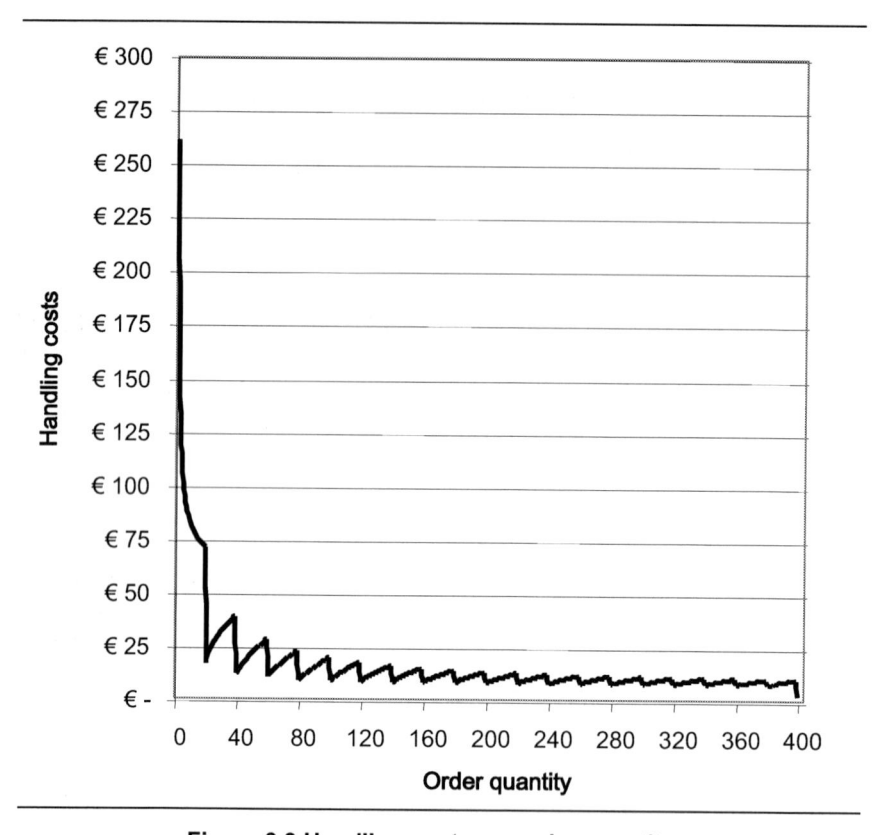

Figure 9.3 Handling costs vs. order quantity.

With this example we want to illustrate that order sizes and frequencies can have a dramatic impact on warehousing costs. If we compare discontinuities to the optimizations that we encountered in the previous stages of *Highly Competitive Warehouse Management,* then we see that their cost effects are more substantial. In this section, we consider the impact of discontinuities in three key areas:
- Order profile
- Volume
- Response time.

If corrected, each of the situations described could lead to substantial savings in the distribution center as well as the overall supply chain.

145. **Order sizes and frequencies can have a dramatic impact on warehousing costs.**
    a. Explain what a discontinuity is.
    b. Which types of discontinuities can be distinguished?

9.1.1 Order Profile Discontinuities

The first type of discontinuity concerns order profiles. The order profile defines what the distribution center has to do to fulfill the order, e.g., the number of order lines, quantities per order line, packaging instructions or special handling requirements (fragile, temperature-controlled, hazardous, etc.). It is obvious that we may find discontinuities in the order profiles. Below we give some examples.

Order Frequency

Order frequency has a significant impact on logistics costs. Each time the customer places an order, it brings about the following activities:
- The order is processed in the administrative systems. If the orders are processed automatically, then these costs are no longer substantial.
- An order-picker has to visit the pick location each time that the customer orders a product.
- A truck has to deliver the product. The number of stops has a substantial impact on transportation costs.

Hence, the costs can be reduced considerably by decreasing the order frequency, i.e., by ordering more different products at the same time and/or ordering larger quantities. Clearly, ordering larger quantities increases the customer's inventory levels. Moreover, if a company delays its orders to accumulate larger quantities, then the response times also increase. However, it is important to make the trade-off between the inventory costs and the costs for transportation and warehouse handling.

Order Line Quantities

We saw in Figure 9.3 that order line quantities have a dramatic impact on warehouse costs. Shipping *full pallets* and *full cases* is relatively much cheaper than shipping less-than-pallet and less-than-case quantities.

In addition to full pallets and full cases, we also view *full pallet layers* as efficient order quantities. Full pallet layer quantities simplify the order-picking process, since it is easier for the order-picker to stack the goods and build a stable pallet. Moreover, we avoid air being added when cases of different sizes are stacked together onto a pallet. This improves the fill rate of the trucks.

The above are efficient handling units inside the distribution center. Likewise a *full truckload* (FTL) is an efficient quantity in transportation. Hence, if possible, orders should be rounded to FTLs.

Packaging

Customers may require specific packaging types for their products, such as different pallet or crate types. This could imply that the goods need to be repacked or restacked in the distribution center. Furthermore, the different crate sizes for different customers lead to poor economies of scale. Also the fill rate of trucks might be affected due to the different sizes that may not always combine well.

Compliance

The cheapest supplier is not necessarily the best choice. If a supplier is unreliable with frequent errors in deliveries and untimely arrivals, then this requires substantially more effort in the distribution center for receiving the goods.

A supplier who provides detailed information on a shipment can further contribute to the efficiency of the receipt process in the distribution center. For instance, if the supplier sends details on the contents of pallets in electronic format, then a simple scan might suffice to register the receipt of a pallet (see Section 3.5.1). This is a significant time saving compared to the regular process where products need to be identified, counted and registered separately. A reliable supplier reduces the time needed for problem solving. It may also be possible to reduce the number of checks required upon receiving, with highly reliable suppliers receiving only occasional random checks on their deliveries.

146. There are various kinds of order profile discontinuities.
   a. *Name four order profile discontinuities.*
   b. *Give an example of each with regard to Foodies' distribution center.*

9.1.2 Volume Discontinuities

The second discontinuity type relates to order and inventory volumes. Fluctuations in volumes require flexibility. However, excessive flexibility may lead to considerable cost levels.

Throughput Volumes

The distribution center is designed to accommodate a certain daily throughput volume. If the order volumes are outside this range, then it may have serious implications for warehouse productivity. On the one hand, if the order volumes exceed the design capacity, then the distribution center requires substantial operator overtime or temporary staff to get the work done in time. Overtime is expensive, since labor rates may increase significantly. Temporary staff usually has relatively low productivity due to the time spent on training and the fact that they are learning by doing. On the other hand, if the order volume is below the design capacity, then this easily leads to underutilization of staff and resources and hence to low productivity as well.

Fluctuations may be incidental or they may be caused by the company itself, due to a marketing campaign or other activity. Some fluctuations are periodic. Think of weekly or monthly patterns, such as a peak volume on Monday or at the end of each month. Throughout the year we may see seasonal highs and lows. Some sectors, e.g., toys, gifts or consumer electronics, realize 50 percent of their sales or more in the last two months of the year.

Fluctuations can also occur during the day. If it is quiet in the morning and busy in the afternoon, then this easily leads to underutilization in the morning and to delays in the afternoon. Moreover, if many trucks arrive at the same time, then this could cause a shortage of receipt docks which dramatically increases waiting times for the truck drivers.

Time Frames

The sell function implicitly or explicitly agrees with the customer on a delivery time for an order. This can be a specific week, a specific day or even a specific hour. The narrower the time frames for the deliveries, the more difficult it is to balance the volume fluctuations in the distribution center as well as in transportation. By leveling the workload between days, we can achieve a steady workload throughout the week. This has a major advantage, since it is much easier to forecast the workload per week than per day. Hence, wide time frames loosen volume discontinuities, while narrow time frames make volume discontinuities tighter. Also balancing the workload within a day can bring substantial benefits. An obvious solution to anticipate peak workloads during a day is to work ahead of schedule as much as possible. However, this requires that orders are known well in advance and that there is sufficient space available to stage the already picked goods.

It might not be possible to arrange wide time frames for all orders. Orders may be urgent or may have to be delivered on a specific date or time. However, if we examine the entire order set, then we might find some subsets with less strict delivery times. Typical examples are a service parts distribution center that differentiates between urgent repair orders and less urgent stock replenishment orders or a retail distribution center that distinguishes between the (less punctual) initial push of a new product to the stores and the subsequent (punctual) store replenishments.

Finally, we emphasize that a wide time frame does not necessarily mean that customers must experience unpredictable response times. It may be that first a relatively wide time frame is arranged upon order acceptance and after the planning cycle a narrower time frame is communicated to the customer. For instance, first the sell function agrees with the customer to deliver next week and later the company informs the customer that it will actually deliver the goods on Wednesday between 2 PM and 4 PM.

Inventory Volumes

Holding inventories is expensive. Think of warehousing costs, interest on the capital employed and the capital loss due to obsolete, expired, damaged or stolen goods. In particular slow and non-moving goods incur relatively high costs. Furthermore, if inventory levels rise to near the maximum storage capacity of the distribution center, then its efficiency might drop severely. We start seeing this effect when more than 85 to 90 percent of the storage locations are occupied. Above 94 percent occupancy, the effect becomes dramatic. Products suddenly need to be stored away from the preferred storage location, e.g., a fast moving product is stored at the back end of the distribution center or a pallet is stored in a bulk location that is far away from the pick location. Clearly, such actions lead to considerably larger travel times for order-picking and for replenishing the pick locations.

Conversely, if the inventory is low and a limited percentage of the storage locations are occupied, then the fixed costs for the building and equipment make the warehouse operation relatively expensive, producing a discontinuity.

147. Consider the inventory and workload fluctuations in your distribution center.
   a. What is your experience with volume discontinuities?
   b. What is their effect on warehousing costs?

9.1.3 Response Time Discontinuities

The third discontinuity type concerns response times. Short response times help to reduce inventory levels and out-of-stocks. It is thus a key challenge for the distribution center to accelerate the inbound and outbound processes. However, short response times also make it increasingly difficult to ship all orders on time, which might harm customer service levels. Moreover, short response times could significantly increase the complexity of the distribution center and thereby its costs. Once again, we have to make a trade-off between the services and costs involved. Below we discuss some common areas for discontinuities in response times.

Planning and Execution Cycle

A short response time makes it hard for the distribution center to anticipate volume fluctuations. For workforce planning, we need a good estimate of the workload at least one day in advance, when we may still have time to hire additional staff or to rearrange the work schedules of the warehouse staff (and truck drivers). We can make a highly reliable workload estimate, if we know all orders at that time. Otherwise, we have to guess the workload and include a safety margin for unexpected peaks. This might increase the costs considerably. Consequently, there is a *discontinuity* when the response time for orders is shorter than the cycle time for planning the workforce.

Figure 9.4 shows the response time for a distribution center, which is defined as the time span between the latest order-entry time and the latest departure time. We see that the response time is sufficiently long to accommodate workforce capacity planning based on the actual orders, transportation planning and order-picking activities. If the response time was any shorter, then we could not use the

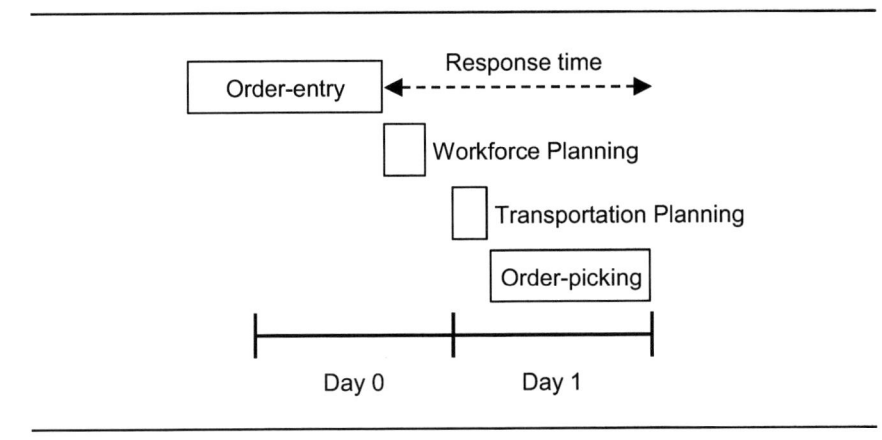

Figure 9.4 Response time accommodates workforce planning time.

actual order set as the input and we would have to plan the workforce capacity against a forecasted workload.

We encounter a second *discontinuity* when the response time affects the cycle time for transportation planning. In Figure 9.5, the response time has not quite encroached upon the transportation planning time, thus we still have time to plan the truck routes before we have to start order-picking. If the response time becomes any shorter (Figure 9.6), then the order-pickers must pick the orders without knowing for which truck route the goods are destined. This implies that the order-pickers cannot deposit the goods directly at the shipping dock, but instead they have to leave them at a *staging area*. Only after the truck routes are known, can the operators sort the goods from the staging area to the correct shipping dock. This requires extra handling of the goods, which is substantially more expensive, making it a discontinuity.

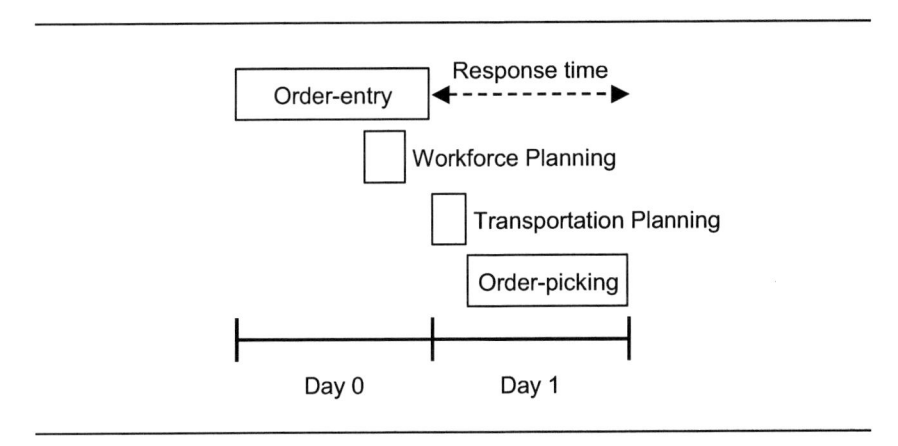

Figure 9.5 Response time accommodates transportation planning time.

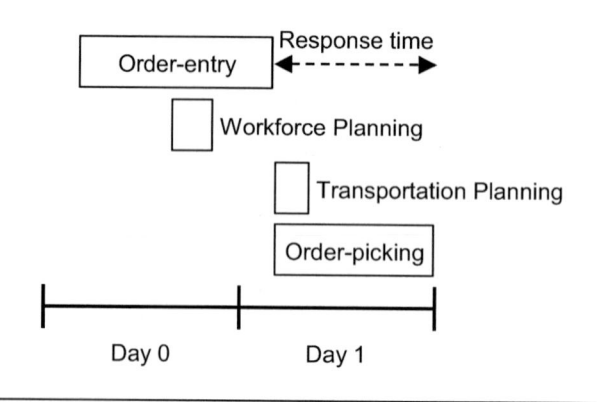

Figure 9.6 Response time accommodates order-picking time.

Figure 9.6 shows the third *discontinuity* in the response times. Here the response time is equal to the order-picking cycle time. If the response time becomes any shorter (Figure 9.7), then the distribution center has to commence the order-picking without knowing all the orders. At this stage, there is the risk that the customer cancels or changes the order, after the order-pickers have commenced their pick tour. Now the order-pickers have to return the picked goods to stock or they have to do another pick tour for the same customer. In the former case, many unnecessary activities are performed, in the latter case two pick tours are needed instead of one. Clearly, this is a discontinuity.

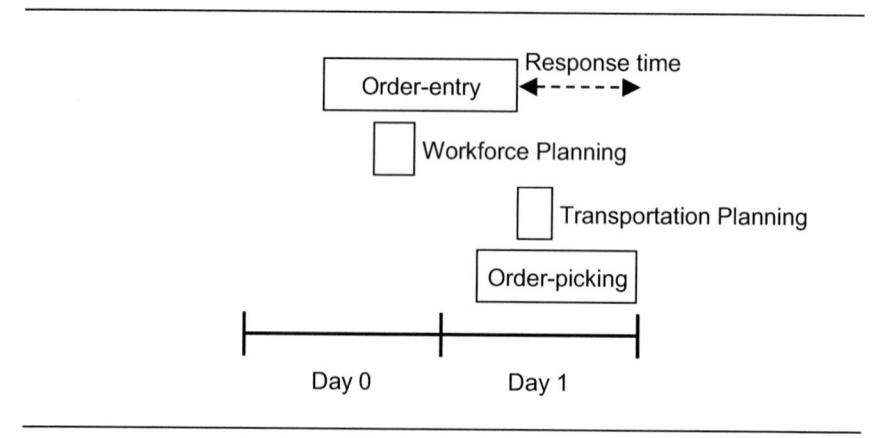

Figure 9.7 Response time shorter than order-picking cycle time.

148. Short response times have advantages and disadvantages.
   a. List several advantages.
   b. Also list some disadvantages.

9.2 Activity-Based Pricing

Activity-based pricing is an approach that makes costs both transparent and realistic. With traditional pricing schemes, the base product is priced and any support services are included within this price. Activity-based pricing separates the product costs and the service costs so that customers pay based on the quantities consumed of both the base product and the support services. The basic idea is that customers/clients start to regard the logistics costs as a variable rather than a fixed cost. Moreover, the underlying use of activity-based costing for determining service fees ensures that the fees give a true reflection of actual costs, possibly including a surcharge for profit margins.

Theories like ECR and JIT encouraged companies to reduce their inventories while ignoring warehousing and transportation costs. De Bie *et al.* (2002) observed this phenomenon and developed an alternative model to ECR, called *supply chain synchronization,* which reduces transportation and handling costs by shipping larger quantities and increasing the fill rate of trucks. Although, this increases inventories downstream in the supply chain (compared to ECR), total costs are typically lower and end-customers experience higher product availability.

Service fees are a powerful instrument for aligning the services in the supply chain. Some distribution centers charge fees for individual services. However, many private warehouses do not do this. Instead they operate on an annual budget. Consequently, other departments consider warehousing costs as a given. These departments focus on their internal costs and service requirements without making a trade-off against warehousing costs. This may result in much inefficiency.

If we want to minimize total costs, distribution centers must know actual costs and establish prices that motivate clients to lower total supply chain costs. This benefits both the company as well as suppliers and customers. We emphasize that substantially over- or undercharging for certain services could make clients either overly reluctant or overly eager to acquire a service, leading to unwanted cost effects. The following *example* shows how an obscure cost structure could lead to misalignment.

> **Example: The Downward Spiral**
> ECR and JIT have successfully accelerated the goods flows and reduced the inventories throughout the supply chain. We use Camp's famous formula (Camp, 1922) for the *economic order quantity* (*EOQ*) to illustrate the impact of these concepts on the warehouse operation. The formula computes the most economic trade-off between the fixed costs for purchasing a product lot and the inventory holding costs. We are not concerned with the mathematics of this formula. Instead we use it to visualize the unexpected effects of improper cost structures.
>
> $$EOQ = \sqrt{\frac{2 \times D \times K}{h}}$$
>
> *D*: Average demand
> *K*: Order costs
> *h*: Inventory holding costs
>
> Note that the demand (*D*) and the order costs (*K*) are in the numerator of the equation so that the order quantity (*EOQ*) decreases when either demand drops or the order costs decrease. The inventory holding costs (*h*) are in the denominator, so that the order quantity (*EOQ*) decreases when the inventory holding costs rise. The following seven steps illustrate what happens when costs are not transparent.
> 1. Process improvements and modern IT systems bring down the order costs (*K*).
> 2. The formula recommends a reduction in the order quantities (*EOQ*).
> 3. Smaller, more frequent orders require more handling activities in the supplier's distribution center to supply the same amount of product.
> 4. The supplier elevates his prices to compensate for these expenses.
> 5. The more expensive products raise the inventory holding costs (*h*), since these costs are directly linked to the inventory value (due to obsolescence, interest, etc.).
> 6. The formula recommends a further reduction in the order quantities (*EOQ*).
> 7. Return to step 3 and the downward spiral continues...
>
> The downward spiral should not be attributed to Camp's formula. We would see the same effect with other inventory control formulas. The effect is actually the result of an improper cost structure as we will explain next.

> **Example: Activity-based Pricing**
>
> $$EOQ = \sqrt{\frac{2 \times D \times K}{h}}$$
>
> The effect of activity-based pricing becomes apparent when we continue with the previous example. The service fees, which originally were hidden in the inventory holding costs (h), now shift to the order costs (K). The following six steps illustrate what happens in this situation.
> 1. Process improvements and modern IT systems bring down the order costs (K).
> 2. The formula recommends a reduction in the order quantities (*EOQ*).
> 3. Smaller, more frequent orders require more handling activities in the supplier's distribution center to supply the same amount of product.
> 4. The supplier elevates his *service fees* to compensate for these expenses.
> 5. The more expensive service fees raise the *order costs* (K).
> 6. The formula recommends an *increase* in the order quantities (*EOQ*).
>
> Note that this avoids the downward spiral. We now have a tool to balance the warehousing costs against inventory and purchasing costs.

As discussed in Section 5.1.3, activity-based costing determines fees per physical unit for physical warehouse services, i.e., a fee per pallet, case or piece. Administrative services, such as order-entry and complaint handling are charged per administrative unit, i.e., a fee per order or order line. However, many distribution centers charge fees for physical warehouse services based on physical volume, weight or order lines. These fees do not represent the actual costs and they are based on assumptions regarding order profiles. Hence, if the order profile changes, then this is not reflected in the fees while it may have a significant impact on the costs.

Highly Competitive Warehouse Management suggests the use of a *service portfolio* (see Section 5.1). This is a menu with all available services and associated fees. The distribution center charges these fees to the source and sell functions. We are effectively suggesting that the distribution center changes from a *cost center* to a *profit center*, i.e., not just the costs are monitored but it is recognized that a well-run distribution center contributes to higher profit margins.

Also, the other departments may want to reconsider their contracts with suppliers and customers. The sell function could decide to pass on the fee structure to customers, so that they will also take the logistics service fees into account. Likewise, we may see that the source function charges penalty fees to suppliers when their delivery does not comply with the *service level agreements*.

In Section 9.1, we considered three types of *discontinuities*. The application of activity-based pricing will automatically optimize *order profile discontinuities*. For *volume discontinuities* and *response time discontinuities*, the distribution center should estimate the effects of the discontinuities on the *cost-to-serve*. Based on this analysis, the source and sell functions can make an informed trade-off between service levels and cost levels.

> **Example: Inventory Increase**
> Philosophies like JIT and ECR have driven companies to order smaller quantities more frequently. In practice we see that uncovering the hidden logistics service costs increases the order sizes once again, which results in higher inventories downstream in the supply chain. However, the overall *cost-to-serve* decreases.
>
> Recent initiatives such as *vendor managed inventories (VMI)* and *factory gate pricing (FGP)* show that order sizes increase when the same company is responsible for both planning the order quantities and holding the inventories. VMI allows the supplier to determine the order quantities while he is responsible for both the deliveries and the customer's inventories. With FGP the customer determines the order quantities while he pays for both the deliveries and the inventories.

149. Activity-based costing charges fees for individual services.
   a. Does your distribution center charge fees for individual services?
   b. Do these fees represent actual warehouse costs?

9.3 Synchronized Planning

Collaboration is the key to improving overall supply chain performance. It is essential that the various departments within the company start to understand the importance of collaboration. Pointing out the discontinuities and charging realistic fees help other departments to better understand the dynamics of logistics. An additional effect is that the distribution center becomes an equal partner to the source and sell functions. It is no longer the case that the distribution center merely has to follow the orders of other departments. The departments, including the distribution function, jointly establish the best result for the company as a whole.

Such a collaboration needs more than just strict arrangements on costs and service levels. It also requires constant communication between the various

departments. The goal is to synchronize their departmental plans. Synchronized planning can be considered on three levels:
- Strategic
- Tactical
- Operational.

9.3.1 Strategic Synchronization

Strategic synchronization relates to the long term. *Highly Competitive Warehouse Management* suggests that the managers of relevant departments meet twice per year to discuss strategic issues. At these meetings the managers discuss their future plans and expectations with respect to the supply chain. The goal of the meetings is to synchronize the plans of each department. The source and sell functions can explain to the logistics department what they want to achieve, and the logistics department has the opportunity to explain the logistical implications. We envision one meeting that relates to supply chain projections and another to service levels.

Supply Chain Projections Meeting

The first strategic meeting on supply chain projections should cover the following topics:
- Projected turnover growth
- Projected assortment proliferation
- Changing supply channels
- Evolving market channels
- Expanding market geographies.

Clearly, the above topics affect the throughput and storage quantities in the distribution center as well as the order profiles. The distribution center may have to increase its capacities to anticipate the expected growth and amend its services to accommodate the new markets.

In the previous stages of *Highly Competitive Warehouse Management* we standardized processes and introduced advanced information systems. Hence, it is essential that the manager of the distribution center assesses whether the new requirements still fit with the standardized processes and systems. If this is not the case, then a discussion should follow to see whether or not the new requirements can be changed or whether new or modified processes are needed. The manager can explain the cost effects. Typically minor modifications to the new requirements or a different focus can result in a better fit. A good time to hold this meeting is during the annual budget rounds. At this time the various departments work out their financial plans for the next year. The meeting should help to refine these plans.

Service Level Meeting

Often companies renegotiate their agreements with suppliers and customers once every year. The second strategic meeting provides the inputs for these negotiations. The negotiations often focus on sales prices and conditions, not on logistics conditions. However, as we discussed before, the logistics service levels have a major impact on costs. Hence, these topics should also be included in the discussions.

In the strategic meeting, the managers discuss the service levels, i.e., response times, accuracy and availability levels, volume fluctuations as well as the service fees. The managers review which service levels have been achieved. Subsequently, the source and sell functions can indicate whether the service levels are still competitive in the market or whether they should be increased. At the same time, the manager of the distribution center can present the *discontinuities* in the service levels, i.e., show how minor changes in the supply chain bring major cost benefits. The result of the meeting is a set of new service levels with new service fees. Subsequently, the distribution center should attempt to keep the fees at an economic level by redesigning the internal operation with respect to the new service levels.

9.3.2 Tactical Synchronization

The tactical meetings are held more frequently – preferably every month or at least every quarter. At these meetings managers discuss service levels and consider any targets that have not been realized. Subsequently, they adjust their plans for the coming months regarding special sales promotions, maintenance of production lines, new product introductions, important projects, etc. The objective of the meetings is to synchronize the plans of the various departments. For example, a major sales promotion should not be scheduled at the same time as the go-live of a new WMS in the distribution center.

9.3.3 Operational Synchronization

There are many informal meetings and discussions between members of the various departments within a company or between the logistics service provider and its clients. These informal contacts are primarily concerned with resolving incidents. The question arises as to what the departments may do to prevent these incidents. There are three basic approaches:
- Operational meetings
- Event management
- Integral planning.

Operational Meetings

It is essential that departments stay in constant contact through regular operational meetings. In these meetings, managers either meet one-to-one or as a group to discuss the current situation and upcoming plans. They may talk about important orders, issues with suppliers or customers, expected volumes, etc. The goal is to synchronize their short-term plans. Moreover, these meetings allow quick feedback on inefficiencies. This is essential, not only to resolve problems quickly, but also to prevent them from reoccurring in the future. At this time, causes of incidents are still fresh in managers' minds, and they can consider ways to reduce the chances of the incident happening again. Thus, the collaboration between departments is continuously improved.

CASE STUDY

150. **Collaboration requires constant communication between the various departments to synchronize the departmental plans on strategic, tactical and operational levels.**
    a. *What could Foodies do on strategic, tactical and operational levels to improve collaboration?*

Event Management

An excellent approach for preventing incidents is to formalize the interaction between departments. Similar to the standardization of the warehouse processes in the stage of effective warehouse management, we can also standardize the processes between departments. Many recurring short-term decisions that involve multiple departments can be formalized. For example, what should be done when customers require more than the available inventory of a product? This may be resolved informally through discussions between representatives of the sell function and the distribution center. However, the process could also be formalized in decision rules that spell out which customers should receive the available merchandise.

Once formalized, we can consider automating these decision processes. In the subsequent section we will introduce new models for order acceptance and transportation planning that consider the available inventories and capacities in various departments. These are examples of systems that make decisions, which affect multiple departments without the need for human interaction.

At the turn of the twenty-first century a number of software vendors introduced so-called *supply chain event management* (SCEM) systems. These systems alert people at various points in the supply chain to special events that require their attention. Some typical examples are a truck that is delayed, a supplier who announces an order is postponed, etc.

The systems were not initially popular and many were discontinued. However, a few systems are still available and are enhanced so that they provide more value to users. Instead of merely alerting the responsible operator, the systems provide decision support and suggest possible solutions. Additionally, they make many standardized decisions automatically.

Intelligent agents are software components that automatically make decentralized decisions based on local data. For example, when a truck is delayed, the agent automatically reschedules its shipment to another truck. Where a centralized system would consider all available data, the intelligent agents only look locally. This reduces the complexity and data requirements of the centralized (ERP) system and at the same time it guarantees instant responses.

Integral Planning

Figure 9.8 shows a traditional order cycle. When the ERP accepts the orders, it considers the available inventories and assigns a delivery time frame to the customer. Order acceptance may determine a time frame that extends a week or a day, for example. Subsequently, the TMS plans the trips, which may narrow down the time frames of the orders to a day or even a few hours. Finally, the WMS organizes the activities in the distribution center such that the orders are picked before the anticipated departure time of the truck.

This description applies to a make-to-stock (MTS) operation. For make-to-order (MTO) operations, order acceptance considers the available production capacity and the availability of components and sub-assemblies. Subsequently, the advanced planning and scheduling (APS) system (or the ERP system) schedules the actual production runs. Both for MTS and MTO, each process step sets the time constraints for the subsequent steps. Since the distribution center is at the end of the order cycle, the various decisions have a major impact on its workload.

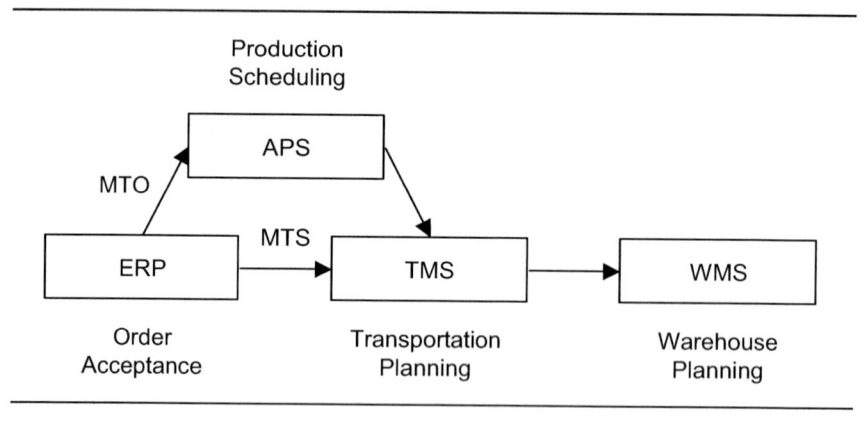

Figure 9.8 Order cycle.

Order acceptance modules offer *available to promise* and *capable to promise* functions. The former function checks whether there is sufficient inventory for an order in stock or in the outstanding purchase orders, while the latter function includes the capabilities to purchase and/or produce the goods.

A more sophisticated variant of functions also considers the capacities and costs in transportation and warehousing. Then, order acceptance performs a *capacity check* on resources, capacities, inventories, costs and service levels. We call this function *capable to deliver*. Few information systems provide support for this function. Hence, companies may need to develop a custom-made module.

The function does not have to be complicated. It should not consider all the minor details in transportation and warehousing. Instead it estimates the capacity requirements for trucks, workforce, docks and storage space at an *aggregated level*. For instance, the capable to deliver function may calculate the capacity requirements for transportation by the number of cubic feet that need to be delivered and the handling capacity of the distribution center by the number of inbound and outbound order lines. Usually these rough measures give an adequate representation of capacity utilization. If not, then they need to be further refined by considering the total weight and number of stops for transportation capacity or the workload of the distribution center in man hours, etc.

The capable to deliver function recommends a time frame by comparing the existing workload to the available capacity. If the workload associated with the order exceeds available capacities for a particular time frame, then the capable to deliver function should suggest a different period.

> **Case Study: Capable to Deliver**
>
> An e-commerce company delivers its bulky products (furniture and white goods) from a central distribution center. Customers order via internet or by phone. Upon order-entry, the system checks the available transportation capacity and suggests the first available delivery date.
>
> The company operates a fleet of 50 trucks. Each truck has a volume capacity of 1,100 ft^3 and each trip may take up to 10 hours. Thus, the total transportation capacity per day is 55,000 ft^3 (volume) and 500 hours (travel time). For each incoming order, the system computes the volume of the ordered goods and the time needed to deliver the goods. The time per delivery consists of a fixed travel time (average estimate) and stop time plus a variable time per item. Consequently, the system selects the first day with sufficient capacity. After all orders have been committed, a vehicle routing and scheduling (VRS) system computes the delivery routes.
>
> During slow periods, the response times can be 1 to 2 days. In busy times they can extend up to 5 workdays. The company has the policy that 95 percent of orders are delivered within 5 workdays. If response times threaten to become longer, then the company increases its fleet capacity by hiring additional trucks.
>
> Balancing the workload for transportation also balances the workload for the distribution center. Moreover, if the order volume rises, the distribution center knows this well in advance so that it has time to increase its labor capacity.

In some situations, the available capacities may need to be further refined. For instance, deliveries to California will never be combined with deliveries to New York. Hence, these regions have separate capacities. Some regions with low volumes may have trucks scheduled on specific days only, for example, the truck for Chicago only departs on Tuesdays and Fridays. Also the system could make a trade-off between costs and response times: sending a single pallet by express courier to Chicago on Monday is more expensive than using the regular carrier on Tuesday.

151. There are various order acceptance routines.
  a. *Explain the available to promise, capable to promise and capable to deliver functions.*

After the *capable to deliver* function has set the time frames, it is up to the TMS and WMS to plan their activities in further detail and execute them. The TMS needs to compute the volume and weight of outbound deliveries before it can decide which deliveries may go together in a truck. With the simple TMS interface discussed in Section 4.4.1, the TMS uses its own product master data to compute the volumes and weights. If a customer only orders full pallet loads, then the volume calculation is straightforward. However, if various individual cases and pieces are stacked onto a pallet or into a container, then the system must add a percentage of *air* to the volume. This addition compensates for the poor fit between different sizes of containers. Also the volume of the pallet itself and other packaging materials add to the gross volume and weight.

WMSs are usually better equipped to perform these volume calculations than TMSs. Some WMSs provide *cubing* functions. This function computes the gross volume and weight of the deliveries before they are actually picked. The WMS knows which products will be picked in the same pick tour and the associated packing rules. Hence, it can determine in advance which products will end up in the same carton or on the same pallet. This enables highly accurate computations. The WMS can communicate the results of the cubing calculations to the TMS. The TMS can then calculate the trips more precisely (Figure 9.9).

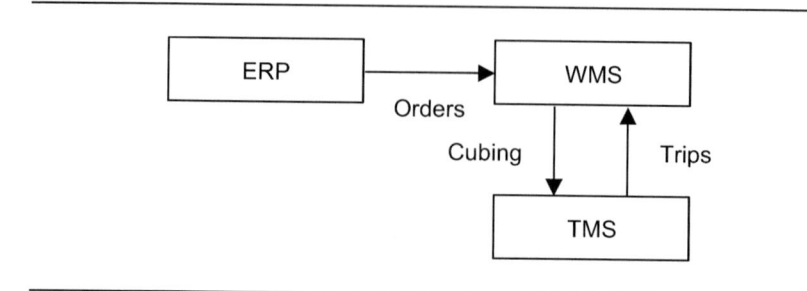

Figure 9.9 Advanced integration.

The transportation planning calculations can be further improved by including the warehousing and dock capacity as constraints when planning the outbound trips. The docking area is often a prominent bottleneck in the distribution center. If all docks are occupied, then the arriving trucks have to wait, which is costly and disrupts their planning. Conversely, when no inbound trucks arrive for some time, then the receipt and putaway processes may become idle. When departures of outbound trucks are clustered within a short time-frame, then this peak volume requires that the orders are picked and staged well in advance. Consequently, the goods occupy the dock area for a considerable period of time. Hence, it is a worthwhile activity to balance the workload at the docks.

The docks are used both for inbound and outbound trips. The inbound trips are typically planned by the suppliers and carriers delivering the goods. The outbound trips are planned by the transportation planning department. As such, the docks are the physical link between the distribution center and the supply chain.

Some distribution centers use a fixed daily or weekly schedule for the arrival and departure of the trucks. In such cases, we could re-examine the schedule and look for opportunities to balance the arrival and departure pattern. Naturally, the haulage firms, suppliers and customers must be consulted during this analysis.

Other distribution centers plan a new schedule every day. Some WMS vendors offer *dock and yard management* modules that help the user schedule the arrivals and departures as well as their stay at the yard. Several of these systems allow the suppliers and carriers to access the plans via the internet. They can view online when docks are available and make a reservation for a time slot. The distribution center therefore knows when to expect the shipment and the truck drivers are certain that a dock will be available when they arrive (on time).

The distribution center might even manipulate the workload, by increasing or decreasing the number of available docks at certain periods. For example, if many trucks arrive in the morning and few in the afternoon, then the distribution center could open all docks in the morning and only a few docks in the afternoon. This smoothes any sudden arrival peaks in the afternoon, so that the receipt process can be handled in the afternoon by a smaller crew with a steady workload.

9.4 Virtual Warehousing

Increased service demands have a great impact on present-day logistics. Smaller orders need to be delivered to an increasingly large geographical market (one of the effects of *globalization*). Assortments proliferate, for example, wholesalers and e-commerce retailers offer an assortment that they themselves do not have in stock. The moment a customer wants a product that is not held in stock, it is ordered from the supplier and subsequently delivered to the customer, sometimes accompanied by several *stock products*. In this manner, the assortment becomes almost limitless.

Virtual warehousing is a possible answer to these challenges. It is a new concept that is particularly well suited to processing small order quantities. Virtual warehousing considers the various distribution centers in the supply chain as a network. It no longer matters where the goods are stored, as long as they can be delivered to the customer on time.

9.4.1 Distribution Centers as a Network

In the 1980's the European supply chain consisted of *regional distribution centers* (RDCs) that supplied the complete assortment to a country (Figure 9.10). In the 1990's, the borders within the European Union were opened, which meant that pan-European transport could proceed more quickly. This presented the opportunity to centralize the stock in a *European distribution center* (EDC) while continuing to guarantee acceptable response times. As a result, companies could reach the same service level with significantly less stock. Similar distribution structures have developed worldwide.

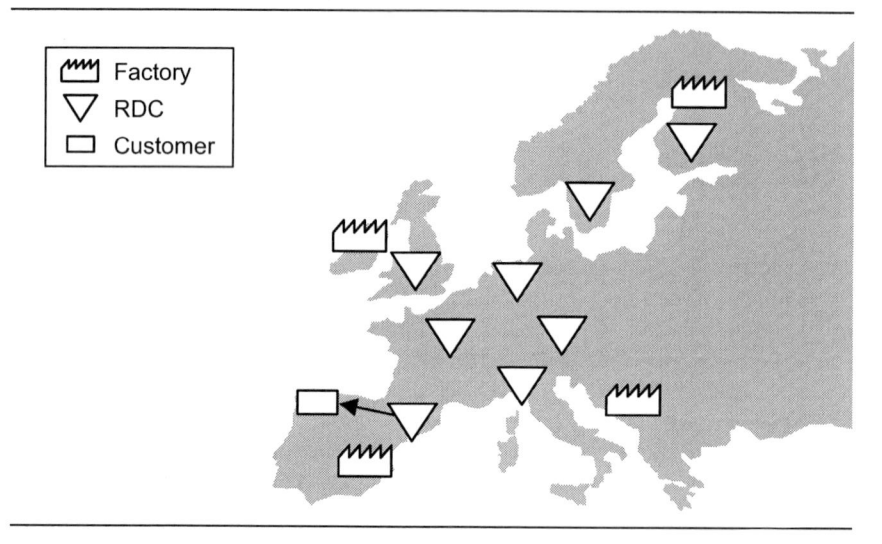

Figure 9.10 RDCs supply complete assortment to region.

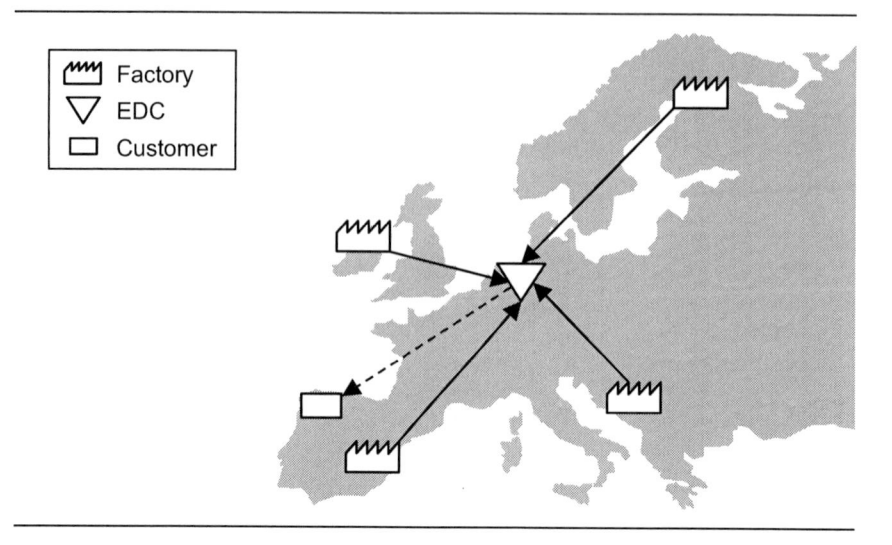

Figure 9.11 EDC supplies all of Europe.

However, the EDC approach has potential drawbacks. For example, a customer in Spain may order a product that is also produced in Spain. This product would be transported to the central European distribution center in The Netherlands first and then transported back to Spain (possibly accompanied by a number of other order lines, Figure 9.11). There is clearly inefficiency in this approach.

Virtual warehousing considers the various distribution centers as a network. The preferred storage location is upstream, close to the factory (Figure 9.12), thereby avoiding unnecessary inbound transportation. Subsequently, the requested goods are transported as efficiently as possible through the network when the order comes in, preferably in full truckloads.

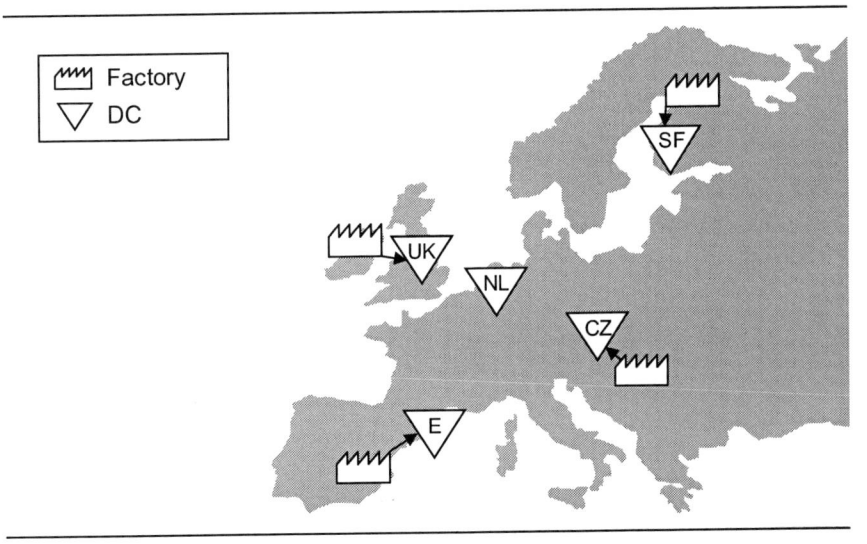

Figure 9.12 Virtual warehousing keeps stock close to the factory.

When full truckloads are not an option, we are faced with a situation such as the one in Figure 9.13. Goods to be transported directly from Finland (SF) to Spain (E) are insufficient for a full truckload. In that case it would be highly expensive to deliver the goods directly. However, by *cross-docking* goods in the distribution center in the Netherlands (NL), we may combine the shipment with goods for other destinations in the network and get full truckloads on both partial hauls. Consequently, the total costs decrease, especially when the individual orders are small. Nevertheless, if an order constitutes a full truckload, then a *direct shipment* from the factory to the customer is also possible.

A European distribution center can consolidate the various products for an order, which is a major advantage. Virtual warehousing takes this a step further via *merge-in-transit*, i.e., the goods for an order come together from various distribution centers at a site in the neighborhood of the delivery address. If necessary, the goods are made country or customer specific there via *value added logistics* (VAL), after which they go to the customer.

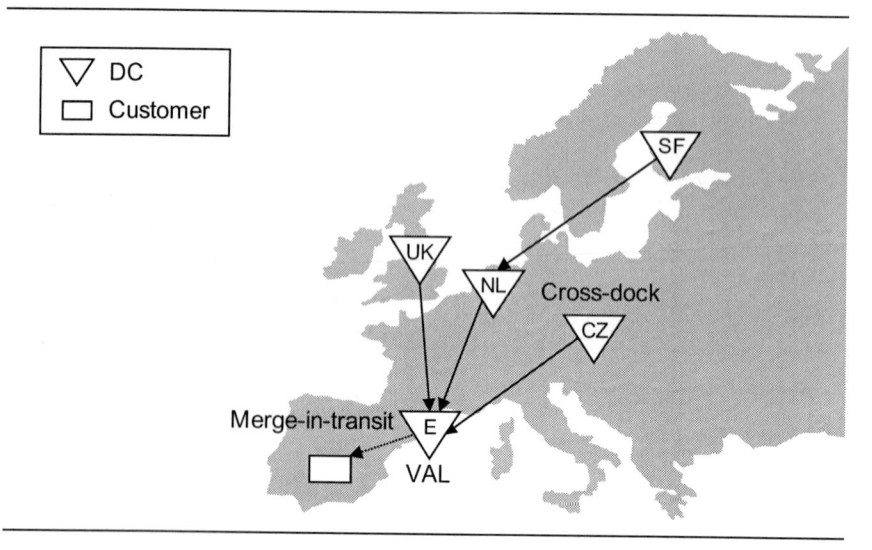

Figure 9.13 Virtual warehousing transports full truckloads through the network.

So far we have examined how we may efficiently transport goods to customers. However, it is important to also consider service levels, particularly response times. Figure 9.14 shows the response times from the various distribution centers to the customer in Spain (E). If we were to store the stock exclusively near the factories, then virtual warehousing would drive up the response times considerably, thus negatively impacting customer service. This can be remedied with limited *forward stock positions* in the distribution centers close to the customer outlets. This stock serves to bridge the demand of nearby customers during stock replenishment. The forward stock quantities are small in comparison to the stock in the regional distribution center of the 1980's. This means that the total stock in the network remains limited.

The virtual warehousing network may be extended by including the distribution centers of suppliers. If we know which stock is available at the supplier's sites, then we may also sell products that we do not currently own. This transforms the supply chain from the traditional *buy-hold-sell* model to the new *sell-source-ship* model. This requires real-time visibility of the availability of goods at suppliers and strict arrangements regarding response times. Large quantities may even be shipped by the supplier directly to the customer (*drop shipments*).

Virtual warehousing can have a significant impact on the distribution center. New processes for *cross-docking*, *merge-in-transit* and *value added logistics* may be required. In particular, it will need to be capable of handling various non-stock products. The distribution center must also operate under tight time constraints to comply with the integral distribution plan.

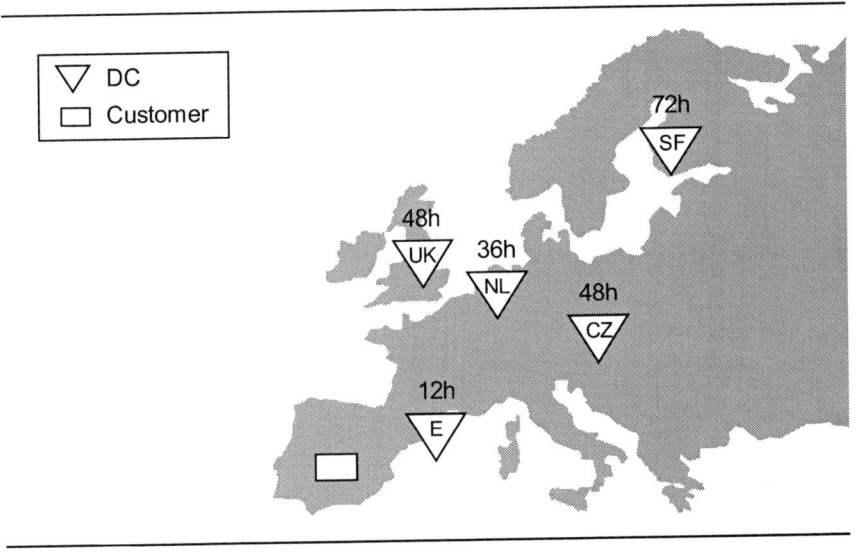

Figure 9.14 Response times from various DCs to the customer.

152. There are various kinds of supply chain structures.
  a. Explain the difference between an RDC network, an EDC network and a virtual warehousing network.

153. Search the internet.
  a. Find an example of a company that uses virtual warehousing.
  b. What kind of companies are using virtual warehousing?

9.4.2 Comparison of Supply Chain Structures

In Table 9.1 we compare the three supply chain structures. If we look at the *response times*, then we see that the transition from regional distribution centers (RDCs) to European distribution centers (EDCs) was purely a cost-saving measure. Especially in the early 1990's, the response times of regional distribution centers were still quite lengthy, typically 3 to 5 days. Nowadays, virtual warehousing aims to reduce delivery lead times.

Turning to the issue of *stock availability*, it is clear that with the RDC structure it may be that a customer cannot be supplied because there is no stock present in the RDC nearby, even though there is stock in another RDC. This problem is remedied both with the EDC and virtual warehousing approaches. The general availability of the inventories also helps to reduce stock levels and thereby *inventory costs*.

Table 9.1 Comparison of supply chain structures.

Criteria	RDC	EDC	VW
Response time	<1-2 days	<3-5 days	<1-2 days
Stock availability	Regional	Complete	Complete
Inventory costs	High	Low	Low
Inbound transportation costs	High	Medium[16]	Low
Outbound transportation costs	Low	High	Medium[16]
Warehousing costs	High	Low	High

The *inbound transportation costs* decrease with virtual warehousing since stock is stored near the factory. With regard to the *outbound transportation costs*, virtual warehousing consolidates the shipments into full truckloads when distributing the goods through the network of distribution centers. The consolidation makes it particularly suitable for delivering small orders. Since a number of distribution centers are needed, the *warehousing costs* may be higher compared to an EDC.

Virtual warehousing is preeminently suitable for organizations that want to deliver small orders within short lead times in an extensive market. We have seen that the warehousing costs can be high when compared to an EDC, however. Costs must be recovered via a higher level of customer service and a better fill rate of the trucks. This explains why virtual warehousing is applied particularly in the high-tech industry where the logistical costs make up a relatively small part of the sale price. Furthermore, we need enough transport volume to combine the small orders effectively. That is why these concepts are primarily used by 3PLs and large shippers. However, as order sizes continue to decrease and information systems evolve, we will encounter virtual warehousing more and more.

154. Consider the following with your distribution center in mind.
   a. Which supply chain structure applies to your distribution center?
   b. What are the advantages and disadvantages of this structure for your distribution center?

Table 9.2 Cost-to-serve analysis for three supply chain structures.

Cost-to-serve	RDC ($ mln)	EDC ($ mln)	VW ($ mln)
Inbound	7.0	6.0	2.0
Storage	7.0	4.0	5.0
Outbound	7.0	10.0	8.5
Inventory	10.0	5.5	6.5
Total	**31.0**	**25.5**	**22.0**

---

[16] Transportation is consolidated.

> **Procedure: Virtual Warehousing**
> Virtual warehousing is achieved gradually. We suggest the following implementation approach.
> 1. Determine the desired service levels. The service levels are in fact the driving force behind the change.
> 2. Design a new supply chain structure with planning and control rules and calculate the associated cost-to-serve (Table 9.2). If the costs turn out to be too high, then review the service levels.
> 3. List the necessary changes in warehousing, transportation, inventory control and in the interaction between these disciplines. The changes define the sub-projects that will have to be executed. Changes may be in the field of IT, planning and control, layout and equipment and organization.
> 4. Implement the sub-projects. An obvious first project is connecting the information systems concerned to establish good visibility of the goods flows.

9.4.3 Information Systems

With virtual warehousing it is necessary to collaborate more closely with suppliers and customers and to exchange information more intensively. If we want to operate a virtual warehousing network, then we need software for:
- Connectivity
- Visibility
- Planning.

Connectivity and Visibility

Virtual warehousing requires an up-to-date view of stocks and goods flows. This *visibility* necessitates interfaces between the various systems involved. If the number of systems increases, the number of crosswise interfaces will rise dramatically. Hence, for a large number of systems, a so-called *enterprise application integration* (EAI) system may be preferred. The enterprise application integration system connects to all systems and takes care of all the messages between the systems.

Planning

Subsequently, we need intelligent logistical information systems to synchronize the flow of goods and information. Advanced planning and scheduling (APS) systems are capable of computing an integral plan for the goods flow through the network. The implementation of an APS system requires a sophisticated model that answers the following questions:
- How much of each product do we stock in each distribution center considering the time delays in the network?
- Where do we source the goods for customer orders and for replenishing forward stock positions?

- How can we round up the product quantities to full truckloads for efficient transportation?
- How do we distribute the goods through the network in the most cost-effective manner via *cross-docking* and *merge-in-transit*?

155. **We need software for connectivity, visibility and advanced planning and scheduling to operate the virtual warehousing network.**
   a. Explain what is meant by connectivity, visibility and advanced planning and scheduling.
   b. Why do we need these sophisticated software systems?

9.5 Summary

Collaborative warehouse management is the fourth and final stage of the maturity grid. In previous stages, we streamlined internal processes and introduced intelligent IT systems. This established a well-organized distribution center. After stage three of the maturity grid, it is no longer possible to improve the internal warehouse operation through better management. However, this chapter has shown that further optimizations can still be achieved through better collaboration with other members of the supply chain, i.e., internal departments as well as suppliers and customers.

The distribution center provides various services to these parties. We observed several minor modifications to services that may achieve major logistics cost reductions. We refer to these changes as *discontinuities*. By definition, discontinuities affect other members of the supply chain. Hence, we have to make a trade-off between the cost savings and the potential impact on service levels. We identified discontinuities in order profiles, throughput and storage volumes, and response times.

Often it is difficult to convince other departments of the importance of collaboration. Instead parties focus on internal objectives rather than the overall results. *Activity-based pricing* is a powerful methodology that makes logistics costs transparent to other parties. When realistic logistics fees are passed on, other members of the supply chain consider the costs in their decision-making processes and automatically optimize overall supply chain performance.

Collaboration also requires a constant conversation between the various departments. Regular meetings should be held to discuss strategic, tactical and operational issues, with the aim of preventing issues rather than solving them once they occur.

Finally, a different supply chain structure can reduce the total cost-to-serve for inventories, warehousing and transportation. *Virtual warehousing* is a new concept that considers the various distribution centers in the supply chain as a network. It no longer matters where goods are stored, as long as they can be delivered to the customer on time.

Chapter 10

Service Alignment

Collaborative warehouse management is the fourth and final stage of the maturity grid. In the previous chapter we introduced several tools associated with this stage. Similar to the previous two stages, collaborative warehouse management may achieve a 10 percent reduction in warehousing costs (Figure 10.1). On top of that, the concepts discussed in Chapter 9 could establish additional savings in *transportation* and *inventory holding costs*.

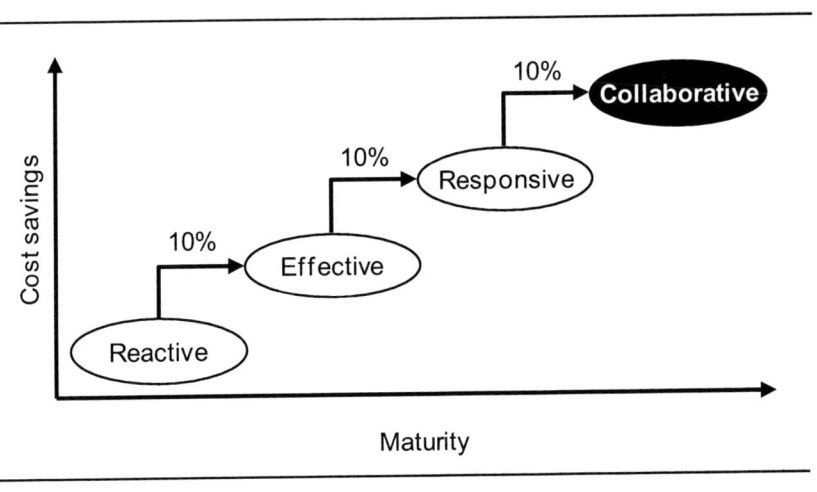

Figure 10.1 Collaborative warehouse management in the maturity grid.

In this stage of *Highly Competitive Warehouse Management* we reconsider the services provided by distribution centers. Some aspects of a service are essential. They give the company a competitive advantage, for example, for rush orders it is vital that they are shipped quickly. For regular orders this may be of less importance. High service levels and special requests add a lot of complexity and cost to the operation. Often these costs are not visible to clients and customers. Were they able to see the true cost, then they might not be willing to pay for these exceptional services. Thus, the question arises as to which services and service levels create the most added value for the company and the supply chain.

In Section 9.1 we identified three types of *discontinuities*, which have a minor effect on services but a major impact on logistics costs. The discontinuities provide great opportunities to improve supply chain performance. We distinguished the following types:
- Order profile discontinuities
- Response time discontinuities
- Volume discontinuities.

Collaborative warehouse management proposes three actions to overcome these three discontinuities. The first action is to *rationalize* order profiles and reduce the complexity of services. The second action is to either *accelerate* or *decelerate* the response times of services. Faster service decreases inventories throughout the supply chain since safety stocks can be reduced. Slower service provides opportunities to better plan and execute. Finally, the third action is to *balance* volumes and reduce workload fluctuations. We show the three actions in Figure 10.2.

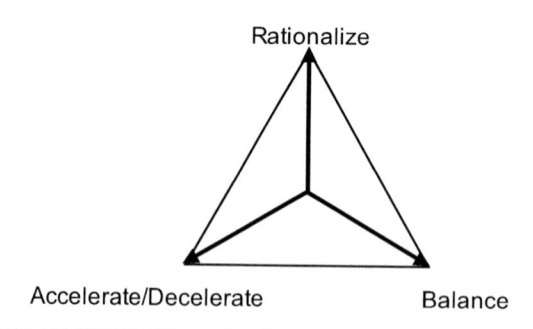

Figure 10.2 Optimization actions for collaborative warehouse management.

10.1 Rationalize

The first action of collaborative warehouse management is to *rationalize* order profiles. As discussed in Section 9.1.1, changing order profiles may substantially cut costs. This requires that the source and sell functions together with suppliers and customers change their order behavior. We suggest a three step approach for rationalizing the order profiles:
- Cost analysis
- Activity-based pricing
- Incentive alignment.

Cost Analysis

Activity-based costing makes costs transparent. This not only applies to the distribution center, but also to other departments within a company. If we apply the *time-driven activity-based costing* model (see Section 5.3.2) to all activities in the value chain, then we may calculate the actual profitability of individual customers, products or orders as well as the actual costs of suppliers. For the distribution center, it quantifies the savings potential of rationalizing the order profiles and identifies the customers, orders and products that cause inefficiencies. Together with the source and sell functions, the manager can search for ways to transform unprofitable activities and relationships. However, the analysis may also identify direct opportunities for streamlining processes and optimizing capacity utilization within other departments.

> **Example: Vendor Managed Inventories**
> *Vendor managed inventories* (VMI) is a popular arrangement in which the supplier determines the order quantities so as to maintain sufficient inventory levels at the customer's distribution center. Clearly, the supplier not only considers the customer's inventories but also its own warehousing and transportation costs. Accordingly, suppliers reduce order frequencies, round order lines to efficient quantities and maximize the fill rate of trucks.

An insightful way to present the outcome of the integral activity-based costing model is the *whale curve* of cumulative customer or product profitability (Kaplan & Anderson, 2007). The whale curve ranks products or customers on the

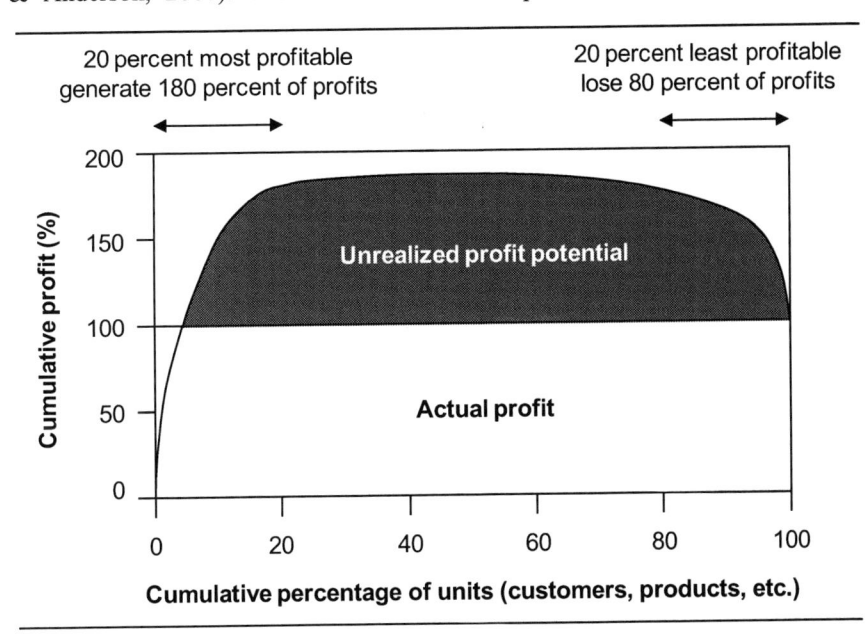

Figure 10.3 The whale curve illustrates unrealized profit potential.

horizontal axis from the most profitable to the least profitable, or largest loss. The vertical axis displays the cumulative profitability of the products or customers. Theoretically, the most profitable 20 percent of customers generate profits between 150 and 300 percent of actually realized profits. The middle 60 to 70 percent break even. The final 10 to 20 percent of customers actually cost the company money, canceling out a lot of the gains of the best customers. This leaves the company with its 100 percent of total profits.

156. The first step to rationalize order profiles is cost analysis.
a. Explain the whale curve of cumulative customer or product profitability.

Activity-Based Pricing

The next step is to introduce activity-based pricing for internal clients and possibly also for suppliers and customers. In Section 9.3 we discussed *activity-based pricing* as a methodology that makes the service fees transparent to other members of the supply chain. Their introduction encourages these parties to consider the overall costs rather than their internal costs only, which in turn automatically rationalizes the order profiles.

In practice, many companies are reluctant to introduce such a pricing scheme internally, let alone externally. Internal departments may obstruct the introduction because they feel that the order profiles are the distribution center's problem, not theirs. A clear analysis of the potential savings is the first step in changing attitudes. If the savings are substantial, then this might entice them to participate.

After the implementation of activity-based pricing, it is important to monitor costs. Perhaps certain departments or customers still insist on their old behavior, because they do not understand the benefits or because the changes cause enormous difficulties. It will take a joint effort to solve these problems.

157. The second step to rationalize the order profiles is activity-based pricing.
a. What is the advantage of the introduction of activity-based pricing?

Incentive Alignment

Although the potential savings are substantial, other departments may still not be motivated to change their behavior. In that case, the disinterest is probably caused by poorly aligned *incentives*. Most companies evaluate the performance of the various departments using performance indicators that exclude the effects of their activities on logistics costs. For instance, the sales department is rewarded based on the sales volume and gross margin that they achieve.

Consequently, they are inclined to sell any order quantity, irrespective of the cost-to-serve. As a final step the manager could suggest that the company's senior management realign the incentives of the various departments. If the logistics costs were included in the sales results, then the sales team would learn that small orders or orders with special requirements might be highly unprofitable.

158. The third step to rationalize the order profiles is incentive alignment.
   a. *How are the incentives aligned within your company?*

10.2 Accelerate/Decelerate

A short response time may provide a competitive advantage. It can also help to reduce inventory costs as illustrated in the *case study* in Section 6.1. It certainly helps to reduce inventories of customers since fast and reliable deliveries require less safety stock. However, short response times also have disadvantages. In Section 9.1.3 we identified several discontinuities with respect to workforce planning, transportation planning and warehouse execution. Hence, by *accelerating* or *decelerating* response times we may overcome the discontinuities.

Optimal Response Times
The question is, what are the most effective response times? Traditionally, managers have not been able to answer this question in a satisfactory manner. How would an increase or decrease in the order response time by one hour affect costs? It is practically impossible to model all the consequences. Fortunately, there is an alternative approach. The introduction of the concept of *discontinuities* has dramatically simplified the problem. Instead of examining all possible response times, we only have to consider the response times that coincide with discontinuities. In Section 9.1.3 we identified three response time discontinuities:
- Workforce planning cycle time
- Transportation planning cycle time
- Order-picking cycle time.

It is quite easy to estimate these cycle times. Consequently, we can develop three alternative scenarios. A first scenario with a response time that accommodates the *workforce planning time* (Figure 9.4), a second scenario with a response time that accommodates the *transportation planning time* (Figure 9.5) and a third scenario with a response time that accommodates the *order-picking time* (Figure 9.6). Companies may observe other response time discontinuities in their wider commercial operations. However, the total number of discontinuities remains limited and, thus, so does the number of alternative scenarios.

We can compare each of these scenarios to the current situation. For example, if the current response time is shorter than the workforce planning cycle time, then the first scenario would save the costs due to inadequate workforce planning. Hence, for each scenario we can identify which inefficiencies are resolved (or added) compared to the current situation, e.g., better workforce utilization, higher fill rates of trucks or the elimination of rework in the distribution center. Also, the effect of the response times on the inventory levels may be quantified. In Section 6.1 we presented a *case study* in which we computed the effects of response times on inventory costs in the supply chain. However, it is not necessarily true that an extended response time increases the inventory costs. If the response times become longer but at the same time more reliable, then customers might need less safety stock.

If the fluctuations in order volumes are severe, then it may be advisable to extend the response times to equal the workforce planning cycle time as shown by the following *case study*.

> **Case Study: e-Commerce Company**
>
> Around the year 2000, a direct-to-consumer company in multimedia products transformed from a catalogue company to an e-commerce company. This had a major impact on its central distribution center. For instance, promoting a wide product range on the internet was much easier (and cheaper) than in a catalogue. Accordingly, the distribution center was redesigned and a WMS and material handling equipment were newly introduced to accommodate 50 percent more products (*SKUs*) within the same facility and to increase productivity by 30 percent. The response time was also reduced from 2 to 3 days to next day delivery.
>
> Within the first year, management re-evaluated the response time and chose to extend it to 2 to 3 days once again. They decided that the increased service level did not adequately compensate for the limited ability to plan the workforce capacities and to balance the workload between days.
>
> However, competition on the internet pressured the company to gradually shorten its response times in the following years. In fact, by 2011, customers could order until 9 PM for next day delivery. This illustrates how the trade-off between costs and competitive service levels may shift.

It is also important to keep in mind that it may not be necessary to extend response times for all orders. We could discriminate between urgent and less urgent orders. Usually, there is a natural distinction between order characteristics, e.g., urgent repair orders and less urgent inventory replenishment orders. If a substantial share of the orders could be treated as non-urgent, then this might give enough flexibility to overcome the response time discontinuities.

We can conclude that a distribution center has an optimal response time for each service. Not only for outbound handling, but also for inbound handling, VAL and cross-docking.

> **Case Study: Food Manufacturer Finds Response Time Mix**
> A food manufacturer delivered products with short shelf-lives within extremely short response times. In fact, orders from retailers and wholesalers were still arriving after the order-pickers had started picking (see Figure 10.4). This caused many inefficiencies in order-picking and transportation.
>
> The manufacturer made a *cost-to-serve* model that not only distinguished discontinuities in transportation planning and order-picking, but also in production. Before, the manufacturing plants only produced to forecast, i.e., *make-to-stock*. An extended response time would enable a shift of the *customer order decoupling point* (Van Goor et al., 2003), so that the plants could produce according to the *make-to-order* policy. This discontinuity significantly reduced inventory levels and improved the freshness of products.
>
> A second discontinuity in production was resolved with the introduction of *vendor managed inventories* (VMI). This was not primarily a response time discontinuity, but rather an order profile discontinuity. The retailers gave insight into their stock positions and the manufacturer arranged for there to be sufficient inventory at the retailers' locations while also optimizing its production runs and transportation capacities. In particular, the need for warehouse handling was reduced since the goods went from the production line directly to the shipping dock. Once 33 pallets were staged, they were shipped immediately. Moreover, the administrative order processes became redundant, both for the manufacturer as well as the retailer.
>
> The manufacturer used the cost-to-serve model in their annual negotiations. The outcome varied between customers. Some retailers insisted on short response times, while others allowed longer response times. In fact, two large retailers and one wholesaler eagerly wanted to adopt VMI. The mix of response times for the various customers enabled the manufacturer to achieve substantial savings in production, transportation and warehousing.

```
                    Response time
         Order-entry ◄---------►
                    □ Transportation Planning
              Order-picking
                         Transport
         ├──────────────┼──────────────┤
              Day 0            Day 1
```

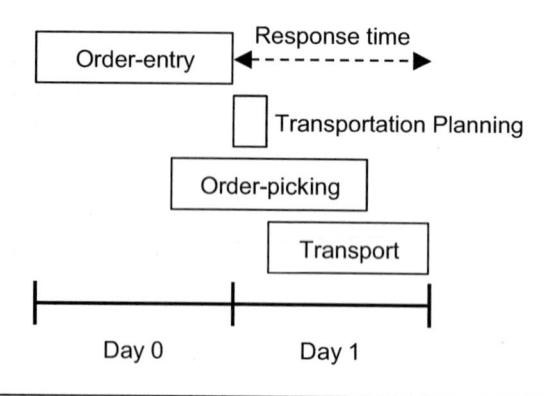

Figure 10.4 Order-pickers start before order cut-off time.

159. For each distribution center it is important to find an optimal response time for its services.
   a. *Why do we only have to consider response times that coincide with discontinuities to find the most effective response times?*

10.3 Balance

Each distribution center has been designed to accommodate certain workload and storage volumes. If the volumes are substantially higher or lower, then this may increase costs and compromise performance. In the previous stage of the maturity grid, responsive warehouse management, we examined ways to tune capacities to the actual workload. Now we do the opposite and investigate how we can adjust the workload and storage volumes to available capacities. In the following two sections we discuss *balancing* throughput volumes and storage volumes, respectively.

10.3.1 Balancing Throughput Volumes

The purchase orders, VAL orders and sales orders on a specific day determine the workload in the distribution center. We present two options for balancing these volumes:
- Order process redesign
- Integral planning and control.

Order Process Redesign

The way in which the orders are processed, could unintentionally cause volume fluctuations. For instance, order acceptance processes often assign a specific delivery date to an order. A common reason for this is that many ERP systems require an exact date to be specified. While some orders need to be shipped as soon as possible or on a specific date in the future, this does not necessarily hold for all orders. If we can find categories of orders that do not need to be shipped on a specific day, then we may use the mix of punctual and non-punctual orders to *balance* the workload in the distribution center. The following *example* shows that it is not necessary to customize the ERP to overcome this problem.

> **Example: Punctual vs. Stretch Orders**
> A consumer-electronics manufacturer assigns a despatch date in its ERP to each outbound order. The ERP communicates the orders to the WMS of the regional distribution center (RDC). The RDC has to ship the orders no later than the specified date.
>
> The company distinguishes two order types: punctual and stretch orders. The punctual orders must be shipped on the specified date. The stretch orders are always assigned to a Friday and may be shipped on any day of that week. Approximately 80 percent of the orders are stretch orders.

160. Foodies' customers from the US have punctual orders, whereas foreign customers have stretch orders.
   a. Explain the difference between punctual orders and stretch orders?
   b. Approximately 20 percent of the sales volume is shipped abroad. Based on this information, how could Foodies balance the workload?

Another common issue in the order process relates to the *order cut-off time*. Customers place orders throughout the day, but only after the cut-off time do the orders become available for transportation planning and warehousing. This approach creates a volume peak at the cut-off time. However, it may sometimes be possible to balance the workload over the day by separating the cut-off times for different customer groups. For example, customers on the east coast order before 12 PM (white segments in Figure 10.5) and customers on the west coast before 4 PM (gray segments in Figure 10.5). The orders in the first group are delivered on the next day before 12 PM and the second group before 4 PM. Consequently, all orders have a 24 hour response time. The customer groups should preferably be separated on geographical grounds, so as not to compromise transportation efficiency.

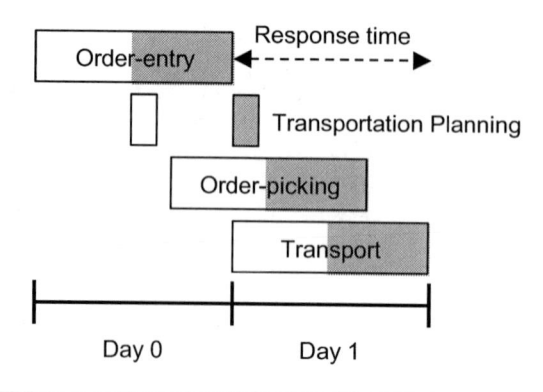

Figure 10.5 Balancing workload with two order cut-off times.

161. Foodies is thinking about separating the cut-off times for different customer groups.
   a. Why would Foodies do this?

Integral Planning and Control

Planning and control decisions are notorious for creating demand fluctuations in the supply chain. A well-known example is the *Forrester Effect* (also known as the *Bullwhip Effect*). Forrester (1961) identified that small disturbances at one link in the supply chain may quickly become magnified as the effect spreads across the supply chain. By transforming the traditional *push* type supply chain based on demand forecasts and sizable orders to a *pull* type supply chain where the end-customer demand triggers orders of just the required quantity, companies have largely managed to smooth this effect. Nevertheless, we still see many fluctuations that are caused by planning and control decisions. We distinguish three types of fluctuations:
- End-customer driven effects
- Business-driven effects
- Incidental effects.

The end-customers, i.e., the customers that actually use the products at the end of the supply chain, determine the real demand. Clearly, the supply chain should be able to anticipate these fluctuations. Nonetheless, end-customers' decisions can be influenced by marketing, sales promotions or pricing strategies. These special promotions are notorious for creating disturbances in the logistics system that might accelerate into a Forrester-type surge. However, they may also be used to balance the flows as shown by the *example* below.

> **Example: Smooth Demand for Candy**
> Dutch candy manufacturers have practically eliminated demand fluctuations. Traditionally, demand dropped between January and April. Nowadays, special promotions during this particular period have smoothed the demand curve throughout the year.

The second type of fluctuation is business-driven. In many companies, we see various daily, weekly, monthly or annual patterns that strongly upset the balance. Ironically, these periodic patterns are not driven by end-customer demand. The effects are typically caused by misaligned incentives or old habits.

> **Example: Fluctuations in Consumer Electronics**
> Multinational consumer electronics manufacturers are notorious for their volume fluctuations. Many of these organizations are driven by monthly sales cycles. To achieve their sales targets, the sales representatives mark down their prices towards the end of each month. This has an enormous effect on sales volumes. A logistics manager at one of these companies once claimed that 10 percent of monthly sales were achieved in the first week, 20 percent in the second week, 30 percent in the third week and 40 percent in the fourth week of the month!

Collaboration could smooth these periodic effects. Similar to the procedure for rationalizing the order profiles in Section 10.1, we suggest the following approach for balancing order volumes:
- Cost analysis
- Activity-based pricing
- Incentive alignment.

The first step is to quantify the cost effects. Compare the costs in the current situation to a situation with a completely balanced goods flow. Compute all costs due to fluctuations, including excess capacities (space, equipment, labor), periodic overtime or underutilization.

The second step is to explain the cost effects to other departments. It might be helpful to calculate an alternative set of service fees, which would apply if the level of demand was smooth. Then, it is up to the source and sell functions to choose between the existing rate (if they continue their current demand pattern) and the reduced rate (if they balance the volumes). Similar arrangements could be set up with suppliers and customers.

Finally, if explaining the consequences does not bring changes in behavior, then the third step might be to realign the incentives of the various departments. As discussed previously, this is a task for senior management.

The third type of fluctuation is incidental. These fluctuations occur because various parties incidentally plan many (or hardly any) orders within the same period. One option to balance these peaks is to incorporate the finite capacity of the distribution center in the control rules of other departments. In Section 9.3.3

we discussed integrated frameworks for *order acceptance, transportation planning* and *dock reservation*.

Furthermore, peaks caused by different departments should be well synchronized. Major sales promotions of different divisions or large inbound and outbound volumes should preferably be separated. This requires good cross-functional coordination and regular meetings.

162. We distinguish three types of fluctuations: End-customer driven effects, business-driven effects and incidental effects.
   a. Explain all three and give a realistic example of each with regard to Foodies.
   b. What could Foodies do to balance these fluctuations?

10.3.2 Storage Volumes

In addition to fluctuations in order volumes, there can also be fluctuations in inventory levels. These fluctuations can be equally disruptive. A high storage volume may significantly increase travel distances. A low volume makes the overhead relatively expensive.

In particular, slow and non-moving stock incur relatively high storage costs. A *Pareto curve* shows the cumulative percentage of demand when products are ranked according to decreasing demand. Figure 10.6 shows an example of a Pareto curve where the 20 percent fastest moving products represent 80 percent of the demand. The subsequent 30 percent medium moving products represent 15 percent of the demand. Then the 30 percent slow moving products represent 5 percent of the demand and the final 20 percent of the products are non-moving.

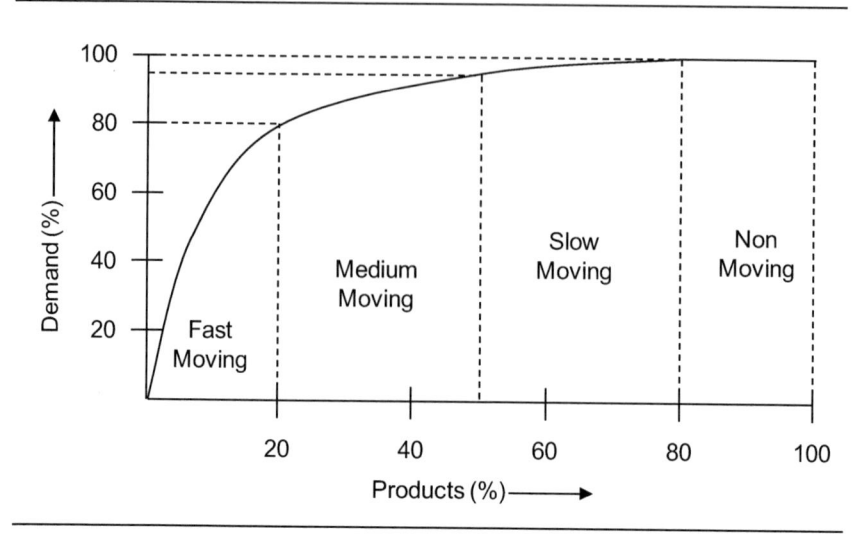

Figure 10.6 Pareto curve.

SERVICE ALIGNMENT

We may compute the number of *days on hand* of every product, i.e., its inventory on hand divided by its average daily demand. For products with many days on hand, we could discuss with the source and sell functions eliminating or reducing inventories. There are various channels for these products, such as mark-downs, junk dealers, factory outlets, etc.

The cost-to-serve analysis in Section 10.1 may be used to identify the profitability of individual products. A notorious cause of increasing inventory volumes is *product proliferation*. Companies introduce new products without rationalizing their existing assortment. Often, inventories can be reduced (and profitability can be increased) by removing unprofitable or redundant products from the assortment. However, unprofitable products cannot always be dropped. They might be *traffic generators,* which encourage customers to purchase additional items. For example, milk cannot be omitted from a supermarket range.

Finally, note that it is possible to create a profitable business with slow moving products. This requires that the costs of slow movers are carefully monitored. Anderson (2006) refers to this huge array of slow movers as the *long tail*. An excellent example of a company that is successful with a long tail is Amazon.

163. **Review Foodies' ABC classification of the juice section (Question 57 on page 113).**
   a. *Draw a Pareto curve for Foodies' juice assortment in Figure 10.7.*
   b. *Compare your Figure 10.7 to Figure 10.6. What do you notice?*
   c. *What could be the reason for the difference between Figure 10.6 and Figure 10.7?*

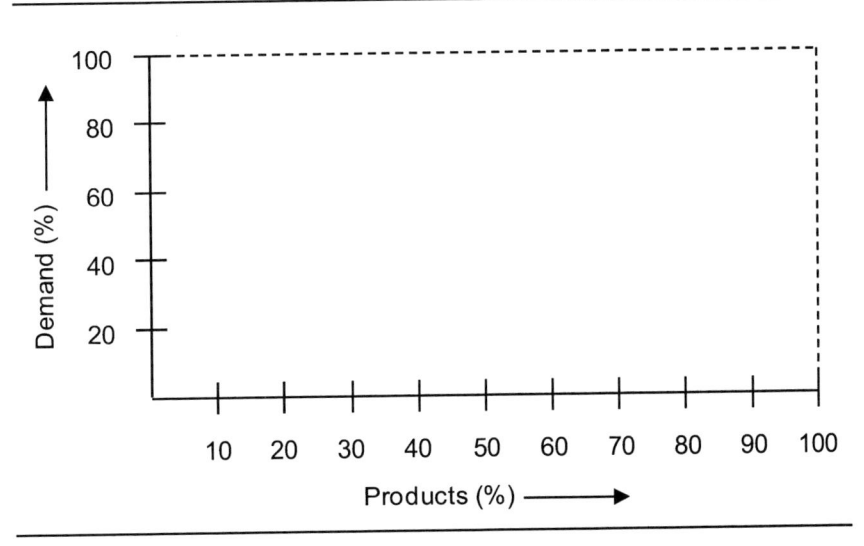

Figure 10.7 Empty graph for Foodies' Pareto curve.

164. Some distribution centers create a profitable business with slow-moving products.
   a. How do the slow moving products influence the business results in your company?

165. Consider Foodies' market.
   a. Would it be possible for Foodies to create a profitable business with slow-moving products?

10.4 Summary

Collaborative warehouse management promotes better collaboration between departments. The goal is to align the services with the overall objectives of the company and the supply chain. In other words, to *do the right things* instead of just *doing things right*. The model investigates three types of discontinuities:
- Order profile discontinuities
- Response time discontinuities
- Volume discontinuities.

Collaborative warehouse management distinguishes three possible actions: *rationalize, accelerate/decelerate* and *balance* to overcome these discontinuities, respectively. Important aspects are the quantification of the cost model, the introduction of activity-based pricing schemes and the alignment of the incentives of various departments. In particular, the model provides a framework to compute optimal response times.

10.5 What's Next?

Are we finished after completing the four stages of the maturity grid? Certainly not. Technological advances and market developments will bring new challenges. However, these challenges can be faced proactively. The framework of *transparency* and *collaboration* should ensure that potential problems will be detected at an early stage. Each problem can be traced back to a specific stage of the maturity grid. Subsequently, the actions prescribed within *Highly Competitive Warehouse Management* can be used to find appropriate solutions. In this way, the distribution center will stay best-in-class.

Appendix A

Maturity Scan

The following survey can be used to assess the maturity of a distribution center. The four answers to each question represent an increasing level of sophistication. If you believe that your operation falls somewhere between two answers, then you should select the lowest answer. For example, if your distribution center almost realizes answer *c* but not completely, then choose answer *b*.

A.1 Effective Warehouse Management

1. Are services and service level agreements (SLAs) formally defined for the distribution center?
   a. No, we do not distinguish services and SLAs.
   b. Somewhat, we do have a few SLAs (response time, accuracy) for some clients/customers.
   c. Yes, we use a complete list of all available warehouse services and associated service levels for all clients/customers.
   d. Yes, we use a complete list of all available warehouse services and associated service levels for all clients/customers and charge fees per individual service.

2. Are the processes in the distribution center formally specified?
   a. No, we do not have standard operating procedures.
   b. Somewhat, we have specified our processes, but they are somewhere in a drawer and/or outdated.
   c. Yes, we do have up-to-date standard operating procedures, which are being actively followed by the operators.
   d. Yes, we do have up-to-date standard operating procedures, which we use for process analysis and for the instruction and operational management of operators.

3. Is activity-based costing actively applied in the distribution center?
   a. No, we do not use activity-based costing.
   b. Somewhat, we have modeled our costs, but we hardly use it.
   c. Yes, we do have an up-to-date activity-based costing model, which we use for the analysis of warehouse-processes.
   d. Yes, we do have an up-to-date activity-based costing model, which we use for process analysis and for our collaboration with other department/supply chain members.

4. Do you report performance indicators in the distribution center?
   a. No, we do not report performance indicators.
   b. Somewhat, we report a few key performance indicators, but not daily.
   c. Yes, each day we report the key performance indicators.
   d. Yes, each day we report the key performance indicators and have direct electronic access to the underlying details for further analysis.

5. Do you report the performance of operators?
   a. No, we do not report the performance of operators.
   b. Somewhat, we report the productivity of teams.
   c. Yes, we report the productivity of individual operators measured against time standards on all major activities.
   d. Yes, we report the productivity (against time standards on all major activities) and accuracy of individual operators.

6. Are performance indicators utilized for the continuous optimization of warehouse processes?
   a. No, performance indicators are not used for achieving improvements.
   b. Somewhat, performance indicators are used for substantiating improvements after we discover them ourselves.
   c. Yes, performance indicators are analyzed regularly to find possible improvements, however, without the use of a standardized methodology.
   d. Yes, performance indicators are used within a standardized methodology for continuous improvement that contains a feedback loop from results to actions (e.g., Deming circle).

A.2 Responsive Warehouse Management

7. Do you use a standard warehouse management system (WMS)?
   a. No, we do not use a WMS.
   b. Somewhat, we do have a WMS, but it is a custom-made system or a heavily customized standard system.
   c. Yes, we do have a standard WMS with only a few minor customizations.
   d. Yes, we do have a standard WMS with only a few minor customizations and our staff can easily reconfigure the system to accommodate process changes without the help of outside experts.

8. Do the warehouse operators communicate with the WMS in real-time?
   a. No, orders are confirmed in the WMS (so that inventory levels can be updated) upfront or some time after their actual completion.
   b. Somewhat, the WMS communicates with the warehouse operators via paper slips. The operators confirm their tasks in the WMS immediately after completing the list.
   c. Yes, a majority of the operators have real-time (paperless) communication with the WMS. The others confirm their tasks immediately after completing the paper list.
   d. Yes, all operators have real-time (paperless) communication with the WMS.

9. Does the WMS communicate with other systems via electronic messages?
   a. No, there are no electronic messages between the WMS and systems outside the distribution center.
   b. Somewhat, the WMS communicates product master data, purchase orders and sales orders with the ERP.
   c. Yes, in addition to the ERP interface for product master data, purchase orders and sales orders, the WMS also communicates despatch advices with all major suppliers/customers.
   d. Yes, the WMS communicates purchase orders, sales orders and despatch advices that include unique pallet identification codes (SSCC) and the contents per pallet.

10. Do you estimate in advance how many operators are required in the distribution center on each day (*capacity planning*)?
    a. No, we make no such estimate.
    b. Somewhat, we manually estimate the workload for the next day/week and use it do determine the number of people that we need.
    c. Yes, we have an information system that computes reasonable estimates of the workload for the next day/week and we have flexible contracts and convenient arrangements with employment agencies.
    d. Yes, we have a sophisticated system that computes accurate estimates of the workload for the next day/week using forecasts and standard times and we have flexible contracts and convenient arrangements with employment agencies.

11. Does the WMS provide a real-time overview of the progress and status of warehouse activities (*wave monitoring*)?
    a. No, the WMS does not provide any real-time progress/status reports.
    b. Somewhat, the WMS shows the number of open orders and order lines.
    c. Yes, the WMS shows the workload expressed in man hours per activity on a central wave monitoring screen. The wave planner can easily exchange operators between different activities from behind the screen.

    d. Yes, the WMS shows the workload per activity and relates it to the number of operators assigned to it and the individual deadlines of tasks. Using the system, the wave planner can easily exchange operators between different activities.

12. Does the WMS assign tasks to operators (*task management*) in an intelligent manner?
    a. No, the WMS does not prioritize the task sequence.
    b. Somewhat, the WMS computes efficient pick tours and it automatically selects putaway locations for incoming goods based on volume, weight and turnover velocity.
    c. Yes, the WMS computes efficient pick tours and it automatically selects putaway locations for incoming goods based on volume, weight and turnover velocity. The system assigns putaway, pallet-pick and replenishment tasks to operators in real-time based on task priorities.
    d. Yes, the WMS computes efficient pick tours per individual pallet by considering the volume, weight and stacking pattern of goods. It automatically selects putaway locations for incoming goods based on volume, weight and turnover velocity. The system interleaves putaway, pallet-pick and replenishment tasks (*dual-command cycles*) while considering urgency, travel distances and congestion.

A.3 Collaborative Warehouse Management

13. Do you charge fees for the logistics services provided by the distribution center?
    a. No, the warehouse costs are on an annual budget.
    b. Somewhat, we charge fees for logistics services, however clients (third party warehouse) or other departments within the company (private warehouse) hardly consider the fees in their decisions.
    c. Yes, we charge fees for logistics services that have been calculated via activity-based costing. The clients or other departments consider the fees in their decisions.
    d. Yes, we separately charge products and logistics services to customers (activity-based pricing). Clients (third-party warehouse) or other departments as well as customers consider the fees in their decisions.

14. Do the various departments regularly meet to synchronize their plans?
    a. No, the distribution center has only reactive discussions with other departments, i.e., after something has already gone wrong.
    b. Somewhat, in exceptional situations, the other departments inform the distribution center of their plans.
    c. Yes, the departments regularly meet and discuss their plans for the next period and attempt to synchronize them.
    d. Yes, the departments have periodic meetings to synchronize their plans on strategic, tactical and operational levels.

15. Do the purchase, sales, production and transportation departments consider integral objectives when planning logistics services?
    a. No, other departments accept and plan orders. The distribution center only executes.
    b. Somewhat, in exceptional circumstances the distribution center may deviate from the plans of other departments after consulting them.
    c. Yes, other departments consider the available storage and throughput capacities of the distribution center when planning orders, production and transportation.
    d. Yes, a *capable to deliver* system considers the integral objectives of the company when accepting orders and planning activities.

16. Are the workload fluctuations in the distribution center properly balanced?
    a. No, the customer is always right and decides when he orders. The purchasing department places orders when inventory is low. The distribution center has nothing to do with that.
    b. Somewhat, the purchasing department attempts to spread inbound orders across the week/month. On busy days the distribution center may shift some orders to the next day.
    c. Yes, the purchasing department levels inbound orders across the days of the week. The distribution center balances the workload of the outbound goods flow via *must-ship* and *can-ship* orders. Special promotions are minimized or planned well in advance.
    d. Yes, the purchasing department levels the inbound orders across the days of the week. The distribution center receives a significant portion of the orders well in advance with broad time frames so that the workload can be balanced. Major customers are supplied via *vendor managed inventories* (VMI).

17. Has a proper trade-off been made between service levels (response times, delivery frequencies, order line quantities) and logistics costs?
    a. No, clients (third party warehouse) or other departments (private warehouse) and customers determine which service levels are required for an order without considering the logistics implications.
    b. Somewhat, service levels have been formally defined with certain restrictions on response times, delivery frequencies and order line quantities.
    c. Yes, service levels have been formally defined with certain restrictions. The service levels may vary between customer groups based on cost considerations.
    d. Yes, a cost-to-serve model has revealed the discontinuities in service levels. The service levels have been revised to represent the optimum trade-off between cost and market requirements for individual customer groups.

18. Do you apply a virtual warehousing approach in your supply chain (including inventories of vendors)?
    a. No, each distribution center has its own independent inventories.
    b. Somewhat, in exceptional situations, inventories are shared between distribution centers.
    c. Yes, inventories are kept in an integrated network. Goods may be sourced from any distribution center and are shipped via a consolidated distribution network (sell-source-ship). Some major vendors supply goods via *vendor managed inventories* (VMI).
    d. Yes, inventories are kept primarily upstream in the supply chain with limited downstream inventories to accommodate short-term demand. Goods are distributed between sites via a consolidated distribution network using concepts like vendor managed inventories, direct shipments, cross-docking, merge-in-transit and postponement.

A.4   Maturity Plot

The survey may be used to estimate the position of a distribution center along the warehouse maturity grid. For each answer, apply the following scores:
   a. 0 points
   b. 3 points
   c. 7 points
   d. 10 points

Now calculate the maturity levels as follows:

$$\text{Effective} = \frac{\text{Total score questions 1 to 6}}{60} \times 100\%$$

$$\text{Responsive} = \frac{\text{Total score questions 7 to 12}}{60} \times 100\%$$

$$\text{Collaborative} = \frac{\text{Total score questions 13 to 18}}{60} \times 100\%$$

In Section 1.6.7 we depicted the scores in a maturity plot. Please refer to this section to find out whether the scores on the three maturity stages are well balanced.

Finally, we estimate the savings potential that can be achieved by applying *Highly Competitive Warehouse Management*.

$$\text{Savings potential} = (30\% - \frac{\text{Effective + Responsive + Collaborative}}{10})$$

Clearly, these are estimates. Make sure that you feel comfortable with the result through further analysis.

Appendix B

Standard Operating Procedures

In this appendix we give the standard operating procedures of Foodies, the fictional food distributor discussed throughout the text. The description can also be used as a template for making your own standard operating procedures. Notice that we use the active form of a verb in all sentences. For example, we state "The receipt operator scans the pallet label with the RF terminal" instead of "The pallet label is scanned." Clearly, the former formulation is more specific. In particular, it clarifies who performs the action (scanning the label).

Figure B.1 shows the processes and flows in Foodies' distribution center. This illustration serves as the basis for the standard operating procedures in this appendix. Due to its generic nature, it can instantly be applied to most distribution centers. The various processes are discussed in Chapter 3.

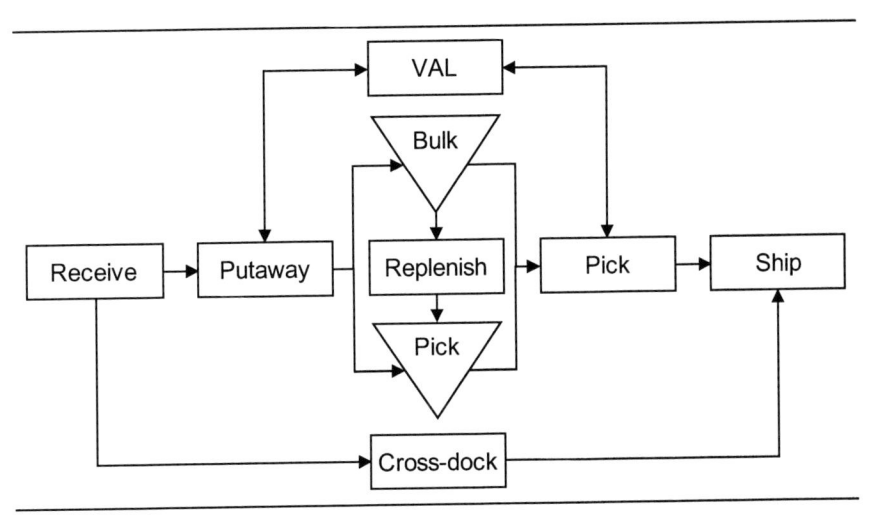

Figure B.1 Processes and flows in a distribution center.

B.1 Receive

Incoming goods are either delivered by truck (Sections B.1.1 and B.1.2) or by a pallet conveyor from an adjacent production plant (Section B.1.3).

B.1.1 Unloading

- The ERP electronically sends the purchase order to the WMS.
- The truck driver arrives and hands the freight documents to the receipt operator.
- The receipt operator registers the arrival of the truck in the WMS.
- The receipt operator assigns a receipt dock to the truck in the WMS.
- The truck driver drives the truck to the receipt dock or to a temporary parking space to wait until the dock becomes available.
- The truck driver unloads the pallets from the truck onto the receipt lane.
- The receipt operator verifies whether the number of handling units (pallets, containers, etc.) is correct and if there is any visible damage.
  - The receipt operator marks any damages or missing handling units on the freight documents.
- The receipt operator signs off on the freight documents and hands a copy to the truck driver.
- The truck driver departs.

This completes the first stage of the receipt process. The goods are now at the receipt lane inside the distribution center. Before the truck driver departs, the receipt operator has performed a superficial check on the delivery. This check prevents the truck driver from having to wait for a more detailed review. The supplier grants a certain *complaint period* during which the distribution center can claim any missing or damaged items.

B.1.2 Receive from Truck

Subsequently, the goods are received.

- The receipt operator enters on the RF terminal which delivery he is going to receive. He refers to the delivery by the purchase order (PO) number on the freight document.
- When products arrive on mixed pallets or containers, the receipt operator first sorts the goods onto pallets or into containers each holding a single product.
- The receipt operator attaches a license plate (LP) label to the pallet or container. The LP label is a unique barcode identification label.
- The receipt operator scans the LP label and registers the product number and quantity received on the RF terminal.
  - For specific products, the operator also enters product attributes such as: lot number, expiration date, quality status and country of origin.
- Once the receipt operator has received all products in the delivery, he closes the receipt of the delivery via the RF terminal.

- The WMS compares the received quantities with the quantities specified in the PO and reports any overages or shortages.
    ○ If the quantities do not match, the WMS asks the receipt operator to re-count the goods to check if there really is a difference.
- The WMS electronically sends a purchase order confirmation (POC) to the ERP.

The goods are at the receipt lane and they have been registered in the WMS. Each *handling unit* (pallet, container or carton) holds a unique license plate (LP) which is used to track its movements through the distribution center.

B.1.3 Receive from Production

- The ERP electronically sends the production order to the WMS.
- The receipt operator travels to the production line output station and picks up a pallet.
- The receipt operator attaches a license plate (LP) label to the pallet. The LP label is a unique barcode identification label.
- The receipt operator scans the LP label and registers the production order number, product number and quantity received on the RF terminal.
- The WMS compares the received quantities with the quantities specified in the production order and reports any overages or shortages.
    ○ If the quantities do not match, the WMS asks the receipt operator to re-count the goods to check if there really is a difference.
- The WMS electronically sends a production order confirmation (POC) to the ERP.

B.2 Putaway

The goods are now ready for putaway.
- The WMS assigns a storage location to each handling unit.
- The WMS displays a putaway task on the RF terminal of the forklift driver to pick up a handling unit from a specific receipt lane or a production line.
- The forklift driver travels to the receipt lane and scans the LP on the handling unit with the RF scanner.
- The RF terminal displays the destination location.
- The forklift driver takes the pallet from the receipt lane and travels to the destination location.
- The forklift driver scans the identification label on the location with the RF terminal.
- If the forklift driver carries multiple handling units simultaneously, then he travels to each location and scans the location as well as the LP on the respective handling units.
- The WMS updates the inventory level in the location.

The goods have arrived at the storage location. This concludes the inbound goods flow.

B.3 Wave Planning

Wave planning starts with the download of sales orders from the ERP.
- The ERP interfaces the sales orders and VAL orders with the WMS.
- The transportation management system interfaces the delivery routes with the WMS, including:
  - Orders/order lines
  - Departure time of the truck
  - Delivery sequence.
- The warehouse planner releases transport orders for wave planning per individual route.
  - The WMS allocates inventory in specific locations to the orders in the wave.
  - The WMS composes pick tours per pallet. The goods may neither exceed the pallet footprint nor the maximum stacking height.
  - If there is insufficient inventory of a product, then the WMS notifies the warehouse planner.
- The warehouse planner or the WMS releases the wave for picking.
  - The WMS generates tasks for replenishing pick locations with insufficient inventory (reactive replenishment).
  - The WMS generates tasks for order-picking and packing.

The WMS has generated replenishment tasks, pick tasks and pack tasks for the orders in the wave. The system has also reserved the required inventory and the tasks have been released.

B.4 Replenish

The WMS has generated replenishment tasks and assigns these to forklift drivers.
- The WMS assigns replenishment tasks to the forklift drivers.
  - The WMS considers the urgency of the replenishment tasks based on the departure times of the associated orders.
  - The WMS considers the travel distance between the current location of the forklift driver and the (bulk) location of the replenishment pallet.
- The WMS displays the bulk location of the replenishment pallet to the forklift driver on the RF terminal.
- The forklift driver travels to the bulk location and scans the pallet label or location label.
- The WMS displays the pick location on the RF terminal.
  - The WMS selects an arbitrary pick location within the zone designated for the product (dynamic pick locations).
- The forklift driver travels to the pick location and scans the location label.
- The forklift driver deposits the pallet in the pick location.

The replenishment has been completed.

B.5 Pick

The processes for pallet picking and case picking are defined separately.

B.5.1 Pallet Pick
- The WMS displays the bulk location to the forklift driver on the RF terminal.
- The forklift driver travels to the bulk location and scans the pallet label/ location label.
- The order-picker travels to the label printer.
- The label printer prints a despatch label.
- The order-picker attaches the despatch label to the pallet.
- The WMS displays the destination on the RF terminal: staging location or VAL station.
- The forklift driver travels to the location and scans the location label.
- The forklift driver deposits the pallet in the location.

B.5.2 Case Pick
- The order-picker selects a pick task on the RF terminal.
- The WMS displays the pallet type on the RF terminal.
- The order-picker takes a pallet.
- The WMS displays the subsequent pick locations on the RF terminal.
  - The WMS sequences the picks so as to create an efficient tour.
- The order-picker scans the location and picks the products.
- When the pallet is complete, the order-picker travels to the label printer.
- The label printer prints a despatch label.
- The order-picker attaches the despatch label to the pallet.
- The WMS displays the destination on the RF terminal: staging location or VAL station via the RF terminal.
- The order-picker travels to the location and scans the location label.
- The order-picker deposits the pallet in the location.

B.6 VAL

- The VAL operator opens a VAL order in the WMS.
- The WMS displays the VAL instructions on the PC.
- The operator scans an incoming pallet with the RF terminal.
- The operator performs the VAL activities.
- The operator registers the completed activities and the packaging materials that have been used in the WMS.
  - The WMS tracks the lot numbers of the products through the VAL process (tracking and tracing).
- The WMS prints the necessary labels for the finished pallets.
- The operator attaches the labels to the pallets.
- The operator deposits the finished pallets on the output location of the VAL station.

B.7 Cross-dock

Cross-docking commences after receiving goods from a truck or from production (see Section B.1).
- The WMS verifies whether there are any back orders for the received goods (opportunistic cross-docking). If this is the case:
  - The WMS allocates the inventory on the receipt dock to the back orders.
  - The WMS generates cross-dock tasks.
- The WMS displays the location of the pallet to the forklift driver on the RF terminal.
- The forklift driver travels to the location and scans the pallet label.
- The WMS displays the destination: staging location or shipping dock on the RF terminal.
- The forklift driver picks up the pallet, travels to the location and scans the location label.
- The forklift driver deposits the pallet in the location.

B.8 Ship

B.8.1 Consolidate
- Some time prior to the scheduled departure time an expedition operator closes the trip in the WMS.
  - The WMS displays any shortages on order lines in the trip.
- The WMS prints the shipping documents.
- The WMS interfaces sales order confirmations to the ERP.
- The WMS interfaces a despatch advice to the customer.

B.8.2 Load
- The truck driver announces his arrival to the expedition operator.
- The expedition operator registers the arrival of the truck in the WMS.
- The expedition operator assigns a shipping dock in the WMS and informs the truck driver of the dock number.
- The truck driver drives the truck to the assigned shipping dock or to a temporary parking space.
- A warehouse operator loads the pallets into the truck.
- The expedition operator hands the shipping documents to the truck driver.
- The truck driver departs.

Appendix C

Create Your Own Action Plan

Highly Competitive Warehouse Management is a methodology that helps to achieve best-in-class performance in distribution centers. Follow the steps in this appendix to make *Highly Competitive Warehouse Management* work for your distribution center.

As stated in Chapter 2, successful change requires the five CDEFG-ingredients:
1. Culture
2. Direction
3. Evolution
4. Fun
5. Guidance

C.1 Culture

As discussed in Section 2.1, a successful implementation of *Highly Competitive Warehouse Management* requires a *culture of change* where people are aware of the potential and feel motivated to change.

166. Organize a meeting with people from within your company. Invite managers and team leaders from the distribution center and other departments that interact with it, e.g., finance, sales, purchasing, transportation, order desk, etc.
   a. Ask all participants to fill out the warehouse maturity scan *in Appendix A[17] in advance*.
   b. Draw the individual maturity and complexity scores in Table C.1 (see Figure 1.5). Explain the scores and discuss with the participants:
      i. Did you expect these scores? What do you notice?
      ii. What are our strengths and weaknesses?
      iii. Are the maturity scores well balanced?
   c. Compare the savings potential of the distribution center to industry averages (Table 1.7 and Table 1.8).
      i. What do you notice? Did you expect these differences?
      ii. Do you believe that warehouse performance can be improved? By how much?
      iii. Do you believe that the company is able to make the necessary changes in the next 1 to 3 years?

Table C.1 Scores from the warehouse maturity scan.

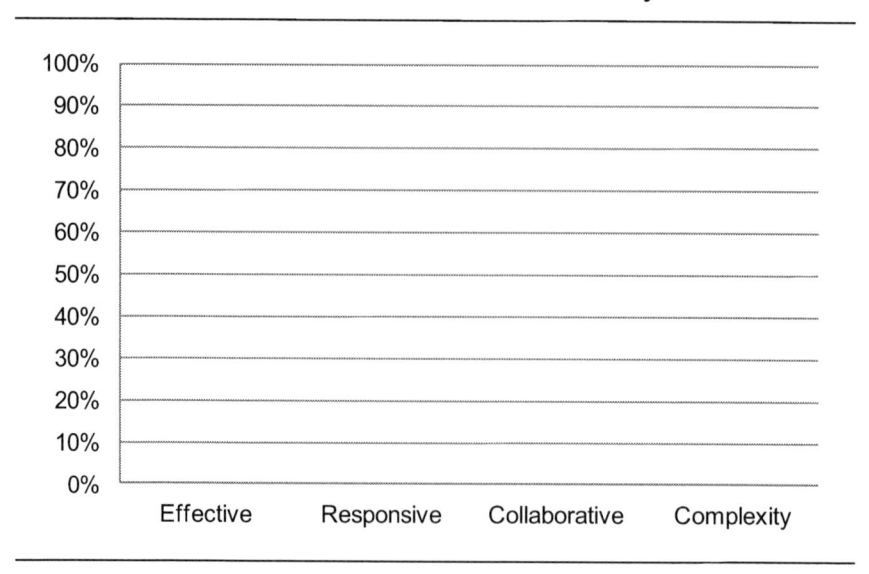

[17] Or use the online version at www.hcwm.net.

167. Participants should consider the activities in their department.
a. Ask each individual participant to list approximately 10 to 15 activities performed by his department.
b. Ask each participant to list bottlenecks in these activities.
c. Classify each bottleneck as either high, medium or low priority.
d. Ask each participant to list measures to overcome the main bottlenecks. Measures may be selected from Table C.2, but other measures are also possible.

Table C.2 Suggested measures by maturity stage (with Section references).

Effective	Responsive	Collaborative
• Logistics strategy (2.2)	• Real-time WMS (4.2)	• Service portfolio review (9.1)
• Service portfolio (5.1)	• Interfaces (4.4)	• Cost analysis (10.1)
• Standard operating procedures (5.2)	• Resource planning (7.2.2)	• Activity-based pricing (9.2)
• Performance indicators (5.4)	• Workload balancing (7.2.3)	• Synchronized planning (9.3)
• Performance management (5.4.5)	• Wave management (7.3)	• Event management (9.3.3)
• Activity-based costing (5.3)	• Task management (7.4)	• Integral planning (9.3.3)
• Change management (2.1)	• Flexible workforce (8.2)	• Virtual warehousing (9.4)
• Project management (2.5)	• Skills matrix (8.3)	• Vendor managed inventories

168. Consider the following points after the meeting.
a. Is there awareness of the potential and motivation to change among participants? In other words, is there a culture of change?
b. Where there is no culture of change, what can you do to create one?

C.2 Direction

Change needs *direction*, otherwise it is futile. In Section 2.2 we discussed how to define a warehouse strategy.

169. Ask senior management to formulate the strategy of your company.
   a. What are the core competencies of your company?
   b. What are the key product/market combinations of your company?
   c. What is the dominant value discipline of your company: Operational excellence, product leadership or customer intimacy?

Now based on the company strategy, define a warehouse strategy for the distribution center.

170. Organize a strategy meeting with managers involved in the distribution center.
   a. Explain the warehouse strategy map in Figure C.2 to the participants.
   b. Start with the financial perspective. Identify how the distribution center can contribute to the company's financial objectives:
      i. Increase the productivity of the warehousing operation
      ii. Improve the cost structure of the warehousing operation
      iii. Increase the throughput capacity of the distribution center
      iv. Increase the value of the goods by providing value added services
      v. Which of these contributions are essential to the company?
      vi. Do you prefer a productivity strategy or a growth strategy?
   c. Continue with the customer perspective. Discuss how the distribution center can contribute to each of the nine elements of the customer value proposition?
      i. Price
      ii. Quality
      iii. Assortment
      iv. Availability
      v. Responsiveness
      vi. Product functionality
      vii. Customer relationship
      viii. Service
      ix. Image
      x. Which of these contributions are key to the company?
      xi. Does this correspond with the value discipline of your company (operational excellence, product leadership or customer intimacy)?
      xii. How does the distribution center perform on these key elements?

d. Next, consider the operational perspective. Discuss how each of the four primary processes contribute to the key elements of the customer perspective.
   i. Inbound handling
   ii. Storage
   iii. Outbound handling
   iv. Value added logistics
   v. Which of these contributions are key to the company?
   vi. How does the distribution center perform with regard to these contributions?
e. Finally, look at the learning and growth perspective. Discuss which elements are key to run the operation effectively:
   i. Competencies of employees
   ii. Technologies
   iii. Culture
   iv. How does the distribution center perform with regard to these elements?

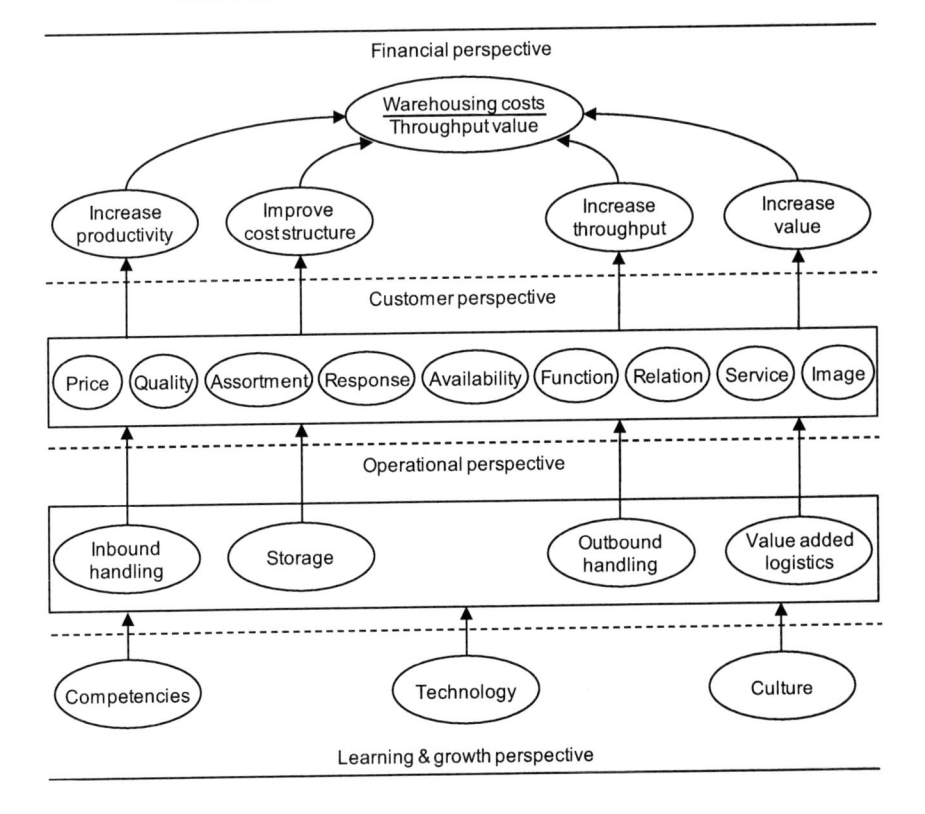

Figure C.2 Warehouse strategy map.

171. Gather the findings of the meeting
   a. Define the warehouse strategy in a formal document that explains the warehouse strategy map and summarizes the key findings of the strategy meeting.
   b. Discuss the warehouse strategy with the other participants in the strategy meeting and seek commitment.
   c. Discuss the warehouse strategy with senior management and seek commitment.
   d. Based on the warehouse strategy, what is the primary direction for change in the next 1 to 3 years?

C.3 Evolution

Based on the outcomes of the previous meetings, it is possible to define an action plan for the next 3 years.

172. Organize a second meeting with the people from Question 166 and 167.
   a. Consider the measures listed by the various participants in Question 167.d and cluster related measures into projects.
   b. Select projects for the next three years and plot the projects in Table C.3.

Table C.3 Action plan for the next three years.

Stage	Year T+1	Year T+2	Year T+3
Effective			
Responsive			
Collaborative			

173. Compare the action plan with the warehouse maturity scan.
   a. Assume that projects are implemented according to the action plan and compute maturity scores for each consecutive year with the warehouse maturity scan in Appendix A[18].
   b. Verify that the action plan develops along the phases defined in Section 2.3.2:
      i. Lay the foundation
      ii. Restore the balance
      iii. Create continuous improvement.
   c. If not, revise the action plan accordingly.
   d. Draw the action plan in Figure C.3.

---

[18] Or use the online scan at www.hcwm.net.

	Year T	Year T+1	Year T+2	Year T+3
■ Effective	..%	..%	..%	..%
▨ Responsive	..%	..%	..%	..%
▨ Collaborative	..%	..%	..%	..%
♦ Savings potential	..%	..%	..%	..%

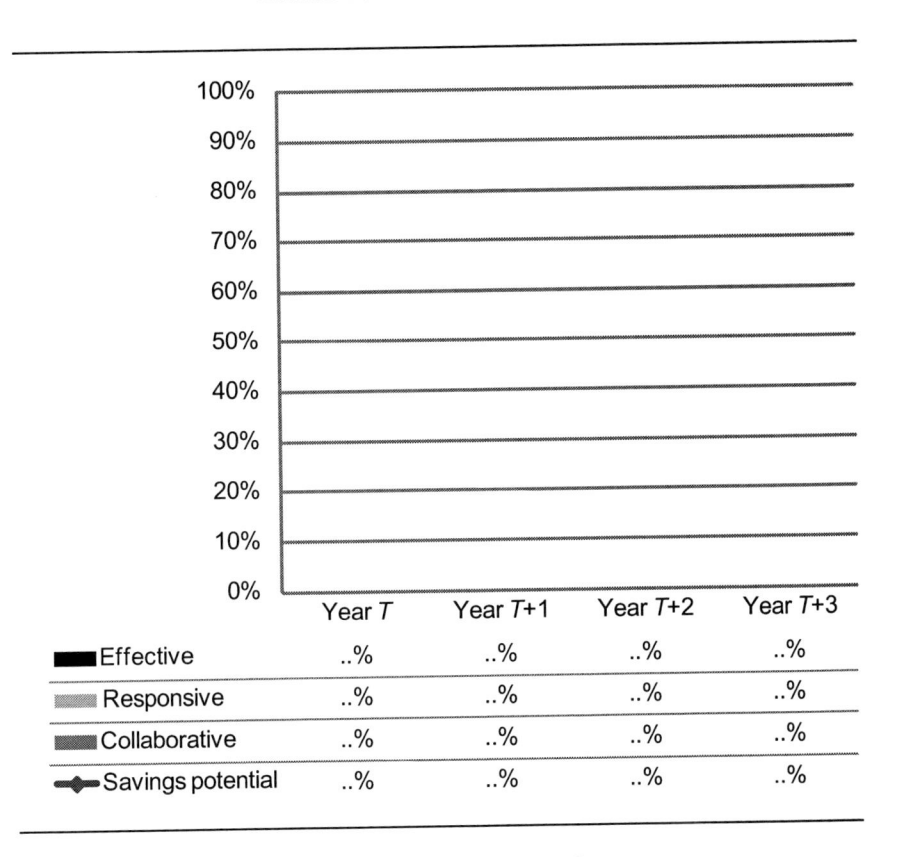

Figure C.3 Action plan for the next three years.

C.4 Fun

The action plan in Section C.3 lists various actions that provide a structure for improving the distribution center. However, we should note that *performance indicators*, *standard operating procedures*, *WMSs* and many other tools and instruments do not create benefits *per se*. The benefits come from using the tools and instruments to streamline processes, to change the behavior of people or to make better decisions. The tools and instruments are merely *enablers*.

In fact, the actual benefits come for instance when we change the warehouse layout, modify the control rules in the WMS or make different arrangements with customers. Successful changes not only create benefits, they also motivate people to continue. Successes are *fun*. They need to be celebrated.

174. Consider ad-hoc actions that can be implemented alongside the action plan defined in Section C.3.
   a. Select a bottleneck in the warehouse activities, preferably by analyzing performance indicators (when available).
   b. Choose an action to overcome the bottleneck by evaluating the following options (ICE-CAP-BAR):
      i. Improve
      ii. Combine
      iii. Eliminate
      iv. Cut
      v. Activate
      vi. Postpone
      vii. Balance
      viii. Accelerate/Decelerate
      ix. Rationalize
   c. Assign a project leader who is responsible for implementing the chosen action.

Typically, these projects have a narrow scope and a short time horizon, e.g., one month. Typical examples are: a project to keep pick locations tidy and organized or a project to obey certain safety rules. These projects are not necessarily led by members of the management team. In fact, these ad-hoc projects may well be led by team leaders or warehouse operators. The project leader writes a simple project plan as defined in Section C.5. After completing the project, the results are evaluated and presented to all staff members. The distribution center should continue to run these ad-hoc projects on a continuous basis.

C.5 Guidance

In Sections C.3 and C.4 we identified structural and ad-hoc projects, respectively. A project implementation is often hard work. A good plan helps to make a project successful.

175. For each project define a project plan.
   a. The project leader writes a project plan with the items in Table C.4.
   b. The project leader discusses the project plan with a sponsor and adjusts the plan where necessary. In particular, the sponsor has to specify the project goal in exact terms.
   c. The project team executes the project. The project leader meets with the sponsor when the original project goals in terms of budget, time or scope cannot be met anymore or when project goals need further clarification.
   d. The project ends with a closure meeting, where the results are presented and the sponsor formally accepts the project.

Table C.4 Items in project plan.

Project name	An inspiring name for the project
Background	How it creates a competitive advantage for the company
Project goal	Precise definition of the end result
Project team	Team members (including the project leader)
Resources	Required budgets and facilities
Benefits	Expected benefits
Kick-off date	Date of the first meeting with all project members
End date	Deadline that is both challenging and realistic
Agreement	Signatures by sponsor and project manager

References

Accenture (2003). *Connecting with the Bottom Line: A Global Study of Supply Chain Leadership and Its Contribution to the High-Performance Business*, white paper, Accenture/INSEAD/Stanford University.

Anderson, C. (2006). *The Long Tail: Why the Future of Business is Selling Less of More*, Hyperion, New York.

Ballou, R. (2003). *Business Logistics/Supply Chain Management*, 5th edition, Prentice Hall, Reading, UK.

Camp, W.E. (1922). Determining the Production Order Quantity, *Management Engineering* (2), p. 17-18.

Christopher, M. (2005). *Logistics and Supply Chain Management: Creating Value - Adding Networks*, 3rd edition, Prentice Hall, London, UK.

Covey, S.R. (2004). *The 7 Habits of Highly Effective People: Restoring the Character Ethic*, Simon & Schuster, New York.

Davis, H.W. (2006). *Logistics Cost and Service 2006*, Presentation CSCMP Conference, San Antonio, TX.

Davis, H.W. (2011). *Logistics Cost and Service 2011*, Presentation CSCMP Conference, Philadelphia, PA.

De Bie, P., R. Broekmeulen, K. de Jong, T. de Kok, J. van Nunen, P. van der Vlist, H. Wortmann & R. Zuidwijk (2002). *Supply Chain Synchronization in Retail* (In Dutch), Deloitte & Touche, Amsterdam, The Netherlands.

De Leeuw, S., & J.P. van den Berg (2011). Improving Operational Performance by Influencing Shop floor Behavior via Performance Management Practices, *Journal of Operations Management*, 29(6), p. 224-235.

Deloitte (2003). *Mastering Complexity in Global Manufacturing: Powering Profits and Growth Through Value Chain Synchronization*, white paper, Deloitte & Touche LLP.

Drickhamer, D. (2005). Census of Distribution: Onward and Upward, *Material Handling Management*, November.

Drickhamer, D. (2006). Census of Distribution: What is World-Class?, *Material Handling Management*, February.

Enslow, B. (2007). *Supply Chain Cost-Cutting Strategies: How Top Process Industry Performers Take Radically Different Actions*, white paper, Aberdeen Group, Boston, MA.

Enslow, B., & J. O'Neill (2006). *The Warehouse Productivity Benchmark Report: A Guide to Improved Warehouse and Distribution Center Performance*, white paper, Aberdeen Group, Boston, MA.

Forrester, J.W. (1961). *Industrial Dynamics*. Productivity Press, Cambridge, MA.

Frazelle, E.H. (2002). *World-Class Warehousing and Material Handling*, McGraw-Hill, New York.

Gabriëls, K. (2011). *The Talent Manager: An Integral Vision on New Leadership* (In Dutch), Het Boekenschap, Zelhem, The Netherlands.

Gattorna, J. (2010). *Dynamic Supply Chains: Delivering Value through People*, Prentice hall, London, UK.

Goedschalckx, M., & H.D. Ratliff (1988). An Efficient Algorithm to Cluster Order Picking Items in a Wide Aisle. *Engineering Costs and Production Economics*, 13(1), p. 263-271.

Graves, S.C., W.H. Hausman & L.B. Schwartz (1977). Storage-Retrieval Interleaving in Automatic Warehousing Systems. *Management Science*, 23(9), p. 935-945.

Gunster, B. (2007), *Yes-but What if it all Works Out?*, A.W. Bruna, Utrecht, The Netherlands.

Hall, R.W. (1983). *Zero Inventories*, McGraw-Hill, New York.

Hamel, G., & C. K. Prahalad (1994). *Competing for the Future*, Harvard Business School Press, Boston, MA.

Hardjono, T.W. & R.J.M. Bakker (2002). *Management of Processes: Identify, Control, Manage and Innovate* (In Dutch), Kluwer/INK, Deventer, The Netherlands.

Hofman, D., K. O'Marah & C. Elvy (2011). *The Gartner Supply Chain Top 25 for 2011*, white paper, Gartner, Stamford, CT.

Kaplan, R.S., & D.P. Norton (1996). *The Balanced Scorecard: Translating Strategy into Action*, Harvard Business School Press, Boston, MA.

Kaplan, R.S., & D.P. Norton (2001). *The Strategy-Focused Organization*, Harvard Business School Press, Boston, MA.

Kaplan, R.S., & D.P. Norton (2004). *Strategy Maps: Converting Intangible Assets into Tangible Outcomes*, Harvard Business School Press, Boston, MA.

REFERENCES

Kaplan, R.S., & R. Cooper (1998). *Cost & Effect: Using Integrated Cost Systems to Drive Profitability and Performance*, Harvard Business School Press, Boston, MA.

Kaplan, R.S., & S.R. Anderson (2007). *Time-Driven Activity-Based Costing: A Simpler and More Powerful Path to Higher Profits*, Harvard Business School Press, Boston, MA.

Kotter, J.P. (1996). *Leading Change*, Harvard Business School Press, Boston, MA.

Kotter, J.P. (2008). *Sense of Urgency*, Harvard Business School Press, Boston, MA.

Lee, H.L. (2002). Aligning Supply Chain Strategies with Product Uncertainties, California Management Review, 44(3), p. 105-119.

Lee, H.L. (2004). The Triple-A Supply Chain, *Harvard Business Review*, October.

Makridakis, S., S.C. Wheelwright & R.J. Hyndman (1998). *Forecasting: Methods and Applications*, 3rd edition, John Wiley, New York.

Porter, M.E. (1980). *Competitive Strategy: Techniques for Analyzing Industries and Competitors*, The Free Press, New York.

Pyzdek, T. (2003). *The Six Sigma Handbook: A Complete Guide for Greenbelts, Blackbelts and Managers at All Levels*, McGraw-Hill, New York.

Ratliff, H.D., & A.S. Rosenthal (1983). Order-picking in a Rectangular Warehouse: A Solvable Case of the Traveling Salesman Problem. *Operations Research*, 31(3), p. 507-521.

Roodbergen, K.J. (2001). *Interactive Warehouse*, www.roodbergen.com/warehouse.

Scheper, W.J., W.V. Bertoen & C.G. Rexwinkel (2005). *In Charge of Complexity with the Business Maturity Model: A Benchmark Study in the Dutch Industry* (In Dutch), white paper, Deloitte Netherlands.

Supply Chain Council (2004). *Supply Chain Operations Reference Model*, version 6.1, www.supply-chain.org.

Treacy, M., & F. Wiersema (1995). *The Discipline of Market Leaders*, Perseus Books, New York.

Van den Berg, J.P. (2002). *Dynamic Routing*, white paper, Jeroen van den Berg Consulting, Buren, The Netherlands.

Van Goor, A.R., M.J. Ploos van Amstel & W. Ploos van Amstel (2003). *European Distribution and Supply Chain Logistics*, Stenfert Kroese, The Netherlands.

Walton, M., & W.E. Deming (1986). *The Deming Management Method*, Penguin Putnam, New York.

Wild, T. (2002). *Best Practice in Inventory Management*, Elsevier, Oxford, UK.

Womack, J.P., & D.T. Jones (2003). *Lean Thinking: Banish Waste and Create Wealth in your Corporation*, Simon & Schuster, New York.

Index

3

3PL · *See* Third party logistics provider

6

6D cubing · 108

A

ABC
  class · 101, 110
  classification · 72, 101, 200
Accelerate/decelerate · 75, 275
Accuracy · 95, 154, 174
  rate · 154
Act · *See* Deming circle
Action plan · 14, 64
Activate · 74, 233
Active
  capacity · 233
  voice · 161
Activity · 90
Activity-based
  costing · 157, 161, 193
  pricing · 253, 274
Add-on module · 123
Advance
  notice of receipt · 137
  replenishments · 236
  shipment notification · 137
Age mix · 235
Alignment · 31
Amazon · 283
ANR · *See* Advance notice of receipt
AS/RS · *See* Automated storage/retrieval system
ASN · *See* Advance shipment notification
Automated storage/retrieval system · 89, 224
Availability · 174
Available to promise · 134, 260

B

Backhaul · 135
Backorder · 134
Balance · 75, 272, 278
Balanced scorecard · 53
Balancing · 101
Barcode label · 98
Batch · *See* Lot
  communication · 127, 220
  processing · 133
Batch-picking · 106, 110, 189, 199, 218, 239
Best practices · 14
Best-of-breed system · 125
Biased fee · *See* Unbiased fee
Big picture, The · 244

Bill of
  lading · 137
  material · 118
  material order · 135
Billing of logistics services · 123
Blind count · 102
Block stacking · 88
BOM · *See* Bill of material
Bottleneck · 222
Brainstorm session · 193
Bulk
  area · 100
  location · 100
Bullwhip Effect · 280
Business intelligence system · 184
Buy-hold-sell · 81, 266

C

Cannibalization · 105
Can-ship order · 235
Capable to
  deliver · 260
  promise · 134, 260
Capacity
  check · 260
  planning · 204, 205, 208, 220
Case · 87
  picking · 115
Cause-and-effect relationship · 19
Change
  management · 184
  process · 183
Check · *See* Deming circle
  digits · 115
Climate of change · 80
Collaboration · 15, 243
Collaborative warehouse
  management · 34, 243
Combine · 73, 192, 199
Combitruck · 90
Committed resource · 162
Company strategy · 51
Complete view · 174
Complexity · 128

Compound task · 106, 221
Constraint · 221
Conveyor · *See* Roller conveyor
Corrective measure · 190, 191
Correlated products · 112
Cost center · 255
Cost-to-serve · 256, 277
Cross-dock · 81, 91, 97, 100, 119, 265, 270
Cubing · 108, 262
Customer · 94
  intimacy · 52, 55
  order · 133
  order decoupling point · 58, 277
  perspective · 55
  value proposition · 55
Customs management · 123
Cut · 74, 232, 233
Cut-off time · 152
Cycle count · 96, 102, 140, 154, 181

D

Days on hand · 283
Deep stacking · 88
Delivery · 135
Deming circle · 69, 186
DESADV · *See* Despatch advice
Despatch advice · 99, 137, 196
Direct shipment · 81, 265
Direction · 47, 80, 300
Discontinuity · 245, 250, 251, 252, 256, 275
Disposition · 99
Do · *See* Deming circle
Dock
  and yard management · 123, 215, 263
  reservation · 282
Dock-to-stock time · 181, 195, 222
Drawer rack · 88
Drop shipment · 266
Dual-command cycle · 189, 200, 218, 222, 239

Dynamic pick location · 112, 197

E

EAI · *See* Enterprise application integration
Earliest
 deadline rule · 226
 starting time · 239
Economic order quantity · 254
Economies of scale · 27
ECR · 27, 253
EDI · 133
Effective warehouse management · 34
Efficiency · 73, 221, 228
Efficient · 72
 consumer response · *See* ECR
Electronic data interchange · *See* EDI
Eliminate · 73, 192, 194
Emergency task · 226
Engineered labor standards · 124
Enterprise
 application integration · 131, 269
 resource planning · *See* ERP
EOQ · *See* Economic order quantity
ERP · 124, 125
European distribution center · 82, 264
Evolution · 48, 80
Excess capacity · 232
Extrinsic motivation · 186

F

Factory gate pricing · 135, 256
Fast mover · 111
FEFO · *See* First expired first out
FIFO · *See* First in first out
Fill rate · 58, 153
Finance · 125
Fire-fighting · 14, 47
First
 carton seen · 98, 143
 expired first out · 105
 in first out · 88, 105
Fixed route · 125, 214
Flexibility · 95, 122, 155, 174, 181
 range · 182, 217
Flexible resource · 162
Follower · 43
Forecast · 210
Forklift truck · 89
Forrester Effect · 280
Forward
 area · *See* Pick area
 stock positions · 266
Frequency · 58, 153
Full
 case · 87, 245, 247
 pallet · 86, 87, 245, 247
 pallet layer · 247
Fun · 48, 71, 80, 303

G

General Food Law · 87
Globalization · 263
Growth strategy · 54
Guidance · 48, 80

H

Hierarchical control rule · 226
Highly competitive warehouse management · 14

I

Idle capacity · 233
Improve · 73, 192, 200
Incentive alignment · 274
Individual
 performance · 186
 piece · 87
Intangible benefits · 77
Integrated system · *See* Best-of-breed system

Intelligent agent · 259
Interface · 131
Interleaving · 221, 225
Internal
   client · 94
   movement · 96, 103
   supply chain · *See* Value chain
Intrinsic motivation · 186
Inventory
   accuracy · 181
   allocation · 104
   allocation rule · 104, 201
   attributes · 143
   discrepancy · 102, 141
   holding costs · 16, 165, 271
   management · 124
   management system · 124

J

JIT · *See* Just in time
Job rotation · 212
Just in time · 16, 28, 111, 198
   replenishment · 114

K

Key performance indicator · 173
Kitting · 92

L

Labor
   management · 124
   management system · 209
Laggard · 43
Last in first out · 88
Latest
   goods issue date · 105
   starting time · 239
Leader · 43
Lean · 16, 28
Legacy system · 121

License plate · 98, 99, 127
LIFO · *See* Last in first out
LMS · *See* Labor management system
Loading dock · *See* Shipping dock
Logistics costs · 22
Long tail · 283
Lost sales · 42
Lot · 87, 138
LP · *See* License plate
   receiving · 99

M

Make-to-order · 118, 277
Make-to-stock · 118, 277
Management information · 124
Mass production · 27
Material handling control system · *See* MHCS
Material handling system · 129
Maturity · 14, 33
Maturity grid · 33
Merge-in-transit · 81, 265, 270
Mezzanine · 88
MHCS · 125
Miniload AS/RS · 89
Modular procedures · 160
Motivation · 49
Movement · 84
Multi-step move · 100, 115
Must-ship order · 235

N

Narrow-aisle truck · 90, 221
Nearest neighbor rule · 225, 226, 228
Negotiated response time · 152
Nesting · 108
Non-stock item · 58

O

Off-the-shelf system · 121
OMS · *See* Order management system
On time in full · 181
Operational excellence · 52, 54
Opportunistic cross-dock · 119, 196
Order · 133
    acceptance · 133, 282
    cut-off time · 279
    disposition · 134
    line · 133
    management · 125
    management system · 125
    profile discontinuity · 247, 256
    promising · 134
Order-pick
    cart · 90
    truck · 90
OTIF · *See* On time in full
Out-of-stock risk · 42
Outsourcing · 206

P

P/D location · 100, 222
Pallet · 87
    picking · 115
    rack · 88
Paperless warehousing · 128
Pareto curve · 282
Pareto's law · 111
Payback period · 76
People · 14, 28
Perfect order (line) rate · 181
Performance
    indicators · 171
    management · 185, 204
Pick · 97
    area · 100
    density · 110
    list · 127
    location · 100
    sequence · 109
    sequencing · 200
    tour · 106
Pick/drop location · *See* P/D location
Pick-and-sort · 106, 199
Pick-to-light · 127
Piece · 87
    picking · 115
Plan · *See* Deming circle
Planned cross-dock · 119, 196
PLC · 129
PO · *See* Purchase order
Postpone · 74, 237
Prearranged response time · 152
Preventive measure · 190, 191
Private warehouse · 92, 123
Proactive replenishment · 111, 236
Problem-solving · 13
Process · 14, 72
Product · 87
    attributes · 142, 143
    definitions · 142
    group · 101, 142
    leadership · 52, 55
    master data · 142
    proliferation · 283
Product/market combination · 56
Production
    costs · 16
    order · 138
Productivity · 73, 174
    strategy · 54
Product-to-picker systems · 89
Profit center · 255
Programmable logic controller · *See* PLC
Project plan · 79, 80
Public warehouse · 155
Purchase
    order · 98, 138, 139
    order confirmation · 140
Putaway · 96, 100
    rule · 201

Q

Quality · 57

R

Radio frequency · 30
   terminal · 127, 194
Rationalize · 75, 272
Reach truck · 90
Reactive
   replenishment · 111, 225
   warehouse management · 34
Real-time
   communication · 127, 200, 220
   processing · 133
Receipt
   advice · 98, 139
   dock · 97
Receiving · 96, 97
Regional distribution center · 264
Relaxed
   FEFO · 105
   FIFO · 105
Replenish · 97
Reserve area · *See* Bulk area
Resource
   planning · 208, 210
   utilization · 170
Response time · 58, 152
Response time discontinuity · 250, 256
Responsive warehouse management · 34
Responsiveness · 58, 95, 152
Return merchandise authorization · 99, 136, 138
Reverse unloading sequence · 117
RF · *See* Radio frequency
RF terminal · *See* Radio frequency terminal
RFID · 147
   tag · 98
RMA · *See* Return merchandise authorization
Roller conveyor · 90
Rolling stock · 196

S

Sales orders · 134
SCM · *See* Supply chain management
Section · 101
Sell function · 93
Sell-source-ship · 81, 266
Separation · 101
Service · 91
   fee · 156, 253
   level agreement · 149, 171, 188, 204, 205, 256
   portfolio · 150, 255
Service level agreement · 90
Shelving rack · 88
Ship · 97
Shipping dock · 117, 119
Shortpick · 102
Simple task · 106, 221
Single-command cycle · 200, 222
Single-order picking · 106, 199
Single-step move · 100
Six dimensional cubing · 108
Six Sigma · 28
SKU · *See* Stock keeping unit
Slotting · 124
Slow mover · 112
Sort-while-pick · 106, 116, 199
Source function · 93
SSCC · 99, 196
S-shape · 109
Staging area · 251
Standard
   operating procedures · 193
   pack configuration · 87
   time · 168, 219, 237
   WMS · 121
Static pick location · 112, 197
Status · 141
Stock
   adjustment · 141
   keeping unit · 87
   product · 263
Storage · 84
Strategy map · 53

Substitution · 105
Supplier · 94
Supply chain
  event management · 259
  life cycle · 84
  management · 27, 31
  manager · 75
  structure · 81
  synchronization · 253
Surprise receipt · 98

T

Task management · 204, 205, 220, 236
Team performance · 186
Technology · 14
Third party
  logistics provider · 92, 206
  warehouse · 92
Threshold level · 228
Throughput value · 53
Time
  and material costs · 161
  bucket · 219, 237
  frame · 58, 153
Time-driven activity-based costing · 163, 273
TMS · 125
Tracking and tracing · 87, 121
Transfer order · 135, 138
Transformation · 84
Transparency · 15, 30, 147, 148
Transport
  order · 135, 136
  order confirmation · 137
Transportation
  costs · 16, 271
  management system · See TMS
  planning · 125, 282
  planning function · 93

U

Unbiased

fee · 157
view · 175
Unloading dock · See Receipt dock
Up-to-date view · 175
Urgency · 221
Utilization · 73, 203

V

Value
  added logistics · 86, 91, 97, 118, 265
  chain · 93
Variable route · 125, 214
Vehicle routing and scheduling system · See VRS
Velocity class · See ABC class
Vendor
  managed inventories · 256, 273, 277
  rating · 99, 196
Virtual warehousing · 263, 265
Visibility · 269
Voice terminal · 68, 127
Voice-picking · 115
Volume discontinuity · 248, 256
VRS · 125

W

Warehouse
  action plan · 80
  function · 84
  management · 28
  management cycle · 204, 205, 232
  management system · 15, 30, 121
  maturity · 14
  maturity scan · 37
  planner · 103
  strategy · 80
Warehousing costs · 16, 22
Waste · 28
Wave · 104, 218
  management · 204, 205, 220, 221

monitoring · 236
monitoring screen · 219
planning · 103
Web portal · 123
Weight-check · 191
Whale curve · 273
WMS · *See* Warehouse management system
Workload balancing · 208

X

XML · 131

Z

Zone · 101
Zone-picking · 107, 199

About the Author

Dr Jeroen P. van den Berg (b. 1967) is a well-known expert in warehouse management. In his work, either as a consultant, author, teacher, speaker or researcher, he challenges people to see the big picture and overcome the obstacles that prevent progress in their companies. People who work with him, will notice his talent for giving structure to complex issues so that they become easy to understand.

In 1996, he earned a Ph.D. from the University of Twente in The Netherlands with his thesis "Planning and Control of Warehousing Systems." He holds a master's degree in Applied Mathematics from the same university.

Mr. Van den Berg can be reached at Jeroen@JeroenvandenBerg.nl.
Follow him on Twitter: @JeroenPvdBerg.
Connect via LinkedIn: www.linkedin.com/in/JeroenPvdBerg.
Visit his website: www.JeroenvandenBerg.nl.